Modern Macroeconomics

Modern Macroeconomics

Edited by Luis Bender

CLANRYE
INTERNATIONAL
www.clanryeinternational.com

Clanrye International,
750 Third Avenue, 9th Floor,
New York, NY 10017, USA

ISBN: 978-1-63240-928-7

Cataloging-in-Publication Data

Modern macroeconomics / edited by Luis Bender.
p. cm.
Includes bibliographical references and index.
ISBN 978-1-63240-928-7
1. Macroeconomics. 2. Economics. I. Bender, Luis.

HB172.5 .M63 2020

339--dc23

For information on all Clanrye International publications
visit our website at www.clanryeinternational.com

CLANRYE
INTERNATIONAL

Contents

Preface

The branch of economics which deals with the structure, performance, behaviour and decision making of an economy as a whole, is known as macroeconomics. Aggregated indicators such as unemployment rates, gross domestic product, national income, price indices, and the correlations among the different sectors of the economy are studied under this field. This helps to understand the functioning of the economy in a thorough manner. The key areas of research under this discipline are the study of the causes and consequences of short-run fluctuations in national income, and the determinants of long-run economic growth. Theories in macroeconomics usually seek to find the relationship between the phenomena of output, unemployment and inflation. This book covers in detail some existent theories and innovative concepts revolving around modern macroeconomics. It is appropriate for students and experts seeking detailed information in this area. Coherent flow of topics, student-friendly language and extensive use of examples make this book an invaluable source of knowledge.

All of the data presented henceforth, was collaborated in the wake of recent advancements in the field. The aim of this book is to present the diversified developments from across the globe in a comprehensible manner. The opinions expressed in each chapter belong solely to the contributing authors. Their interpretations of the topics are the integral part of this book, which I have carefully compiled for a better understanding of the readers.

At the end, I would like to thank all those who dedicated their time and efforts for the successful completion of this book. I also wish to convey my gratitude towards my friends and family who supported me at every step.

Editor

1

Business Cycles in European Post-Communist Countries

Karol Szomolányi[1], Martin Lukáčik[1], Adriana Lukáčiková[1]

ABSTRACT The European post-communist countries that have integrated into the European Union are emerging market economies. However, their short-run economic performance does not correspond to the observed business cycles of other global emerging markets. The business cycles of the studied countries are longer, and their recessions are more pronounced. Moreover, economic activity in the studied countries is relatively low and volatile, and the trade balance and government purchases have a relatively significant countercyclical character. These are the core conclusions from our business cycle study of the chosen European post-communist countries. In the study, we use both traditional and contemporary business cycle definitions. Using traditional definitions, we determine the peaks, troughs, expansions and contractions and quantify the durations and amplitudes of their expansions, recessions and business cycles. Using contemporary definitions, we measure cyclical properties by computing the first and second moments of the chosen macroeconomic cyclical components and growth rates. Differences in the business cycles and characteristics between European post-communist countries and other emerging countries are discussed with reference to the works of other authors.

KEY WORDS: business cycles, emerging markets, European post-communist countries

[1] University of Economics in Bratislava - Department of Operations Research and Econometrics, Slovakia

1. Introduction

In this paper, we analyze the cyclical properties of selected post-communist countries in the European Union using two simple characteristics. First, using the definition of Burns and Mitchell (1946), we identify business cycles based on turning points in the aggregate time series; second, using Lucas's (1977) definition, we identify business cycles based on movements about trends. The definition of Burns and Mitchell (1946) is used to identify business cycles, whereas the definition of Lucas (1977) is used to discern the cyclical properties of the chosen aggregate time series by computing the moments of cyclical components. In accordance with Lucas's definition, we state that the aggregate time series is pro-cyclical (counter-cyclical) if the cyclical component of the series is positively (negatively) correlated with the cyclical component of the output time series. If the cyclical component of the aggregate data series is not correlated with that of the output, the series is acyclical. The volatility of the data series is measured using the standard deviation of its cyclical component. The persistency of the data series is measured by the serial correlation coefficient of its cyclical component.

Correspondence concerning this article should be addressed to: **Karol Szomolányi**, University of Economics in Bratislava - Department of Operations Research and Econometrics, Dolnozemská cesta 1, Bratislava 852 35, Slovakia. E-mail: karol.szomolanyi@euba.sk

The results obtained are compared with the results of analyses of business cycles around the world. Uribe and Schmitt-Grohé (2017) and Montiel (2013) state that the aforementioned simple business cycle characteristics differ across countries of different sizes, wealth, and openness. In the comparative analysis, we must consider that according to the definition of Uribe and Schmitt-Grohé (2017), all the studied post-communist countries are emerging. Their average purchasing power parity (PPP) converted into GDP per capita over the period 1990-2009 falls within the 3,000-25,000 range. Presented below is a summary of the Uribe and Schmitt-Grohé (2017) conception of the relationship between a country's wealth and its business cycle:

- business cycles in rich countries are approximately one-half as volatile as business cycles in emerging or poor countries.
- consumption volatility is higher in poor and emerging countries than in rich countries.
- the trade balance-to-output ratio is more negatively correlated with output as the level of economic development increases.
- the share of government consumption in relation to output is counter-cyclical in rich countries but acyclical in emerging and poor countries.
- expansions are on average longer in developed countries than in emerging countries.
- contractions are more pronounced in emerging countries than in developed countries.

The authors obtained the last two items in the above list from Calderón and Fuentes (2010). Uribe and Schmitt-Grohé (2017) also take into account the higher volatility of economic activity in small open countries than that in large countries.

Assuming that these simple characteristics of business cycles in emerging countries around the world coincide with those of post-communist countries, it is useful to review the empirical and theoretical literature analyzing the business cycles of emerging countries. Numerous authors have successfully explained many of the aforementioned characteristics. The basic principles can be understood based on a simple real business cycle model developed by Kydland and Prescott (1982), which is resistant to the Lucas (1976) critique. Mendoza (1991) made an important modification to the model by forming a real business cycle model of a small open economy to study Canadian business cycles. In interpreting the model, Uribe and Schmitt-Grohé identify certain theoretical principles to explain consumption volatility and trade balance cyclicality:

- the more persistent the productivity shocks are, the more volatile consumption is and thus the more counter-cyclical the trade balance is.
- the more pronounced capital costs are, the more pro-cyclical the trade balance is.

Using these principles, the authors tried to empirically explain the characteristics of business cycles in emerging countries. According to Aguiar and Gopinath (2007), high consumption volatility in emerging economies derives from non-stationary productivity shocks. However, García-Cicco, Pancrazi and Uribe (2010) argue that the data range used in the paper of Aguiar and Gopinath is too small to study the non-stationarity of the variables. Furthermore, using the persistent productivity shock principle, the real business cycle model of the small open economy with nonstationary output shocks predicts not only highly volatile consumption but also a relatively strongly counter-cyclical trade balance. The trade balance is indisputably less counter-cyclical in emerging countries than it is in developed countries.

García-Cicco et al. (2010) consider several shocks to explain the business cycles of emerging economies. In addition to various productivity shocks, agents in emerging and poor countries face interest rate and interest rate spread premium changes. According to the authors, in poor and emerging countries, interest rate and interest rate spread shocks are significant whereas non-stationary productivity shocks are negligible. Uribe and Yue (2006) show that interest rate and interest rate spread shocks significantly influence business cycles in poor and emerging countries. The interest rate spread is considered partially exogenous and partially endogenous. Access of domestic agents to international financial markets is better (and capital adjustment costs are lower) if domestic economic policy is credible. Agents may borrow funds at a relatively low interest rate, and the country's interest rate spread is low. Therefore, the reason for the high economic volatility of poor and emerging countries is international financial market friction. The low economic activity of emerging and poor countries and their more severe economic contractions stem from the low credibility of their economic policies. Therefore, capital cost changes in emerging countries are rather persistent. The correctly calibrated interactivity of the capital cost severity and related income shock persistency may explain why the trade balance is not countercyclical and consumption is highly volatile in emerging countries.

Based on these facts and theoretical concepts, Uribe and Schmitt-Grohé (2017) explain the short-term economic performance of Latin American countries using dynamic stochastic general equilibrium models with stochastic changes in the total factors of productivity, interest rates, interest rate spreads and investment. They also discuss possible expansion of the model by including trade shocks.

If the economic perspective of post-communist countries is similar to that of emerging countries, one might expect that financial friction is the main source of business cycles in post-communist countries. However, a quick look at the European economic reality does not support this suggestion. In particular, other European Union countries have experienced higher interest rates than post-communist European Union countries in the past two decades. Szomolányi, Lukáčik and Lukáčiková (2014a) and Szomolányi, Lukáčik and Lukáčiková (2014b) conducted studies with a VAR model similar to that of Uribe and Yue using Slovak and Czech data. The authors show that interest rate and interest rate spread shocks have had a very small impact on Slovak and Czech business cycles and that more than 90% of these business cycles may be explained by supply shocks.

Therefore, we consider it useful to identify simple characteristics of business cycles and to compare them with the data presented in the relevant literature. Our results and the implications thereof are discussed in the Results and Discussion section.

2. Data and Methodology

In our research, we focus on two business cycle characteristics. Specifically, we identify business cycles using peaks and troughs, in accordance with the definition of Burns and Mitchell (1946), and quantify the cyclical properties of business cycles using Lucas's (1977) definition. Using the first approach, we compute the durations and extents of business cycles. Calderón and Fuentes (2010) suggest that this method is appropriate for determining the business cycles of emerging countries.

We analyze business cycles in eleven European post-communist countries. The choice of countries was based on the availability of published data; we chose countries for which most of the selected data series were published for the period 1995-2013. The countries studied are Bulgaria (BG), the Czech Republic (CZ), Estonia (EE), Croatia (HR), Hungary (HU), Latvia (LV), Lithuania (LT), Poland (PL), Romania (RO), Slovakia (SK) and Slovenia (SI). All analyzed countries are members of the European Union and are classified as emerging according to the definition of Uribe and Schmitt-Grohé (2017). Many authors, including Uribe and Schmitt-Grohé (2017), measure a country's openness by its international trade-to-output ratio, where international trade is the sum of exports and imports. If a country's average international trade-to-output ratio is more than 1 in the period 1995-2013, the country is deemed to be open. We conclude that this ratio is less than 1 for three studied countries: Croatia, Poland and Romania. Uribe and Schmitt-Grohé (2017) consider a country small if its population is less than 20 million. The populations of Poland and Romania are in the 20-50 million range; therefore, Poland and Romania are considered medium-sized countries.

To determine business cycles, we used quarterly GDP data in millions of the national currency units at constant prices, with reference to 2005 prices obtained from the Eurostat portal. We determined business cycles using the algorithm of Calderón and Fuentes (2010). Letting y_t denote the logarithm of real GDP, a peak occurs when $y_t > y_{t+j}$ for j = -2, -1, 1, 2. The duration of a cycle is the period of time from one peak to the next. The duration of a contraction is the period of time from a peak to the next trough. The extent of a contraction is the percentage decrease in output between a peak and the next trough. Letting y_t denote the logarithm of real GDP, a trough occurs when $y_t < y_{t+j}$ for j = -2, -1, 1, 2. The duration of an expansion is the period of time from a trough to the next peak. The extent of an expansion is the percentage increase in output between a trough and the next peak. Durations are averaged arithmetically, and amplitudes are medians. Following Calderón and Fuentes (2010), we estimated the cumulative variation of the cycle as

Table 1. Durations and Amplitudes of Contractions and Expansions in Three Country Groups

	country groups	developed	emerging	post-communist
durations	contraction	4.2	4.8	5.0
	expansion	14.3	16.3	25.6
amplitudes	contraction	3.4	4.4	8.4
	expansion	7.5	19.4	30.4
cumulative gain/loss	contraction	9.2	12.8	33.0
	expansion	55.1	224.3	445.3

Note: The quarterly time series of post-communist countries for the period 1995-2013 are adapted from "GDP and main components (output, expenditure and income)" by Eurostat database (2014). Retrieved from http://appsso.eurostat.ec.europa.eu/nui/show.do?dataset=namq_10_gdp&lang=en
The quarterly time series of developed countries for the period 1995-2012 are adapted from "Quarterly National Accounts" by OECD database (2014).

the area of the triangle formed by the duration and amplitude of the cycle. This method reflects the idea of foregone output from peaks to troughs during contractions and output gains during expansion periods. We needed to compare these results with observations around the world. One possibility was to use the results of Calderón and Fuentes (2010) as referenced facts about business cycle durations and amplitudes in emerging and developed countries around the world. Although these results cover the two characteristics mentioned in the introduction, Calderón and Fuentes (2010) use data with a different range, excluding recent world financial crises. Therefore, we repeated the analysis with OECD quarterly data for the period 1995-2012.[1] We divided countries into emerging and developed groups based on the definitions of Uribe and Schmitt-Grohé (2017). The developed countries are Australia, Austria, Belgium, Canada, Denmark, Finland, France, Germany, Hong Kong, Italy, Japan, Netherlands, Norway, Sweden, Switzerland, the United Kingdom and the United States. The emerging countries are Argentina, Israel, South Korea, Mexico, New Zealand, Peru, Portugal, South Africa, Spain, Turkey and Uruguay. The results are presented in Table 1.

We analyzed the cyclical properties of aggregate data series using annual GDP data, the final consumption expenditures of households and non-profit institutions serving households, the final consumption of the general government, gross capital formation, exports and imports of goods and services in millions of the national currency units at constant prices with reference to 2005, and population size. Aggregate data series of the nominal current account of the payment balance in millions of the national currency units were adjusted by the trade balance index volume with reference to 2005. For our analysis, we used data sets expressed intensively (per capita), i.e., divided by population size. Data from the period 1995-2013 were obtained from the Eurostat portal.

Macroeconomic textbooks such as Williamson (2014) and Uribe and Schmitt-Grohé (2017) use two approaches to measure the cyclical properties of aggregate data series according to Lucas's (1977) definition. The first approach is to compute the moments of cyclical components, and the second approach is to compute the moments of growth rates. The cyclical component time series of GDP (output; denoted by the letter y), household consumption (c), gross capital formation (i), government consumption (g), exports (x) and imports (m) is expressed as the difference between logs of corresponding intensively expressed observed and trend time series. The cyclical component time series of the trade balance (tb), current account (ca) and share of government consumption (gy) are expressed

Table 2. Moments of the Cyclical Components Computed Using the Log-Quadratic Trend

standard deviations	**BG**	**CZ**	**EE**	**HR**	**HU**	**LV**	**LT**	**PL**	**RO**	**SK**	**SI**	**weighted average**
σ_y	6.51	4.51	6.19	4.06	3.14	7.90	6.43	2.14	15.12	4.44	3.51	5.92
σ_c/σ_y	1.19	0.69	1.31	1.13	1.44	1.37	1.38	0.89	0.71	0.84	0.74	0.94
σ_g/σ_y	1.35	0.70	0.65	0.69	1.19	0.55	0.46	1.45	0.28	0.91	0.58	0.98
σ_i/σ_y	3.69	2.06	3.50	3.56	2.24	2.59	3.22	5.61	1.18	3.00	3.58	3.50
σ_x/σ_y	1.61	1.17	1.51	1.27	1.76	0.86	1.37	2.25	0.43	1.62	1.88	1.54
σ_m/σ_y	1.88	1.06	2.08	2.26	1.71	1.72	1.85	3.73	0.87	1.51	2.15	2.25
$\sigma_{tb/y}$	5.17	1.23	5.02	2.76	1.23	5.95	4.09	1.87	4.93	2.40	1.47	2.86
$\sigma_{ca/y}$	10.43	2.57	17.08	–	1.72	10.83	59.76	–	–	19.18	3.33	–
correlations with *y*	**BG**	**CZ**	**EE**	**HR**	**HU**	**LV**	**LT**	**PL**	**RO**	**SK**	**SI**	**weighted average**
c	0.94	0.90	0.95	0.96	0.90	0.97	0.96	0.88	0.15	0.92	0.76	0.75
i	0.81	0.94	0.93	0.92	0.53	0.89	0.83	0.95	-0.02	0.78	0.96	0.69
x	0.18	0.71	0.63	0.72	0.39	0.73	0.66	0.39	-0.24	0.49	0.91	0.33
m	0.60	0.67	0.88	0.92	0.43	0.89	0.88	0.85	-0.01	0.66	0.96	0.60
tb	-0.85	0.40	-0.94	-0.86	-0.41	-0.92	-0.89	-0.89	-0.14	-0.26	-0.69	-0.53
ca	-0.76	-0.08	-0.28	–	-0.15	-0.93	-0.23	–	–	0.07	-0.83	–
gy	-0.05	-0.76	-0.61	-0.68	-0.02	-0.78	-0.91	-0.17	-0.96	-0.52	-0.81	-0.46
serial correlations	**BG**	**CZ**	**EE**	**HR**	**HU**	**LV**	**LT**	**PL**	**RO**	**SK**	**SI**	**weighted average**
y	0.70	0.78	0.57	0.72	0.63	0.66	0.61	0.67	-0.17	0.72	0.61	0.51
c	0.71	0.77	0.70	0.60	0.65	0.67	0.71	0.65	0.80	0.76	0.61	0.70
g	0.20	0.49	0.72	0.69	0.65	0.45	0.66	0.75	-0.07	0.38	0.64	0.48
i	0.22	0.56	0.50	0.61	-0.05	0.49	0.22	0.61	0.70	0.30	0.54	0.50
x	0.11	0.31	0.28	0.36	0.40	0.37	0.35	0.18	0.46	0.30	0.46	0.29
m	0.24	0.23	0.41	0.55	0.21	0.50	0.44	0.42	0.66	0.30	0.49	0.42
tb	0.61	0.45	0.64	0.45	0.34	0.51	0.53	0.62	0.63	0.04	0.42	0.53
ca	0.70	0.04	-0.40	–	-0.09	0.49	-0.20	–	–	-0.02	0.09	–
Average	**BG**	**CZ**	**EE**	**HR**	**HU**	**LV**	**LT**	**PL**	**RO**	**SK**	**SI**	**weighted average**
$(x+m)/y$	113.22	119.32	147.97	83.79	134.68	108.74	118.39	69.93	71.90	145.73	119.78	93.07

Note: The annual time series of post-communist countries for the period 1995-2013 are adapted from "GDP and main components (output, expenditure and income)" by Eurostat database (2014). Retrieved from http://appsso.eurostat.ec.europa.eu/nui/show.do?dataset=nama_10_gdp&lang=en

Table 3. Moments of Cyclical Components – the Hodrick-Prescott Filter (λ = 100)

standard deviations	**BG**	**CZ**	**EE**	**HR**	**HU**	**LV**	**LT**	**PL**	**RO**	**SK**	**SI**	**weighted average**
σ_y	5.15	3.59	6.07	3.86	2.89	7.31	5.84	2.04	15.22	3.73	3.44	5.62
σ_c/σ_y	1.22	0.72	1.28	1.12	1.44	1.34	1.34	0.99	0.55	0.89	0.74	0.95
σ_g/σ_y	1.57	0.82	0.54	0.63	1.10	0.60	0.44	1.24	0.28	1.00	0.60	0.92
σ_i/σ_y	4.37	2.23	3.46	3.62	2.77	2.76	3.53	5.55	0.95	3.43	3.67	3.59
σ_x/σ_y	1.99	1.44	1.51	1.42	2.09	0.91	1.47	2.31	0.38	1.85	1.78	1.66
σ_m/σ_y	2.30	1.34	2.08	2.30	2.23	1.80	1.94	4.03	0.72	1.82	2.08	2.45
$\sigma_{tb/y}$	4.65	1.21	4.68	2.51	1.39	5.59	3.80	1.80	4.35	2.59	1.49	2.67
$\sigma_{ca/y}$	9.23	2.55	16.61	–	1.77	10.22	59.21	–	–	18.36	3.14	–
correlations with *y*	**BG**	**CZ**	**EE**	**HR**	**HU**	**LV**	**LT**	**PL**	**RO**	**SK**	**SI**	**weighted average**
c	0.90	0.85	0.95	0.95	0.89	0.97	0.95	0.87	0.22	0.86	0.77	0.75
i	0.76	0.92	0.94	0.92	0.65	0.89	0.84	0.95	0.02	0.77	0.97	0.70
x	0.16	0.70	0.70	0.79	0.52	0.74	0.64	0.47	-0.15	0.48	0.88	0.38
m	0.55	0.67	0.90	0.93	0.59	0.89	0.88	0.86	0.08	0.67	0.94	0.63
tb	-0.78	0.31	-0.91	-0.79	-0.53	-0.91	-0.87	-0.91	-0.19	-0.29	-0.70	-0.56
ca	-0.67	-0.13	-0.29	–	-0.22	-0.93	-0.23	–	–	-0.05	-0.79	–
gy	0.10	-0.73	-0.75	-0.75	-0.26	-0.74	-0.90	-0.31	-0.97	-0.49	-0.79	-0.52
serial correlations	**BG**	**CZ**	**EE**	**HR**	**HU**	**LV**	**LT**	**PL**	**RO**	**SK**	**SI**	**weighted average**
y	0.63	0.72	0.58	0.69	0.69	0.65	0.57	0.63	-0.27	0.65	0.61	0.46
c	0.65	0.68	0.70	0.56	0.75	0.63	0.67	0.58	0.75	0.69	0.57	0.66
g	0.19	0.50	0.64	0.65	0.63	0.50	0.60	0.69	-0.09	0.27	0.64	0.44
i	0.29	0.44	0.50	0.55	0.20	0.51	0.20	0.58	0.62	0.21	0.56	0.48
x	0.08	0.32	0.27	0.42	0.48	0.33	0.33	0.13	0.42	0.30	0.41	0.27
m	0.24	0.24	0.41	0.53	0.45	0.46	0.39	0.38	0.59	0.29	0.47	0.41
tb	0.63	0.44	0.62	0.36	0.59	0.47	0.48	0.58	0.56	0.03	0.42	0.52
ca	0.67	0.03	-0.38	–	-0.05	0.45	-0.22	–	–	-0.07	-0.01	–
average	**BG**	**CZ**	**EE**	**HR**	**HU**	**LV**	**LT**	**PL**	**RO**	**SK**	**SI**	**weighted average**
(x+m)/y	113.22	119.32	147.97	83.79	134.68	108.74	118.39	69.93	71.90	145.73	119.78	93.07

Note: The value λ = 100 used in these calculations is suggested by Hodrick and Prescott (1997).
The annual time series of post-communist countries for the period 1995-2013 are adapted from "GDP and main components (output, expenditure and income)" by Eurostat database (2014). Retrieved from http://appsso.eurostat.ec.europa.eu/nui/show.do?dataset=nama_10_gdp&lang=en

Table 4. Moments of Cyclical Components – the Hodrick-Prescott Filter (λ = 6.25)

standard deviations	BG	CZ	EE	HR	HU	LV	LT	PL	RO	SK	SI	weighted average
σ_y	2.41	1.69	4.25	2.09	1.45	4.73	3.97	1.12	12.43	2.09	1.95	3.88
σ_c/σ_y	1.37	0.73	1.13	1.31	1.30	1.38	1.21	0.87	0.29	0.78	0.64	0.85
σ_g/σ_y	2.44	1.15	0.43	0.65	1.13	0.70	0.41	1.05	0.30	1.34	0.48	0.97
σ_i/σ_y	7.07	3.25	3.71	4.50	4.14	3.05	4.28	6.18	0.66	4.83	4.10	4.33
σ_x/σ_y	3.75	2.41	1.79	1.77	2.98	1.13	1.78	3.27	0.30	2.73	2.28	2.38
σ_m/σ_y	4.03	2.27	2.32	2.86	3.10	2.11	2.21	4.83	0.50	2.58	2.52	3.08
$\sigma_{tb/y}$	2.91	0.95	3.13	1.88	0.86	3.94	2.51	0.98	2.61	2.12	1.05	1.67
$\sigma_{ca/y}$	5.55	2.31	15.04	–	1.56	7.50	54.99	–	–	15.66	2.51	–
correlations with *y*	**BG**	**CZ**	**EE**	**HR**	**HU**	**LV**	**LT**	**PL**	**RO**	**SK**	**SI**	**weighted average**
c	0.66	0.53	0.93	0.91	0.67	0.95	0.92	0.78	0.46	0.72	0.54	0.68
i	0.82	0.92	0.96	0.88	0.76	0.85	0.86	0.93	0.15	0.75	0.95	0.73
x	0.26	0.77	0.76	0.76	0.70	0.75	0.65	0.58	0.04	0.57	0.88	0.50
m	0.60	0.83	0.94	0.92	0.77	0.87	0.86	0.82	0.14	0.81	0.94	0.67
tb	-0.75	0.20	-0.88	-0.70	-0.29	-0.84	-0.83	-0.85	-0.14	-0.22	-0.47	-0.50
ca	-0.61	-0.37	-0.29	–	-0.01	-0.92	-0.18	–	–	-0.46	-0.78	–
gy	0.53	-0.80	-0.87	-0.80	-0.55	-0.60	-0.91	-0.56	-0.98	-0.49	-0.91	-0.61
serial correlations	**BG**	**CZ**	**EE**	**HR**	**HU**	**LV**	**LT**	**PL**	**RO**	**SK**	**SI**	**weighted average**
y	0.07	0.25	0.37	0.29	0.13	0.44	0.29	0.40	-0.33	0.27	0.17	0.17
c	0.25	0.09	0.51	0.17	0.23	0.41	0.41	0.31	0.21	0.32	0.06	0.25
g	-0.08	0.14	0.25	0.22	0.10	0.28	0.27	0.15	-0.20	-0.07	0.13	0.06
i	-0.02	0.05	0.30	0.27	-0.24	0.26	-0.01	0.36	0.20	-0.03	0.17	0.17
x	-0.08	0.09	0.09	-0.07	0.23	0.17	0.16	-0.27	-0.15	0.15	0.09	-0.09
m	0.01	-0.03	0.22	0.18	0.08	0.27	0.16	0.07	0.08	0.07	0.11	0.07
tb	0.37	0.30	0.43	0.04	0.10	0.21	0.09	0.31	0.20	-0.03	0.10	0.23
ca	0.45	-0.10	-0.63	–	-0.22	0.24	-0.32	–	–	-0.27	-0.31	–
average	**BG**	**CZ**	**EE**	**HR**	**HU**	**LV**	**LT**	**PL**	**RO**	**SK**	**SI**	**weighted average**
(x+m)/y	113.22	119.32	147.97	83.79	134.68	108.74	118.39	69.93	71.90	145.73	119.78	93.07

Note: The value λ = 6.25 used in these calculations is suggested by Ravn and Uhlig (2002).
The annual time series of post-communist countries for the period 1995-2013 are adapted from "GDP and main components (output, expenditure and income)" by Eurostat database (2014). Retrieved from http://appsso.eurostat.ec.europa.eu/nui/show.do?dataset=nama_10_gdp&lang=en

Table 5. Moments of Growth Rates

standard deviations	**BG**	**CZ**	**EE**	**HR**	**HU**	**LV**	**LT**	**PL**	**RO**	**SK**	**SI**	**weighted average**
σ_y	4.65	3.08	6.34	4.00	2.89	6.84	5.89	1.86	21.26	3.37	3.76	6.67
σ_c/σ_y	1.23	0.78	1.14	1.19	1.35	1.34	1.20	1.12	0.32	0.92	0.74	0.95
σ_g/σ_y	2.04	1.04	0.48	0.58	1.03	0.71	0.42	1.17	0.30	1.36	0.60	0.96
σ_i/σ_y	5.80	2.92	3.60	3.81	3.97	3.27	4.66	5.75	0.64	4.83	3.75	4.01
σ_x/σ_y	3.10	2.13	1.84	1.77	2.46	1.15	1.74	3.58	0.31	2.50	1.91	2.35
σ_m/σ_y	3.28	2.12	2.31	2.51	2.83	2.12	2.23	5.15	0.52	2.57	2.18	3.08
$\sigma_{tb/y}$	4.68	1.17	4.73	2.58	1.25	4.82	3.63	1.81	4.52	2.35	1.46	2.66
$\sigma_{ca/y}$	9.47	2.63	17.27	–	1.69	9.52	61.78	–	–	19.01	3.11	–
correlations with y	**BG**	**CZ**	**EE**	**HR**	**HU**	**LV**	**LT**	**PL**	**RO**	**SK**	**SI**	**weighted average**
c	0.69	0.72	0.92	0.91	0.81	0.93	0.92	0.80	0.29	0.70	0.75	0.69
i	0.78	0.90	0.95	0.88	0.77	0.83	0.85	0.93	0.02	0.76	0.96	0.70
x	0.23	0.73	0.75	0.81	0.73	0.71	0.64	0.61	-0.02	0.58	0.84	0.49
m	0.51	0.76	0.91	0.90	0.79	0.84	0.86	0.84	0.09	0.77	0.93	0.66
tb	-0.22	0.16	-0.34	-0.06	-0.42	-0.47	-0.21	-0.36	-0.16	-0.22	-0.07	-0.24
ca	-0.01	-0.01	-0.34	–	-0.17	-0.52	-0.11	–	–	-0.66	-0.26	–
gy	0.54	-0.24	-0.71	-0.59	-0.13	-0.51	-0.62	0.13	-0.60	-0.41	-0.52	-0.16
serial correlations	**BG**	**CZ**	**EE**	**HR**	**HU**	**LV**	**LT**	**PL**	**RO**	**SK**	**SI**	**weighted average**
y	0.47	0.42	0.39	0.57	0.38	0.45	0.23	0.45	-0.35	0.28	0.35	0.27
c	0.37	0.46	0.62	0.32	0.65	0.39	0.41	0.57	0.32	0.53	0.43	0.48
g	0.26	0.07	0.32	0.32	0.16	0.29	0.15	0.20	-0.36	-0.16	0.53	0.07
i	0.19	0.02	0.26	0.38	-0.15	0.25	-0.11	0.36	0.26	-0.05	0.29	0.21
x	-0.25	0.03	-0.06	0.09	0.25	0.04	0.02	-0.31	-0.14	0.03	0.01	-0.13
m	-0.08	-0.02	0.09	0.25	0.22	0.18	0.01	0.08	0.17	-0.06	0.12	0.09
tb	0.59	0.43	0.64	0.43	0.31	0.44	0.52	0.62	0.65	0.04	0.41	0.53
ca	0.71	0.05	-0.39	–	-0.10	0.44	-0.20	–	–	-0.02	0.10	–
average	**BG**	**CZ**	**EE**	**HR**	**HU**	**LV**	**LT**	**PL**	**RO**	**SK**	**SI**	**weighted average**
(x+m)/y	113.22	119.32	147.97	83.79	134.68	108.74	118.39	69.93	71.90	145.73	119.78	93.07

Note: The annual time series of post-communist countries for the period 1995-2013 are adapted from "GDP and main components (output, expenditure and income)" by Eurostat database (2014). Retrieved from http://appsso.eurostat.ec.europa.eu/nui/show.do?dataset=nama_10_gdp&lang=en

as the difference between corresponding intensively expressed observed and trend time series.

There are several possible methods for expressing the trends of the data series. Like Uribe and Schmitt-Grohé (2017), we utilize the log-quadratic trend and the Hodrick and Prescott (1997) filter. It is important to correctly choose the weights for the Hodrick-Prescott filter. Generally, the value of $\lambda = 100$ is used, but Ravn and Uhlig (2002) suggest using the value of $\lambda = 6.25$. We use all three methods to detrend the data series.

Using the second approach, we compute the data series of growth rates of GDP (y), household consumption (c), gross capital formation (i), government consumption (g), exports (x) and imports (m) as the first difference of logs of intensively expressed corresponding data series. The data series of growth rates of the trade balance (tb), current account (ca) and share of government consumption (gy) are computed from the data series of the exports and imports difference, current account and government consumption share of the GDP.

Tables 2-5 present the second moments of data series aggregates; standard error (in percentage terms) measuring relative volatilities; the serial correlation coefficient measuring persistence; and the correlation coefficient with the GDP cyclical component (growth rate for Table 5). Each table refers to different computation methods. In Table 2, cyclical components are computed using the log-quadratic trend; in Table 3, they are computed using the Hodrick-Prescott filter with $\lambda = 100$; and in Table 4, they are computed using the Hodrick-Prescott filter with $\lambda = 6.25$. Table 5 shows the second moments of growth rates of data series. Average second moments weighted by the countries' population sizes are computed in the last columns of Tables 2-5. Average international trade balance-to-output ratios are in the bottom row. We could not compute the current account moments for Romania and Poland because the corresponding data series are incomplete for the period 1995-2013.

3. Results and Discussion

Using the methodology of Calderón and Fuentes (2010) and quarterly data from the period 1995-2012, we cannot fully confirm their results, which were obtained using more extensive quarterly data from the period 1970-2007. From Table 1, it follows that contractions are more pronounced in emerging countries than in developed countries and that expansions are longer in emerging countries than in developed countries. Different results come from our post-communist business cycle analysis using quarterly Eurostat data from the period 1995-2013. We can see that both expansions and contractions are longer and more pronounced in post-communist countries than in both emerging and developed countries. The estimated variation of the cycle confirms this view. Cumulative gains and losses in post-communist countries are higher than in both emerging and developed countries. Moreover, comparing amplitude-to-duration ratios, post-communist contractions are more pronounced than post-communist expansions and more pronounced than contractions in developed and other emerging countries. It is necessary to note that the data range studied is short. Using these limited data, we cannot confirm the results of Calderón and Fuentes. The limited availability of official post-communist data stems from the fact that these countries transformed their economic system only 25 years ago. It is reasonable to assume that business cycle characteristics have evolved with changes in the system. Countries and agents are now more open to international goods and services and financial markets. Trade shocks, which have characteristic effects on short-term economic performance, are now more pronounced.

The average cyclical component moments of 11 post-communist countries in the last columns of Tables 2-5 confirm several global business cycle characteristics proposed by Uribe and Schmitt-Grohé (2017):

- exports and imports are more volatile than output.
- on average, household consumption, gross capital formation, exports and imports are positively correlated with output.
- trade balance is negatively correlated with output.
- the components of aggregate supply (output and imports) and aggregate demand (household and government consumption, gross capital formation and exports) are positively serially correlated.

All four methods used in this study confirm these propositions. If we focus on consumption volatility and trade balance correlation with output, all four methods roughly generate the same results. Therefore, we used only one approach in our further analysis. To compare our results with other analyses in the literature, we chose a log-quadratic trend to compute cyclical components.

In Table 6, we present a comparison of the average moments of cyclical components using a log-quadratic trend of 11 post-communist, emerging, and developed countries (i.e., the last column of Table 2). The results for poor, emerging, and developed countries are obtained from Uribe and Schmitt-Grohé (2017), who used data from the period 1965-2010 and employed the same methodology.

It follows from Table 6 that the aggregate economic activity of 11 post-communist countries in the period 1995-2013 was less volatile than the aggregate economic activity of emerging countries in the period 1965-2010. Notice that this period includes the shorter period of 1982-2008, which has been labeled by many authors (e.g., Williamson, 2014) as "the Great Moderation" because U.S. output was less volatile in this period. The post-communist trade balance is relatively strongly counter-cyclical, contradicting the argument in the introduction that the trade balance-to-output ratio is more negatively correlated with output as the level of economic development increases. Post-communist countries are similar to other emerging countries in terms of the volatility of consumption.

For a more detailed view, we should divide emerging countries according to population size because economic activity in larger countries is less volatile. We should compare the cyclical component moments of similarly sized countries. As stated earlier, using the definition of Uribe and Schmitt-Grohé (2017), Poland and Romania are medium-sized countries. The weighted averages of the moments of cyclical components in small countries (i.e., 9 small post-communist countries in the period 1995-2013) are computed in Table 7. The results for poor, emerging, and developed countries are obtained from Uribe and Schmitt-Grohé (2017), who used data from the period 1965-2010 and employed the same methodology.

The results of the analysis are similar: output volatility in post-communist countries in the period 1995-2013 is lower than that in poor and emerging countries from 1965-2010. The volatility of government share of GDP in post-communist countries (1995-2013) is similar to that in developed countries (1965-2010). Consumption is highly volatile and the trade balance or current account is more strongly counter-cyclical in post-communist countries (1995-2013).

We reach the same conclusions if we compare the results of Poland with those of other medium-sized countries (see Table 8). In contrast, the results for Romania are unique. Romanian output is very volatile and the trade balance is weakly counter-cyclical. Furthermore, output in Romania is negatively serially correlated. We can conclude that Romanian business cycles differ from those of other post-communist countries and that this analysis is less helpful in the case of Romania than it is in the cases of other post-communist countries.

Assisted by other studies, we can put forth several observations from this "first look at the data" as our contribution to the discussion of results.

We cannot overlook the long-term development of post-communist countries. Szomolányi, Lukáčiková and Lukáčik (2011) show that post-communist countries were in a transitional state in the period 1997-2009 and that they were converging to a higher level expressed by steady state GDP per capita. The steady state was similar for European Union countries.[2] In other words, post-communist European Union members may be as rich as Germany several decades from now. It follows from neoclassical growth theory that as post-communist countries have been in a transitional state, their steady state has changed (risen) dramatically. This change stems from events such as economic system transformation, opening up to international markets, price liberalization, privatization, tax reformation and legal system transformation, among others. All these events have been present in some form in all post-communist countries during the period studied. Moreover, there were currency transformations in many countries. As explained by neoclassical growth theory, events causing changes in steady states are themselves mostly caused by permanent real shocks. Indeed, the afore-mentioned events have the character of permanent real shocks, which may explain why post-communist business cycles last longer than those of other countries (see Table 1). It follows from the real business cycle principles

Table 6. Cyclical Properties of Post-Communist, Poor, Emerging and Developed Countries

	Countries			
standard deviations	**post-communist**	**poor**	**emerging**	**developed**
σ_y	5.92	6.08	8.71	3.32
σ_c/σ_y	0.94	1.12	0.98	0.87
σ_g/σ_y	0.98	2.46	2.00	1.73
σ_i/σ_y	3.50	3.24	2.79	3.20
σ_x/σ_y	1.54	3.08	2.82	3.36
σ_m/σ_y	2.25	3.30	2.72	3.64
$\sigma_{tb/y}$	2.86	2.12	3.80	1.25
$\sigma_{ca/y}$	–	2.06	3.08	1.39
correlations with *y*	**post-communist**	**poor**	**emerging**	**developed**
c	0.75	0.66	0.75	0.76
i	0.69	0.60	0.77	0.77
x	0.33	0.14	0.35	0.17
m	0.60	0.14	0.50	0.34
tb	-0.53	-0.11	-0.21	-0.26
ca	–	-0.28	-0.24	-0.30
gy	-0.46	0.08	-0.08	-0.39
serial correlations	**post-communist**	**poor**	**emerging**	**developed**
y	0.51	0.65	0.87	0.76
c	0.70	0.62	0.74	0.75
g	0.48	0.71	0.80	0.89
i	0.50	0.49	0.72	0.67
x	0.29	0.65	0.74	0.74
m	0.42	0.61	0.74	0.69
tb	0.53	0.59	0.62	0.69
ca	–	0.55	0.52	0.71
average	**post-communist**	**poor**	**emerging**	**developed**
$(x+m)/y$	93.07	32.50	46.40	40.40

Source: Uribe and Schmitt-Grohé (2017) and authors' calculations.

Note: The annual time series of post-communist countries for the period 1995-2013 are adapted from "GDP and main components (output, expenditure and income)" by Eurostat database (2014). Retrieved from http://appsso.eurostat.ec.europa.eu/nui/show.do?dataset=nama_10_gdp&lang=en

Table 7. Cyclical Properties of Small Countries

	small countries			
standard deviations	**post-communist**	**poor**	**emerging**	**developed**
σ_y	4.80	8.17	9.50	4.31
σ_c/σ_y	1.09	1.39	0.97	0.92
σ_g/σ_y	0.91	2.92	1.85	1.66
σ_i/σ_y	2.83	4.68	2.97	3.07
σ_x/σ_y	1.47	2.81	2.23	2.23
σ_m/σ_y	1.66	2.96	2.25	2.36
$\sigma_{tb/y}$	2.72	5.62	4.00	2.29
$\sigma_{ca/y}$	10.47	4.84	3.55	2.37
correlation with *y*	**post-communist**	**poor**	**emerging**	**developed**
c	0.92	0.58	0.73	0.55
i	0.80	0.45	0.72	0.63
x	0.53	0.53	0.53	0.58
m	0.67	0.53	0.62	0.63
tb	-0.42	-0.04	-0.21	-0.11
ca	-0.31	-0.17	-0.20	-0.11
gy	-0.46	0.02	0.03	-0.26
serial correlations	**post-communist**	**poor**	**emerging**	**developed**
y	0.69	0.76	0.89	0.83
c	0.70	0.61	0.70	0.73
g	0.51	0.61	0.78	0.87
i	0.32	0.62	0.67	0.71
x	0.31	0.58	0.74	0.68
m	0.31	0.68	0.71	0.66
tb	0.42	0.50	0.52	0.67
ca	0.13	0.36	0.40	0.56
average	**post-communist**	**poor**	**emerging**	**developed**
$(x+m)/y$	121.60	57.70	69.20	116.80

Source: Uribe and Schmitt-Grohé (2017) and authors' calculations.

Note: The annual time series of post-communist countries for the period 1995-2013 are adapted from "GDP and main components (output, expenditure and income)" by Eurostat database (2014). Retrieved from http://appsso.eurostat.ec.europa.eu/nui/show.do?dataset=nama_10_gdp&lang=en

Table 8. Cyclical Properties of Medium-sized Countries

			medium-sized countries		
standard deviations	**Poland**	**Romania**	**poor**	**emerging**	**developed**
σ_y	2.14	15.12	9.46	8.99	3.05
σ_c/σ_y	0.89	0.71	1.05	0.93	0.93
σ_g/σ_y	1.45	0.28	2.86	2.05	1.71
σ_i/σ_y	5.60	1.18	4.01	2.86	3.07
σ_x/σ_y	2.25	0.43	3.94	2.92	3.33
σ_m/σ_y	3.73	0.87	3.45	2.68	3.80
$\sigma_{tb/y}$	1.87	4.93	3.82	4.39	1.47
$\sigma_{ca/y}$	–	–	3.40	3.45	1.47
correlation with *y*	**Poland**	**Romania**	**poor**	**emerging**	**developed**
c	0.88	0.15	0.74	0.70	0.70
i	0.95	-0.02	0.55	0.76	0.74
x	0.39	-0.24	0.58	0.36	0.37
m	0.85	-0.01	0.62	0.57	0.47
tb	-0.89	-0.14	-0.25	-0.24	-0.24
ca	–	–	-0.11	-0.34	-0.08
gy	-0.17	-0.96	0.24	0.00	-0.40
serial correlations	**Poland**	**Romania**	**poor**	**emerging**	**developed**
y	0.67	-0.17	0.84	0.84	0.80
c	0.65	0.80	0.61	0.71	0.75
g	0.75	-0.07	0.74	0.80	0.89
i	0.61	0.70	0.64	0.70	0.61
x	0.18	0.46	0.73	0.76	0.75
m	0.42	0.66	0.68	0.72	0.71
tb	0.62	0.63	0.51	0.58	0.68
ca	–	–	0.42	0.46	0.67
average	**Poland**	**Romania**	**poor**	**emerging**	**developed**
$(x+m)/y$	69.93	71.90	48.90	49.70	45.20

Source: Uribe and Schmitt-Grohé (2017) and authors' calculations.
Note: The annual time series of Poland and Romania for the period 1995-2013 are adapted from "GDP and main components (output, expenditure and income)" by Eurostat database (2014). Retrieved from http://appsso.eurostat.ec.europa.eu/nui/show.do?dataset=nama_10_gdp&lang=en

outlined in the introduction that higher consumption volatility and trade balance (current account) counter-cyclicality occur if permanent real shocks occur.

García-Cicco et al. (2010), Uribe and Yue (2006) and Uribe and Schmitt-Grohé (2017) state that the business cycles of emerging countries are driven by interest rate and interest rate spread shocks, but our study cannot confirm that financial friction is an important determinant of the business cycle in post-communist countries. Consumption is relatively highly volatile in post-communist countries, but their trade balance is too counter-cyclical. For example, Szomolányi et al. (2014a; 2014b) conducted SVAR analysis that shows that interest rate and interest rate spread shocks have had a very small impact on Slovak and Czech business cycles.

Financial friction is a significant factor in the short- and medium-term economic performance of emerging and poor countries around the world. As the credibility of domestic economic policy decreases, domestic interest rate spreads increase. Low output is one of the consequences of decreased policy credibility. The limited ability of agents to borrow causes a cumulative fall in output. Interest rate and interest rate spread shocks cause high domestic output volatility. Therefore, output volatility is higher in emerging and poor countries around the world than in post-communist countries.

4. Conclusion

Even if we consider European post-communist countries to be emerging, their business cycle characteristics differ slightly from those of emerging countries around the world:

- post-communist countries' expansions and recessions are longer.
- post-communist countries' recessions are more pronounced.
- post-communist countries' output is relatively low in volatility.
- post-communist countries' household consumption is relatively highly volatile.
- the government share of GDP is countercyclical in post-communist countries.
- trade balances (current accounts) are relatively strongly counter-cyclical in post-communist countries.

We understand that business cycle analysis in post-communist countries is more complex because of differences related to the level of economic (monetary) integration into European structures, their financial links to the rest of the world, etc. However, the results obtained herein reveal that the simple characteristics of business cycles are similar across post-communist countries, with the exception of Romania.

When analyzing business cycles, we attempted to use as long a time series as possible. This analysis focused on the characteristics of the economic cycles of European post-communist countries. Our intention was thus partly thwarted by the lack of sufficiently long and reliable data for these economies. Nevertheless, this paper identifies particularities in these post-communist countries despite the data limitations. We also wanted to contrast our results with previously known and accepted conclusions regarding other types of economies that are in many ways different from post-communist economies. The reasons for these differences are the focus of ongoing research and continuous discussions, and our goal was not to analyze any changes that occurred after the period of Great Moderation. Rather, our intent was to use the available data on European post-communist countries to reveal the characteristics of their economic cycles. Furthermore, we tried to intuitively form conclusions regarding why a group of European post-communist countries differs from its closest typological group, i.e., small emerging economies.

References

Aguiar, M., & Gopinath, G. (2007). Emerging market business cycles: The cycle is the trend. *Journal of Political Economy, 115(1)*, 69-102.

Burns, A. F., & Mitchell, W. C. (1946). *Measuring business cycles.* New York, NY: National Bureau of Economic Research. Retrieved from http://papers.nber.org/books/burn46-1

Calderón, C., & Fuentes, R. (2010). Characterizing the business cycles of emerging economies (Policy Research Working Paper No. 5343). The World Bank. Retrieved from https://papers.ssrn.com/sol3/papers.cfm?abstract_id=1629052

Eurostat (2014). database (2014). GDP and main components (output, expenditure and income).

Retrieved from http://appsso.eurostat.ec.europa.eu/nui/show.do?dataset=namq_10_gdp&lang=en

García-Cicco, J., Pancrazi, R., & Uribe, M. (2010). Real business cycles in emerging countries? *American Economic Review, 100*(5), 2510-2531.

Hodrick, R. J., & Prescott, E. C. (1997). Postwar U.S. business cycles: An empirical investigation. *Journal of Money, Credit and Banking, 29*(1), 1-16.

Kydland, F. E., & Prescott, E. C. (1982). Time to build and aggregate fluctuations. *Econometrica, 50*(2), 1345-1370.

Lucas, R. E. Jr. (1976). Econometric policy evaluation: A critique. *Carnegie-Rochester Conference Series on Public Policy, 1(1)*, 19-46.

Lucas, R. E. Jr. (1977). Understanding business cycles. *Carnegie-Rochester Conference Series on Public Policy, 5*(1), 7-29.

Mendoza, E. (1991). Real business cycles in a small open economy. *American Economic Review, 81*(4), 797-818.

Montiel, P. J. (2013). *Macroeconomics in Emerging Markets* (2nd ed.). New York, NY: Cambridge University Press.

OECD database (2014). Quarterly National Accounts. Retrieved from http://stats.oecd.org/BrandedView.aspx?oecd_bv_id=na-data-en&doi=data-00017-en

Ravn, M. O., & Uhlig, H. (2002). On adjusting the Hodrick-Prescott filter for the frequency of observations. *The Review of Economics and Statistics, 84*(2), 371-375.

Szomolányi, K., Lukáčiková, A., & Lukáčik, M. (2011). The β-convergence of the EU27 countries. In M. Dlouhý & V. Skočdopolová (Eds.), *Proceedings of the 29th International Conference Mathematical Methods in Economics 2011* (Vol. 2, pp. 287-291). Praha: Professional Publishing.

Szomolányi, K., Lukáčik, M., & Lukáčiková, A. (2014a). Slovak Economy and Interest Rates Shocks. In M. Reiff, & M. Lukáčik (Eds.), *Proceedings of the 17th International Conference Quantitative Methods in Economics. Multiple Criteria Decision Making XVII* (pp. 263-269). Bratislava: Ekonóm.

Szomolányi, K., Lukáčik, M., & Lukáčiková, A. (2014b). World Financial Frictions and the Czech Economy. In O. Deev, V. Kajurová, & J. Krajíček (Eds.), *Proceedings of the 11th International Scientific Conference European Financial Systems* (pp. 638645). Brno: Masaryk University.

Uribe, M., & Schmitt-Grohé, S. (2017). *Open Economy Macroeconomics.* Princeton, NJ: Princeton University Press.

Uribe, M., & Yue, V. Z. (2006). Country spreads and emerging countries: Who drives whom? *Journal of International Economics, 69*(1), 6-36.

Williamson, S. D. (2014). *Macroeconomics* (5th ed.). Upper Saddle River, NJ: Pearson Education.

Endnotes

1 *Longer data series were not published at the time of processing.*

2 *Croatia was not a member of the European Union at the time of the paper's completion (2011). Hungary seemed to converge to a statistically significantly lower steady state than other European Union members.*

Acknowledgements

This paper is supported by the Grant Agency of the Slovak Republic - VEGA, grant no. 1/0444/15 "Econometric Analysis of Production Possibilities of the Economy and the Labour Market in Slovakia".

2

A new measure of international product innovation

Valeska V. Geldres-Weiss[1], Joaquín Monreal-Pérez[2], Dirceu Tornavoi-Carvalho[3], Jorge Tello-Gamarra[4]

ABSTRACT

It is important for firms to undertake product innovation since this will enable them to incorporate additional value to its market offer and, consequently, will increase their international competitiveness. Thus, the aim of this article is to develop a new index, the Export Product Innovation Index (EPII), a metric that associates product innovation to export activity according to the value of new export products / goods traded abroad at a single company level. The proposed index is built on official export data and based on the Harmonized System Codes. Therefore, the EPII may be widely generalized and calculated for every export firm all over the world for which export shipping data is available, enabling benchmarks for companies, international comparative studies and policy making. This article uses data on Chilean fruit exporters to illustrate EPII calculation and use. Through the comparison of this new index with some previous ones measuring product innovation overall population of Chilean fruit exporters, it is demonstrated that the EPII provides more accurate information to appraise a firm´s export product innovation performance.

KEY WORDS: Product Innovation, International Competitiveness, Export Product Innovation Index, Harmonized System Codes, Fruit Exports, Chile

[1] Universidad de La Frontera, Chile
[2] Murcia University, Spain
[3] University of Sao Paulo, Brazil
[4] University of Rio Grande, Brazil

1. Introduction

Various theoretical frameworks address sources of value creation (Amit & Zott, 2011). In the scope of export business, the question is: Which sources of value are of particular importance? Hence, we first measure the export product innovation through a new index.

Although recent decades have seen the emergence of innovation indexes applied to different types of innovation, levels of aggregation and sources of data, in the export context there have been few studies on the elaboration of individual innovation indexes. In the literature, the most studied types of innovation refer to production, processing, management and marketing (OECD, 2005). However, when it comes to exports, product innovation allows us to capture most accurately the results of this activity. Therefore, this research will be focused on product innovation.

Why choose product innovation among the different types of innovation outputs? It is considered to be the most important kind of innovation. since it is said to be an antecedent of any firm innovation strategy of the firm. In the words of Boer and During (2001), "in most cases the main motive for starting the innovation

Correspondence concerning this article should be addressed to: **Joaquín Monreal-Pérez**, Murcia University, Spain. E-mail: joaquinmonreal@hotmail.com

process was the need to develop (a) new product(s), often driven by the demands of just one customer, or the desire to penetrate new markets by developing new products or adapting existing products" (p. 14).

Thus, the objective of this article is to develop a new index, the Export Product Innovation Index (EPII), a metric that associates product innovation to export activity according to the value of new products traded abroad by export firms over time.

The purpose of this new index (EPII) is to define a product innovation metric associated with firms' export activity. It is an approach that seeks to capture product innovation in international markets and to contribute to traditional product innovation indicators as well. Dutta, Lanvin and Wunsch-Vincent (2017) also refers to this gap, which is both conceptual and empirical, in the annual editions of the Global Innovation Index (GII): "finding metrics that capture innovation as it happens in today's world remains a key challenge, since direct official measures that quantify innovation outputs are still scarce". Thus, the present article contributes to narrowing down such gaps by focusing on product innovation from an export perspective, since most studies focus on classical indicators of innovation (e.g. R&D investment per year, number of patents registered per year, etc.)

The EPII is proposed as a way of measuring how much export value is created by product innovations by a company, measured by its impact on total export revenues. It is not a full model with causal or enabling factors, but a performance measure based on official data, which enables us to compare individual firms, build a ranking and identify case studies for future research on the underlying factors for the EPII index level achieved. EPII is proposed in such a way that it can be calculated using existing governmental data in most countries. Moreover, the article brings empirical results which add to official statistics on the amount of innovative activity in a given sector (fruit), and country level (Chile). Chile is the leading fruit exporter in the southern hemisphere and the world's leading exporter of table grapes and blueberries. The Chilean fruit area occupies 294,000 hectares, the sector produces around 5 million tons of fruit, of which 2.6 million are exported as fresh fruit, generating more than USD 4,000 million annually. (ODEPA, 2018). Product innovation is especially significant for fruit producers from Chile, who mostly sell standardized products to international intermediaries and therefore with limited profitability. Moreover, small size companies, which predominate in a country like Chile, are the type of organizations carrying out mainly product innovations (Boer & During, 2001).

Thus, for the empirical example and analysis, we have used as our example a country with a clear exporting vocation - Chile - and a sector that is relevant for this country in its international performance -the fruit sector.

The motivations behind this research are first that innovation is important to boost economic progress and competitiveness. In the field of international business, many governments are putting export promotion and innovation at the centre of their growth strategies. Second, there is the awareness that the definition of innovation has been broadened to recognize innovation in more areas, and we seek to provide an indicator of product innovation based on export markets, which is a topic that has not been treated in the literature.

The EPII provides a key tool that uses detailed metrics based on the international definitions of the Harmonized Commodity Designation and Coding System (HS) of the World Customs Organization (WCO). The innovative activity of exporting firms enables export promotion policies to be refined.

The rest of the paper is organized as follows: section 2 reviews the literature related to innovation indexes; section 3 establishes the conceptual foundations of the proposed index; section 4 provides its formulation and an example of its calculation; section 5 offers the results and an empirical comparison with other indexes of innovation are presented; finally, section 6 gives the discussion and conclusions.

2. Innovation Indexes

Innovation, and in particular its measurement, has been approached from a wide number of perspectives. These belong to two groups, according to the public or private objectives that the measure seeks to achieve, and the ownership of the information. From a firm's perspective, this means setting Key Performance Indicators (KPIs), based on firm-level data, which access its innovation capabilities and results. By doing so, it handles what is considered a strategic asset, which requires attention and investment, which is why detailed information about KPIs is seldom made available to academic researchers. From a policy maker perspective, it allows setting a good environment for innovation to take place. It means working with composite indicators to measure a complex phenomenon that is not directly measurable and not uniquely defined. It means developing a conceptual and operational model that is used for different purposes, including policy-making and monitoring, public communication, and building rankings.

As stated by Becker, Saisana, Paruolo and Vandecasteele (2017, p. 12) "The popularity of rankings is due to two main reasons. First, because of their simplicity: they provide a summary picture of the multiple facets or dimensions of complex, multidimensional phenomena in a way that facilitates evaluation and comparison. Second, because rankings force institutions and governments to question their standards; rankings are drivers of behaviour and of change".

A very well-known innovation ranking is The Global Innovation Index (GII). Published yearly since 2012. GII has evolved to shape the model that measures the five enabling pillars and two innovation outputs which compose the conceptual model. "Today innovation capability is seen more as the ability to exploit new technological combinations; it embraces the notion of incremental innovation and 'innovation without research'. Non-R&D innovative expenditure is an important component of reaping the rewards of technological innovation" (Dutta et al., 2017, p.48).

A recent publication reports a bibliometric analysis on the theme by using "innovation index" as keyword in a number of open academic databases, e.g., Scopus. Results indicate that although there have been referenced publications since 1973, the number of articles has greatly increased since 2009, and had reached more than one hundred in 2013 (Speroni, Dandolini, Souza, & Gauthier, 2015). Using the same approach with the closed database Science Direct in January 2018, and adding the keyword "export", our query returned 115 articles since 2009. The results are listed in Table 1.

The results are in agreement with Speroni et al. (2015), who also point to a similarly large increase in the number of articles since 2009. This leads to the conclusion that innovation indexes are built and used mainly for technological forecasting and policy-making. However, the presence of the Journal of Business Research and the Brazilian RAI in Table 1, unlike in Speroni et al. (2015), reveals an increase in the interest of business academics in this topic. This interest focuses on how public policies affect innovation in companies. For example, DiPietro and Anoruo (2006) suggest that a country should focus at least a portion of its export promotion efforts on establishing a favorable environment for creativity as an effective strategy for its development. The authors "test whether creativity and its four components - innovation, technology, technology transfer, and business startups - have any impact on the total value of a country's exports and on their composition" (DiPietro & Anoruo, 2006, p. 133).

The cited authors are among the few who treat export as an innovation output. In most of the articles found by our literature review, export is an independent variable used in composite measures for a country´s overall innovation performance. For example, Becker et al. (2017) assess the importance of different factors used in composite indicators for environmental performance, such as the Resource Governance Index, the Good Country Index, and the Water Retention Index. Another use is made by Esteves and Feldmann (2016), who seek to identify the most relevant factors explaining the allocation of countries in the Global Innovation Index (GII) ranking. They conclude that "the order of the variables is as follows: (1) GDP per capita, (2) public expenditure on R&D, (3) exports of high-tech products, (4) public expenditure on education, (5) number of large companies and (6) number of patents".

Similarly, the country-level innovation indexes recognize that innovation happens at company level because it has to be accompanied by entrepreneurial results to be relevant. However, they focus on "external factors that can also boost and/or hinder the emergence of innovation. Such factors can be attributed to specific institutional characteristics of the countries in which innovative companies originate from" (Esteves & Feldmann, 2016, p. 34).

On the other hand, the Global Innovation Index (GII) attempts to explain relative country performances by a conceptual and operational data model that measures five enabling pillars and two innovation outputs which compose the conceptual model.

Table 1. Top 10 journals by number of papers on Innovation Indexes and export in Science Direct

Publication title	Articles	Publication title	Articles
Technological Forecating and Social Change (*)	20	Rai Revista de Administração e inovação	6
Procedia Economics and Finance	14	Journal of Business Research	4
Research Policy (*)	11	Journal of Cleaner Production	3
Procedia - Social and Behavioral Sciences	10	World Patent Information	3
Technovation (*)	9	Procedia Computer Science	3

Note: The journals also reviewed by Speroni et al. (2015) are marked with (*).

Thus, it considers export as an output of innovation, not an antecedent.

According to this index, exports, and only those of the high tech products, are part of the output pillar "Knowledge & technology outputs", which encompasses three sub-pillars. To compose the "third sub-pillar, namely knowledge diffusion, the GII includes: (a) intellectual property receipts as a percentage of total trade; (b) high-tech net exports as a percentage of total exports; (c) exports of ICT services as a percentage of total trade; and (c) net outflows of FDI" (Dutta et al. 2017, p. 53).

Our study adopts the same perspective as the GII, considering export as an output, but not limited to high-tech products. Our literature review found a few scientific publications studying innovation in the export scenario, but none on how the indexes are elaborated. To address this gap, this article develops a new index, the Export Product Innovation Index (EPII), a metric that associates innovation to export activity by the value of new products traded abroad by exporting firms over time.

In doing so, we return to the basics, to the definition given by the Oslo Manual developed by the European Communities and the Organization for Economic Co-operation and Development (OECD): "An innovation is the implementation of a new or significantly improved product (good or service), a new process, a new marketing method, or a new organizational method in business practices, workplace organization, or external relations"(OECD, 2005, p. 146). Thus, in considering innovation, we consider not only the traditional categories of incremental and radical innovation, but innovation that change the architecture of a product without changing its components (Henderson & Clark, 1990).

We argue that there are indirect official measures that quantify innovation outputs available that may build a metric that captures innovation outputs as they occur in the world today, and so address the gap, stated by Dutta et al. (2017), and hence, accomplish the stated objective of this article.

3. Conceptual basis for calculating the EPII

EPII calculation is based on the Harmonized System Code (HS Code). This index is conceptualized so as to be calculated at a single company level, based on official export data, and described by the HS Code, which is the most successful legally binding instrument of the World Customs Organization (WCO) and is a code used worldwide and consists of six digits.

3.1. Harmonized System or HS (WCO, 2018a)

The Harmonized Commodity Description and Coding System generally, referred to as "Harmonized System" or simply "HS", is a multipurpose international product nomenclature developed by the World Customs Organization (WCO). It comprises about 5,000 commodity groups, each identified by a six-digit code, arranged in a legal and logical structure and is supported by well-defined rules for uniform classification.

Table 2. Sections and Chapters of HS Code

Section	Name of Section	Total Chapters by Section
I	LIVE ANIMALS; ANIMAL PRODUCTS	5
II	VEGETABLE PRODUCTS	9
III	ANIMAL OR VEGETABLE FATS AND OILS AND THEIR CLEAVAGE PRODUCTS; PREPARED EDIBLE FATS; ANIMAL OR VEGETABLE WAXES	1
IV	PREPARED FOODSTUFFS; BEVERAGES, SPIRITS AND VINEGAR; TOBACCO AND MANUFACTURED TOBACCO SUBSTITUTES	9
V	MINERAL PRODUCTS	3
VI	PRODUCTS OF THE CHEMICAL OR ALLIED INDUSTRIES	11
VII	PLASTICS AND ARTICLES THEREOF; RUBBER AND ARTICLES THEREOF	2
VIII	RAW HIDES AND SKINS, LEATHER, FURSKINS AND ARTICLES THEREOF; SADDLERY AND HARNESS; TRAVEL GOODS, HANDBAGS AND SIMILAR CONTAINERS; ARTICLES OF ANIMAL GUT (OTHER THAN SILK-WORM GUT)	3
IX	WOOD AND ARTICLES OF WOOD; WOOD CHARCOAL; CORK AND ARTICLES OF CORK; MANUFACTURES OF STRAW, OF ESPARTO OR OF OTHER PLAITING MATERIALS; BASKETWARE AND WICKERWORK	3
X	PULP OF WOOD OR OF OTHER FIBROUS CELLULOSIC MATERIAL; RECOVERED (WASTE AND SCRAP) PAPER OR PAPERBOARD; PAPER AND PAPERBOARD AND ARTICLES THEREOF	3
XI	TEXTILES AND TEXTILE ARTICLES	14
XII	FOOTWEAR, HEADGEAR, UMBRELLAS, SUN UMBRELLAS, WALKING-STICKS, SEAT-STICKS, WHIPS, RIDING-CROPS AND PARTS THEREOF; PREPARED FEATHERS AND ARTICLES MADE THEREWITH; ARTIFICIAL FLOWERS; ARTICLES OF HUMAN HAIR	4
XIII	ARTICLES OF STONE, PLASTER, CEMENT, ASBESTOS, MICA OR SIMILAR MATERIALS; CERAMIC PRODUCTS; GLASS AND GLASSWARE	3
XIV	NATURAL OR CULTURED PEARLS, PRECIOUS OR SEMI-PRECIOUS STONES, PRECIOUS METALS, METALS CLAD WITH PRECIOUS METAL AND ARTICLES THEREOF; IMITATION JEWELLERY; COIN	1
XV	BASE METALS AND ARTICLES OF BASE METAL	12
XVI	MACHINERY AND MECHANICAL APPLIANCES; ELECTRICAL EQUIPMENT; PARTS THEREOF; SOUND RECORDERS AND REPRODUCERS, TELEVISION IMAGE AND SOUND RECORDERS AND REPRODUCERS, AND PARTS AND ACCESSORIES OF SUCH ARTICLES	2
XVII	VEHICLES, AIRCRAFT, VESSELS AND ASSOCIATED TRANSPORT EQUIPMENT	4
XVIII	OPTICAL, PHOTOGRAPHIC, CINEMATOGRAPHIC, MEASURING, CHECKING, PRECISION, MEDICAL OR SURGICAL INSTRUMENTS AND APPARATUS; CLOCKS AND WATCHES; MUSICAL INSTRUMENTS; PARTS AND ACCESSORIES THEREOF	3
XIX	ARMS AND AMMUNITION; PARTS AND ACCESSORIES THEREOF	1
XX	MISCELLANEOUS MANUFACTURED ARTICLES	3
XXI	WORKS OF ART, COLLECTORS' PIECES AND ANTIQUES	1
TOTAL CHAPTERS		**97**

Source: Adapted from "HS Nomenclature 2017 edition" by WCO. (2018c). Available at http://www.wcoomd.org/en/topics/nomenclature/instrument-and-tools/hs-nomenclature-2017-edition/hs-nomenclature-2017-edition.aspx

The system is used by more than 200 countries and economies as a basis for their Customs tariffs and for the collection of international trade statistics. Over 98 % of the merchandise in international trade is classified in terms of the HS (WCO, 2018a). The HS contributes to the harmonization of Customs and trade procedures, and the non-documentary trade data interchange in connection with such procedures, thus reducing the costs related to international trade. It is also extensively used by governments, international organizations and the private sector for many other purposes such as internal taxes, trade policies, monitoring of controlled goods, rules of origin, freight tariffs, transport statistics, price monitoring, quota controls, compilation of national accounts, and economic research and analysis. The HS is thus a universal economic language and code for goods, and an indispensable tool for international trade. The Harmonized System is governed by "The International Convention on the Harmonized Commodity Description and Coding System".

The WCO published a new version of the Harmonized System on 1 January 2017, following a five-year review cycle. This new instrument allows all Customs administrations to monitor and control the goods trade, especially those having a social and environmental impact. The nature of this review also highlights the partnerships maintained by the WCO with international organizations such as the Food and Agricultural Organization of the United Nations. This trend should continue as new issues are raised that require clear and appropriate responses (WCO, 2018b).

3.2. HS Nomenclature (2017 edition) (WCO, 2018c)

The text of the Nomenclature established under the International Convention on the Harmonized Commodity Description and Coding System, amended as at 1 January 2017. The Nomenclature includes the General Rules for the Interpretation of the Harmonized System, the Section, Chapter and Subheading Notes, and the headings and subheadings. The HS Code is organized in 21 sections, ranging from "live animals; animal products ", up to" works of art, collectors' and antiques ", categorized in 97 chapters (WCO, 2018c) (See Table 2).

Each heading is identified by four digits, the first two indicating the Chapter number and the second two the numerical order in which the heading appears within that Chapter. The heading numbers are shown in the first column. The second column contains the texts of the headings in upper case. The third column contains the number of sections of the chapter.

4. EPII definition and calculation (EPII has been registered by the Chilean "Departamento de Derechos Intelectuales".

The EPII is used to measure the relative weight that the introduction of new products has in the exports of a company. If the company shows EPII in the year, it means that it has done a previous job to be able to export new products, so it is innovating to cover a larger market and meet the demand that they have abroad for those products. A higher the EPII means that there is a higher percentage of exports due to the innovation of new products.

The EPII allows an appraisal of the innovative behaviour of companies over the years in relation to exports, which can be used to generate public policies, promotion programs and benchmarks for goal setting. At a more aggregate level, EPII can provide an overview of innovation export trends in the country.

The EPII may take values from 0% to 100%, where 0% indicates that the company has not introduced new products in a given year, and 100% indicates that all of the exports of the company are due to the introduction of new goods.

4.1. EPII Components

- Product / Good = materials and/or products, which can be wholly obtained or produced, even if they are intended for later use as materials in another production process, need to be included. The terms "goods" and "products" can be used interchangeably (ASEAN definition, WCO, 2018d).
- FOB = means the free-on-board value of the goods, including the costs of transport to the port or site of final shipment abroad. The valuation shall be made in accordance with Article VII of GATT 1994 and the Agreement on the Implementation of Article VII of GATT 1994 as contained in Annex 1A to the WTO Agreement (WCO, 2018d).

- Harmonized System (HS) = means the Harmonized Commodity Description and Coding System (six-digit codes), including its General Rules of Interpretation, Section Notes, Chapter Notes and Subheading Notes as adopted and implemented by the Parties in their respective laws. HS are organized in chapters (two-digit codes) and headings (four-digit codes) (WCO, 2018d).

4.2. EPII Calculation

For an individual (specific) export company

- For a year t:

We can identify products / goods that a company exports, measured by the number of products / goods calculated according to the number of different HS that the company exports (by their FOB value).

- For a year t+1

We want to know if the company innovates in its products / goods portfolio. We calculate the new HS code products the company exports in t+1.We use the total HS with 6 digits, where the first 2 digits designate the "H.S. Chapter", the second 2 digits designate the "HS heading", and the third 2 digits designate the "HS Code" or "HS subheading". Thus, under the assumption that a firm competes in a broad sector, defined by a specific HS Chapter (such as Chapter 08 - Fruits and nuts), the export innovation is identified when the firm launches a new product / good, identified by a new 6 digits H.S. Code (for example if the firm usually exports apples, classified under HS 0808.10 and starts selling pears, classified under HS 0808.30). The interesting thing about the HS code is that it allows the scanning of all exports based on internationally recognized and standardized nomenclatures.

However, the company must not only export a new product, but also have relevant sales of that product. Then, we calculate the sales associated to the number of new HS exports in the year t valued it by FOB value. Thus, we argue that there is an innovation when the company has incorporated new HS codes and has sold any quantity of them.

- The equation is the following:

$$EPII(t) =$$

$$= \frac{FOB\,value\,of\,new\,HS\,codes\,of\,product\,/\,goods\,in\,year\,t}{Total\,FOB\,value\,of\,product\,/\,goods\,in\,year\,t} \text{x}100$$

EPII is the percentage change in the FOB value of new HS Code produced by the innovation in new products / goods. It is a performance measure based on official data, which enables us to compare individual firms, and rank them, and it is calculated using existing governmental data in most countries.

The calculation of the EPII for a company in a given year is defined by total sales FOB due to new products with a different H.S. Code, and by comparing these with the previous ones and dividing by overall FOB sales of the firm. The index measures the contribution that the new products / goods makes to the firm's exports. The index is calculated for each year, allowing us to measure the degree of innovation in companies, sectors and even countries over time. The EPII seeks to show the degree of innovation over time of the firms, and with this we intend to estimate the innovation profile of the firm in its export activity, and thus also analyze the creation of value of both the company and of a particular sector. The conceptual definition of "Export Product Innovation" is the Innovation due to the incorporation of a new HS code in the firm's export portfolio between one year and another.

4.3. EPII example

For the example we analyze a Chilean exporting company exporting fruit and its exports in 2011 and 2012. Fruit exports are classified under chapter 8 of the HS. Chapter 8, which has 68 HS codes (See Table 3).

In this example the exporting company exported during 2011 "Cranberries, bilberries and other fruits of the genus Vaccinium" under the HS code 0810.40, and in the year 2012 continued exporting this product, but introduced other products: apples (HS code 0808.10) and cherries (HS code 0809.29). The FOB values exported for each HS code can be seen in Table 4.

Taking into account the calculation algorithm of the EPII and having the following data (See Table 2):

FOB value of new HS codes of product / goods in year t+1 = 353701 US$ FOB

Total FOB value in year t+1 = 2225293 US$ FOB

$$EPII = \frac{US\$353701}{US\$2225293} x100 = 15{,}90\%$$

Thus, 15,90% of the company exports are due to new products.

Table 3. Description of HS codes of Chapter 8

Heading		H.S. Code	
Coconuts, Brazil nuts and cashew nuts, fresh or dried, whether or not shelled or peeled.	0801	Coconuts: Desiccated	0801.11
		Coconuts: In the inner shell (endocarp)	0801.12
		Coconuts: Other	0801.19
		Brazil nuts : In shell	0801.21
		Brazil nuts : Shelled	0801.22
		Cashew nuts : In shell	0801.31
		Cashew nuts : Shelled	0801.32
Other nuts, fresh or dried, whether or not shelled or peeled.	0802	Almonds : In shell	0802.11
		Almonds : Shelled	0802.12
		Hazelnuts or filberts (Corylus spp.) : In shell	0802.21
		Hazelnuts or filberts (Corylus spp.) : Shelled	0802.22
		Walnuts : In shell	0802.31
		Walnuts : Shelled	0802.32
		Chestnuts (Castanea spp.) : In shell	0802.41
		Chestnuts (Castanea spp.) : Shelled	0802.42
		Pistachios : In shell	0802.51
		Pistachios : Shelled	0802.52
		Macadamia nuts : In shell	0802.61
		Macadamia nuts : Shelled	0802.62
		Kola nuts (Cola spp.)	0802.70
		Areca nuts	0802.80
		Other	0802.90
Bananas, including plantains, fresh or dried.	0803	Plantains	0803.10
		Other	0803.90
"Dates, figs, pineapples, avocados, guavas, mangoes and mangosteens, fresh or dried."	0804	Dates	0804.10
		Figs	0804.20
		Pineapples	0804.30
		Avocados	0804.40
		Guavas, mangoes and mangosteens	0804.50
Citrus fruit, fresh or dried.	0805	Oranges	0805.10
		Mandarins (including tangerines and satsumas); clementines, wilkings and similar citrus hybrids: Mandarins (including tangerines and satsumas)	0805.21
		Mandarins (including tangerines and satsumas); clementines, wilkings and similar citrus hybrids: Clementines	0805.22
		Mandarins (including tangerines and satsumas); clementines, wilkings and similar citrus hybrids: Other	0805.29
		Grapefruit, including pomelos	0805.40
		Lemons (Citrus limon, Citrus limonum) and limes (Citrus aurantifolia, Citrus latifolia)	0805.50
		Other	0805.90

Table 3. Description of HS codes of Chapter 8 (Continued)

Heading		H.S. Code	
Grapes, fresh or dried.	0806	Fresh	0806.10
		Dried	0806.20
Melons (including watermelons) and papaws (papayas), fresh.	0807	Melons (including watermelons) : watermelons	0807.11
		Melons (including watermelons) : others	0807.19
		Papaws (papayas)	0807.20
Apples, pears and quinces, fresh.	0808	Apples	0808.10
		Pears	0808.30
		Quinces	0808.40
Apricots, cherries, peaches (including nectarines), plums and sloes, fresh.	0809	Apricots	0809.10
		Cherries : Sour cherries (Prunus cerasus)	0809.21
		Cherries: Other	0809.29
		Peaches, including nectarines	0809.30
		Plums and sloes	0809.40
Other fruit, fresh.	0810	Strawberries	0810.10
		Raspberries, blackberries, mulberries and loganberries	0810.20
		Black, white or red currants and gooseberries	0810.30
		Cranberries, bilberries and other fruits of the genus Vaccinium	0810.40
		Kiwifruit	0810.50
		Durians	0810.60
		Persimmons	0810.70
		Other	0810.90
Fruit and nuts, uncooked or cooked by steaming or boiling in water, frozen, whether or not containing added sugar or other sweetening matter.	0811	Strawberries	0811.10
		Raspberries, blackberries, mulberries, loganberries, black, white or red currants and gooseberries	0811.20
		Other	0811.90
Fruit and nuts, provisionally preserved (for example, by sulphur dioxide gas, in brine, in sulphur water or in other preservative solutions), but unsuitable in that state for immediate consumption.	0812	Cherries	0812.10
		Other	0812.90
Fruit, dried, other than that of headings 08.01 to 08.06; mixtures of nuts or dried fruits of this Chapter.	0813	Apricots	0813.10
		Prunes	0813.20
		Apples	0813.30
		Other fruit	0813.40
		Mixtures of nuts or dried fruits of this Chapter	0813.50
Peel of citrus fruit or melons (including watermelons), fresh, frozen, dried or provisionally preserved in brine, in sulphur water or in other preservative solutions.	0814	Peel of citrus fruit or melons (including watermelons), fresh, frozen, dried or provisionally preserved in brine, in sulphur water or in other preservative solutions.	0814.00
TOTAL H.S. Codes	**14**		**68**

Source: Adapted from "HS Nomenclature 2017 edition" by WCO. (2018c). Available at http://www.wcoomd.org/en/topics/nomenclature/instrument-and-tools/hs-nomenclature-2017-edition/hs-nomenclature-2017-edition.aspx

Table 4. Example of Chilean exporting company exporting fruit (Chapter 8): Total HS codes and FOB value 2011-2012

Chapter 8: H.S. Code	Total HS Codes 2011	FOB 2011	Total HS Codes 2012	FOB 2012
Coconuts: Desiccated	0801.11		0801.11	
Coconuts: In the inner shell (endocarp)	0801.12		0801.12	
Coconuts: Other	0801.19		0801.19	
Brazil nuts : In shell	0801.21		0801.21	
Brazil nuts : Shelled	0801.22		0801.22	
Cashew nuts : In shell	0801.31		0801.31	
Cashew nuts : Shelled	0801.32		0801.32	
Almonds : In shell	0802.11		0802.11	
Almonds : Shelled	0802.12		0802.12	
Hazelnuts or filberts (Corylus spp.) : In shell	0802.21		0802.21	
Hazelnuts or filberts (Corylus spp.) : Shelled	0802.22		0802.22	
Walnuts : In shell	0802.31		0802.31	
Walnuts : Shelled	0802.32		0802.32	
Chestnuts (Castanea spp.) : In shell	0802.41		0802.41	
Chestnuts (Castanea spp.) : Shelled	0802.42		0802.42	
Pistachios : In shell	0802.51		0802.51	
Pistachios : Shelled	0802.52		0802.52	
Macadamia nuts : In shell	0802.61		0802.61	
Macadamia nuts : Shelled	0802.62		0802.62	
Kola nuts (Cola spp.)	0802.70		0802.70	
Areca nuts	0802.80		0802.80	
Other	0802.90		0802.90	
Plantains	0803.10		0803.10	
Other	0803.90		0803.90	
Dates	0804.10		0804.10	
Figs	0804.20		0804.20	
Pineapples	0804.30		0804.30	
Avocados	0804.40		0804.40	
Guavas, mangoes and mangosteens	0804.50		0804.50	
Oranges	0805.10		0805.10	
Mandarins; clementines, wilkings and similar citrus hybrids: Mandarins	0805.21		0805.21	
Mandarins; clementines, wilkings and similar citrus hybrids: Clementines	0805.22		0805.22	
Mandarins; clementines, wilkings and similar citrus hybrids: Other	0805.29		0805.29	
Grapefruit, including pomelos	0805.40		0805.40	
Lemons (Citrus limon, Citrus limonum) and limes (Citrus aurantifolia, Citrus latifolia)	0805.50		0805.50	

Table 4. Example of Chilean exporting company exporting fruit (Chapter 8): Total HS codes and FOB value 2011-2012 (Continued)

Chapter 8: H.S. Code	Total HS Codes 2011	FOB 2011	Total HS Codes 2012	FOB 2012
Other	0805.90		0805.90	
Fresh	0806.10		0806.10	
Dried	0806.20		0806.20	
Melons (including watermelons) : watermelons	0807.11		0807.11	
Melons (including watermelons) : others	0807.19		0807.19	
Papaws (papayas)	0807.20		0807.20	
Apples	0808.10		0808.10	85803
Pears	0808.30		0808.30	
Quinces	0808.40		0808.40	
Apricots	0809.10		0809.10	
Cherries : Sour cherries (Prunus cerasus)	0809.21		0809.21	
Cherries: Other	0809.29		0809.29	267898
Peaches, including nectarines	0809.30		0809.30	
Plums and sloes	0809.40		0809.40	
Strawberries	0810.10		0810.10	
Raspberries, blackberries, mulberries and loganberries	0810.20		0810.20	
Black, white or red currants and gooseberries	0810.30		0810.30	
Cranberries, bilberries and other fruits of the genus Vaccinium	0810.40	135470	0810.40	1871592
Kiwifruit	0810.50		0810.50	
Durians	0810.60		0810.60	
Persimmons	0810.70		0810.70	
Other	0810.90		0810.90	
Strawberries	0811.10		0811.10	
Raspberries, blackberries, mulberries, loganberries, black............	0811.20		0811.20	
Other	0811.90		0811.90	
Cherries	0812.10		0812.10	
Other	0812.90		0812.90	
Apricots	0813.10		0813.10	
Prunes	0813.20		0813.20	
Apples	0813.30		0813.30	
Other fruit	0813.40		0813.40	
Mixtures of nuts or dried fruits of this Chapter	0813.50		0813.50	
Peel of citrus fruit or melons*	0814.00		0814.00	
TOTAL H.S. Codes & FOB	**1**	**135470**	**3**	**2225293**

Note: *(including watermelons), fresh, frozen, dried or provisionally preserved in brine, in sulphur water or in other preservative solutions.

Source: Adapted from "HS Nomenclature 2017 edition" by WCO. (2018c). Available at http://www.wcoomd.org/en/topics/nomenclature/instrument-and-tools/hs-nomenclature-2017-edition/hs-nomenclature-2017-edition.aspx

Table 5. Comparison between the EPII and other indexes on Chilean product innovation performance

Index	Sample	Main value	Observations
EPII (Export Product Innovation Index)	Firm level: 249 firms	0.23 (mean value)	Fruit Sector. 2006-2015
SIF (Survey on Innovation in Firms)	Firm level: 4,940 firms	7.87 % firms performed product innovations	Official source: Ministry of Finance of Chile, based on OECD and on CIS (Community Innovation Survey). Last four Innovation Surveys (2009-2016)
GII (Global Innovation Index)	Country level	41.2 (ranking 42 out of 143 countries)	GII 2015

5. Results

In Table 5, we describe the main value obtained with our new index, the EPII, applied to our sample of Chilean fruit exporting firms, compared to that of the SIF (Survey on Innovation in Firms) and to the one of the GII (Global Innovation Index).

As can be seen, while the EPII and the SIF are at the firm level, the GII is at the country level. The former two indexes at a micro level enable us to disentangle the firms' innovative behaviour, without considering other innovation actors included in a generic country's innovation measure, as these activities are carried out by public institutions.

Moreover, the EPII is an internationally standardized way of approaching the firm's innovative result, since it is based on the international HS codes. Its final advantage is that, thanks to its quantitative nature, the EPII allows us to measure the intensity of the obtention of product innovation outputs in a dynamic way (since it compares one year with the previous one), while other indexes, such as the SIF, have the limitation that they only point statically (in a given year) to the proportion of product innovating firms. Therefore, we argue that the EPII provides richer information.

6. Discussion and conclusions

The objective of this article was to develop a new index, the EPII, a metric that associates innovation to export activity by the value of new products / goods traded abroad by exporting firms. Since Chile is a largely export-oriented economy –specially the fruit sector where it is a world leader in exports-, and its firms address a deep concern of lack of added value in their products, which we argue can be solved with product innovation, we have applied the analysis to a sample of Chilean fruit manufacturers.

After explaining how the EPII is calculated (basically a measure of the exports result of new products / goods relative to total exports), we have compared this index with two other important indexes in the literature that explore innovation and that can be applied to the case of Chile: the SIF index, which can be calculated from the Survey on Innovation in Firms and the GII (Global Innovation Index). As argued in the previous section, the EPII shows three main advantages: first, since it is based on the Harmonized System codes, it can be universally applied (to almost any country, sector and performance measure); second, it is implemented at the firm level, thus allowing us to measure how competitive (in innovative terms) the firms from a specific country are; third, since it measures exactly and quantitatively the degree of the firm product innovation activity, we argue that the information provided is more ample than with other qualitative indexes that only appraise whether the firm innovates or not..

Because of all these arguments, we argue that we successfully contribute to the literature by developing a new reliable, quantitative and universalistic index that can be used to test any country's firm competitive level in terms of product innovation.

The implications of our proposal are explained below: At a public policy level, the EPII would make decisions regarding the allocation of public funds to improve the innovative performance of certain industrial sectors and the promotion of exports. At a company level, the EPII allows us to measure the degree of innovation in the company's export activity and its role in the firm's export performance. Thus, managers can use this measure to identify if the firm really faces a lack of innovation problem, and therefore how the firm may improve its competiveness. Additionally, the new products innovation activity (measured through the EPII) allows the firm to overcome its traditional core capabilities that may be named core rigidities since they usually limit these disruptive new projects (Leonard-Barton, 1992).

The main limitations are now detailed. First, the index algorithm is based only on one innovation final output (product innovation) and does not consider other ways of innovating (such as process, marketing, ...). Second, we focus only on one mode of entry (exports), in one country (Chile) and in one sector (fruit exports). This may limit the generalization of the results. Other industrial sectors may present results based on their own characteristics, such as the specific Regional Innovation System, their innovative culture, technological paradigms, regulatory aspects, etc. As a consequence, as future lines of research we suggest applying this research to other contexts.

Additionally, since product development is a dynamic capability that requires to involve some routines for superior performance, as a cross functional team (Eisenhardt & Martin, 2000). In this line, Ardito and Petruzzelli (2017) analyze the role of strategic HR practices on product innovation. Consequently, further research could target not only the gathering of new products but also the study of all these complementary routines and practices.

References

Amit, R., & Zott, C. (2001). Value creation in e-business. *Strategic Management Journal, 22*(6-7), 493-520.

Ardito, L., & Petruzzelli, A. M. (2017). Breadth of external knowledge sourcing and product innovation: the moderating role of strategic human resource practices. *European Management Journal*, 35(2), 261-272.

Becker, W., Saisana, M., Paruolo, P., & Vandecasteele, I. (2017). Weights and importance in composite indicators: Closing the gap. *Ecological Indicators, 80*, 12–22.

Boer, H., & During, B. E. (2001). Innovation, what innovation? A comparison between product, process and organizational innovation. *International Journal of Technology Management, 22*(1/2/3), 83-107.

Dutta, S., Lanvin, B. & Wunsch-Vincent, S. (Eds.). (2017). The Global Innovation Index 2017: Innovation Feeding the World (10th ed.). Ithaca, NY: Cornell University.

DiPietro, W. R., & Anoruo, E. (2006). Creativity, innovation, and export performance. *Journal of Policy Modeling, 28*(2), 133-139.

Eisenhardt, K. M., & Martin, J. A. (2000). Dynamic capabilities: what are they?. *Strategic management journal*, 21(10-11), 1105-1121.

Esteves, K., & Feldmann, P. R. (2016). Why Brazil does not innovate: a comparison among nations. *RAI Revista de Administração e Inovação, 13*(10), 29-38.

Henderson, R. M., & Clark, K. B. (1990). Architectural innovation: The reconfiguration of existing product technologies and the failure of established firms. *Administrative Science Quarterly, 35*(1), 9-30.

Leonard-Barton, D. (1992). Core capabilities and core rigidities: A paradox in managing new product development. *Strategic Management Journal*, 13, 111-125.

ODEPA. (2018). Frutas frescas [Fresh fruit]. Available at https://www.odepa.gob.cl/rubros/frutas-frescas

OECD. (2005). *The Oslo manual: Guidelines for collecting and interpreting innovation data* (3rd ed.). Paris: OECD.

Speroni, R. M, Dandolini, G. A., Souza, J. A. & Gauthier, F. A. O. (2015). Estado da arte da produção científica sobre indicadores e índices de inovação [State of art of the scientific production of innovation indicators and indexes]. *RAI – Revista de Administração e Inovação, 12*(4), 50-75.

WCO. (2018a). What is the Harmonized System (HS)? Available at http://www.wcoomd.org/en/topics/nomenclature/overview/what-is-the-harmonized-system.aspx

WCO. (2018b). HS Multi-Purposes Tool. Available at http://www.wcoomd.org/en/topics/nomenclature/overview/hs-multi-purposes-tool.aspx.

WCO. (2018c). HS Nomenclature 2017 edition. Available at http://www.wcoomd.org/en/topics/nomenclature/instrument-and-tools/hs-nomenclature-2017-edition/hs-nomenclature-2017-edition.aspx

WCO. (2018d). Definitions. Available at http://www.wcoomd.org/en/topics/origin/instrument-and-tools/comparative-study-on-preferential-rules-of-origin/specific-topics/study-topics/def.aspx

3

On the causal links between the stock market and the economy of Hong Kong

Sin-Yu Ho[1], Bernard Njindan Iyke[1]

ABSTRACT A bulk of literature has identified the major economic drivers of Hong Kong's rapid and steady economic performance over the last three decades. Of the major economic drivers identified, the performance of the stock market has received less attention. This paper examines the causal links between the stock market performance and economic performance of Hong Kong in an augmented VAR setting. Using an extended quarterly dataset that covers the period of 1986Q2–2014Q4 and the Toda-Yamamoto causality test, we find that stock market performance as proxied by the market capitalization ratio and economic performance stimulate each other. In addition, stock market performance as proxied by the total value traded ratio and economic performance influence each other. However, the causal links between stock market performance and economic performance dissipate if stock market performance is proxied by the turnover ratio. This finding suggests that the causal links between stock market performance and economic performance are highly dependent on the proxy used for stock market performance in the case of Hong Kong.

KEY WORDS: Causality, Economic Performance, Stock Market Performance, Toda-Yamamoto

[1] University of South Africa - Economics, South Africa

1. Introduction

The growing importance of stock markets around the world has generated diverse research in the finance and economic literature, most of which has identified a strong positive association between the performance of stock markets and the performance of economies. The theoretical contributions suggest that the stock market is an important component of financial sector development in promoting economic growth in different ways. By reducing the cost of mobilizing savings, the stock market may facilitate investment into the most productive technologies, thereby leading to economic growth (Greenwood & Smith, 1997). As the stock market develops, it may improve corporate governance by addressing the principal-agent problem, which is beneficial to economic growth (Jensen & Murphy, 1990). Well-developed stock markets also allow world portfolios to shift from safer low-return capital to riskier high-return capital, which can create substantial welfare gain through the effects on expected consumption growth (Obstfeld, 1994). In addition, the stock market provides market liquidity, which allows investors to trade financial assets in a less risky manner. Such an increase in liquidity also provides companies with easy access to capital, thereby contributing to long-term growth (Bencivenga, Smith, & Starr, 1996; Levine, 1991).

Correspondence concerning this article should be addressed to: **Bernard Njindan Iyke**, University of South Africa - Economics, P.O. Box 392, 0003, Hazelwood, Brooklyn, Pretoria 0003, South Africa. E-mail: benitoflex@gmail.com

There are equally opposing theoretical views about the association between stock market performance and the performance of an economy. In terms of stock market liquidity, Demirgüc-Kunt, and Levine (1996) identify various channels through which stock market development hurts economic performance. First, greater stock market liquidity may reduce the savings rate by increasing the returns on investment. Second, by reducing the uncertainty associated with investment, it may make investment more attractive to risk-averse agents and decrease the demand for precautionary savings. Third, a highly liquid stock market encourages dissatisfied investors to sell quickly, which can lead to a disincentive to exert corporate control and therefore compromise the quality of corporate governance (Jensen & Murphy, 1990). In addition, excessive price volatility in stock markets may lead to an inefficient allocation of resources and upward pressure on interest rates to compensate for higher uncertainty. Therefore, the quantity and productivity of investment may be compromised, which will hinder growth (Arestis, Demetriades, & Luintel, 2001; DeLong, Schleifer, Summers, & Waldmann, 1989).

Indeed, the role of stock market development in the performance of economies is an inconclusive subject. This leaves room for further research. In this paper, we attempt to answer an important country-specific question that has received less attention in the literature: Is the performance of the stock market crucial to Hong Kong's rapid and dominant economic performance over the last three decades? There are existing papers that investigate this question in panel and cross-country data settings, but the worry is that country-specific information is lost due to the "lumping" of countries. Panel data analysis usually entails a single dataset composed of several countries that may not share the same economic fundamentals. This means that the ability of panel data to isolate the effects of country-specific information or more general policies depends on making appropriate assumptions and selecting the "right models" (Hsiao, 2005). We cannot be sure that these previous studies made the appropriate assumptions and selected the right models in their empirical analysis. In addition, cross-country data are limited in that they usually have one historical context and therefore do not allow the researcher to examine economic relationships over time (Kramer, 1983). To eliminate these uncertainties, time series techniques may be very useful. Our study aims to utilize time series techniques to re-assess the above question.

To the question at hand, there are existing studies that provide different answers. For example, Atje and Jovanovic (1993), using 40 countries for the period of 1980-1988, conclude that there is a large effect of stock market development on the level and growth rate of economic activities. Levine and Zervos (1996), in a study of 41 countries, including Hong Kong, over the period of 1976-1993, find that stock market development is positively associated with economic growth. In another study, Levine and Zervos (1998) utilize cross-country regressions for 47 countries, including Hong Kong, covering the period of 1976-1993. They demonstrate that stock market liquidity is positively correlated with economic growth. Rousseau and Wachtel (2000) examine the relationship between stock markets, banks and growth for a set of 47 countries from 1980-1995. Their findings indicate that stock market development and banking sector development explain subsequent growth. A similar result is supported by Beck and Levine (2004), who studied a panel of 40 countries for the period of 1976-1998. Minier (2003), using the data of Levine and Zervos (1998), claims that there is a positive correlation between stock market development and economic growth in countries with high levels of market capitalization such as Hong Kong. A similar view is also held by Rioja and Valev (2004), who conclude that the nexus differs at various stages of economic development. Recent studies such as Masoud and Hardaker (2012), Naik and Padhi (2015), Phiri (2015), Sehrawat and Giri (2015) also indicate that stock market development and economic growth are positively related. In direct contrast, Singh (1997), studying the role of stock markets on the economic growth of developing countries during the 1980s and 1990s, concludes that stock market development does not promote faster long-term economic growth. This view is also supported by Harris (1997), who studied 49 countries from 1980-1991. In the whole sample and in the sub-sample of developing countries, the study yields no hard evidence that the level of stock market activity can explain economic growth.

We add to this burgeoning literature by arguing that the performance of the Hong Kong stock market has contributed greatly to the rapid and steady performance of its economy over the past three decades. To provide firm support for our argument, we regressed the indices of stock market performance on economic performance in an augmented VAR setting. Using the Toda-Yamamoto test for causality, we find that the performance of the Hong Kong stock market, as proxied by the market capitalization ratio, and the performance of the Hong Kong's economy influence each other. In addition, we find that, if proxied by the total value traded ratio, the stock market and the economy of Hong Kong influence each other. However, the causal links between stock market performance and economic performance vanish if stock market performance is proxied by the turnover ratio. This suggests that the causal links between stock market performance and economic performance are highly dependent on the proxy of stock market performance in the case of Hong Kong.

In the next section, we briefly discuss the stock market development in Hong Kong. Section 3 presents the methodology and the data. Section 4 reports our main empirical results. Section 5 performs a sensitivity analysis of the results, and section 6 provides the conclusion.

2. Stock Market Development in Hong Kong

Hong Kong has experienced more than a hundred years of stock market development. The first formal stock exchange, the Association of Stockbrokers in Hong Kong, was established early in 1891. In 1914, it was renamed the Hong Kong Stock Exchange. However, the activities of the Exchange were generally regarded as insignificant until the 1970s. During the 1970s, Hong Kong was regarded as the Euro-Dollar market in a different time zone, and the flows of international capital into Asia boosted its financial activities (Jao, 2003). There was an influx of foreign banking and non-bank financial institutions that contributed to the rapid growth of the stock market. As a result, three other stock exchanges were established in the late 1960s and early 1970s (Tsang, 2004).

The global market crash in 1987 revealed various flaws that led to major reforms in the stock market of Hong Kong. One of them was the unification of four stock exchanges to become the Hong Kong Stock Exchange in 1986 to avoid destructive competition among them (Hong Kong Exchanges and Clearing Limited (HKEx), 2011). In 1999, the Stock Exchange, the Futures Exchange and its associated clearing houses were merged to form the Hong Kong Stock Exchange and Clearing Limited (HKEx) to reduce operation costs through achieving economies of scale. In the same year, a second board known as the Growth Enterprise Market was launched to provide start-up companies with a capital formation platform and an alternative market to the Main Board (HKEx, 1999). In 2000, the HKEx was demutualized to become one of the first stock exchanges in the world to go public (Ghosh, 2006; HKEx, 2011). In 2012, a joint venture known as the China Exchange Service Company Limited was formed between the HKEx, the Shanghai Stock Exchange and the Shenzhen Stock Exchange to strengthen the linkage of stock market activities between Hong Kong and Mainland China. In the same year, the London Metal Exchange was acquired as the HKEx's first overseas member, with a vision of developing the HKEx into a global vertically integrated multi-asset class exchange (HKEx, 2015a).

The Hong Kong stock market responded positively to the reforms and became one of the most highly developed markets as indicated by the size and the liquidity of the market. The size of the stock market, as measured by the stock market capitalization, increased significantly from US$608 billion in 1999 to US$3101 billion in 2013. In 2013, it was ranked as the fifth largest stock market in the world and the second largest in Asia (World Federation of Exchanges, 2015). The major reason for the phenomenal growth in the market capitalization is that Hong Kong has been established as a preferred center for initial public offering (IPOs) internationally. The amount raised by IPOs increased significantly from HK$17 billion in 1999 to the highest level of HK$449 billion in 2010. In 2013, HK$169 billion was raised through IPOs, contributing 45% to the total equity fund raised in that year (HKEx, 2013). The growth of Hong Kong as an IPO fund-raising center has been driven largely by the listing of companies from Mainland China. In 2013, Hong Kong became the second largest IPO fund-raising center in the world, just behind the New York Stock Exchange (Ernst & Young, 2013).

The performance of the Hong Kong stock market becomes more impressive when the comparison is

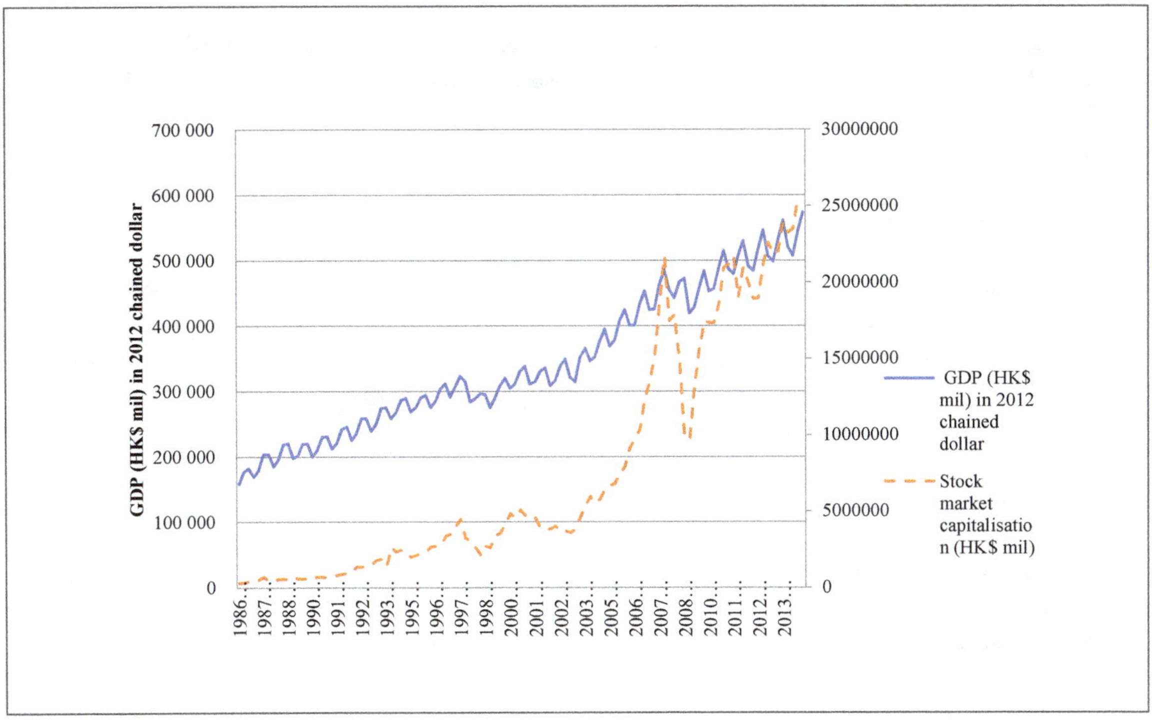

Figure 1. Economic performance and stock market development in Hong Kong during 1986Q2 to 2014Q4
Source: Adapted from "Securities Statistics Archive" by Hong Kong Exchanges and Clearing Limited (2015b). Available from http://www.hkex.com.hk/eng/stat/smstat/statarch/statarchive.htm and "Gross Domestic Product (GDP), implicit price deflator of GDP and per capita GDP" by Census and Statistics Department of Hong Kong (2017, May 11). Available from http://www.censtatd.gov.hk/hong_kong_statistics/statistical_tables/index.jsp?tableID=030

based on the market capitalization as a percentage of GDP. Figures from the World Development Indicators (WDI, 2014) indicate that Hong Kong has been the home of the largest stock market in the world during the period of 1999 to 2012, in terms of the market capitalization ratio, for the following reasons. First, there has been substantial increase in the number of listed enterprises from Mainland China on the Exchange. In 2013 alone, Mainland Chinese enterprises accounted for 41% of the total market capitalization (HKEx, 2013). Second, there has been an expansion in the activities of Hong Kong companies in overseas territories. Many listed companies in Hong Kong have substantial investment in countries overseas. Their sources of earning are outside Hong Kong and do not necessarily have a direct relationship with the GDP in Hong Kong (Lee & Poon, 2005).

The stock market in Hong Kong has also recorded impressive growth in terms of liquidity, as indicated by the total value traded ratio and the turnover ratio (Levine & Zervos, 1996; 1998). The HKEx had the most liquid stock market in the world during the period of 2007 to 2012, as measured by the total value traded ratio (WDI, 2014). It was also the seventh most liquid market globally in 2012 by the turnover ratio, according to figures from the WDI (2014). On these accounts, we could argue that Hong Kong has an extremely liquid stock market with low transaction costs.

The magnificent growth in the stock market is also accompanied by the rapid growth of economic activities in Hong Kong. Hong Kong has achieved an "economic miracle" over the past few decades. The real GDP has increased more than threefold from HK$ 157,823 million in 1986Q2 to HK$ 573,280 million in 2014Q4, comparable to the advanced market economies. Figure 1 shows the economic performance and stock market development in Hong Kong during 1986Q2 to 2014Q4.

3. Methodology and Data

In this section, we present the preliminary tests employed, the models and the data used to examine the relationship between the stock market performance and the performance of the Hong Kong economy. To examine the stationary properties of the stock market and the economic performance series, we use two sets of stationarity tests: (i) stationarity tests without structural breaks, i.e., the Augmented Dickey-Fuller (ADF) and the Dickey-Fuller generalized least squares (DF-GLS) tests, and (ii) stationarity tests with structural breaks, i.e., the Perron and the Zivot-Andrews tests. We then examine whether the series are causally linked using the Toda-Yamamoto test developed by Toda and Yamamoto (1995).

3.1 Stationarity Tests without Structural Breaks

As a preliminary analysis, prior to examining the nature of the relationship between stock market performance and the performance of the economy, we examine their stationary properties. We utilize the ADF and DF-GLS tests. The DF-GLS test is proposed by Elliot, Rothenberg, and Stock, (1996). We use this test to compensate for the drawback of the ADF test. The ADF test has been found to over-reject the null hypothesis of unit root when the time series under consideration has a large and negative moving average (MA) component, even when there is a unit root (Caner & Killian, 2001; Schwert, 1986). Elliot et al. (1996) demonstrate that the DF-GLS test has substantially higher power, even when the root of the time series is closer to unity. To estimate results that are based on parsimonious regressions, we determine the optimal lags for both tests using the Modified Akaike Information Criterion (MAIC). The regressions and test statistics underlying DF-GLS tests have been discussed thoroughly in various studies. Thus, we preserve space by not discussing it here.

3.2 Stationarity Tests with Structural Breaks

Macroeconomic time series, such as the ones we use in this paper, are found to be characterized by structural breaks. The presence of structural breaks has been found to distort the statistical power of the stationarity tests we have discussed so far. Perron (1989), for example, found that these tests accept the null hypothesis of unit roots in time series, even when there are clear indications of no unit roots. Since this discovery, various stationarity tests have been developed to take into account structural breaks in time series. In this paper, we utilize the Perron (1997) test and the Zivot and Andrews (1992) test as robust alternatives for examining the stationary properties of the series considered in this paper.

The Perron test, which was originally derived by Perron (1989) and later modified by Perron (1997), proceeds by fitting the following Augmented Dickey-Fuller (ADF) regression with shifts in mean and trend,

$$\Delta y_t = \alpha + \beta y_{t-1} + \sum_{i=1}^{k} \rho_i \Delta y_{t-i} + \mu_t + \epsilon_t, \quad (1)$$

where $\mu_t = \mu_0 + \mu_0^s d_{tT_B} + \mu_1 t + \mu_1^s (t - T_B) d_{tT_B}$ are potential deterministic terms and T_B is the break date. The test has three null hypotheses: (i) y_t is non-stationary with a structural break in the intercept, (ii) y_t is non-stationary with a structural break in the trend, and (iii) y_t is non-stationary with a structural break in the intercept and trend.

Zivot and Andrews (1992) argue that the Perron test suffers because the break date is determined exogenously. They argue that the identification of a break date may be unassociated with the data. Thus, if the critical values computed under the null hypothesis are computed on the basis that the break date is determined *ex ante*, then there could be substantial size distortions. Under this kind of situation, the Perron test will frequently reject the null hypothesis of unit root. The Zivot-Andrews test differs from the Perron test by explicitly modeling the break date endogenously. The Zivot-Andrews test also uses the ADF regression in *Eq.* (1). The test applies the Perron (1989) procedure for each break date in the dataset and selects the break date for which the support for the null hypothesis is the strongest (Zivot & Andrews, 1992). The null hypotheses under the Zivot-Andrews test are the same as those under the Perron test.

3.3 Specification for Testing Granger Causality

The traditional test for causality proposed by Granger (1969) in the vector autoregressive (VAR) setting requires the researcher to first establish the integration properties of the time series. In cases where the series are I(1), the researcher will need to test whether there are any co-integrating relationships before carrying out the test for causality. However, most of the diagnostic tests for unit roots and co-integration are known to have low power against the alternative hypotheses of stationarity and cointegration. Toda and Yamamoto (1995), in particular, stress that the traditional way of testing for causality by first testing for unit root and cointegration exposes this approach to pretesting bias. This view is supported by He and Maekawa (2001), who argue that testing for causality using *F*-statistics when one or both time series are non-stationary can lead to spurious causality.

Thus, according to Toda and Yamamoto (1995), the problems inherent in the traditional testing for Granger causality can be avoided by fitting an augmented VAR model that adds the highest order of integration to the optimal lag of the VAR model. This technique ensures that the test statistic for the causality test has a standard asymptotic distribution. We specify a modified vector autoregressive model, $VAR(m+d_{max})$, following Yamada (1998), of the form

$$y_t = \gamma_0 + \sum_{i=1}^{m} \gamma_{1i} y_{t-i} + \sum_{i=m+1}^{m+d_{max}} \gamma_{2i} y_{t-i} + \sum_{i=1}^{m} \varphi_{1i} x_{t-i} + \sum_{i=m+1}^{m+d_{max}} \varphi_{2i} x_{t-i} + u_{1t} \quad (2)$$

$$x_t = \Theta_0 + \sum_{i=1}^{m} \Theta_{1i} x_{t-i} + \sum_{i=m+1}^{m+d_{max}} \Theta_{2i} x_{t-i} + \sum_{i=1}^{m} \delta_{1i} y_{t-i} + \sum_{i=m+1}^{m+d_{max}} \delta_{2i} y_{t-i} + u_{2t}, \quad (3)$$

where y_t and x_t are the series under consideration; δ, γ, Θ and φ are the parameters of the model; and u_1 and u_2 are the white-noise innovations.

From *Eq.* (2), x_t causes y_t if $\varphi_{1i} \neq 0, \forall i = 1,2,\ldots,m$. Similarly, in *Eq.* (3), y_t causes x_t if $\delta_{1i} \neq 0, \forall i = 1,2,\ldots,m$. The test statistic for these hypotheses follows a *chi-squared* distribution. Take the hypothesis $\delta_{1i} = 0, \forall i = 1,2,\ldots,m$, for example, and let $\delta = vec(\delta_1, \delta_2, \ldots, \delta_m)$ be a vector of m VAR parameters. Toda and Yamamoto (1995) demonstrate that for a suitably selected Z, the modified *Wald*-statistic for testing this hypothesis is of the form

$$W = T(\hat{\delta}' Z' (Z \hat{\Sigma}_u Z')^{-1} Z \hat{\delta}) \quad (4)$$

where $\hat{\delta}$ is the OLS estimate of δ; $\hat{\Sigma}_u$ is a consistent estimate of the variance-covariance matrix of $\sqrt{T}(\hat{\delta} - \delta)$; and T is the sample size. W, the test statistic, is *chi-squared* distributed with m degrees of freedom.

3.4 Data

3.4.1 Data Sources

The period covered in this paper is from the second quarter of 1986 to the fourth quarter of 2014. The data are obtained from the World Federation of Exchanges (2015), the HKEx (2015b), and the Census and Statistics Department of Hong Kong (2017). These data sources are preferred to other sources because they provide the original data on each of the variables employed in this paper.

3.4.2 Definitions of Variables

(i) Economic Performance (GDP)

There are various proxies for economic performance in the literature. In this paper, economic performance is proxied by real GDP, which is an indicator of output based on GDP after controlling for the inflationary effect. It captures the size of the output of the economy in a given year. This proxy has also been used by Cheng (2012), Hondroyiannis, Lolos, and Papapetrou (2005), Malik and Amjad (2013), and Marques, Fuinhas, and Marques (2013), among others.

(ii) Stock Market Performance (MCR, TVR and TOR)

Stock market performance is a multifaceted concept that captures the size, liquidity, degree of international integration, and volatility (Levine & Zervos 1998). In this paper, we choose three proxies that are frequently used in the empirical literature to measure stock market performance. These are the stock market capitalization ratio (MCR), the total value traded ratio (TVR), and the turnover ratio (TOR). MCR shows the size of a stock market, whereas TVR and TOR show the liquidity of a stock market. MCR is the value of equities traded on the domestic stock market as a percentage of GDP. The variable has also been used by studies such as Arestis and Demetriades (1997), Boyd, Levine, and Smith (2001), Deb and Mukherjee (2008), Enisan and Olufisayo (2009), Levine and Zervos (1996; 1998), Malik and Amjad (2013), Masoud and Hardaker (2012), and Marques et al. (2013). TVR shows the value of trades of domestic shares on the domestic stock market as a percentage of GDP. It measures trading volume as a share of economic output, thereby positively reflecting the liquidity of the stock market on an economy-wide basis. The variable has been used by studies such as Atje and Jovanovic (1993), Boyd et al. (2001), Deb and Mukherjee (2008), Enisan and Olufisayo (2009), Levine and Zervos (1996; 1998), and Masoud and Hardaker (2012). TOR shows the value of trades of domestic shares on the stock market as a percentage of the size of the stock market. A high turnover ratio may indicate low transaction costs in the stock market. The variable has also been used by studies such as Boyd et al. (2001), Jeffus (2004), Levine and Zervos (1996; 1998), Masoud and Hardaker (2012), and Minier (2003).

4. Empirical Results

4.1 Results of the Tests for Stationarity

To examine the effect of stock market performance on the performance of the Hong Kong economy, we first test whether the proxies for stock market performance and economic performance are stationary. We employ the ADF and DF-GLS tests and perform our stationarity analysis by considering the drift and trend options. The tests for the stationarity of the series in their levels are presented in Tables 1 and 2. The evidence in favor of stationarity or no unit roots in the series using the ADF and DF-GLS is weak at the conventional levels of significance. The drawback here is that the ADF and the DF-GLS have substantial size distortion when these series contain structural breaks. In practice, there are various reasons that we should expect breaks in the stock market and the economic performance variables we utilize in this paper. The oil price shocks of 1973 and 1979, the Gulf war in 1990, the Asian financial crisis of the 1997, and the recent global financial and economic crisis could have caused substantial shocks to the path of these variables. The ADF and the DF-GLS tests are unable to detect these breaks. To present robust stationarity evidence, we employ two alternative stationarity tests that cater to structural breaks in our series. These are the Perron and the Zivot-Andrews tests. The results of these tests presented in Table 1 also indicate that all the variables, except *LNTOR*, contain unit roots. Therefore, we difference the non-stationary variables once and again examine their stationary status. The results, presented in Table 2, show that the variables are first-difference stationary at conventional levels of significance.

4.2 Lag Selection and Model Diagnostics

To perform the Toda-Yamamoto test, the appropriate lag length needs to be selected. In this paper, we select the lag length using the Akaike Information Criterion (AIC), the Hannan-Quinn Criterion (HQC), the Schwartz Information Criterion (SIC), and the Final Prediction Error (FPE). For all three VAR models, the optimal lag selected is 5. Thus, we fit the three *VAR* models by including 5 lags. In addition to selecting the lags, our models must be structurally stable and free of serial correlation. The inverses of the roots of the characteristic equations are greater than unity (i.e., for *LNGDP* and *LNMCR* equations, the inverse of the root is 1.0077; for *LNGDP* and *LNTVR*, it is 1.0099; and for *LNGDP* and *LNTOR*, it is 1.0113) indicating that the models are structurally stable. Figures A.1, A.2 and A.3 in the appendix show the cumulative sum of recursive residual plots, which also support this evidence. The models are also free of serial correlation. For example, the *chi-squared statistic* is 35.635 with a *p-value* of 0.8114 for the *LNGDP* and *LNMCR* model; 44.496 and 0.4507 for the *LNGDP* and *LNTVR* model; and 57.027 and 0.143 for the *LNGDP* and *LNTOR* model.

4.3 Results of the Tests for Causality

Having satisfied the necessary requirements for the Toda-Yamamoto test, we fitted a *VAR*(6) for each of the three models (i.e., $m = 5$ and $d_{max} = 1$). The results of the tests for Granger causality between *LNGDP* and *LNMCR* are reported in Table 3. The results show that there is a bidirectional causal relationship between *LNMCR* and *LNGDP* at a 1% level of significance. This is indicated by the *chi-squared statistics* of 35.60 and 24.10, with corresponding *p-values* of 0.00 and 0.00 for the *LNGDP* and *LNMCR* equations, respectively. The implication is that the performance of the stock market, as proxied by the market capitalization ratio, can stimulate the performance of the Hong Kong economy. In a similar fashion, economic performance can also influence the performance of the stock market. This finding is consistent with the existing findings (Atje & Jovanovic, 1993; Beck & Levine, 2004; Levine & Zervos, 1996; 1998).

Next, we analyze the causal relationship between *LNGDP* and *LNTVR*. The results for this are reported in Table 3. Similar to the first model, we find bidirectional causality between *LNGDP* and *LNTVR* at a 5% level of

Table 1. Tests for Unit Roots for Variables in Levels

Test	Level Variables			
	LNGDP	LNMCR	LNTOR	LNTVR
ADF[Drift]	-1.156	-0.702	-2.061	-1.225
ADF[Trend]	-2.399	-3.220*	-3.032	-3.908**
DF-GLS[Drift]	1.893	0.229	-1.116	-0.044
DF-GLS[Trend]	-1.0588	-3.152**	-3.051**	-3.866***
Perron[Drift]	-3.668	-4.778	-5.501**	-4.672
	[1997Q2]	[2005Q4]	[2005Q2]	[2005Q4]
Perron[Trend]	-2.187	-4.199	-5.281**	-4.196
	[2001Q4]	[1990Q3]	[2010Q2]	[1990Q3]
Zivot-Andrews[Drift]	-3.721	-4.778	-5.544***	-4.729*
	[1997Q4]	[2006Q1]	[2006Q1]	[2006Q1]
Zivot-Andrews[Trend]	-2.474	-3.286	-5.223	NA
	[2002Q2]	[2006Q1]	[2009Q3]	NA

Note: *, ** and *** denote significance at the 10%, 5% and 1% levels, respectively. NA denotes non-applicable. Items in block parentheses are break dates.

Table 2. Tests for Unit Roots for Variables in First-Difference

	First-difference Variables			
	ΔLNGDP	ΔLNMCR	ΔLNTOR	ΔLNTVR
ADF[Drift]	-10.808***	-12.049***	-13.177***	-12.180***
ADF[Trend]	-10.753***	-11.997***	-13.122***	NA
DF-GLS[Drift]	-0.140	-4.333***	-4.287***	-5.545***
DF-GLS[Trend]	-1.282	-11.85675***	NA	NA
Perron[Drift]	-5.323**	-12.889***	NA	-12.429***
	[2003Q2]	[2008Q4]	NA	[1990Q4]
Perron[Trend]	-4.928**	-12.176***	NA	-9.277***
	[1997Q1]	[2006Q4]	NA	[2007Q1]
Zivot-Andrews[Drift]	-5.412***	-9.499***	NA	-6.610***
	[2003Q3]	[2008Q1]	NA	[2008Q2]
Zivot-Andrews[Trend]	-4.653**	-9.278***	NA	-6.301***
	[2007Q1]	[2007Q1]	NA	[2007Q1]

Note: ** and *** denote significance at the 5% and 1% levels, respectively. NA denotes non-applicable. Items in block parentheses are break dates. Δ denotes the first-difference operator.

Table 3. Tests for Granger Causality using the Full Sample

	Wald-statistic [p-value]			Inverse Roots
Variable	LNGDP	LNMCR		
LNGDP	NA	35.60[0.00] ***		1.008
LMCR	24.10[0.00]***	NA		1.008
Variable	LNGDP	LNTVR		
LNGDP	NA	12.80[0.025]**		1.010
LNTVR	13.40[0.02]**	NA		1.010
Variable	LNGDP	LNTOR		
LNGDP	NA	3.00[0.70]		1.011
LNTOR	6.00[0.31]	NA		1.011
Lag Selection	AIC = 5	BIC = 5	HQC = 5	FPE = 5
Serial Correlation	χ^2-statistic	p-value		
	35.635	0.811		
	44.496	0.451		
	57.027	0.143		

Note: ** and *** denote significance at the 5% and 1% levels, respectively. NA denotes non-applicable.

significance. This is indicated by the *chi-squared statistics* of 12.80 and 13.40, with corresponding *p-values* of 0.025 and 0.02 for the *LNGDP* and *LNTVR* equations, respectively. Thus, stock market performance defined in terms of total value traded ratio and economic performance influence each other. This finding is also documented in the literature (Beck & Levine, 2004; Minier, 2003; Rousseau & Wachtel, 2000).

Finally, we analyze the causal relationship between *LNGDP* and *LNTOR*. This is reported in Table 3 as well. The causality test reveals no causal flow between *LNGDP* and *LNTOR*. This is indicated by the *chi-squared statistics* of 3.00 and 6.00, with corresponding *p-values* of 0.70 and 0.31 for the *LNGDP* and *LNTOR* equations, respectively. Thus, the performance of the stock market, as proxied by the turnover ratio, does not influence the performance of the Hong Kong economy at the conventional level of significance. This conclusion holds, conversely, and is consistent with some previous findings (Harris, 1997; Singh, 1997).

It is important to note that the results reported so far rest on the assumption that the variables have maintained constant slopes over time. In reality, these variables experienced sharp changes in their slopes during the Asian financial crisis, which started in July 1997. To make our results reliable, we divided our sample into two periods: 1986Q2–1997Q2, marking the period before the crisis, and 1997Q3–2014Q4, marking the period during and after the crisis. Then, we perform a causality test for these subsamples. These results are reported in Tables 4 and 5. The results are basically the same as those reported in Table 3 for the full sample. We find evidence of bidirectional causality between stock market development and economic performance when stock market performance is proxied by either the market capitalization ratio (MCR) or total value

Table 4. Tests for Granger Causality (1986Q2–1997Q2)

	Wald-statistic [p-value]			**Inverse Roots**
Variable	LNGDP	LNMCR		
LNGDP	NA	22.39[0.00] ***		1.240
LMCR	18.46[0.00]***	NA		1.240
Variable	LNGDP	LNTVR		
LNGDP	NA	10.84[0.03]**		1.142
LNTVR	16.55[0.00]***	NA		1.142
Variable	LNGDP	LNTOR		
LNGDP	NA	6.83[0.28]		1.102
LNTOR	4.69[0.62]	NA		1.102
Lag Selection	AIC = 3	BIC = 3	HQC = 3	FPE = 3
Serial Correlation	χ^2-statistic	p-value		
	38.201	0.741		
	41.526	0.497		
	53.441	0.180		

Note: ** and *** denote significance at the 5% and 1%, respectively. NA denotes non-applicable.

traded ratio (TVR). However, the evidence dissipates once we proxy stock market performance by the turnover ratio (TOR). Therefore, regime shifts are not driving the results reported for the full sample.

In summary, the causal links between stock market performance and economic performance are highly dependent on the proxy of stock market performance in the case of Hong Kong. One plausible explanation of this finding may stem from the way the proxies of stock market performance are calculated. The first two proxies of stock market performance, namely, MCR and TVR, are calculated as percentages of GDP, whereas the third proxy, TOR, is calculated as the total value of shares traded as a percentage of stock market capitalization. Hence, by their construction, it is obvious that MCR and TVR are correlated with GDP so that factors that may drive GDP may also be driving MCR and TVR. This implies that any model containing GDP and any of these stock market variables should exhibit reverse causality. This may not necessarily be the case if such a model contains TOR instead. Second, unlike TOR, MCR and TVR are dependent on stock prices. Therefore, if stock prices increase – with the number of transactions in the stock market unchanged – MCR and TVR will increase. In this sense, MCR and TVR are susceptible to the "price effect", whereas this price effect is factored away when calculating TOR. The price effect may play an important role when examining the causal linkages between the stock market and the economy (Levine & Zervos 1998). Our results appear to confirm this assertion.

5. Sensitivity Analysis

The results obtained thus far rest on the assumption that the tests for causality that entail testing for unit roots and cointegration are exposed to pre-testing bias

Table 5. Tests for Granger Causality (1997Q3–2014Q4)

	Wald-statistic [p-value]			Inverse Roots
Variable	LNGDP	LNMCR		
LNGDP	NA	25.83[0.00] ***		1.153
LMCR	14.22[0.01]**	NA		1.153
Variable	LNGDP	LNTVR		
LNGDP	NA	11.90[0.03]**		1.137
LNTVR	19.78[0.00]***	NA		1.137
Variable	LNGDP	LNTOR		
LNGDP	NA	5.42[0.34]		1.046
LNTOR	5.65[0.32]	NA		1.046
Lag Selection	AIC = 3	BIC = 4	HQC = 3	FPE = 3
Serial Correlation	χ^2-statistic	p-value		
	29.516	0.879		
	32.307	0.583		
	35.894	0.468		

Note: ** and *** denote significance at the 5% and 1%, respectively. NA denotes non-applicable.

and therefore not appropriate. It is important to note that by not accounting for cointegration, additional information, i.e., the short-run dynamics of the model, is lost. Hence, this section provides a sensitivity analysis of our results when cointegration properties of the model are accounted for. We first perform three cointegration tests on our specifications and then explore the causal dynamics of the variables. Here, we employ the Johansen, the Engel-Granger, and the Phillips-Ouliaris tests (Engle & Granger, 1987; Johansen & Juselius, 1990; Johansen, 1991; Phillips & Ouliaris, 1990) to perform the cointegration analysis. The results are presented in Tables 6 and 7. Using the Johansen trace and maximum eigen value test, we can conclusively state that *LNGDP* and *LMCR* are cointegrated at 5% (see Table 6). This is also confirmed by the Engel-Granger and the Phillips-Ouliaris tests (see Table 6). The results reported by the Johansen test, however, do not show any cointegrating relationship between *LNGDP* and *LNTVR*. This contrasts the evidence reported by the Engel-Granger and the Phillips-Ouliaris tests. Since the Johansen test provides better results than these single-equation–based tests, we conclude that *LNGDP* and *LNTVR* are not cointegrated (see Table 7).

The presence of a cointegrating relationship between *LNGDP* and *LNMCR* provides a hint of causality between these variables in the short and long runs. The absence of any cointegrating relationship between *LNGDP* and *LNTOR* and between *LNGDP* and *LNTVR* implies that if there is any causal flow, then it occurs in the long run. To test for causality between *LNGDP* and *LNMCR*, we fit a VECM in the spirit of the Engel-Granger representation theorem. Additionally, to test for causality between *LNGDP* and *LNTOR* and between *LNGDP* and *LNTVR*, we fit two small-scale unrestricted VAR models. We then use these esti-

Table 6. Tests for Cointegration between LNGDP and LNMCR

Item	**Johansen Test**			
Hypothesized No. of CE(s)	Eigen value	Trace Statistic	Critical Value (5%)	P-value♦
None	0.135	18.181	15.494	0.019
At most 1	0.019	2.175	3.841	0.140
Hypothesized No. of CE(s)	Eigen value	Max-Eigen Statistic	Critical Value (5%)	P-value♦
None	0.135	16.006	14.264	0.026
At most 1	0.019	2.175	3.841	0.140
		Engle-Granger		
Dependent	tau-statistic	P-value♠	z-statistic	P-value♠
LNGDP	-3.566	0.033	-16.716	0.093
LNMCR	-2.017	0.522	-11.259	0.276
		Phillips-Ouliaris		
Dependent	tau-statistic	P-value♠	z-statistic	P-value♠
LNGDP	-6.813	0.000	-61.401	0.000
LNMCR	-6.716	0.000	-62.167	0.000

Note: ♠MacKinnon (1996) p-values. ♦MacKinnon-Haug-Michelis (1999) p-values.

mates to perform the causality analysis. The results for the tests of Granger causality between the variables are reported in Table 8. The results show that there is a distinct causal flow from *LNMCR* to *LNGDP* in the long run. The results also indicate bidirectional causality between *LNGDP* and *LNMCR* and between *LNGDP* and *LNTVR* in the short run at a 1% significance level. Finally, we find no causal flow between *LNGDP* and *LNTOR*. In light of this, the results are not sensitive to the approach used for testing the causal links between the variables in this study.

6. Conclusion

The arguments surrounding the role of stock markets in the performance of economies have remained inconclusive. Today, there are a number of studies that find a strong positive association between the stock market and economic performance (Bencivenga et al., 1996; Greenwood & Smith, 1997; Jensen & Murphy, 1990; Levine, 1991; Obstfeld, 1994). However, other studies have found that strong stock market performance hurts the performance of the economy in some ways (Arestis et al., 2001; DeLong et al., 1989;

Table 7. Tests for Cointegration between LNGDP and LNTVR

Item	Johansen Test			
		Trace		
No. of CE(s)	Eigen value	Statistic	Critical Value (5%)	P-value♦
None	0.097	12.426	15.495	0.138
At most 1	0.011	1.185	3.841	0.277
		Max-Eigen		
No. of CE(s)	Eigen value	Statistic	Critical Value (5%)	P-value♦
None	0.097	11.242	14.265	0.143
At most 1	0.011	1.185	3.841	0.276
		Engle-Granger		
Dependent	tau-statistic	P-value♠	z-statistic	P-value♠
LNGDP	-2.981	0.123	-16.648	0.094
LNTVR	-3.057	0.106	-20.241	0.043
		Phillips-Ouliaris		
Dependent	tau-statistic	P-value♠	z-statistic	P-value♠
LNGDP	-4.797	0.001	-37.341	0.001
LNTVR	-5.062	0.000	-41.702	0.000

Note: ♠MacKinnon (1996) p-values. ♦MacKinnon-Haug-Michelis (1999) p-values

Demirgüc-Kunt & Levine, 1996). The inconclusive nature of these studies makes the links between stock market performance and economic performance worthy of empirical re-investigation. Additionally, Hong Kong is among the countries whose stock market and economy have experienced tremendous advancements in the last three decades, making it a worthy candidate for this empirical investigation. In this paper, we ask the following question: Is the strong performance of the stock market in Hong Kong essential to the performance of its economy? This question has received less attention in the literature, perhaps due to the inconclusive nature of the links between stock markets and real economic activities. We explore this question in this paper in an augmented VAR setting by making use of the Toda-Yamamoto test for causality. Using an extended quarterly dataset that covers the period 1986Q2-2014Q4, we find bidirectional causal linkages between stock market performance, as proxied by the market capitalization ratio, and the performance of the Hong Kong economy. In addition, we find bidirectional causal flow between stock mar-

Table 8. Tests for Granger Causality – Alternative Approach

	F-statistic		[t-statistic]
Variable	LNGDP	LNMCR	ECT
LNGDP	---	11.518***	-0.172[-4.988]***
LMCR	8.174***	---	0.858[4.005]***
Variable	LNGDP	LNTVR	ECT
LNGDP	---	4.414***	---
LNTVR	3.366***	---	---
Variable	LNGDP	LNTOR	ECT
LNGDP	---	1.191	---
LNTOR	0.722	---	---

Note: * and *** denote significance at the 10% and 1% levels, respectively.

ket performance, as proxied by the total value traded ratio, and the performance of the Hong Kong economy. However, the causal links between stock market performance and economic performance vanish if stock market performance is proxied by the turnover ratio. This suggests that the causal links between stock market performance and economic performance are highly dependent on the proxy used for stock market performance in the case of Hong Kong. This paper clearly shows that the choice of the proxies for stock market performance matters. Proxies of stock market performance based on the total value traded and market capitalization ratio may exhibit strong correlation with measures of economic performance, thereby generating reverse causality *a priori*, whereas proxies of stock market performance based on the turnover ratio may not. Moreover, the inherent price effects in proxies of stock market performance based on the total value traded and market capitalization ratio imply that the results based on these proxies may differ from those based on the turnover ratio. Hence, for an empirical researcher, care must be taken when selecting the proxies of stock market performance. Perhaps a robust way to proxy stock market performance is pulling the information contents of these three proxies to construct a single multifaceted proxy for stock market performance. The results based on this new proxy may then be compared with those based on the three proxies to make a proper judgment. Future studies may shift toward this direction.

References

Arestis, P. & Demetriades, P. (1997). Financial development and economic growth: Assessing the evidence. *The Economic Journal, 107*(442), 783-799.

Arestis, P., Demetriades, P. O., & Luintel, K. B. (2001). Financial development and economic growth: The role of stock markets. *Journal of Money, Credit and Banking, 33*(1), 16–41.

Atje, R. & Jovanovic, B. (1993). Stock market and development. *European Economic Review 37*(2-3), 623-640.

Beck, T. & Levine, R. (2004). Stock markets, banks and growth: Panel evidence. *Journal of Banking and Finance, 28*(3), 423-442.

Bencivenga, V. R., Smith, B. D., & Starr, R. M. (1996). Equity markets, transactions costs, and capital accumulation: An illustration. *World Bank Economic Review, 10*(2), 241-65.

Boyd, J. H., Levine, R., & Smith, B. D. (2001). The impact of inflation on financial market performance. *Journal of Monetary Economics, 47*(2), 221–248.

Caner, M. & Kilian, L. (2001). Size distortion of tests of the null hypothesis of stationarity: Evidence and implication for the PPP debate. *Journal of International Money and Finance, 20*, 639-657.

Census and Statistics Department of Hong Kong. (2017, August 11). Gross Domestic Product (GDP), implicit price deflator of GDP and per capita GDP. Available from http://www.censtatd.gov.hk/hong_kong_statistics/statistical_tables/index.jsp?tableID=030

Cheng, S. Y. (2012). Substitution or complementary effects between banking and stock markets: Evidence from financial openness in Taiwan. *Journal of International Financial Markets*, Institutions and Money, *22*(3), 508-520.

Deb, S. G. & Mukherjee, J. (2008). Does stock market development cause economic growth? A time series analysis for Indian economy. *International Research Journal of Finance and Economics, 21*, 142-149.

DeLong, J. B., Schleifer, A., Summers, L. H., & Waldmann, R. J. (1989). The size and incidence of the losses from noise trading. *Journal of Finance, 44*(3), 681-96.

Demirgüc-Kunt, A., & Levine, R. (1996). Stock markets, corporate finance, and economic growth: An overview. *World Bank Economic Review, 10*(2), 223-39.

Elliot, G., Rothenberg, T. J., & Stock, J. H. (1996). Efficient tests for an autoregressive unit root. *Econometrica, 64*(4), 813-836.

Enisan, A. A., & Olufisayo, A. O. (2009). Stock market development and economic growth: Evidence from seven sub-Sahara African countries. *Journal of Economics and Business, 61*(2), 162-171.

Engle, R. F., & Granger, C. W. J. (1987). Cointegration and error correction: Representation, estimation, and testing. *Econometrica, 55*(2), 251–276.

Ernst and Young. (2013). EY global IPO trends. Retrieved from http://www.ey.com/Publication/vwLUAssets/EY_-_Global_IPO_Trends_Q4_2013/$FILE/EY-Global-IPO-Trends-Q4-2013.pdf

Ghosh, S. R. (2006). *East Asian finance: The road to robust markets*. Washington, DC: World Bank.

Granger, C. W. J. (1969). Investigating causal relations by econometric models and cross-spectral methods. *Econometrica, 37*(3), 424–438.

Greenwood, J. & Smith, B. (1997). Financial markets in development and the development of financial markets. *Journal of Economic Dynamics and Control, 21*(1), 145-82.

Harris, R. D. F. (1997). Stock market and development: A re-assessment. *European Economic Review, 41*(1), 139-146.

He, Z. & Maekawa, K. (2001). On spurious granger causality. *Economic Letters, 73*(3), 307–313.

Hondroyiannis, G., Lolos, S., & Papapetrou, E. (2005). Financial markets and economic growth in Greece, 1986–1999. *Journal of International Financial Markets, Institutions and Money, 15*(2), 173-188.

Hong Kong Exchanges and Clearing Limited. (1999). Hong Kong Exchange Fact Book. Retrieved from http://www.hkex.com.hk/eng/stat/statrpt/factbook/1999/FB_1999.pdf

Hong Kong Exchanges and Clearing Limited. (2011, May). *A Glimpse of the Past*, Hong Kong. Available from https://docslide.com.br/download/link/l07-hk-stock-exchangea-glimpse-of-the-past

Hong Kong Exchanges and Clearing Limited. (2013). *Hong Kong Exchange Fact Book*, Hong Kong. Available from http://www.hkex.com.hk/eng/stat/statrpt/factbook/factbook2013/fb2013.htm

Hong Kong Exchanges and Clearing Limited. (2015a). History of HKEX and its market. Available from http://www.hkexgroup.com/eng/abouthkexgroup/history.htm

Hong Kong Exchanges and Clearing Limited. (2015b). Securities Statistics Archive. Available from http://www.hkex.com.hk/eng/stat/smstat/statarch/statarchive.htm

Hsiao, C. (2005). Why Panel Data? *Singapore Economic Review, 50*(2), 143–154.

Jao, Y.C. (2003). Financial Reform in Hong Kong. In Maximilian J.B. Hall (ed.), *The International Handbook on Financial Reform* (pp. 113-130), Cheltenham: Edward Elgar Publishing.

Jeffus, W. M. (2004). FDI and stock market development in selected Latin American countries. *International Finance Review, 5*, 35–44.

Jensen, M. C., & Murphy, K. J. (1990). Performance pay and top management incentives. *Journal of Political Economy, 98*(2), 225-64.

Johansen, S. (1991). Estimation and hypothesis testing of cointegration vectors in Gaussian vector autoregressive models. *Econometrica, 59*(6), 1551–1580.

Johansen, S. &Juselius, K. (1990). Maximum likelihood estimation and inference on cointegration with applications to the demand for money. *Oxford Bulletin of Economics and Statistics, 52*(2), 169–210.

Kramer, G. H. (1983). The ecological fallacy revisited: Aggregate versus individual-level findings on economics and elections and sociotropic voting. *The American Political Science Review, 77*(1), 92-111.

Lee, J. & Poon, J. (2005, November). Alternative measures of the size of the stock market (Research Paper No. 27). Research Department of the Supervision of Markets Division.

Levine, R. (1991). Stock markets, growth, and tax policy. *Journal of Finance, 46*(4), 1445-1465.

Levine, R. & Zervos, S. (1996). Stock market development and long run growth. *World Bank Economic Review, 10*(2), 323-339.

Levine, R. & Zervos, S. (1998). Stock markets, banks and economic growth. *The American Economic Review, 88*(3), 537-58.

MacKinnon, J. G. (1996). Numerical distribution functions for unit root and cointegration tests. *Journal of Applied Econometrics, 11*(6), 601-618.

MacKinnon, J. G., Haug, A. A., & Michelis, L. (1999). Numerical distribution functions of likelihood ratio tests for cointegration. *Journal of Applied Econometrics, 14*(5), 563-577.

Malik, I. A. & Amjad, S. (2013). Foreign direct investment and stock market development in Pakistan. *Journal of International Trade Law and Policy, 12*(3), 226- 242.

Marques, L. M., Fuinhas, J. A., & Marques, A. C. (2013). Does the stock market cause economic growth? Portuguese evidence of economic regime change. *Economic Modelling, 32*, 316-324.

Masoud, N. & Hardaker, G. (2012). The impact of financial development on economic growth: Empirical analysis of emerging market countries *Studies in Economics and Finance, 29*(3), 148-173.

Minier, J. (2003). Are small stock markets different? *Journal of Monetary Economics, 50*(7), 1593-1602.

Naik, P. K. & Padhi, P. (2015). On the linkage between stock market development and economic growth in emerging market economies. Dynamic panel evidence. *Review of Accounting and Finance, 14*(4), 363- 381.

Obstfeld, M. (1994). Risk-taking, global diversification, and growth. *The American Economic Review, 84*(5), 1310-1329.

Perron, P. (1989). The great crash, the oil price shock, and the unit root hypothesis. *Econometrica, 57*(6), 1361-1401.

Perron, P. (1997). Further evidence on breaking trend functions in macroeconomic variables. *Journal of Econometrics, 80*(2), 355-385.

Phillips, P. C. B. & Ouliaris, S. (1990). Asymptotic properties of residual based tests for cointegration. *Econometrica, 58*(1), 165–193.

Phiri, A. (2015). Asymmetric cointegration and causality effects between financial development and economic growth in South Africa. *Studies in Economics and Finance, 32*(4), 464- 484.

Rioja, F. K. & Valev, N. T. (2004). Finance and the sources of growth at various stages of economic development. *Economic Inquiry, 42*(1), 127- 140.

Rousseau, P. L. & Wachtel, P. (2000). Equity markets and growth: Cross-country evidence on timing and utcomes, 1980-1995. *Journal of Business & Finance, 24*(12), 1933-1957.

Schwert, G. W. (1986). Test for unit roots: A Monte Carlo investigation. *Journal of Business and Economic Statistics, 7*(2), 147-159.

Sehrawat, M. & Giri, A. K. (2015). Financial development and economic growth: empirical evidence from India. *Studies in Economics and Finance, 32*(3), 340- 356.

Singh, A. (1997). Financial liberalization, stock markets and economic development. *The Economic Journal, 107*(442), 771-782.

Toda, H. Y. and Yamamoto T. (1995). Statistical inference in vector autoregressions with possibly integrated processes. *Journal of Econometrics, 66*(1-2), 225–250.

Tsang, S. (2004). *A Modern History of Hong Kong*. London, UK: I.B. Tauris & Co Ltd.

World Federation of Exchanges. (2015). The Global Voice in a Global Conversation. Available from http://www.world-exchanges.org

The World Bank. (2014). World Development Indicators. Available from http://data.worldbank.org/data-catalog/world-development-indicators

Yamada, H. (1998). A note on the causality between exports and productivity: An empirical re-examination. *Economics Letters, 61*(1), 111-114.

Zivot, E. & Andrews, D. W. K. (1992). Further evidence on the great crash, the oil-price shock, and the unit-root hypothesis. *Journal of Business and Economic Statistics, 10*(3), 251-270.

Acknowledgments

We thank, without implicating, the editor of ***ERSA Working Papers***, Professor Jan van Heerden, and an anonymous referee for helpful comments and suggestions on an earlier version. We also thank participants at the Western Economic Association International's 12th International Conference (7–10 January, 2016; Nayang Technological University, Singapore) for their useful suggestions. Finally, we thank Professor Staniewski and three anonymous referees of this journal for helpful comments and suggestions. All remaining shortcomings are regretfully ours.

Appendix

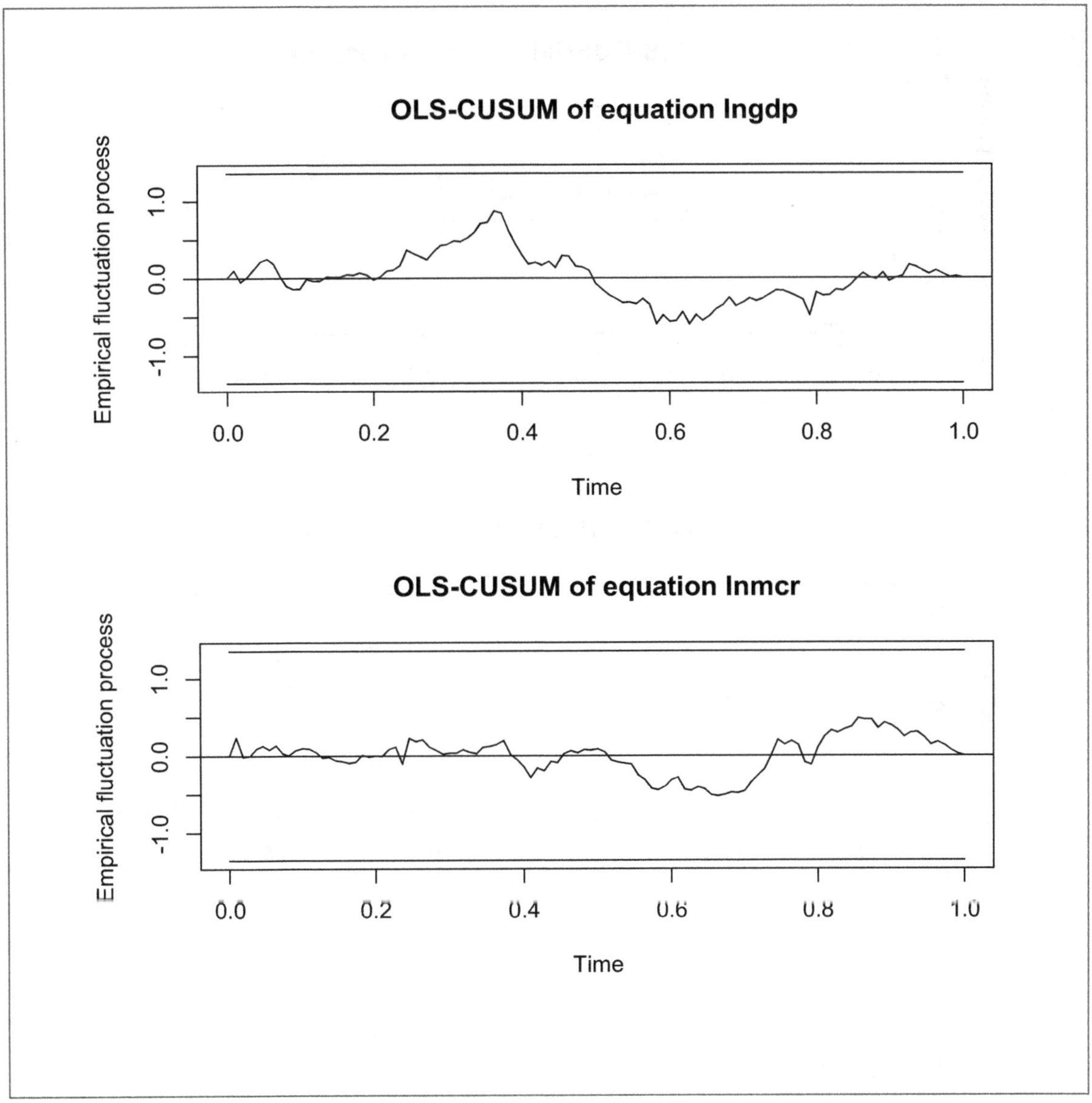

Figure A.1. Model Diagnostic Test for Structural Stability

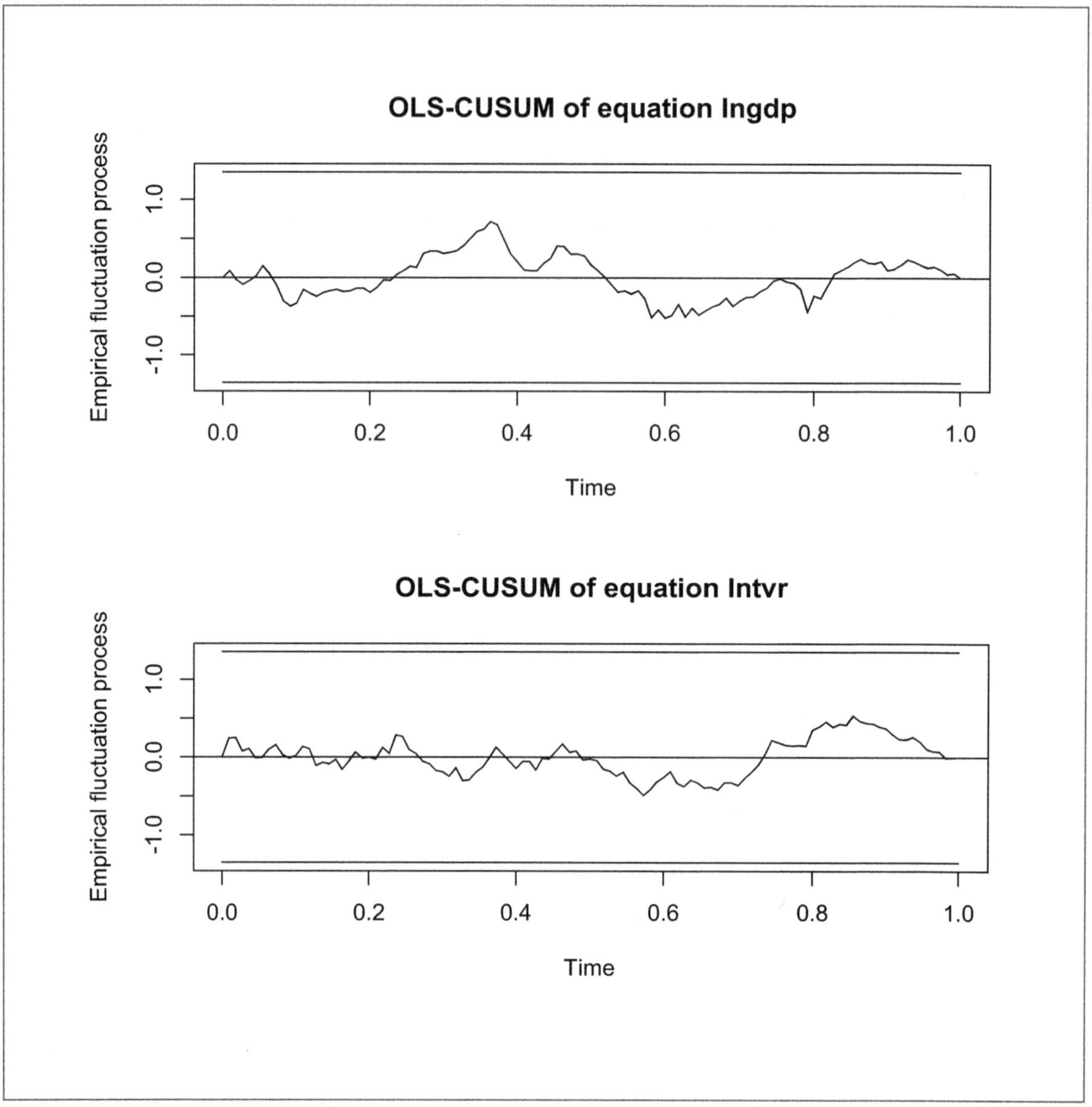

Figure A.2. Model Diagnostic Test for Structural Stability

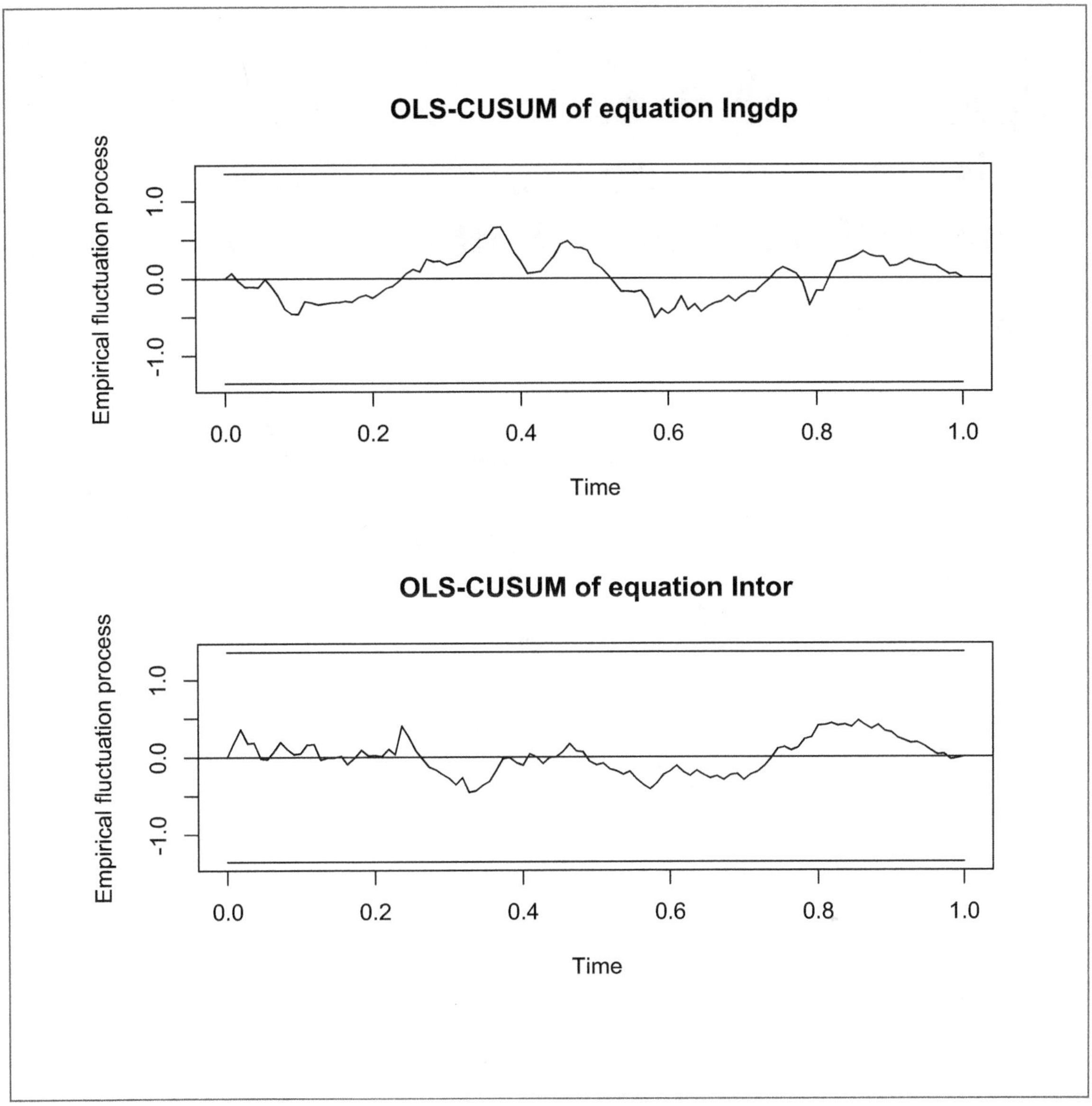

Figure A.3. Model Diagnostic Test for Structural Stability

4

Tripartite Analysis of Financial Development, Trade Openness and Economic Growth: Evidence from Ghana, Nigeria and South Africa

Kizito Uyi Ehigiamusoe[1], Hooi Hooi Lean[1]

ABSTRACT

This study examines the tripartite relationship between financial development, trade openness and economic growth in Ghana, Nigeria and South Africa for the 1980-2014 period. The study reveals a long-run causal relationship between financial development, trade openness and economic growth, thereby supporting finance- and trade-led growth hypotheses for Ghana, Nigeria and South Africa. Moreover, long-run causality from financial development and economic growth to trade openness is found for Ghana. In the short-run, there is evidence of causality from growth to financial development for Ghana, from trade openness to financial development for Nigeria and from growth and financial development to trade openness for South Africa. The findings of this study are robust to alternative proxies of financial development and various diagnostic tests. The study shows that financial development and trade openness can be deployed to accelerate growth, while growth and financial development can be used to promote trade openness. Additionally, trade openness spurs financial development. Therefore, a tripartite relationship exists between the three variables. Hence, interdependence between financial development, trade openness and economic growth is found and consequent policy recommendations are made.

KEY WORDS: Financial development, Trade openness, Economic growth

[1] Universiti Sains Malaysia - Economics Program, School of Social Sciences, Malaysia

1. Introduction

One of the greatest economic challenges currently confronting most developing countries concerns how to make economic growth more inclusive. Many developing countries in Africa, Asia and Latin America are growing faster than most high-income economies in Europe, Asia and North America, but unemployment, income inequality and poverty rates have remained obstinately high in these regions despite their impressive growth (Central Inteligence Agency [CIA], 2014). Though some level of growth and strong average growth are necessary for poverty reduction, these are not sufficient conditions for economic development, as most people do not benefit equally from such growth. Ali and Son (2007) noted that economic growth can

Correspondence concerning this article should be addressed to: **Kizito Uyi Ehigiamusoe**, Universiti Sains Malaysia - Economics Program, School of Social Sciences, 11800 Penang, Malaysia. E-mail: ehiuyikizexcel@yahoo.com

worsen the living conditions of the poor and of marginalized groups, thereby exacerbating inequality, unemployment and poverty rates. Therefore, growth is inclusive when it facilitates equal access to opportunities without social exclusion linked to institutional, market and policy factors (Ali & Zhuang, 2007). Inclusive growth and development boost the social opportunity function (social welfare function), which is dependent on how the average population is granted equity and access to resources such as employment, basic infrastructure, education and healthcare.

According to Todaro and Smith (2009), economic development involves the efficient allocation of existing productive resources and sustained growth overtime as well as economic, political, social and institutional mechanisms (both public and private) needed to bring about rapid and large-scale improvements in people's quality of life. It measures the overall well-being of individuals in terms of how many real goods and services are available to them for investment and consumption. It seeks to trickle down economic growth to the general population in terms of job and economic opportunities; the broader distribution of social and economic benefits; and reductions in discrimination, poverty, unemployment and inequality. A commonly used index of development uses the levels and growth rates of real per capita income by considering a country's capacity to enhance output faster than the rate of population growth (Beck & Levine, 2004; Jhingan, 2010; Todaro & Smith, 2009). Consequently, many low-income countries are grappling with development policy options aimed at accelerating economic growth with a view to achieving inclusive growth and development. In achieving this, there has been a renewed emphasis on sectors of the economy that create job opportunities and that reduce inequality and poverty rates such as the agricultural, industrial, financial and external sectors.

The foregoing emphasizes the importance of economic growth for the achievement of economic development and inclusiveness. Neither economic development nor inclusive growth can be attained without economic growth. Hence, the achievement of sustained and long-term economic growth remains a fundamental macroeconomic objective of most developing countries. However, the theoretical literature contends that financial development can accelerate economic growth and development through its influence on technological innovation, capital accumulation, resource allocation and productivity growth. Through savings mobilization and the allocation of capital to productive investments, the financial sector promotes growth (Beck, Levine, & Loayza, 2000; Chortareas, Magkonis, Moschos, & Panagiotidis, 2015; Muhammad, Islam, & Marashdeh, 2016). The theory of finance and growth focuses on how finance impacts growth and development via resource allocation decisions by delivering on specific functions such as the mobilization of savings, the provision of extant information, the delivery of corporate governance, the allocation of capital and monitoring investments, the facilitation of trade, and the diversification and management of risks (Levine, 2002).

Similarly, theoretical and empirical evidence lays credence to the fundamental role that trade openness plays in economic growth and development (Baltagi, Demetriades, & Law, 2009; Sbia, Shahbaz, & Hamdi, 2014). The classical theory of international trade developed by Adam Smith, David Ricardo and J.S Mill stresses that trade openness broadens markets and enhances investment, productivity, the division of labor and specialization, vents for surplus, and the efficient use of resources and welfare (Jhingan, 2010). Additionally, the endogenous growth model opines that by granting access to global markets through international trade, an open economy is more likely to grow faster and more efficiently than a closed economy. This is the case because international markets allow producers to purchase inputs and sell outputs at competitive prices and grant consumers access to a variety of goods and services.

Furthermore, theoretical evidence supports a link between financial development and trade openness. For instance, Rajan and Zingales' (2003) hypothesis states that for financial development to occur, trade and financial openness are fundamental. Svaleryd and Vlachos (2002) also opined that positive interdependence exists between financial development and liberal trade policies, and this had been corroborated by Shahbaz, Hye, Tiwari, and Leitão, (2013). Baltagi et al. (2009) also posited that trade and financial openness can significantly impact financial development. In essence, there is a link between the finance-growth nexus, the trade-growth nexus and the finance-trade nexus.

For Sub-Saharan Africa however, the tripartite relationship between financial development, trade openness and economic growth remains unclear. This may be related to low levels of financial development and dominant trade deficits (or a chronic balance of payments deficits) observed alongside impressive levels of economic growth found in much of this region. Gries, Kraft, and Meierrieks, (2009) and Menyah, Nazlioglu, and Wolde-Rufael (2014) attempted to examine the causal relationship between these variables by applying a panel Granger causality approach to certain African countries, but their findings are quite conflicting even though most results support an absence of causal relationships between the variables for nearly all of the countries surveyed. Therefore, this study contributes to the existing literature by investigating relationships between financial development, trade openness and economic growth. Specifically, the objectives of this study are: (i) to examine the long-run relationship between financial development, trade openness and economic growth for Ghana, Nigeria and South Africa (hereafter GNS) and (ii) to investigate the direction of the causal relations between financial development, trade openness and economic growth in GNS.

In this regard, the contributions of this study to the existing literature are two-fold. First, unlike previous studies that mainly focus on the trade-growth or finance-growth nexus and that merely use trade openness as a control variable, this study examines the long-run relationship between financial development, trade openness and economic growth under a tripartite framework. In turn, the cointegration relationship between these three variables is identified. Second, the direction of the causal relationship between financial development and trade openness for developing countries remains unclear. Empirical evidence on whether more trade openness is beneficial for the development of the financial sector or whether more financial development is necessary to facilitate trade openness remains scant. This study represents an attempt to address this gap. Interestingly, the study finds that financial development and trade openness spur economic growth and thereby support finance- and trade-led growth hypotheses for Ghana, Nigeria and South Africa. There is also evidence of long-run causality from financial development and economic growth to trade openness for Ghana. For the short-run, the study finds evidence in support of the openness-finance and finance-openness hypotheses for Nigeria and South Africa, respectively. These results reveal a tripartite relationship between financial development, trade openness and economic growth.

The scope of this study is limited to GNS for the following reasons. First, these countries are likely the largest economies of Sub-Sahara Africa and any force that affect their economies will definitely have adverse effects on the continent. Second, these countries have embarked on financial sector reforms over the past decades and consequently have the most developed financial systems in Africa. Third, they have the largest volumes of imports and exports and are more open than other countries of the continent. Finally, our findings on GNS will prove useful to other developing countries in Africa, Asia and Latin America that are vigorously pursuing financial and trade sectors reforms.

The remainder of this paper is divided into five sections. Section 2 presents stylized facts on financial development, trade openness and economic growth for GNS. Section 3 examines empirical issues. The methodology employed in the study is presented in section 4, and section 5 presents the study's empirical results and findings. The final section concludes the paper with policy recommendations.

2. Stylized Facts on Financial Development, Trade Openness and Economic Growth for GNS

Over the past three decades several Sub-Sahara African countries have embarked on reforms in the financial and external sectors with a view to accelerating economic growth and development. Although such reforms have enhanced sector development, levels of development achieved have remained low compared to levels achieved in the financial and external sectors of advanced economies. Moreover, the financial systems of most Sub-Sahara African countries are dominated by the banking sector with stock markets remaining relatively underdeveloped. The failure of government interventions into financial systems in West African countries (e.g., Ghana, Nigeria, etc.) in the 1980s prompted most of these countries to embark on structural reforms involving interest rate liberalization, credit control elimination, the restructuring and privatization of commercial banks, the adoption of indirect instruments of monetary policy and the development of financial systems (Mehran et al., 1998; Ncube, 2007).

For instance, banking sector reforms applied in Ghana in the 2000s consolidated the financial sector and repositioned it for efficiency and effectiveness. The regulator of commercial banks (Bank of Ghana) recapitalized commercial banks to prevent bank insolvency and to restore the confidence of customers of the system. In a bid to adhere to the new capitalization scheme, many banks injected new capital and retained earnings, thereby substantially increasing shareholders' funds. Financial development indicators for Ghana show that credit to the private sector as a ratio of GDP increased from 2.19% in 1980 to 13.97% in 2000 and to 20.44% in 2015. Broad money supply as a ratio of GDP also increased from 18.55% to 28.16% and to 33.95% in the same period. Furthermore, liquid liabilities as a ratio of GDP improved from 16.54% to 23.22% and to 29.15% during this period (Federal Reserve Bank of St. Louis, 2016; The World Bank, 2016). These figures reveal the occurrence of steady improvements in financial development indicators during this period.

In Nigeria, banking consolidation (reforms) occurring in 1991, 2005 and 2009 repositioned the banking sector for efficiency and boosted customer confidence. Prior to this consolidation, the system was characterized by incessant bank failures and insolvency, which resulted in a loss of customer deposits and confidence. The financial system was characterized by suspicion and uncertainty because many bank executives were running financial institutions as private businesses without recourse to customers' deposits and interests. Transparency, accountability and the adequate disclosure of banks' financial positions were lacking. Thus, the bank regulator (Central Bank of Nigeria) embarked on bank consolidation, which increased the share capital of commercial banks and which led to the emergence of stronger and larger banks through mergers and acquisitions. Improvements in technological and financial innovations rendered the financial sector more efficient in the performance of its functions (see Todaro & Smith, 2009). These financial reforms and policies have resulted in greater supply and demand for financial services. However, no remarkable improvements in financial development indicators were made during the 1980-2015 period. For instance, credit to the private sector as a ratio of GDP marginally increased from 12.22% in 1980 to 12.35% in 2000 and to 14.21% in 2015. Broad money supply as a ratio of GDP decreased from 28.62% in 1980 to 21.96% in 2000 and to 19.54% in 2015. Liquid liabilities relative to GDP experienced a similar trend, as they decreased from 23.96% in 1980 to 19.05% in 2000 before slightly increasing to 19.75% in 2015 (Federal Reserve Bank of St. Louis; The World Bank, 2016).

South Africa has experienced more financial development than Ghana and Nigeria. In terms of regulations and capitalization levels, South Africa's banking sector is ranked one of the best in Africa. Thus, reforms and policies introduced by the regulatory authority (South African Reserve Bank) have continued to ensure further improvements to promote system stability and soundness. Local banks have closed, customer confidence has been enhanced and consumer credit has increased. Consequently, financial development indicators for this country have substantially improved. For instance, credit to the private sector as a ratio of GDP increased from 55.6% in 1980 to 130.3% in 2000 and to 149.18% in 2015. Broad money supply as a ratio of GDP also increased from 53.67% to 57.31% and to 74.13% during this period. Additionally, liquid liabilities as a ratio of GDP respectively reached 48.19%, 52.70% and 40.74% during this period (Federal Reserve Bank of St. Louis, 2016; The World Bank, 2016).

Unlike those of the financial sector, reforms made in the external sector have not substantially altered the composition and direction of international trade in many African countries. The composition of international trade shows that exports mainly involve primary goods (agricultural and mineral products) while imports mainly involve manufactured goods. As noted by Gries at al. (2009), countries specializing in the production and export of primary products are less likely to obtain learning spill overs, dynamic externalities and industrial linkages that promote productivity and sustainable economic growth. Specifically, Ghana's main exports are gold, cocoa (beans, paste and butter), crude petroleum, etc. whereas its main imports include refined petroleum, rice, military technologies, industrial equipment, etc. Substantial improvements in trade openness have been achieved in Ghana overs the years. Statistically, The World Bank (2016) shows that trade openness as a ratio of GDP reached 17.62%, 116.05% and 99.25% in 1980, 2000 and 2015, respectively.

Moreover, Nigeria's main exports include crude petroleum, cocoa, oil palm, rubber, leather, etc. while its main imports include industrial supplies, machinery appliances, vehicles, refined petroleum products, rice, processed food, etc. According to The World Bank (2016), trade openness in Nigeria reached 48.57%, 71.38% and 21.45% in 1980, 2000 and 2015, respectively. For South Africa, international trade increased remarkably after the end of Apartheid and with the subsequent lifting of sanctions and boycotts imposed during the Apartheid period. Thus, South Africa's main exports include gold, coal, diamonds, metals, agricultural products (fruits, corn and sugar), etc. while its main imports include machinery and transportation equipment, manufactured goods, chemicals, petroleum, etc. Thus, The World Bank (2016) notes that trade openness levels in South Africa respectively reached 62.72%, 46.86% and 62.85% in 1980, 2000 and 2015.

However, Ghana, Nigeria and South Africa have recently experienced impressive levels of GDP growth despite income level variations. For instance, Ghana's real GDP per capita reached USD411, USD264 and USD1369 in 1980, 2000 and 2015, respectively. Corresponding GDP growth rates reached 0.47%, 3.70% and 3.91%, respectively. Additionally, Nigeria's real GDP per capita respectively reached USD871, USD377 and USD2640 in 1980, 2000 and 2015, respectively. Corresponding GDP growth rates respectively reached 4.20%, 5.31% and 2.65%. Finally, South Africa's real GDP per capita increased from USD2920 in 1980 to USD3099 in 2000 and to USD5723 in 2015. Corresponding GDP growth rates for the period respectively reached 6.62%, 4.20% and 1.26% (The World Bank, 2016). From these figures it is unclear whether financial development or/and trade openness are preconditions for economic growth for these countries. Moreover, there is no evidence to suggest that trade openness enhances economic growth by influencing financial sector development or that financial development enhances growth through its effects on trade openness in these countries.

3. Literature Review

The findings of empirical literature on the finance-growth nexus, trade-growth nexus and finance-trade nexus are mixed, conflicting and inconclusive. However, it has been argued that countries with developed financial systems tend to grow faster and to exhibit stronger economic performance than countries with poorly developed financial systems (Baltagi et al., 2009; Fung, 2009). Additionally, Ndulu, Chakraborti, Lijane, Ramachandran, and Wolgin (2007) asserted that inadequate financial development and poor international trade are partly responsible for the poor economic performance of most developing countries in Africa. Thus, through capital accumulation and productivity growth, financial development accelerates economic growth, and this has been documented by some empirical studies (Beck et al., 2000; Christopoulos & Tsionas, 2004; Shan & Jianhong, 2006). Muhammad et al. (2016) found a positive and significant impact of finance on economic growth, though Arcand, Berkes, and Panizza (2015) opined that when credit to the private sector exceeds 100% of GDP, the positive effect of finance on growth vanishes. However, some empirical studies (Ang & McKibbin, 2007; Blanco, 2009; Esso, 2010; Gozgor, 2015) report that the direction of the causal relationship runs from economic growth to financial development. These studies show that as the economy grows, more financial products, services and instruments are demanded, promoting financial system development. Furthermore, Apergis, Fillippidis, and Economidou, (2007), Adusei (2013) and Chortareas et al. (2015) found a bidirectional causal relationship between financial development and growth. Furthermore, evidence of the absence of a causal relationship between financial development and economic growth is documented in Atindehou, Gueyie, and Amenounve (2005); Kar, Nazlioglu, and Ağır, (2010) and Menyah et al. (2014). Thus, Rapp and Udoieva (2016) found that while stock markets accelerate economic growth and mitigate economic risks, private sector credit does not have any significant impact on growth. This is corroborated by Kalaitzoglou and Durgheu (2016) who also found an insignificant relationship between financial development and economic growth. Badeeb and Lean (2017) found that financial development does not play any significant role in enhancing real sector activities of a resource-based economy. This literature reveals an absence of consensus among scholars on the direction of the causal relationship between financial development and economic growth.

On the finance-trade nexus, Baltagi et al. (2009) noted that trade and financial openness have significant impacts on financial development. Thus, in enabling international trade and capital accounts, a relatively closed economy can benefit significantly. Their study corroborates Rajan and Zingales' hypothesis that for financial development to occur, trade and financial openness are fundamental. Rajan and Zingales (2003) contended that industrial opposition to financial development can be weakened by trade openness and capital flows. This hypothesis however refutes the views of McKinnon (1993), which posit that financial liberalization should be preceded by trade liberalization and that capital account opening should be the last stage of the liberalization process. Law and Demetriades (2006) concluded that middle-income countries that are simultaneously opened in terms of capital flows and trade can enhance financial development while the link is weaker for low income countries. Kim, Lin, and Suen (2010a) found a positive long-run relationship and a negative short-run link between trade openness and financial development for relatively low- and high-income countries. Through a similar study Kim, Lin, and Suen (2010b) found long-run complementarity and short-run substitutionarity between trade openness and financial development for non-OECD countries while the effect of financial development on trade was found to be negligible for OECD countries. They found non-linearity in the long-run relationship, as trade responses decline with financial development. Moreover, Chortareas et al. (2015) reported that the long-run relationship between finance and output only holds after accounting for economic openness. Trade openness appears to be more essential for developing countries while financial openness appears to be more fundamental for advanced countries.

Huang and Temple (2005) concluded that trade openness promotes financial development. Wolde-Rufael (2009) found a strong unidirectional causal relation from financial development to import and export growth (trade) but weak causality from trade to financial development for Kenya. Chinn and Ito (2006) also found that trade openness is a sine qua non for capital account liberalization while banking sector development is a prerequisite of equity market development. Furthermore, positive interdependence between financial development and liberal trade policies was unearthed by Svaleryd and Vlachos (2002). Beck (2002) also found that financial development significantly affects exports and the trade balance of manufactured goods. This confirms the theoretical postulation that countries with better developed financial sectors enjoy a comparative advantage in manufacturing industries. Levine (2001) contended that stock market liquidity can be enhanced through liberal restrictions on international portfolio flows and banking sector efficiency can be enhanced through the stronger presence and participation of foreign banks. Shahbaz et al. (2013) found a short-run unidirectional causal relation from financial development to trade openness for Indonesia while Farhani and Ozturk (2015) found short-run Granger causality from financial development to trade openness for Tunisia. Conversely, Gries et al. (2009) found little to no evidence in support of any causal relation between financial development and trade openness for 16 Sub-Sahara African countries, and similar results (absence of causality) were found by Menyah et al. (2014) for 21 Sub-Sahara African countries.

On the trade-growth nexus, Blackburn and Hung (1998) reported a bidirectional causal relationship between financial development and economic growth and found that the development of intermediation efforts can be accelerated through financial and trade liberalization with the latter having a positive impact on economic growth. Klein and Olivei (2008) found that economic growth can be accelerated through capital account liberalization and by deepening a country's financial sector. This view had previously been canvassed by Bekaert, Harvey, and Lundblad (2001) who found a strong relationship between capital account liberalization and economic growth. While Khan, Qayyum, and Ghani (2006) found that trade and financial liberalization play a fundamental role in enhancing long-run growth, Naceur and Ghazouani (2007) found a negative relationship between trade openness and economic growth. Sbia et al. (2014) found a long-run unidirectional causal relation from trade openness to economic growth and a short-run bidirectional causal relationship between the two variables. However, Farhani and Ozturk (2015) found no causal relationship between trade openness and economic growth.

Nevertheless, relationships between financial development, trade openness and economic growth for Sub-Sahara Africa remain unclear due to limited research conducted on the subject and due to the conflicting and inconclusiveness results of empirical studies. Two notable previous studies (Gries et al., 2009; Menyah et al., 2014) found no causal relation from financial development or trade openness to economic growth for most of the countries examined. However, given reforms made to the financial and trade sectors of Sub-Saharan African countries over the past three decades, development brought about through these reforms should be positively related to economic growth. Hence, the present study measures the tripartite relationship between financial development, trade openness and economic growth for Ghana, Nigeria and South Africa.

4. Methodology

We conduct an Autoregressive Distributed Lagged (ARDL)-bounds test (developed by Pesaran and Shin (1999) and later extended by Pesaran, Shin, and Smith, 2001) to investigate the long-run relationship between financial development, trade openness and economic growth for Ghana, Nigeria and South Africa. The ARDL bound test can be applied irrespective of whether the model variables are endogenous, integrated at order one or zero, and even when the sample size considered is small. However, the ARDL-bound test approach requires that all variables of the model be integrated in the order of zero [I(0)] and one [I(1)]. Hence, we conduct Augmented Dickey Fuller and Phillip Perron unit root tests to determine the order of integration for the studied variables before conducting our cointegration test. When a long-run cointegration relationship was found between the variables, we examined long-run effects and short-run dynamics via the Error Correction Model (ECM). Data on economic growth, financial development and trade openness used in this study for 1980-2014 were sourced from the World Bank's World Development Indicators.

4.1 Model Specification

The ARDL model used to examine the cointegration relationship between financial development, trade openness and economic growth (following Beck et al., 2000; Beck & Levine, 2004) is written as follows:

$$\Delta Y_t = \alpha_0 + \sum_{i=1}^{p} \alpha_1 \Delta Y_{t-i} + \sum_{j=0}^{q} \alpha_2 \Delta FDE_{t-j} + \sum_{k=0}^{r} \alpha_3 \Delta TOP_{t-k} +$$

$$+ \alpha_4 Y_{t-1} + \alpha_5 FDE_{t-1} + \alpha_6 TOP_{t-1} + \mu_t \qquad (1)$$

where: Y= economic growth (proxied by real GDP per capita growth rates; FDE= financial development (proxied by credit to the private sector as a ratio of GDP); TOP= trade openness as a ratio of GDP; and μ_t = the disturbance term. All of the variables are given as natural logarithms.

Following Baltagi et al. (2009) and Chinn and Ito (2006) and Kim et al. (2010a) and Law and Demetriades (2006), Equation 1 can also be written with financial development and trade openness as dependent variables as follows:

$$\Delta FDE_t = \beta_0 + \sum_{i=0}^{p} \beta_1 \Delta Y_{t-i} + \sum_{j=1}^{q} \beta_2 \Delta FDE_{t-j} + \sum_{k=0}^{r} \beta_3 \Delta TOP_{t-k} +$$

$$+ \beta_4 Y_{t-1} + \beta_5 FDE_{t-1} + \beta_6 TOP_{t-1} + \mu_t \qquad (2)$$

$$\Delta TOP_t = \delta_0 + \sum_{i=0}^{p} \delta_1 \Delta Y_{t-i} + \sum_{j=0}^{q} \delta_2 \Delta FDE_{t-j} + \sum_{k=1}^{r} \delta_3 \Delta TOP_{t-k} +$$

$$+ \delta_4 Y_{t-1} + \delta_5 FDE_{t-1} + \delta_6 TOP_{t-1} + \mu_t \qquad (3)$$

In Equation 1, if α_5 and α_6 are positive and statistically significant, financial development and trade openness impact economic growth. Similarly, if β_4 and β_6 in Equation 2 are positive and statistically significant, it suggests that economic growth and trade openness affect financial development. In the same vein, economic growth and financial development can be seen as having impact on trade openness if δ_4 and δ_5 in Equation 3 are positive and statistically significant.

Furthermore, the first section of Equation 1 $(\alpha_1, \alpha_2, \alpha_3)$ examines the short-run dynamic relationship while the second section $(\alpha_4, \alpha_5, \alpha_6)$ investigates long-run associations between the variables. The same goes for parameters of Equations 2 and 3. In selecting the number of lags denoted by p, q, r, we consider the Akaike information criterion (AIC). To test for the cointegration relationship between the variables via the ARDL approach, the null hypothesis of no cointegration is stated against the alternative hypothesis of cointegration between the variables in the models as follows:

$H_0: \alpha_4 = \alpha_5 = \alpha_6 = 0 \quad H_1: \alpha_4 = \alpha_5 = \alpha_6 \neq 0$

$H_0: \beta_4 = \beta_5 = \beta_6 = 0 \quad H_1: \beta_4 = \beta_5 = \beta_6 \neq 0$

$H_0: \delta_4 = \delta_5 = \delta_6 = 0 \quad H_1: \delta_4 = \delta_5 = \delta_6 \neq 0$

Once a cointegration relationship is established between the variables, we examine the direction of long- and short-run causal relations between the variables using Error Correction Model (ECM) equations given as follows:

$$\Delta Y_t = \phi_0 + \sum_{i=1}^{m} \phi_1 \Delta Y_{t-i} + \sum_{j=0}^{n} \phi_2 \Delta FDE_{t-j} + \sum_{k=0}^{o} \phi_3 \Delta TOP_{t-k} + + \varpi ECT_{t-1} + \mu_t \quad (4)$$

$$\Delta FDE_t = \delta_0 + \sum_{i=0}^{m} \delta_1 \Delta Y_{t-i} + \sum_{j=1}^{n} \delta_2 \Delta FDE_{t-j} + \sum_{k=0}^{o} \delta_3 \Delta TOP_{t-k} + + \lambda ECT_{t-1} + \mu_t \quad (5)$$

$$\Delta TOP_t = \theta_0 + \sum_{i=0}^{m} \theta_1 \Delta Y_{t-i} + \sum_{j=0}^{n} \theta_2 \Delta FDE_{t-j} + \sum_{k=1}^{o} \theta_3 \Delta TOP_{t-k} + + \sigma ECT_{t-1} + \mu_t \quad (6)$$

Thus, the null hypothesis of no long- or short-run causality is tested against the alternative hypothesis of causality using the ECM equations. In Equations 4-6, long-run causality is examined based on the statistical significance of the coefficient of the lagged error correction term (ECT_{t-1}) at the 5% level. In other words, the null hypothesis is rejected based on the joint statistical significance of the regressors and based on the significance of the coefficient of the lagged error correction term (ECT_{t-1}), which should also be negative. The long-run null hypotheses of Equations 4-6 are stated against the alternative hypotheses as follows:

$H_0: \varpi_1 = 0;\ H_1: \varpi_1 \neq 0$

$H_0: \lambda_1 = 0;\ H_1: \lambda_1 \neq 0$

$H_0: \sigma_1 = 0;\ H_0: \sigma_1 \neq 0$

Conversely, short-run causality is examined from the statistical significance of the F-statistic of each coefficient of the independent variables. The short-run null hypotheses for financial development is stated against the alternative hypotheses as follows:

$H_0: \phi_2 = 0;\ H_1: \phi_2 \neq 0$

$H_0: \delta_2 = 0;\ H_1: \delta_2 \neq 0$

$H_0: \theta_2 = 0;\ H_1: \theta_2 \neq 0$

The short-run null hypotheses for trade openness are stated against the alternative hypotheses as follows:

$H_0: \phi_3 = 0; H_1: \phi_3 \neq 0$

$H_0: \delta_3 = 0;\ H_1: \delta_3 \neq 0$

$H_0: \theta_3 = 0;\ H_1: \theta_3 \neq 0$

Similarly, the short-run null hypotheses for economic growth are stated against the alternative hypotheses as follows:

$H_0: \phi_1 = 0;\ H_1: \phi_1 \neq 0$

$H_0: \delta_1 = 0;\ H_1: \delta_1 \neq 0$

$H_0: \theta_1 = 0;\ H_1: \theta_1 \neq 0$

4.2 Justification of the Model Variables

Various monetary aggregates have been proposed and employed in the literature as proxies for measuring financial development. However, credit to the private sector as a ratio of GDP remains as a primary proxy because it defines credit to economic agents (producers and consumers) as against credit to the public sector (Beck et al., 2000; Beck & Levine, 2004; Levine & Zervos, 1998). To measure the robustness of the results, we use broad money supply as a ratio of GDP as an alternative proxy for financial development (Kar et al., 2010; Odhiambo, 2008; Wolde-Rufael, 2009). Financial development is expected to be positively related to economic growth and trade openness.

To measure trade openness, we use the addition of exports and imports as a ratio of GDP. Theory suggests that because international trade allows for flows of foreign capital into and out of a country, a more open economy is likely to develop faster and more efficiently through its access to global markets (Herwartz & Walle, 2014; Shan & Jianhong, 2006; Yilmazkuday, 2011). Hence, trade openness is expected to be positively related to economic growth and financial development.

The GDP per capita growth rate is used to proxy economic growth because it takes into account a country's GDP and population. The rate at which a country's GDP and population grows has serious implications for unemployment, inequality and poverty rates (Beck et al., 2000; Beck & Levine, 2004).

Thus, financial development and trade openness are fundamental determinants of economic growth. In modeling the relationship between financial development and economic growth, most previous studies have used trade openness and income level as control variables (Beck et al., 2000; Levine et al., 2000; Herwartz & Walle, 2014). Moreover, in modeling the relationship between financial development and trade openness, previous studies have typically used income levels and one-period lagged financial development as control variables (Baltagi et al., 2009; Chinn & Ito, 2006). The present study follows previous empirical studies of the modeling framework. However, as we focus on the tripartite relationship between financial development, trade openness and economic growth using the Error Correction Model-based causality approach, the number of control variables considered is kept to a minimum to retain the interpretability of the relationships examined (Chinn & Ito, 2006; Gries et al., 2009; Menyah et al., 2014; Wolde-Rufael, 2009).

5. Empirical Results

Table 1 presents descriptive statistics on variables measured in this study. It shows broad variations in financial development, trade openness and economic growth across the samples for the three countries. While Ghana experienced an average growth rate of 1.79% during the period, Nigeria and South Africa experienced average growth rates of 1.06% and 0.41%, respectively. In addition, average credit to the private sector as a ratio of GDP reached 8.93% in Ghana compared to 15% in Nigeria and 110.2% in South Africa. Furthermore, trade openness averaged at 62.8% in Ghana but hovered at approximately 52% in Nigeria and South Africa. This shows that Ghana experienced the highest average growth rate and levels of trade openness while South Africa experienced the highest average levels of financial development during the period.

The results of the unit root tests using the Augmented Dickey Fuller (ADF) and Philip-Perron (PP) to ascertain the order of integration of model variables are presented in Table 2. GDP per capita growth is integrated at an order of zero [I(0)] for Ghana, Nigeria and South Africa while financial development and trade openness are integrated at an order of one [I(1)] for Ghana, Nigeria and South Africa at the 1% significance level. This shows that the model variables represent a mixture of [I(0)] and [I(1)] and that the ARDL bound test can be applied.

To determine the appropriate lag order of differenced variables included in the model, we apply the Akaike Information Criterion (AIC) via the unrestricted ARDL equation. The ADRL-bounds testing approach is then used to determine the existence of a cointegration relationship between financial development, trade openness and economic growth. The results presented in Table 3 show that according to Equation 1, a cointegration relationship exists between financial development, trade openness and economic growth when the latter is used as a dependent variable for Ghana, Nigeria and South Africa. Thus, the calculated F-statistic is greater than upper bound critical values at the 10 percent significance level. Hence, we reject our null hypothesis on the absence of a cointegration relationship between the variables and we fail to reject our alternative hypotheses supporting the existence of cointegration relationships between financial development, trade openness and economic growth for all of the countries examined.

In Equation 2, where financial development is the dependent variable, the cointegration relationship was only found for Nigeria. Hence, the null hypothesis is rejected in favor of the alternative hypothesis. Conversely, we fail to reject the null hypothesis of no cointegration for Ghana and South Africa, implying the absence of a cointegration association. Similarly, for Equation 3, wherein trade openness was used as a dependent variable, a cointegration relationship between the variables was only found for South Africa, thus rejecting the null hypothesis, and no such cointegration relationship was found for Nigeria. The calculated F-

Table 1. Summary of Descriptive Statistics

	Y	FDE	M2	TOP
		Ghana		
Mean	1.794	8.930	22.890	62.794
Maximum	11.251	19.907	34.108	116.048
Minimum	-9.925	1.542	11.304	6.320
Standard Deviation	3.782	5.609	7.053	30.299
		Nigeria		
Mean	1.061	15.021	24.439	51.903
Maximum	30.342	38.386	43.266	81.812
Minimum	-15.458	8.7096	13.230	23.608
Standard Deviation	7.4737	6.187	6.646	15.768
		South Africa		
Mean	0.401	110.165	59.636	52.549
Maximum	4.171	160.124	80.799	72.865
Minimum	-4.330	55.600	45.500	38.645
Standard Deviation	2.455	32.683	10.148	8.185

Notes: Y= real GDP per capita growth rates, FDE= financial development proxy based on credit given to the private sector as a ratio of GDP M2= broad money supply as a ratio of GDP (alternative proxy of financial development) TOP= trade openness as a ratio of GDP.

statistic is lower than lower bound critical values of the 10 percent significant level. However, for Ghana it cannot be determined whether a cointegration relationship exists because the calculated F-statistic lies within the lower and upper bound critical values at the 5 percent significance level. The Error Correction Model can be used to determine the existence of a long-run association between the variables.

Furthermore, the presence of a cointegration relationship between two variables implies that one variable Granger causes the other, though cointegration does not determine the direction of causality. We thus use the Error Correction Model to determine the direction of Granger causality between financial development, trade openness and economic growth, and corresponding results are presented in Table 4. We show that long-run causality runs from financial development and trade openness to economic growth for Ghana, Nigeria and South Africa. This is supported by the statistical significance of the coefficient of the lagged Error Correction Term [ECT(-1)] at the 5% level. This implies that economic growth tends to converge to its long-run equilibrium path in response to variations in financial development and trade openness. Bannerjee, Dolado, and Mestre, (1998) found that a negative and highly significant coefficient of lagged error correction terms further proves the existence of a cointegration relationship between variables.

A long-run causal relation runs from financial development and economic growth to trade openness for Ghana, but such causality was not found for Nigeria and South Africa. Similarly, we found no evidence of long-run causality from economic growth and trade openness to financial development for the examined countries. However, we found evidence of short-run causality running from financial development and

Table 2. Unit Root Test Results

Variables	Augmented Dickey Fuller (ADF)		Philip-Perron (PP)	
	Level [I(0)]	1st Difference [I(1)]	Level [I(0)]	1st Difference [I(1)]
		Ghana		
Y	-3.415**	-6.465***	-3.324**	-15.164***
FDE	-0.870	-6.398***	-0.618	-7.844***
M2	-0.852	-6.462***	-0.714	-6.462***
TOP	-1.430	-4.737***	-1.446	-4.744***
		Nigeria		
Y	-4.877***	-12.956***	-4.911***	-15.309***
FDE	-2.594	-5.107***	-2.431	-8.749***
M2	-3.249**	-4.876***	-2.139	-7.178***
TOP	-1.944	-7.459***	-1.958	-7.414***
		South Africa		
Y	-3.922***	-7.188***	-3.916***	-9.466***
FDE	-1.698	-6.545***	-2.073	-7.188***
M2	-0.893	-4.124***	-0.728	-4.143***
TOP	-1.619	-5.287***	-1.753	-5.352***

Notes: *** and ** denote statistical significance at the 1% and 5% levels, respectively, and a rejection of the null hypothesis of the unit root. Y= real GDP per capita growth rates, FDE= a financial development proxy based on credit given to the private sector as a ratio of GDP, M2= broad money supply as a ratio of GDP (alternative proxy of financial development), TOP= trade openness as a ratio of GDP.

Table 3. Cointegration Test Results

Dependent variable	Function	**Ghana**	**Nigeria**	**South Africa**
		F-Statistic	F-Statistic	F-Statistic
Y	Y= f(FDE, TOP)	12.816***	8.650***	9.388***
FDE	FDE= f(Y, TOP)	1.675	4.435*	1.527
TOP	TOP= f(Y, FDE)	3.798	2.038	5.991**

Bounds test critical values

	Lower Bounds	Upper Bounds
1%	5.15	6.36
5%	3.79	4.85
10%	3.17	4.14

Notes: ***, ** and * denote statistical significance at the 1%, 5% and 10% levels, respectively. Y= real GDP per capita growth rates, FDE= financial development proxy based on credit given to the private sector as a ratio of GDP, TOP= trade openness as a ratio of GDP.

Table 4. Granger Causality Tests

Dependent variable	Causal Flow	F- Statistic (Short-run causality)	ECT [T- Statistic] (Long-run causality)	R^2
		Ghana		
Y	FDE → Y	4.471 (0.107)	-0.628*** [-18.929]	0.975
Y	TOP → Y	5.319* (0.070)		
FDE	Y → FDE	5.518* (0.063)	-0.043 [-0.917]	0.384
FDE	TOP → FDE	2.462 (0.292)		
TOP	Y → TOP	1.893 (0.338)	-0.158*** [-3.907]	0.519
TOP	FDE → TOP	0.308 (0.858)		
		Nigeria		
Y	FDE → Y	4.952* (0.084)	-0.749*** [-3.289]	0.534
Y	TOP → Y	1.213 (0.545)		
FDE	Y → FDE	2.249 (0.325)	0.432*** [3.222]	0.343
FDE	TOP → FDE	7.227** (0.027)		
TOP	Y → TOP	3.114 (0.210)	0.075 [0.575]	0.260
TOP	FDE → TOP	0.742 (0.690)		
		South Africa		
Y	FDE → Y	3.370 (0.185)	-0.774 *** [-2.903]	0.558
Y	TOP → Y	4.391 (0.111)		
FDE	Y → FDE	0.546 (0.761)	0.003 [0.251]	0.190
FDE	TOP → FDE	4.475 (0.107)		
TOP	Y → TOP	9.791*** (0.008)	-0.010 [-0.996]	0.512
TOP	FDE → TOP	11.494*** (0.003)		

Notes: ***, ** and * denote statistical significance at the 1%, 5% and 10% levels, respectively. Figures shown in parenthesis are probability values while T-statistics are shown in square brackets. Y= real GDP per capita growth rates, FDE= financial development proxy based on credit given to the private sector as a ratio of GDP, TOP= trade openness as a ratio of GDP.

economic growth to trade openness for South Africa. Short-run causal relations were also found running from trade openness to financial development and from financial development to economic growth for Nigeria. In the case of Ghana, short-run causality runs from trade openness to economic growth and from economic growth to financial development. These findings are supported by the statistical significance of calculated F-statistics of the variables at the 10% level.

Our findings on causality running from financial development to economic growth for South Africa are consistent with those of Gries et al. (2009) and Menyah et al. (2014). This implies that the supply-leading hypothesis prevails for this country, as the financial sector can be used to accelerate economic growth. This can likely be attributed to the development of the financial sector in South Africa. However, our findings on causal relations between financial development and

Table 5. Granger Causality Tests based on an alternative proxy for financial development

Dependent variable	Causal Flow	F- Statistic (Short-run causality)	ECT [T- Statistic] (Lon-run causality)	R^2
		Ghana		
Y	M2 → Y	2.457 (0.293)	-0.455*** [-16.004]	0.972
Y	TOP → Y	4.864* (0.088)		
M2	Y → M2	0.552 (0.759)	0.066*** [2.723]	0.467
M2	TOP → M2	1.077 (0.583)		
TOP	Y → TOP	2.004 (0.367)	-0.122*** [-3.706]	0.528
TOP	M2 → TOP	0.419 (0.811)		
		Nigeria		
Y	M2 → Y	2.280 (0.319)	-0.745*** [-3.072]	0.438
Y	TOP → Y	3.779 (0.151)		
M2	Y → M2	0.302 (0.859)	0.049 [0.410]	0.145
M2	TOP → M2	2.039 (0.361)		
TOP	Y → TOP	1.855 (0.395)	0.242 [1.716]	0.227
TOP	M2 → TOP	4.381 (0.112)		
		South Africa		
Y	M2 → Y	0.378 (0.828)	-0.541 [-1.468]	0.379
Y	TOP → Y	2.459 (0.292)		
M2	Y → M2	6.415** (0.041)	0.243*** [4.551]	0.576
M2	TOP → M2	1.381 (0.501)		
TOP	Y → TOP	4.951* (0.084)	-0.171 [-1.365]	0.303
TOP	M2 → TOP	3.208 (0.201)		

Notes: ***, ** and * denote statistical significance at the 1%, 5% and 10% levels, respectively. Figures shown in parenthesis are probability values while T-statistics are shown in square brackets. Y= real GDP per capita growth rates, M2= financial development proxy based on broad money supply as a ratio of GDP, TOP= trade openness as a ratio of GDP.

economic growth for Ghana and Nigeria contradict those of Gries et al. (2009), who report a demand-following hypothesis for Ghana and a feedback hypothesis for Nigeria. In general, we find that financial development and trade openness can be used to enhance economic performance.

On causal relations between financial development and trade openness, the findings of this study are consistent with the finance-openness hypothesis reported for Nigeria in Gries et al. (2009) but contrast with trade openness-finance and feedback relationships reported for Ghana and South Africa, respectively. Generally, there is evidence of causal relations between financial development and trade openness, and this is consistent with Huang and Temple (2005) and Wolde-Rufael (2009). Finally, overwhelming evidence found in support of causality between economic growth and trade openness is consistent with Berthelemy and Varoudakis (1996). Thus, trade openness induces economic growth, and the reverse causation is also found.

To measure the robustness of our results we use broad money supply as a ratio of GDP as an alternative proxy for financial development and corresponding results are reported in Table 5. The results are similar to those obtained when credit to the private sector was used as a proxy for financial development.

For our robustness check of the cointegration results, we conducted a structural breaks test using the method proposed by Bai and Perron (2003) to measure the presence of structural breaks in the series. After controlling for structural breaks, the co-integration results were not significantly altered. We also conducted various diagnostic tests (the results are available on request) to further measure the robustness of the results. We found no signs of autocorrelation or heteroscedasticity, and the models are generally stable. The stability tests show that the models are stable, as plots of the charts lie within the critical bounds at the 5% significance level. Bahmani-Oskooee and Nasir (2004) found that the null hypothesis stating that the regression equation is correctly specified cannot be rejected when plots of these statistics fall within critical boundaries at the 5% significance level.

In sum, the findings of this study are three-fold. First, there is a long-run causal relation running from financial development and trade openness to economic growth, thereby supporting the finance- and trade-led growth hypotheses. This implies that financial development and trade openness are jointly growth-enhancing in Ghana, Nigeria and South Africa. This strongly refutes the notion that financial development and trade openness do not affect or hinder economic growth in Sub-Sahara African countries. Unlike previous studies, this study finds joint long-run causality from financial development and trade openness to economic growth. This finding is consistent with theories emphasizing the positive role of financial development and trade openness in economic growth. In terms of individual causality, there is evidence of short-run causality running from financial development and trade openness to economic growth.

Second, there is a joint long-run causal relation running from financial development and economic growth to trade openness, thereby confirming the finance- and growth-openness hypotheses. There is also evidence of individual short-run causality from financial development and economic growth to trade openness. The implication of this finding is that financial development and economic growth can be deployed to accelerate trade openness. Thus, policies and reforms that boost financial development and economic growth can also spur trade openness in these countries. Finally, there is no strong evidence for joint long-run causal relations from trade openness and economic growth to financial development, but we find marginal evidence of short-run causality from trade openness to financial development. This contrasts with the results of Kim et al. (2010b), who found long-run complementarity and short-run substitutionarity between trade openness and financial development for non-OECD countries and a negligible effect of financial development on trade in OECD countries. Thus, the tripartite relationship found between financial development, trade openness and economic growth is evident, as finance and trade spur growth; finance and growth spur trade; and trade spurs finance.

The findings of this paper are robust to alternative proxies of financial development and to various diagnostic tests (e.g., structural break, autocorrelation, heteroscedasticity and stability tests). Econometrically, the techniques used in this study reveal the presence of joint and individual causality and of long-run and short-run causality between the examined variables.

6. Conclusion

This study examines cointegration and causal relationships between financial development trade openness and economic growth for Ghana, Nigeria and South Africa. The study results support the existence of cointegration relationships between the variables. We found that a long-run causal relation runs from financial development and trade openness to economic growth for all of the examined countries, thereby supporting the finance- and trade-led growth hypotheses. We also found long-run causality running from financial development and economic growth to trade openness for Ghana. Though we found no long-run causality from trade openness to financial development, we found evidence of short-run causality. Hence, a tripartite relationship between finance, trade and growth is evident from this study. These findings are robust to alternative proxies of financial development and to various diagnostic tests.

This study shows that financial development and trade openness can be deployed to accelerate economic growth in all of the countries examined. This rejects the notion that financial development and trade openness are unimportant to economic growth in developing countries. Thus, long-run economic benefits in terms of economic growth and trade openness can be attained by developing countries when they embark on reforms/ restructuring that can stimulate the development of their financial sectors. Furthermore, countries with relatively closed economies can derive long-term economic benefits in terms of financial development and economic growth by encouraging trade. However, the examined countries would secure more long-term economic benefits in terms of economic growth and development if they facilitated trade while developing their financial sectors. Hence, policies focused on the development of the financial sector and on trade openness to enhance economic growth appear justified. In other words, we justify development strategies that underscore economic openness and/or financial sector development as feasible options for countries. Additionally, policies directed at stimulating financial development are likely to shape trade as an additional outcome. To stimulate economic growth, the financial and trade sectors must be developed owing to their fundamental role in economic growth. Policies and reforms that enhance (or dampen) economic growth will also enhance (or dampen) the development of the financial and trade sectors due to the essential role of economic growth in promoting finance and trade. Thus, policymakers must understand the tripartite relationship between finance, trade and in making policy decisions.

Though the findings of this study show that financial development and trade openness are fundamental for economic growth, we do not conclude that these are the only variables required for economic growth and development in all countries. Evidence from other countries may indicate that other variables (besides finance and trade) contribute to economic growth. Thus, employing a more balanced development approach that considers various fundamental determinants of economic growth and development should be the most appropriate development strategy for different countries.

References

Adusei, M. (2013). Finance-growth nexus in Africa: A panel generalized method of moments (GMM) Analysis. *Asian Economic and Financial Review, 3*(10), 1314-1324.

Ali, I., & Son, H. H. (2007). Measuring inclusive growth. *Asian Development Review, 24*(1), 11-31.

Ali, I., & Zhuang, J. (2007). Inclusive growth toward a prosperous Asia: Policy implication (Working Paper No. 97). Asian Development Bank (ADB). Retrieved from https://www.adb.org/sites/default/files/publication/28210/wp097.pdf

Ang, J. B., & McKibbin, W. J (2007). Financial liberalization, financial sector development and growth: Evidence from Malaysia. *Journal of Development Economics, 84*(1), 215-233.

Apergis, N., Fillippidis, I., & Economidou, C. (2007). Financial deeping and economic growth linkages: A panel data analysis. *Review of World Economics, 143*(1), 179-198.

Arcand, J. L., Berkes, E., & Panizza, U. (2015). Too much finance? *Journal of Economic Growth, 20*(2), 105-148.

Atindehou, R. B., Gueyie, J. P., & Amenounve, E. K. (2005). Financial intermediation and economic growth: Evidence from Western Africa. *Applied Financial Economics, 15*(11), 777–790.

Badeeb, R. A., & Lean, H. H. (2017). Natural resources, financial development and sectoral value added in a resource-based economy. In V. Kreinovich, S. Sriboonchitta, V. N. Huynh (Eds.), *Robustness in Econometrics* (pp. 401-417). New York, NY: Springer International Publishing.

Bahmani-Oskooee, M. & Nasir, A. B. M. (2004). ARDL approach to test the productivity bias hypothesis. *Review of Development Economics, 8*(3), 483-488.

Bai, J., & Perron, P. (2003). Computation and analysis of multiple structural change models. *Journal of Applied Econometrics, 18*(1), 1-22.

Baltagi, B. H., Demetriades, P. O., & Law, S. H. (2009). Financial development and openness: Evidence from panel data. *Journal of Development Economics, 89*(2), 285-296.

Bannerjee, A,. Dolado, J., & Mestre, R. (1998). Error correction mechanism tests for cointegration in single equation framework. *Journal of Time Series Analysis, 19*(3), 267-283.

Beck, T. (2002). Financial development and international trade: Is there a link? *Journal of International Economics, 57*(1), 107-131.

Beck, T., Levine, R., & Loayza, N. (2000). Finance and the sources of growth. *Journal of Financial Economics, 58,* 261-300.

Beck, T., & Levine, R. (2004). Stock markets, banks and growth: Panel evidence. *Journal of Banking and Finance, 28*(3), 423-442.

Bekaert, G., Harvey, C. R., & Lundblad, C. (2001). Emerging equity markets and economic development. *Journal of Development Economics, 66*(2), 465-504.

Berthelemy, J. C., & Varoudakis, A. (1996). Economic growth, convergence clubs, and the role of financial development. *Oxford Economic Papers, 48*(2), 300-328.

Blackburn, K., & Hung, V. T. (1998). A theory of growth, financial development and trade. *Economica, 65*(257), 107-124.

Blanco, L. (2009). The finance-growth link in Latin America. *Southern Economic Journal, 76*(1), 224-248.

Central Inteligency Agency. (2014). The World Factbook 2014. Available at https://www.cia.gov/library/publications/download/download-2014/index.html

Chinn, M., & Ito, H. (2006). What matters for financial development? Capital controls, institutions, and interactions. *Journal of Development Economics, 81*(1), 163-192.

Chortareas, G., Magkonis, G., Moschos, D., & Panagiotidis, T. (2015). Financial development and economic activity in advanced and developing open economies: Evidence from panel cointegration. *Review of Development Economics, 19*(1), 163–177.

Christopoulos, D. K., & Tsionas, E. G. (2004). Financial development and economic growth: Evidence from panel unit root and cointegration test. *Journal of Development Economics, 73*(1), 55-74.

Esso, L. J. (2010). Re-examining the finance-growth nexus: Structural break, threshold cointegration and causality, evidence from the ECOWAS. *Journal of Economic Development, 35*(3), 57-79.

Farhani, S., & Ozturk, I. (2015). Causal relationship between CO_2 emissions, real GDP, energy consumption, financial development, trade openness, and urbanization in Tunisia. *Environmental Science and Pollution Research, 22*(20), 15663-15676.

Federal Reserve Bank of St. Louis (2016). Economic Data. Available at https://fred.stlouisfed.org/

Fung, M. K. (2009). Financial development and economic growth: Convergence or divergence? *Journal of International Money and Finance, 28*(1), 56-67.

Gozgor, G. (2015). Causal relation between economic growth and domestic credit in the economic globalization: Evidence from the Hatemi-J's test. *The Journal of International Trade & Economic Development, 24*(3), 395-408.

Gries, T., Kraft, M., & Meierrieks, D. (2009). Linkages between financial deepening, trade openness, and economic development: Causality evidence from Sub-Saharan Africa. *World development, 37*(12), 1849-1860.

Herwartz, H., & Walle, Y. M. (2014). Openness and the finance-growth nexus. *Journal of Banking & Finance, 48,* 235-247.

Huang, Y., & Temple, J. (2005). Does external trade promote financial development? (Discussion Paper No. 05575). Department of Economics, University of Bristol. Retrieved from http://www.efm.bris.ac.uk/economics/working_papers/pdffiles/dp05575.pdf

Jhingan, M. L. (2010). International Economics (6th ed.). Delhi: Vrinda Publications Ltd.

Kalaitzoglou, I., & Durgheu, B. (2016). Financial and economic growth in Europe: Is the euro beneficial for all countries? *Journal of Economic Integration, 31*(2), 414-471.

Kar, M., Nazlioglu, S., & Ağır, H. (2010). Financial development and economic growth nexus in the MENA countries: Bootstrap panel granger causality analysis. *Economic Modelling, 28,* 685-693.

Kim, D. H., Lin, S. C., & Suen, Y. B. (2010a). Dynamic effects of trade openness on financial development. *Economic Modelling, 27*(1), 254-261.

Kim, D. H., Lin, S. C., & Suen, Y. B. (2010b). Are financial development and trade openness complements or substitutes? *Southern Economic Journal, 76*(3), 827-845.

Klein, M. W., & Olivei, G. P. (2008). Capital account liberalization, financial depth, and economic growth. *Journal of International Money and Finance, 27*(6), 861-875.

Khan, M. A., Qayyum, A., & Ghani, E. (2006). Trade liberalisation, financial sector reforms, and growth. *The Pakistan Development Review, 45*(4), 711-731.

Law, S. H., & Demetriades, P. (2006, May). Openness, institutions and financial development (Working Paper No. 0012). Word Economy & Finance Research Programme. Available at https://ssrn.com/abstract=941387

Levine, R. (2001). International financial liberalization and economic growth. *Review of International Economics, 9*(4), 688-702.

Levine, R. (2002). Bank-based or market-based financial systems: Which is better? *Journal of Financial Intermediation, 11*(4), 398-428.

Levine, R., Loayza, N., & Beck, T. (2000). Financial intermediation and growth: Causality and causes. *Journal of monetary Economics, 46*(1), 31-77.

Levine, R., & Zervos, S. (1998). Stock market development and economic growth. *American Economic Review, 88*(3), 537-558.

McKinnon, R. I. (1993). *The order of economic liberalization: Financial control in the transition to a market economy* (2nd ed.). London, UK: Johns Hopkins University Press.

Mehran, H., Ugolini, P., Briffaux, J. P., Iden, G., Lybek, T., Swaray, S., & Hayward, P. (1998). Financial sector development in Sub-Saharan African countries (Working Paper No. 169). Washington, DC: International Monetary Fund.

Menyah, K., Nazlioglu, S., & Wolde-Rufael, Y. (2014). Financial development, trade openness and economic growth in African countries: New insights from a panel causality approach. *Economic Modelling,* 37, 386-394.

Muhammad, N., Islam, A. R. M., & Marashdeh, H. A. (2016). Financial development and economic growth: an empirical evidence from the GCC countries using static and dynamic panel data. *Journal of Economics and Finance, 40*(4), 773-791.

Naceur, S. B., & Ghazouani, S. (2007). Stock markets, banks and economic growth: Empirical evidence from the MENA region. *Research in International Business and Finance, 21*(2), 297-315.

Ncube, M. (2007). Financial services and economic development in Africa. *Journal of African Economies, 16*(1), 13-57.

Ndulu, B., Chakraborti, L., Lijane, L., Ramachandran, V., & Wolgin, J. (2007). *Challenges of African growth. Opportunities, Constraints and Strategic Directions.* Washington, DC: The World Bank.

Odhiambo, N. M. (2008). Financial depth, savings and economic growth in Kenya: A dynamic causal linkage. *Economic Modelling, 25*(4), 704-713.

Pesaran, M. H. & Shin, Y. (1999). An Autoregressive Distributed Lag Modelling Approach to Cointegration Analysis. In S. Strom (Ed.), Econometrics and Economic Theory in the 20th century: The Ragnar Frish Centennial Symposium (pp. 371-413). Cambridge: Cambridge University Press.

Pesaran, M. H., Shin, Y., & Smith, R. J. (2001). Bounds testing approach to the analysis of level relationships. *Journal of Applied Econometrics, 16*(3), 289-326.

Rajan, R. G., & Zingales, L. (2003). The great reversals: The politics of financial development in the twentieth century. *Journal of Financial Economics, 69*(1), 5-50.

Rapp, M. S., & Udoieva, I. (2016). What Matters in the Finance-Growth Nexus of Developed Economies? Evidence from OECD Countries (MACIE Paper Series No. 2016/12. Marburg Centre for Institutional Economics. Available at https://papers.ssrn.com/sol3/papers.cfm?abstract_id=2813587

Sbia, R., Shahbaz, M., & Hamdi, H. (2014). A contribution of foreign direct investment, clean energy, trade openness, carbon emissions and economic growth to energy demand in UAE. *Economic Modelling, 36*, 191-197.

Shahbaz, M., Hye, Q. M. A., Tiwari, A. K., & Leitão, N. C. (2013). Economic growth, energy consumption, financial development, international trade and CO_2 emissions in Indonesia. *Renewable and Sustainable Energy Reviews, 25*, 109-121.

Shan, J., & Jianhong, Q. (2006). Does financial development lead economic growth? The case of China. *Annals of Economics and Finance, 1*, 197-216.

Svaleryd, H., & Vlachos, J. (2002). Markets for risk and openness to trade: How are they related? *Journal of International Economics, 57*(2), 369-395.

The World Bank. (2016). World Development Indicators. Available at https://data.worldbank.org/products/wdi

Todaro, M. P., & Smith, C. S. (2009) *Economic Development* (10th ed.). New York, NY: Addison-Wesley Publications.

Wolde-Rufael, Y. (2009). Re-examining the financial development and economic growth nexus in Kenya. *Economic Modelling, 26*(6), 1140-1146.

Yilmazkuday, H. (2011). Thresholds in the finance-growth nexus: A cross-country analysis. *World Bank Economic Review Revenue, 25*(2), 278-295.

Acknowledgement:

Kizito Uyi Ehigiamusoe acknowledges support received from Universiti Sains Malaysia (USM) through Teaching Fellowship.

5

Tolerable Level of Corruption for Foreign Direct Investment in Europe and Asia

Anselm Komla Abotsi[1,2]

ABSTRACT In 2009, Foreign Direct Investment (FDI) flows to developed countries experienced the largest decline among all regions and sub-regions. However, South, East and Southeast Asia showed the smallest decline among developing economies and remained the largest recipient of FDI inflows. Meanwhile, approximately 68% of the countries in Asia scored less than the tolerable level of corruption for investment (TLCI) in Africa (-0.27) over recent years. Moreover, corruption has been observed to be significant in virtually all Asian countries, but, despite this, the region remains the number one global investment destination. This study, therefore, estimates the TLCI in Asia and Europe to enable comparison across these regions. Secondary data from the World Development Indicators were used in this study. The frequency of the data is annual, and it is available from 1996 to 2013. The dynamic panel data estimation technique was deployed while controlling for other variables. The estimated TLCIs for Europe and Asia are 0.534 and -0.735, respectively, on the control of corruption scale, which ranges from approximately -2.5 (weak) to 2.5 (strong). Despite the lower TLCI in Asia, the region is still able to attract relatively more FDI inflow than Africa. This scenario may be attributed to the presence of sound policy factors that drive FDI inflows. Another reason may be due to the nature, scope, social role and the perception of corruption across these regions.

KEY WORDS: corruption, tolerable level of corruption for investment, foreign direct investment, institutions

[1] University of Education, Winneba - Department of Economics Education, Ghana; [2] P. O. Box AC 101 Arts Centre, Accra, Ghana

1. Introduction

In 2009, Foreign Direct Investment (FDI) flows to developed countries experienced the largest decline (44%) among all regions and sub-regions. South, East and Southeast Asia showed the smallest decline (17%) among developing economies and remained the largest recipient, while Africa recorded a decrease of 19%. According to the United Nations Conference on Trade and Development [UNCTAD] (2010), Asia was expected to experience faster investment recovery because Asia seemed to be the most attractive region for FDI inflow and therefore played a leading role in the global economic recovery, while a relatively weaker investment recovery was expected in Europe and Africa (UNCTAD, 2010). The steady improvement of macroeconomic conditions, recovering corporate profits and stock market valuations, and policies promoting openness to FDI were expected to be enhanced by the countries in all the regions over the next few years in order to boost speedy investment recovery. According to Abotsi and Iyavarakul (2015), a non-policy factor that enhances the attraction of FDI inflow into a country is its level of institutional quality.

Correspondence concerning this article should be addressed to: **Anselm Komla Abotsi**, University of Education, Winneba - Department of Economics Education, P. O. Box 25 Winneba, Winne-ba, Ghana. E-mail: agrivetent@gmail.com

In fact, Abotsi (2016) postulates that at a high level of institutional quality, corruption is expected to have a positive impact on FDI inflow, and at a low level of institutional quality, corruption is expected to have a negative impact on FDI inflow. Empirical literature on the effect of institutional quality on FDI inflows reveals that countries that have weak institutions, especially high corruption and unreliable legal systems, tend to receive less FDI inflow (Gastanaga, Nugent & Pashamiova, 1998; Wei, 2000b). Recent theory on corruption and FDI inflow postulates that there is a corruption threshold with respect to the attraction of FDI inflow. Corruption is expected to have a positive impact on FDI inflows below the threshold and a negative impact above the threshold (Abotsi, 2016). An empirical study by Abotsi and Iyavarakul (2015) estimated the corruption threshold (referred to as the tolerable level of corruption for investment (TLCI) in their study) in Africa to be -0.27 on the control of corruption scale. In relation, approximately 68% of the countries in Asia scored less than the tolerable level of corruption for investment in Africa (-0.27) in 2009 and 2010 (in Europe, approximately 23% of the countries scored less) on the control of corruption index. In 2011, approximately 70% of Asian countries scored less than the TLCI in Africa (in Europe, approximately 19% of the countries scored less). In 2012, the number of Asian countries that scored less than the TLCI in Africa plummeted to 66% and remained at this figure until 2014 while that of Europe rose to 21%. Rent-seeking has been found to be endemic in both developing and developed countries, though the rent-seeking in developing countries can be more extensive and can include illegal forms (Khan & Sundaram, 2000). In fact, corruption has been observed to be significant in virtually all Asian countries (Khan & Sundaram, 2000), but, despite this, Asia remains the number one global investment destination. UNCTAD (2014) indicates that developing countries improved their global share of FDI inflows to a record level of 54% in 2013 with developing Asia attracting more inward FDI than either the EU or the United States. In 2014, the FDI inflows to developing Asia grew 9% to historically high levels, which further consolidated the region's position as the largest FDI recipient in the world (UNCTAD, 2015). This is contrary to empirical literature that states that high corruption actually deters foreign direct investment (Aizenman & Spiegel, 2003; Barassi & Zhou, 2012; Cuervo-Cazurra, 2008; Habib & Zurawicki, 2002; Hakkala, Norback & Svaleryd, 2008; Javorcik & Wei, 2009). The question that comes to mind is, "what is the tolerable level of corruption for investment in Asia and Europe?" It is thought-provoking to know the TLCI in Asia and Europe, as this enables comparison of the tolerable level of corruption for investment across these regions and fills the lacuna in the literature with respect to the threshold of corruption in attracting FDI inflow in other regions. This is the motivation for this study. The TLCI will motivate leaders of the countries on these continents to control corruption in their various countries to levels that will not deter FDI inflows. Additionally, the findings of this study will help potential investors in making an informed decision with respect to the destination of their investments.

Using a dynamic panel data estimation technique while controlling for other variables, the estimated TLCI is 0.534 and -0.735 for Europe and Asia, respectively, on the control of corruption scale, which ranges from approximately -2.5 (weak) to 2.5 (strong). This paper continues with a literature review on FDI inflow, corruption and other determinants of FDI used as control variables. These control variables include GDP growth rate, trade openness, inflation rate, exchange rate, rents on total natural resources (in the case of Europe) and rents on natural gas (in the case of Asia). This is followed by a presentation of the methodology used in the study, the results, a discussion, and finally, the conclusion.

2. Literature review

2.1. FDI inflow to Asia and Europe

South, East and Southeast Asia were the first to bottom out from the downturn in 2009. Intraregional FDI gained momentum and accounted for as much as half of the region's inward FDI stock after investment from developed countries plummeted. FDI inflows to China and India started recovering as early as mid-2009, and their continued FDI outflows were anticipated to bring the region's outward investment back to a place of growth in 2010. Apart from intraregional FDI, FDI flows from developing countries in Asia and Africa account for a major part of interregional FDI flows among developing countries. One of the most significant foreign investors in some sub-Saharan African countries is China. In Southeast Europe and the Commonwealth of Independent States (CIS), FDI inflows declined by 43% in 2009 after an eight-year upward trend. Also in the same year, FDI flows into the 27 European Union (EU) countries declined by 33% (to $362 billion) (UNCTAD, 2010).

FDI flows to South Asia continued to fall, but at the same time, major emerging regions, such as East and Southeast Asia, experienced strong growth in FDI inflows in 2010. FDI inflows to ASEAN more than doubled; those to East Asia saw a 17% rise while FDI to South Asia declined by one-fourth. Inflows to East, South, and Southeast Asia as a whole rose by 24% in 2010, reaching $300 billion. Similarly, in 2010, flows to the Commonwealth of Independent States (CIS) rose marginally by 0.4% while FDI flows to Southeast Europe plummeted sharply for the third consecutive year (UNCTAD, 2011). A 10% increase in Asia accounted for the rising FDI inflow to developing countries in 2011. In East Asia and Southeast Asia, FDI inflows reached new records, with total inflows amounting to $336 billion, accounting for 22% of global inflows. Southeast Asia continued to experience faster FDI growth than East Asia. FDI inflows to Europe, which had declined until 2010, showed a turnaround. In economies in transition in Southeast Europe and the Commonwealth of Independent States (CIS), FDI experienced some recovery after two years of stagnant flows, reaching $92 billion, which was driven in large part by cross-border M&A deals (UNCTAD, 2012).

Global FDI fell by 18% to $1.35 trillion in 2012. Developing economies in 2012 absorbed more FDI than developed countries for the first time ever, accounting for 52% of global FDI flows. FDI inflows to developing Asia fell by 7% to $407 billion but remained at a high level. The majority of developed countries saw significant drops in FDI inflows, especially the European Union, which alone accounted for two-thirds of the global FDI decline (UNCTAD, 2013). According to the UNCTAD (2014), after a decline in 2012, global foreign direct investment flows rose by 9% to $1.45 trillion in 2013, with growth expected to continue in the years to come. With a 3% increase, developing Asia remains the number one global investment destination. The report further states that Europe, which is traditionally the largest FDI recipient region, is at less than one-third of its 2007 inflows and one-fourth of its outflows. The European Union (EU) and the United States saw their combined share of global FDI inflows decline from well over 50% pre-crisis to 30% in 2013 (UNCTAD, 2014).

2.2. Influence of corruption on FDI inflow

The investment recovery in all regions has not been smooth since its downturn in 2009, with some regions experiencing an increase while others have experienced a decline over the period. Apart from the policy factors that drive FDI inflow, there are non-policy factors that also account for the inflow of FDI into these regions. These non-policy factors are corruption, factor endowments, market size of the host country, distance/transport costs, and political and economic stability (Mateev, 2009; Touchton, 2016). Whereas some studies (Egger & Winner, 2005) found a positive impact of corruption on FDI, studies elsewhere (Aizenman & Spiegel, 2003; Barassi & Zhou, 2012; Cuervo-Cazurra, 2008; Habib & Zurawicki, 2002; Hakkala et al., 2008; Javorcik & Wei, 2009) show that corruption actually deters foreign direct investment. These findings are consistent with the argument that the quality of the existing institutions in a foreign country has the potential to attract or repel FDI inflow (Abotsi, 2016). This is because firms exploit their ownership and location advantages in the foreign countries to minimize their transaction costs. Therefore, with the existing quality of institutions in a country, if firms are not able to exploit their ownership and location advantages, they will not be motivated to invest in the country. Empirical findings indicate that the corruption has a negative and highly significant impact on foreign ownership of firms in Africa (Abotsi, 2015). The control of the corruption variable is captured in this study as perceptions of the extent to which public power is exercised for private gain and is expected to have both negative and positive effects on the inflows of FDI into a country depending on the levels of institutional quality and corruption.

2.3. Other control variables

In addition to the control of the corruption variable and its squared values, some other variables identified in the literature to determine FDI inflow were included in the model as independent variables to serve as controls. These variables include GDP growth rate, trade openness, inflation rate, exchange rate, rents on total natural resources (in the case of Europe) and rents on natural gas (in the case of Asia). A country with more stable macroeconomic conditions and a high and sustained growth rates is expected to attract more FDI inflows than a more volatile economy (Ranjan & Agrawal, 2011). Proxies for the macroeconomic stability of a country include GDP growth rates and inflation rates (Dasgupta & Ratha, 2000). High inflation rates are associated with economic disarray and lower purchasing power, so inflation risk becomes an important factor in long-run investment plans. Inflation has been found to have a negative relation with FDI inflows, though its magnitude is much smaller (Abotsi & Iyavarakul, 2015; Ranjan & Agrawal, 2011). The impact of exchange rates on FDI inflows has shown mixed results. The literature on exchange rates shows that the real exchange rate has both negative (Kyereboah-Coleman & Agyire-Tettey, 2008) and positive (Abotsi & Iyavarakul, 2015; Jeon & Rhee, 2008) influence on FDI inflows. Trade openness is an important vehicle for technological spillovers. Therefore, trade openness is generally a positive and significant determinant of FDI inflows (Sahoo, 2006). Jadhav (2012) opines that resource-seeking FDI is motivated by the availability of natural resources in host countries. However, according to Asiedu and Lien (2011), the presence of natural resources in host countries may affect the FDI-democracy relationship. Asiedu and Lien (2011) found that democracy has a negative effect on FDI inflows to countries where exports are dominated by natural resources. It is therefore expected in this study that GDP growth rate and trade openness will have a positive impact on FDI inflow. The inflation rate is expected to have a negative influence on FDI inflow. The influence of exchange rate, rents on total natural resources (in the case of Europe) and rents on natural gas (in the case of Asia) will be determined empirically.

3.0 Methodology

3.1 Data

Secondary data from the World Development Indicators (The World Bank, 2013) was used in this study. The frequency of the data is annual, and it is available from 1996 to 2013. In all, 43 countries were sampled from Europe and 39 from Asia. The control of the corruption index is drawn from the Worldwide Governance Indicators DATABANK (The World Bank, 2014), and it is one of the six dimensions of governance in the Worldwide Governance Indicators. The choice of this variable in determining the tolerable level of corruption is because of its authenticity and its free availability on the internet.

3.2 Data Analysis

A dynamic panel data estimation technique is used in this study as deployed in a similar study by Abotsi and Iyavarakul (2015) to allow for comparison of results. This dynamic panel model includes exogenous and endogenous variables in addition to the lagged dependent variable. The dynamic panel estimation technique is one of many panel data analysis techniques used in many studies in economics. This is because many economic relationships are dynamic in nature. Nerlove (2002) argues that economic behavior is inherently dynamic, and so most econometrically interesting relationships are either implicitly or explicitly dynamic. Bond (2002) also posits that dynamic models are of interest in a wide range of economic applications. In fact, the inclusion of lag of dependent variables as an explanatory variable is a parsimonious way of accounting for the effects of explanatory variables in the past, and this can also help to remove serial correlation in the disturbance term (Beck & Katz, 1996). Additionally, models including lagged dependent variables can also control for many omitted variables to a large extent (Abotsi & Iyavarakul, 2015). Empirical literature shows that firms tend to locate where other firms with similar characteristics are already established (Crozet, Mayer & Mucchielli, 2004; Head, Ries & Swenson, 1999; Pusterla & Resmini, 2007). This confirms the fact that current FDI depends on its own past realizations, and therefore the use of the dynamic panel model is appropriate. All of these informed the choice of the dynamic panel data estimation technique in this study.

The general model is of the form presented in equation (1).

$$y_{it} = \alpha y_{i,t-1} + x_{it}^{'}\beta + \varepsilon_{it} \qquad (1)$$

where $\varepsilon_{it} = u_i + v_{it}$, for i = 1,..., N and t = 2,..., T, with $|\alpha| < 1$. The disturbance term ε_{it} has two orthogonal components. These components are the fixed effects u_i and the idiosyncratic shocks v_{it}. $E(u_i) = E(v_{it}) = E(u_i v_{it}) = 0$ for i = 1,..., N and t = 2,..., T.

The framework for evaluating the relations between FDI, corruption, and other determinants of FDI is presented in equation (2).

$$y_{it} = \beta_1 + \beta_2 x_{it} + \beta_3 x_{it}^2 + \omega z_{it} + \alpha_1 y_{i,t-1} + \varepsilon_{it} \quad (2)$$

where y_{it} is a measure of FDI in country i at time period t, $y_{i,t-1}$ is a measure of FDI in country i at time period $t-1$, x_{it} is an index of the control of corruption in country i at time t, x_{it}^2 is the squared index of control of corruption in country i at time period t, z_{it} are a set of control variables in country i at time period t, β_1, β_2, β_3, α_1 and ω (set of parameters) are parameters to be estimated, and finally, ε_{it} denotes the disturbance term. StataCorp 2013 is the statistical software used in the data analysis.

3.3 Model One: The System GMM Model of FDI (Europe)

The benchmark FDI equation for Europe in a linear form with a constant term is presented in equation (3).

$$\begin{aligned} &FDI\_netinflows\_perGDP_{it} = \\ &= \beta_1 + \beta_2 Control\_of\_Corruption_{it} + \\ &+ \beta_3 Control\_of\_Corruption\_Sqr_{it} + \\ &+ \beta_4 FDI\_netinflows\_perGDP\_1_{it} + \\ &+ \beta_5 GDP\_growth_{it} + \beta_6 Trade\_perGDP_{it} + \\ &+ \beta_7 Inflation_{it} + \beta_8 Official\_exchange\_rate_{it} + \\ &+ \beta_9 Total\_natural\_resources\_rents_{it} + \\ &+ Time(Dummies) + \varepsilon_{it} \end{aligned} \quad (3)$$

3.4 Model Two: The System GMM Model of FDI (Asia)

The benchmark FDI equation for Asia in a linear form with a constant term is presented in equation (4).

$$\begin{aligned} &FDI\_netinflows\_perGDP_{it} = \\ &= \beta_1 + \beta_2 Control\_of\_Corruption_{it} + \\ &+ \beta_3 Control\_of\_Corruption\_Sqr_{it} + \\ &+ \beta_4 FDI\_netinflows\_perGDP\_1_{it} + \\ &+ \beta_5 GDP\_growth_{it} + \beta_6 Trade\_perGDP_{it} + \\ &+ \beta_7 Inflation_{it} + \beta_8 Official\_exchange\_rate_{it} + \\ &+ \beta_9 Natural\_gas\_rents_{it} + \\ &+ Time(Dummies) + \varepsilon_{it} \end{aligned} \quad (4)$$

The net FDI inflow per GDP is used as the dependent variable in the system dynamic model. The control of corruption and its squared values are included as independent variables together with other control variables that were chosen based on previous research and data availability for the selected period. These control variables include GDP growth rate, trade openness, inflation rate, exchange rate, rents on total natural resources (in the case of Europe), rents on natural gas (in the case of Asia) and time-related shock variables (time dummies). It must be noted that infrastructure was captured in the model as fixed telephone subscriptions but was dropped by the Stata software due to collinearity.

The control of corruption variable is defined as the perception of the extent to which public power is exercised for private gain, including both petty and serious forms of corruption, as well as the "capture" of the state by elites and private interests (The World Bank, 2014). The control of corruption variable is transformed from its original scale, which ranges from approximately -2.5 (weak) to 2.5 (strong), to a new scale ranging from 0 to 100 for computational purposes and to allow for easy interpretation of the results. The formula; $x = (a + 2.5) * 20$, was used where x is the value of the transformed variable, and a refers to the value of the original scale (Abotsi & Iyavarakul, 2015).

This means that the higher a country is on the scale, the better the governance performance against corruption, which is an indication of a lower level of corruption. Trade openness refers to the sum of exports and imports of goods and services measured as a share of the gross domestic product. Total natural resource rents include the sum of oil, natural gas, coal (hard and soft), mineral, and forest rents. Natural gas rents are the difference between the value of natural gas production at world prices and total costs of production. Inflation, as measured by the consumer price index, reflects the annual percentage change in the cost to the average consumer of acquiring a basket of goods and services that may be fixed or changed at specified intervals. The official exchange rate refers to the exchange rate determined by national authorities or to the rate determined in the legally sanctioned exchange market. GDP growth rate refers to the annual percentage growth rate of GDP at market prices based on constant local currency, and the aggregates are based on constant 2005 U.S. dollars (The World Bank, 2014).

The two-step estimator is deployed in the estimation because the standard covariance matrix is robust to panel-specific autocorrelation and heteroskedasticity and is thus asymptotically efficient. Control of corruption and trade openness are treated as endogenous in this study, as in a previous study (Abotsi & Iyavarakul, 2015). All other independent variables are treated as strictly exogenous. No external instruments are used. In the case of the European panel, there are 46 countries (N), and in the case of the Asian countries, there are 39 countries (N) that are analyzed over a period of 19 years (T). This means there are more countries (N) than years (T) in both cases, which supports the argument made by many authors (Baltagi, 2008; Baum, 2006; Bond, 2002; Roodman, 2006; 2007; Sarafidis, Yamagata & Robertson, 2006) that dynamic panel models are specially designed for situations where T is smaller than N to control for dynamic panel bias.

3.5 System Generalized Method of Moments

The dynamic panel model is made up of System GMM (Generalized Method of Moments) and Difference GMM (Generalized Method of Moments). The System GMM estimate has an advantage over the Difference GMM with respect to variables that exhibit "random walk" or are close to random-walk variables (Baum, 2006; Bond, 2002; Roodman, 2006; 2007). Empirical research with dynamic models indicates that the System GMM is a good estimator, or at least better than the Difference GMM, which is severely downwardly biased (Hoeffler, 2002; Nkurunziza & Bates, 2003; Presbitero, 2005). Therefore, the System GMM estimator is chosen over the Difference GMM estimator in this study because it is consistent and asymptotically more efficient.

3.6 Specification Testing in Dynamic Panel Models

Specification testing in dynamic panel models is conducted to address problems of over-identification restrictions and serial correlation due to the inclusion of the lag of the dependent variable as an explanatory variable. The tests deployed are the standard Sargan and Hansen J test for over-identification restrictions and the Arellano-Bond test for autocorrelation. Roodman (2009) expounds that if the model is over-identified, a test statistic for the joint validity of the moment conditions falls out of the GMM framework. The null hypothesis in both of these tests is that all of the instruments are valid and the alternative is that some subsets are not valid. When the number of instruments i is large relative to the cross section sample size n, these tests lose power. The rule of thumb is to keep the number of instruments less than or equal to the number of groups (see Abotsi & Iyavarakul, 2015).

3.7 The Estimation of the Tolerable Level of Corruption for Investment

A common empirical test of the relationships between two economic variables that are predicted to be non-monotonic in various economic theories is to estimate an equation using a polynomial of the variable that is supposed to have the nonlinear relationship according to Plassmann & Khanna (2007). To empirically estimate the Tolerable Level of Corruption for Investment in both Europe and Asia, a power term of the control of corruption index is introduced into the dynamic model. The response variable in this study is foreign direct investment (FDI_netinflows_perGDP) and Control of Corruption and Control of Corruption Sqr variables are the control of corruption index and its square, respectively. The TLCI is obtained by estimating the equation and taking the derivative of the estimated equation with respect to the control of corruption variable.

$$\frac{\delta \hat{y}_{it}}{\delta x_1} = \hat{\beta}_2 + 2\hat{\beta}_3 x_1 = 0 \quad (5)$$

Solving this equation gives the turning point of the relationship indicating an inverse U-shape if $\hat{\beta}_2 < 0$ and vice versa. The turning point is given by $\varphi = -\frac{\hat{\beta}_2}{2\hat{\beta}_3}$, which is referred to as the threshold point or the Tolerable Level of Corruption for Investment (Abotsi & Iyavarakul, 2015).

3.8 Test of the U-Shaped Relationship

Lind and Mehlum (2007), explained that to properly test for the presence of a U-shaped relationship on some interval of values, there is the need to test whether the relationship is decreasing at low values within this interval and increasing at high values within the interval. Assuming that ε_{it} ~ NID (0, σ2), a test based on likelihood ratio principle (Sasabuchi, 1980) takes the form:

For min(x)

$$H_0: \quad \beta_2 + \beta_3 f'(x_l) \geq 0$$

$$H_1: \quad \beta_2 + \beta_3 f'(x_l) < 0$$

For max(x)

$$H_0: \quad \beta_2 + \beta_3 f'(x_h) \leq 0$$

$$H_1: \quad \beta_2 + \beta_3 f'(x_h) > 0$$

The rejection of the null hypotheses in both cases is a confirmation of a U-shaped relationship on the interval of values. This test gives the exact necessary and sufficient conditions for the test of a U shape. An equivalent test is to check whether the confidence interval for the minimum point and is contained within the interval $[x_l, x_h]$ (Lind & Mehlum, 2007). The U-shaped relationship will be confirmed in this study using both tests. This procedure was also deployed by Abotsi and Iyavarakul (2015).

4.0 Results

4.1 Descriptive statistics

The descriptive statistics of the variables deployed for Europe and Asia in the study are presented in Table 1 and Table 2, respectively. The total number of observations is 462 for Europe and 519 for Asia. The period under study is from 1996 to 2013. The mean official exchange rates for Europe and Asia are 143.1281 and 1314.178, respectively, and the standard deviations are 693.4735 and 3480.971, respectively. This shows that the official exchange rate observations are widely dispersed in both Europe and Asia.

The results also show that over the period under consideration, some countries in both Europe and Asia experienced negative FDI inflow, GDP growth and inflation. Also worthy of mention are the mean trade openness (90.16152 and 95.33428 for Europe and Asia respectively) and standard deviation (30.05845 and 64.52994 for Europe and Asia respectively), which shows that these observations are widely dispersed within the period of observation.

4.2 Empirical Results of the Dynamic Panel Model Estimation

The estimated results of the dynamic panel model for Europe and Asia are presented in Table 3. The FDI net inflow per GDP is used as the dependent variable in the estimations, and the control of corruption variable and its squared values, as well as other control variables, are used as independent variables. The two-step estimator is deployed in the estimations with the control of corruption and trade openness variables treated as endogenous in both models. All the other independent variables are treated strictly as exogenous. No external instruments are used.

4.3 Model Specification Diagnostics Test

The validity of the estimated results in System GMM depends on the statistical diagnostics tests. If the model is well specified, the expectation is that the null hypothesis of no autocorrelation of the second order, AR(2), is not rejected. Therefore, the Arellano-Bond test for serial correlation supports the validity of the model specification (Basu 2008). The p-value of 0.494 and 0.818 for Europe and Asia, respectively, shows that the null hypothesis of no autocorrelation of the second order, AR(2), is not rejected. Since the number of instruments (42 and 37 for Europe and Asia, respectively) is less than the number of groups (43 and 39 for Europe and Asia, respectively), the assumptions underlying the two procedures are not violated. In the case of Europe, the 43 instruments came from the restriction of using two lags for levels and two for differences in the data (i.e., the restriction is set to (2 2) in *xtabond2*). However, in the case of Asia, the 37 instruments came from the restriction of using one lag for levels and one lag for differences in the data (i.e., the restriction is set to (1 1) in *xtabond2*).

The Hansen J-statistic tests the null hypothesis of the correct model specification and valid over-identifying restrictions, i.e., the validity of instruments. The rejection of the null hypothesis indicates that either or both assumptions are violated. The Hansen J-test of over-identifying restrictions does not reject the null hypothesis in either the Europe or Asia models at any conventional level of significance (p = 0.884 and 0.569

Table 1. Descriptive statistics (Europe)

Variable	Obs	Mean	Std. Dev.	Min	Max
FDI_netinflows_perGDP	462	5.336405	6.364192	-16.1545	50.96784
Control_of_corruption	462	58.05281	22.73689	25	101
GDP_growth	462	3.777827	4.662255	-14.814	34.5
Trade_perGDP	462	90.16152	30.05845	24.17033	169.9286
Inflation	462	7.766153	14.5344	-2.41026	168.6202
Official_exchange_rate	462	143.1281	693.4735	0.081405	8880.052
Total_natural_resources_rents	462	4.694349	10.06215	0	68.35304

Table 2. Descriptive statistics (Asia)

Variable	Obs	Mean	Std. Dev.	Min	Max
FDI_netinflows_perGDP	519	3.768904	5.032905	-3.46865	45.28994
Control_of_corruption	519	44.27746	18.14811	13.4	98.4
GDP_growth	519	5.609956	4.559997	-13.1267	54.15777
Trade_perGDP	519	95.33428	64.52994	18.93944	439.6567
Inflation	519	7.045173	9.6846	-18.1086	90.98073
Official_exchange_rate	519	1314.178	3480.971	0.081405	20933.42
Total_natural_resources_rents	519	2.725519	4.835469	0	29.56645

for Europe and Asia, respectively), giving an indication that the models in both cases have valid instrumentation. Efendic, Pugh and Adnett (2009) postulates that the check for the "steady state" assumption suggested by (Roodman, 2006) can also be used to investigate the validity of instruments in System GMM. The results show that the estimated coefficients on the lagged dependent variable (FDI_netinflows_perGDP_1) are 0.671 and 0.626 for Europe and Asia, respectively. This means that the steady-state assumption holds. The evidence from the various tests above satisfies the key assumptions of System GMM estimation.

The Wild Chi-square test of joint significance indicates that the null hypothesis, which states that independent variables are jointly equal to zero at any conventional level of significance, may also be rejected (p=0.000) in both models (Europe and Asia).

4.4 Interpretation and discussion of results

The results show that control of corruption is negative and significant (at the 5% significance level for both Europe and Asia) while the square of control of corruption is positive and highly significant (at the 1% significance level for both Europe and Asia) in both models. The control of corruption scale ranges from approximately -2.5 (weak) to 2.5 (strong), which means the higher the score of the country, the less corrupt it is. This result is consistent with the findings by Abotsi and Iyavarakul (2015), which indicate that at low scores, corruption has a negative impact on FDI inflows, and at high scores, corruption has a positive impact on FDI inflows. This finding is also consistent with earlier studies that show corruption deters foreign direct investments (Aizenman & Spiegel 2003; Barassi & Zhou 2012; Cuervo-Cazurra 2006; 2008; Habib & Zurawicki, 2002; Hakkala, et al. 2008; Javorcik & Wei 2009; Voyer & Beamish 2004; Wei 2000a) and a few other studies by Egger and Winner (2005), who found a positive impact of corruption on FDI.

Table 3 shows that the lag of FDI inflow, GDP growth rate, trade openness, inflation rate and official exchange rate are statistically significant in both the Europe and Asia models. Total natural resources is also significant in the Europe model. The probability value associated with the t statistics of the coefficients of these variables is less than 0.05, which shows that the estimated value of the coefficient is statistically significant. Coefficients of lag of FDI inflow, GDP growth rate, trade openness, and inflation rate are positive, which implies that these variables have a positive effect on total inward FDI. The official exchange rate and total natural resources rents (in the case of Europe) are negative, which implies that these variables have a negative effect on total inward FDI. Even though the coefficient of natural gas rents (in the case of Asia) is negative, it is not statistically significant.

The results on the lag of FDI seem to confirm the empirical literature that finds that firms tend to locate where other firms with similar characteristics are already established (Crozet et al., 2004; Head et al., 1999; Pusterla & Resmini, 2007). The finding on trade openness supports the assertion that trade liberalization leads to increased FDI inflow (Anyanwu 2012; Anyanwu & Erhijakpor 2004; Asiedu 2002; Ranjan & Agrawal 2011; Sahoo 2006). This result on inflation is consistent with Jadhav (2012) but inconsistent with other findings by Abotsi and Iyavarakul (2015) and Ranjan and Agrawal (2011), who found inflation to have a negative relation with FDI inflow. The findings on GDP growth rate are also consistent with the earlier assertion that market size is a positive and significant determinant of FDI flows (Abotsi & Iyavarakul, 2015; Garibaldi et al. 2002; Nunes, Oscategui, & Peschiera, 2006; Sahoo 2006). This is because GDP growth rate represents a country's economic track record and serves as an indicator of profitable investment opportunities to the outside world.

The global economy experienced a severe recession inflicted by a massive financial crisis and an acute loss of confidence in 2009 (Abotsi & Iyavarakul, 2015). Therefore, time dummy variables were included in both models to capture universal time-related shocks before and after the global economic recession. The results show that the dummy for 2009 is positive and highly statistically significant, which seems to suggest that FDI inflow to Europe and Asia did not suffer a time-related shock in 2009 due to the severe global economic recession as in the case of Africa. The finding in a similar study by Abotsi and Iyavarakul (2015) suggests that FDI inflow to Africa suffered a time-related shock in 2009 due to the severe global economic recession.

4.5 The Estimated Tolerable Level of Corruption for Investment

The results in Table 3 show that at low scores, corruption has a negative impact on FDI inflows, and at high scores, corruption has a positive impact on FDI inflows. The TLCI of a country will determine whether or not FDI is likely to flow to a country. The coefficient $\hat{\beta}_2$ of the control of corruption variable tells both the direction and steepness of the curvature. As $\hat{\beta}_2$ is a positive value, it indicates that the curvature is upwards but less steep. Using equation 5, the turning point is 60.68 for Europe and 35.30 for Asia. These turning points are highly statistically significant with a 95% confidence interval between 53.08 at the minimum and 68.29 at the maximum for the Europe model and between 19.75 at the minimum and 50.85 at the maximum for the Asia model. This is shown in Table 4.

The usual criteria used by most researchers to test the precision of a turning point are that if both $\hat{\beta}_1$ and $\hat{\beta}_2$ are significant and if the implied extreme point is within the data range, then they have found a U-shaped relationship (Abotsi & Iyavarakul, 2015). This test is satisfied in this study because the results in Table 3 show that both the control of corruption and the square of control of corruption are significant. However, Lind and Mehlum (2007) argue that though these criteria are sensible, they are neither sufficient nor necessary and are too weak. Using the joint test in finding out whether the relationship is decreasing at low values within this interval and increasing at high values within the interval, the results of the combined test (Table 5) re-

Table 3. Results of the Dynamic System GMM Estimation

Dependent variable	**FDI_netinflows_perGDP**	
Variables	**Europe**	**Asia**
Control_of_corruption	-0.534**	-0.0951**
	(0.238)	(0.0424)
Control_of_corruption_Sqr	0.00440**	0.00135***
	(0.00177)	(0.000431)
FDI_netinflows_perGDP_1	0.671***	0.626***
	(0.0353)	(0.0215)
GDP_growth	0.724***	0.410***
	(0.0406)	(0.0322)
Trade_perGDP	0.0655***	0.0249***
	(0.00840)	(0.00175)
Inflation	0.0636**	0.0687***
	(0.0279)	(0.0238)
Official_exchange_rate	-0.00106**	-0.000197***
	(0.000469)	(6.67e-05)
Total_natural_resources_rents	-0.268***	
	(0.0622)	
Natural_gas_rents		-0.00185
		(0.0260)
2008 (year dummy)	-1.116***	-0.958***
	(0.332)	(0.142)
2009 (year dummy)	3.875***	1.504***
	(0.412)	(0.195)
2010 (year dummy)	-0.937**	0.530***
	(0.377)	(0.0949)
Constant	8.029	-2.551***
	(6.788)	(0.944)
OIR test (p-value)	0.884	0.569
Arellano-Bond test for AR(1)	0.012	0.001
Arellano-Bond test for AR(2)	0.494	0.818
Number of instruments	42	37
Observations	461	495
Number of groups	43	39

Standard errors in parentheses
*** p<0.01, ** p<0.05, * p<0.1

Table 4. The Turning Point Estimate

	Turning point	Std. Err.	z	P>z	[95% Conf. Interval]	
Europe	60.68375	3.8792	15.64	0.000	53.08075	68.28676
Asia	35.2993	7.93559	4.45	0.000	19.74583	50.85277

Table 5. Joint hypothesis test results

Control of corruption	**Turning point**	
	Europe	**Asia**
$H_0: \beta_1 + \beta_2 f^{'}(x_l) \geq 0$	-0.3141378** (0.1507288)	-0.0589969** (0.0283805)
$H_0: \beta_1 + \beta_2 f^{'}(x_h) \leq 0$	0.346116*** (0.1202149)	0.1699939*** (0.0518314)

Standard errors in parentheses
*** p<0.01, ** p<0.05, * p<0.1

ject the null hypothesis ($H_0: \beta_1 + \beta_2 f^{'}(x_l) \geq 0$ and/or $\beta_1 + \beta_2 f^{'}(x_h) \leq 0$) and confirms a U-shaped relationship for the observed data range. This test gives the exact necessary and sufficient conditions for the test of a U shape. The confidence intervals for the turning point of Europe ($53.08075 \leq \varphi \leq 68.28676$) and that for Asia ($19.74583 \leq \varphi \leq 50.85277$) are contained within the observed respective data range, which further confirms this U-shaped relationship.

The estimated TLCI is 60.68 for Europe and 35 for Asia. These figures translate to 0.53 and -0.74 for Europe and Asia, respectively, on the original control of corruption scale, which ranges from approximately -2.5 (weak) to 2.5 (strong). This means that all the countries in Europe and Asia falling below the corresponding TLCI are less likely to attract FDI inflow and those falling above are more likely to attract FDI inflow. This follows the theory proposed by Abotsi (2016), which postulates that there is a corruption threshold with respect to the attraction of FDI inflow. Below the threshold, corruption is expected to have a positive impact on FDI inflows and above the threshold, corruption is expected to have a negative impact on FDI inflows. All the countries falling below the TLCI are above the threshold of corruption, and those falling above the TLCI are conversely below the threshold of corruption. Specifically, the findings in this study are consistent with research by Cole, Elliott and Zhang (2009) on the determinants of province-level FDI in China, which found that foreign capital prefers to locate in regions in which the government has made more effort to fight corruption and the local government is considered to be more efficient. Abotsi (2016) postulates that, at a high level of institutional quality, corruption is expected to have a positive impact on FDI inflow and at a low level of institutional quality, corruption is expected to have a negative impact on FDI inflow. The confidence interval for the TLCI translates to ($0.15 \leq \varphi \leq 0.91$) for Europe and ($-1.51 \leq \varphi \leq 0.04$) for Asia on the original control of corruption scale. Therefore, countries that fall within this range can be referred to as transition countries.

A similar study by Abotsi and Iyavarakul (2015) found the TLCI for Africa to be -0.27. The TLCI in Europe (0.53) is higher than the TLCI in Africa and is consistent with the report that Europe is traditionally the largest FDI recipient region (UNCTAD, 2014). This is also consistent with the postulation by Abotsi

(2016) that, at a high level of institutional quality, corruption is expected to have a positive impact on FDI inflow. However, in the case of Asia, the TLCI (-0.74) is lower than the TLCI in Africa, but FDI inflow to Asia is greater than that to Africa. This implies that even at high level of corruption, FDI inflow to Asia is higher than Africa. This suggests that despite the corruption levels in Asia, the region is still able to attract relatively more FDI inflow. A similar result by Touchton (2015) shows that while economic growth rates have remained relatively high in Southeast Asia, which indicates continued investment in markets, empirical literature provides evidence of a strong negative relationship between barriers to entry and the rule of law. This scenario may be attributed to the presence of sound policy factors that drive FDI inflows such as trade openness, product market regulations, labor market arrangements, corporate tax rates, trade barriers, and infrastructure in Asia. With the existing quality of institutions in a country, as long as firms are able to exploit their ownership and location advantages, they will be motivated to invest in the country. According to Khan and Sundaram, (2000), businesspeople may subjectively evaluate corruption to be less serious if the system works and they make large profits. For example, the improved economic growth in Thailand in the face of high corruption was attributed to the dynamics of Thai clientelism, which led to competitive market structures in addition to collective action problems resolved by their institutions (Khan & Sundaram, 2000). Another reason may be due to the nature, scope, social role and the perception of corruption across these regions. Comparing corruption across regions is a difficult task, both due to the secretive nature of corruption and the variety of forms it takes. A common explanation of differential corruption among sociologists is that social norms are very different in different countries. Therefore, what is deemed in one culture as corrupt may be considered a part of routine transactions in another (Bardhan, 1997). According to Bardhan (1997), gift-exchange is a major social norm in business transactions in developing countries.

5.0 Conclusion

Corruption has been observed to be significant in virtually all Asian countries (Khan & Sundaram, 2000), but, irrespective of this observation, Asia remains the number one global investment destination, which is contrary to the empirical literature that states that high corruption actually deters foreign direct investment. This study, therefore, sought to determine the TLCI in Asia and Europe to enable comparison of the tolerable level of corruption for investment across these regions since the TLCI for Africa is already known. This study also sought to fill the lacuna in the literature with respect to the threshold of corruption in attracting FDI inflow in the various regions. The findings of this study show that the estimated TLCI for Europe is 0.534 and that for Asia is -0.735 on the control of corruption index, which ranges from approximately -2.5 (weak) to 2.5 (strong). Despite the corruption levels in Asia, the region is still able to attract relatively more FDI inflow than Africa. It is recommended that leaders of the countries on these continents enact policies to control corruption in their various countries to levels that will not deter FDI inflows. Additionally, the findings of this study will assist potential investors in making an informed decision with respect to the destination of their investments.

The findings suggest that leaders in African countries should not only concentrate on the control of corruption but also consider policy factors that drive FDI inflows such as trade openness, product market regulations, labor market arrangements, corporate tax rates, trade barriers, and infrastructure. The limitation of this study is the assumption that foreign investors choose a country based solely on the level of corruption of the host country because there are other country-based business risks and individual-specific shocks that investors take into consideration before an investment decision is made. It is recommended that further studies should explore the nature, scope, social role and the perception of corruption across the regions. This will give a better understanding of the dynamics of corruption across these regions.

References

Abotsi, A. K. & Iyavarakul, T. (2015). Tolerable level of corruption forforeign direct investment in Africa. *Contemporary Economics*, *9*(3), 249–270. https://doi.org/10.5709/ce.1897-9254.240

Abotsi, A. K. (2015). Foreign ownership of firms and corruption in Africa. *International Journal of Eco-*

nomics and Financial Issues, 5(3), 647–655. http://dx.*doi*.org/*10.2139/ssrn.2693490*

Abotsi, A. K. (2016). Theory of foreign direct investment and corruption. *International Journal of Asian Social Science, 6*(6), 359-378.

Aizenman, J., & Spiegel, M. (2003). *Institutional efficiency, monitoring costs, and the investment share of FDI* (Working Paper No. 9324). Retrieved from http://www.nber.org/papers/w9324

Anyanwu, J. C., & Erhijakpor, A. E. O. (2004). Trends and determinants of foreign direct investment in Africa. *West African Journal of Monetary and Economic Integration*, second half, 21–44.

Anyanwu, J. C. (2012). Why does foreign directinvestment go where it goes ? New evidence from african countries. *Annals of Economics and Finance, 13*(2), 425–462.

Asiedu, E., & Lien, D. (2011). Democracy, foreign direct investment and natural resources. *Journal of International Economics, 84*(1), 99–111. https://doi.org/10.1016/j.jinteco.2010.12.001

Asiedu, E. (2002). On the determinants of foreign direct investment to developing countries: Is Africa different? *World Development, 30*(1), 107–119.

Baltagi, B. H. (2008). *Econometric analysis of panel data* (4th ed.). Chichester, UK: John Wiley & Sons Ltd.

Barassi, M.R., & Zhou, Y. (2012). The effect of corruption on FDI: A parametric and non-parametric analysis. *European Journal of Political Economy, 28*(3), 302–312. https://doi.org/10.1016/j.ejpoleco.2012.01.001

Bardhan, P. (1997). Corruption and development: A review of issues. *Journal of Economic Literature, 35*(3), 1320–1346.

Basu, S. R. (2008). *A new way to link development to institutions, policies and geography*. Retrieved from http://unctad.org/en/ Docs/itcdtab38_en.pdf

Baum, F. C. (2006). *An Introduction to Modern Econometrics Using Stata*. College Station, TX: Stata Press.

Beck, N., & Katz, J. N. (1996). Nuisance vs substance: Specifying and estimating time series cross sectional models. *Political Analysis, 6*(1), 1–36. http://dx.doi.org/10.1093/pan/6.1.1

Bond, S. (2002). *Dynamic panel models: A guide to micro data methods and practice. Institute for Fiscal Studies*. Retrieved from http://cemmap.ifs.org.uk/wps/cwp0209.pdf

Cole, M. A., Elliott, R. J. R., & Zhang, J. (2009). Corruption, governance and FDI location in China: A province-level analysis. *The Journal of Development Studies, 45*(9), 1494–1512. https://doi.org/10.1080/00220380902890276

Crozet, M., Mayer, T., & Mucchielli, J. L. (2004). How do firms agglomerate? A Study of FDI in France. *Regional Science and Urban Economics, 34*, 27–54. http://dx.doi.org/10.1016/S0166-0462(03)00010-3

Cuervo-Cazurra, A. (2006). Who cares about corruption? *Journal of International Business Studies, 37*(6), 803–822.

Cuervo-Cazurra, A. (2008). Better the devil you don't know: Types of corruption and FDI in transition economies. *Journal of International Management, 14*(1), 12–27. https://doi.org/10.1016/j.intman.2007.02.003

Dasgupta, D., & Ratha, D. (2000). *What Factors Appear to Drive Private Capital Flows to Developing Countries and How Does Official Lending Respond?* Retrieved from http://www-wds.worldbank.org/servlet/WDSContentServer/WDSP/IB/2000/08/19/000094946_00080705302231/Rendered/PDF/multi_page.pdf

Efendic, A., Pugh, G., & Adnett, N. (2009). *Institutions and economic performance: System GMM modelling of institutional effects in transition*. Retrieved from http://www.riinvestinstitute.org/pdf/Efendic_et_al.pdf

Egger, P., & Winner, H. (2005). Evidence on corruption as an incentive for foreign direct investment. *European Journal of Political Economy, 21*(4), 932– 952. https://doi.org/10.1016/j.ejpoleco.2005.01.002

Garibaldi, P., Mora, N., Sahay, R., & Zettelmeyer, J. (2002). *What moves capital to transition economies?(Working Paper No. 02/64)*. International Monetary Fund. Retrieved from https://www.imf.org/external/pubs/ft/wp/2002/wp0264.pdf

Gastanaga, V., Nugent, J., & Pashamiova, B. (1998). Host country reforms and FDI inflows: How much difference do they make? *World Development, 26*(7), 1299–1314.

Habib, M., & Zurawicki, L. (2002). Corruption and Foreign Direct Investment. *Journal of International Business Studies, 33*(2), 291–307.

Hakkala, K.N., Norback, P., & Svaleryd, H. (2008). Asymmetric effects of corruption on FDI: evidence from Swedish multinational firms. *The Review of Economics and Statistics, 90*(4), 627–642. https://doi.org/10.1162/rest.90.4.627

Head, K., Ries, J., & Swenson, D. (1999). Agglomeration benefits and location choice: Evidence from Japanese manufacturing investments in the United States. *Journal of International Economics, 38*(3-4), 223–247. https://doi.org/10.1016/0022-1996(94)01351-R

Hoeffler, A. E. (2002). The augmented Solow model and the African growth debate. *Oxford Bulletin of Economics and Statistics, 64*(2), 135–158. https://doi.org/10.1111/1468-0084.00016

Jadhav, P. (2012). Determinants of foreign direct investment in BRICS economies: Analysis of economic, institutional and political factor. *Procedia - Social and Behavioral Sciences, 37*, 5 – 14. https://doi.org/10.1016/j.sbspro.2012.03.270

Javorcik, B. S., & Wei, S. J. (2009). Corruption and cross-border investment in emerging markets: firm-level evidence. *Journal of International Money and Finance, 28*(4), 605–624. https://doi.org/10.1016/j.jimonfin.2009.01.003

Jeon, B. N., & Rhee, S. (2008). The determinants of Korea's foreign direct invest ment from the United States, 1980-2001: An empirical investigation of firm level data. *Contemporary Economic Policy, 26(1)*, 118–131. https://doi.org/10.1111/j.1465-7287.2007.00061.x

Khan, M. H., & Sundaram, J. K. (2000). *Rents, rent-seeking and economic development: Theory and evidence in Asia.* Cambridge, UK: Cambridge University Press.

Kyereboah-Coleman, A., & Agyire-Tettey, K. F. (2008). Effect of exchange rate volatility on foreign direct investment in Sub-Saharan Africa: The case of Ghana (Case study). *Journal of Risk Finance, 9*(1), 52–70. https://doi.org/10.1108/15265940810842410

Lind, J. T., & Mehlum, H. (2007). *With or Without U? - The appropriate test for a U shaped relationship.* (MPRA Working Paper No. 4823). University Library of Munich, Germany. Retrieved from http://mpra.ub.uni-muenchen.de/4823/

Mateev, M. (2009). Determinants of foreign direct investment in Central and Southeastern Europe: New empirical tests. *Oxford Journal, 8*(1), 133–149.

Nerlove, M. (2002). *Essays in Panel Data Econometrics.* Cambridge, UK: Cambridge University Press.

Nkurunziza, J. D., & Bates, R. H. (2003). *Political Institutions and Economic Growth in Africa* (Working Paper No. 2003-03). Centre for the Study of African Economies, University of Oxford. Retrieved from http://econwpa.repec.org/eps/dev/papers/0409/0409028.pdf

Nunes, C. L., Oscategui, J., & Peschiera, J. (2006). *Determinants of FDI in Latin America. Documento De Trabajo 252.* Retrieved from http://www.pucp.edu.pc/ economia/pdf/DDD252.pdf

Plassmann, F., & Khanna, N. (2007). Assessing the precision of turning point estimates in polynomial regression functions. *Econometric Reviews, 26*(5), 503– 528. https://doi.org/10.1080/07474930701512105

Presbitero, A. F. (2005). *The debt-growth nexus: A dynamic panel data estimation.* Retrieved from http://utenti.dea.univpm.it/presbitero/pubblicazioni/Presbitero_RIE.pdf

Pusterla, F., & Resmini, L. (2007). Where do foreign firms locate in transition countries? An empirical investigations. *The Annals of Regional Science, 41*(4), 835–856. https://doi.org/10.1007/s00168-007-0144-4

Ranjan, V., & Agrawal, G. (2011). FDI inflow determinants in BRIC countries: A panel data analysis. *International Business Research, 4*(4), 225–263.

Roodman, D. (2006). *How To Do xtabond2: An Introduction to "Difference" and "System" GMM in Stata.* Retrieved from http://www.nuffield.ox.ac.uk/users/bond/file_HowtoDoxtabond8_with_foreword.pdf.

Roodman, D. (2007). *A Short Note on the Theme of Too Many Instruments.* Retrieved from http://www.cgdev.org/files/14256_file_Instruments.pdf

Roodman, D. (2009). How to do xtabond2: An introduction to difference and system GMM in Stata. *The Stata Journal, 9*(1), 86–136.

Sahoo, P. (2006). *Foreign Direct Investment in South Asia: Policy, Trends, Impact and Determinants.* Retrieved from http://www.adbi.org/files/dp56_fdi_in_south_asia.pdf

Sarafidis, V., Yamagata, T., & Robertson, R. (2006). *A Test of Cross-Section Dependence for a Linear Dynamic Panel Model with Regressors. Faculty of Eco-*

nomics, University of Cambridge. Retrieved from http://www.econ.cam.ac.uk/faculty/robertson/HCSDtest14Feb06.pdf

Sasabuchi, S. (1980). A test of a multivariate normal mean with composite hypotheses determined by linear inequalities. *Biometrika*, *67*(2), 429–439. https://doi.org/10.1093/biomet/67.2.429

Touchton, M. (2015). Trapping the tigers: Regulation of market entry and the rule of law in SE Asia. *The Social Science Journal*, *52*(1), 8–21. https://doi.org/10.1016/j.soscij.2013.10.010

Touchton, M. (2016). Campaigning for capital: Fair elections and foreign investment in comparative perspective. *International Interactions*, *42*(2), 271–294. https://doi.org/10.1080/03050629.2016.1093475

Voyer, P. A., & Beamish, P. W. (2004). The effect of corruption on Japanese foreign direct investment. *Journal of Business Ethics*, *50*(3), 211–226. https://doi.org/10.1023/B:BUSI.0000024737.57926.bf

Wei, S. J. (2000a). How Taxing is Corruption on International Investors. *The Review of Economics and Statistics*, *82*(1), 1–11. https://doi.org/10.1162/003465300558533

Wei, S. J. (2000b). Local Corruption and Global Capital Flows. *Brookings Papers on Economic Activity*, *20*(2), 303–346. https://doi.org/10.1353/eca.2000.0021

The World Bank. (2013). *World Development Indicators. Washington, DC: World Bank*. Available at http://www.worldbank.org/data/

The World Bank. (2014). *Worldwide Governance Indicators*. Available at http://info.worldbank.org/governance/wgi/index.aspx#home

UNCTAD. (2010). *Investing In a Low-Carbon Economy*. Geneva: United Nations. Retrieved from http://unctad.org/en/Docs/wir2010_en.pdf

UNCTAD. (2011). *Non-Equity Modes of International Production and Development*. Geneva: United Nations. Retrieved from http://unctad.org/ en/PublicationsLibrary/wir2011_en.pdf

UNCTAD. (2012). *Towards A New Generation of Investment Policies*. Geneva: United Nations. Retrieved from http://unctad.org/en/ PublicationsLibrary/wir2012_embargoed_en.pdf

UNCTAD. (2013). *Global Value Chains: Investment and Trade for Development*. Geneva: United Nations. Retrieved from http://unctad.org/en/ PublicationsLibrary/wir2013_en.pdf

UNCTAD. (2014). *Investing In the SDGs: An Action Plan*. Geneva: United Nations. Retrieved from http://unctad.org/en/PublicationsLibrary / wir2014_en.pdf

UNCTAD. (2015). *Reforming International Investment Governance*. Geneva: United Nations. Retrieved from http://unctad.org/en/PublicationsLibrary/wir2015_en.pdf

6

The impact of a trend pattern for sustainable marketing budgets on turnover dynamics

Alexandru Capatina[1], Adrian Micu[1], Nicoleta Cristache[1], Angela Eliza Micu[2]

ABSTRACT

In business practice, sustainable marketing seeks to meet environmental and social sustainability needs. Sustainable marketing budgets should create a balance between market needs and the need to use existing resources as rationally as possible.

By recognizing that certain internal and external factors may cause fluctuations in sustainable marketing budgets and have a direct impact on the expected turnover, managers could capture opportunities to channel these budgets into business areas with higher return on investment (ROI).

This study highlights the trends of sustainable marketing budgets in the case of one company and assesses their impact on its business turnover. Based on the assumed objective, this study provides explanations regarding the efficiency of sustainable marketing budgets in terms of benefits and, more precisely, on turnover dynamics. From the methodological perspective, the use of the coefficient of variation method allows the assessment of the longitudinal data homogeneity, reflecting the dynamics of the indicators, sustainable marketing budgets and turnovers. The results reveal that monthly sustainable marketing budgets have a significant impact on monthly turnover dynamics, considering the quadratic trend in the case of monthly sustainable marketing budgets and the exponential trend of monthly turnovers. From a managerial perspective, the implications of this study reveal that the more you invest in sustainable marketing, the more revenue your company could earn.

KEY WORDS: sustainable marketing, sustainable development, trend pattern, coefficient of variation

[1] Universitatea Dunarea de Jos din Galati, Romania; [2] Universitatea Ovidius din Constanta, Romania

1. Introduction

Major concerns at national and international forums have increased due to exponential population growth, the dynamics of industry, excessive consumerism and numerous ecological disasters. The expectations of civil society regarding the impact of economic activity on sustainable development are higher.

The concept of sustainable development belongs to the new theory of economic development. From this perspective, an explanation, even an exhaustive one, is required, given the abundant use of this theory for sustainable development.

In business practice, the use of sustainability assessment methodology occurs when relevant decision makers measure environmental and social issues

Correspondence concerning this article should be addressed to:
Alexandru Capatina, str. Traian 89 B3B, sc. 2, ap. 22, Galati 800003, Romania.
E-mail: alexandru.capa-tana@ugal.ro

using an evaluation scale and integrate all aspects of the business processes to enable an overview of the rated domain (Lee & Grewall, 2004).

The conceptualization of sustainable marketing orientation has been focused on the micromanagement of ecological issues. Key performance indicators related to corporate sustainability have only been developed in the past decade (Mitchell, Wooliscroft, & Higham, 2010).

Sustainable marketing has pushed companies towards new forms of 'green consumerism', which reinforce awareness of environmental standards and inform companies about the benefits of a 'green' image (Redclift, 2005).

The research question addresses the following topic: How do sustainable marketing budgets adopted by a company that is characterized by a sustainable market orientation influence its turnover dynamics?

The primary objective of this study is the identification of trend patterns related to the dynamics of sustainable marketing budgets, as well as their effects on the dynamics of business turnovers, in the case of a Romanian company in the retailing industry.

This study contributes to extant literature for two reasons: first, we present evidence on the statistical relations between trends of monthly sustainable marketing budgets and monthly turnovers. Our results extend the understanding of the role played by sustainable marketing budgets on the increase of revenues. Second, our empirical results indicate that the type of trend (linear, quadratic or exponential) related to the variables (monthly sustainable marketing budgets and respective monthly turnovers) have substantial higher explanatory power than other metrics.

This paper is organized as follows: First, we provide a theoretical background on sustainable marketing and highlight the most relevant research outcomes in this field. Then, the framework for a qualitative research, based on coefficient of variation method, is developed. Finally, the trend patterns for both sustainable marketing budgets and turnovers are discussed, illustrating how the proposed methodological framework can bring valuable contributions to the body of knowledge related to sustainable marketing.

2. Theoretical background

The core of sustainable marketing reveals the decisions in which environmental issues are emphasized and environmental strengths are used as a competitive advantage (Karna, Hansen, & Juslin, 2003).The concept of sustainable marketing is extended towards fulfilling the needs of future generations, which implies creating, communicating and delivering sustainability-based value to the next generations (Kumar, Rahman, Kazmi, & Goyal, 2012).

The difference between corporate social responsibility (CSR) and the strategically based marketing view of sustainability must be emphasized, considering that market-focused sustainability can be a strategic resource that leads to competitive advantages (Hult, 2011). The primary challenge given by this context is to integrate aspects related to environmental and social issues into marketing processes (Figge & Hahn, 2004; Pautard, 2004). According to specialists, a detailed guidance on the relative weighting given to indicators of sustainable marketing (Baker, 2007) is part of a series of priorities for business and is meant to offer insights into decision-making processes in the marketing policies of companies.

Marketing efforts regarding sustainable development include a better quality of life at the present and for future generations (Purcarea, 2008). The need for sustainable development monitoring systems for the effective governance of marketing activities has no headline indicator (Urbaniec, 2016) because no indicator is considered strong enough and important for policies to be able to provide a broad overview of the assessment of sustainable marketing.

Therefore, it is assumed that in marketing, "sustainability is a value - it is a moral choice to accept equity between generations, regarded as superior ethics" (Capron, 2005). We observe the emphasis on the moral value terms, ethics and fairness. However, these terms do not provide consistency in debates regarding sustainable development.

More issues related to sustainable marketing are increasingly institutionalized (Bansal, 2002). The adoption of standardized management systems, such as the ISO 14,000 (Morrow & Rondinelli, 2002; Rondinelli & Vastag, 2000) and official guidelines and recommendations for environmental and social reports, such as the Global Reporting Initiative (2011), are examples of best practices for the sustainable marketing policies of companies.

From the sustainable marketing perspective, for many people today, products just appear in a shop and there is little or no awareness of where they came from or how they were made – thus, many sustainability issues arise (Giddings, Hopwood, & O`Brien, 2002). Moreover, consumers who express a preference for sustainable marketing report that they are not always able to identify and/or apply information that could help them exercise this preference (Cairns & Macdonald, 2016).The sustainability dimension considers labeling of products or services an effective tool of marketing that a company can use to attempt to improve its competitive position. The societal pressures highly interact with market forces to shape this sustainability dimension (De Boer, 2003).

The creation of value, beyond the financial value embedded in profits, has changed the debate in managerial issues, which may include the socially responsible marketing practices of firms to reinforce their reputations or create real value for all stakeholders (Gallego-Alvarez, Prado-Lorenzo, Rodríguez-Domínguez, & García-Sánchez, 2010). The effects of large investments in sustainable marketing on financial metrics were noted by a major result of a study, which highlights that high sustainability firms outperform traditional firms when we consider accounting rates of return, such as turnover (Eccles, Ioannou, & Serafeim, 2014).

Marketing concepts should interface with the concept of sustainability to strive towards meeting global development requirements and balancing the business ecosystem (Nkamnebe, 2011). To determine the degree of corporate sustainability in terms of commitment to sustainable initiatives and the ability to communicate them through targeted marketing efforts, self-assessment tools for sustainable initiatives are frequent used by high sustainability firms (Baldassarre & Campo, 2016). Christofi, Leonidou and Vrontis (2014) propose an integrated framework for organizations to gain a sustainable competitive advantage by implementing sustainability through marketing, product innovation and leadership.

As a concluding remark regarding the body of knowledge dedicated to sustainable marketing, companies pursuing the sustainability dimension engage in marketing activities related to managing environmental and social issues (Sun, Garrett, & Kim, 2016).

3. Research Methodology

To achieve the research goalmentioned in the introduction, we conducted a qualitative study aimed at determining the temporal evolution of sustainable marketing budgets' dynamics within the analyzed firm. We focused our attention on building a panel, represented by the sustainable marketing budgets, and apply repeated monthly measurements during two consecutive years: 2012 and 2013.

The conceptual architecture of trend patterns considers marketing budgets as investments, enabling the company selected for the current study to confront the temporal relationship between marketing actions and marketplace reactions, an approach consistent with Sheth and Sisodia (2002).

Given the confidentiality related to financial data, it was difficult to find a Romanian company from the retailing industry whose manager would agree to provide us with the required information for addressing the research question. We selected the company based on its manager's willingness to provide us financial reports regarding monthly sustainable marketing budgets and turnovers.

We were particularly interested in analyzing the trend patterns related to the correlations between sustainable marketing budgets and turnover to better understand the issues regarding the effective assignment of sustainable marketing budgets in a real-life context.

During the first preliminary meeting, the following three hypotheses were stated:

Null hypothesis - H_0 - the trend pattern for the monthly sustainable marketing budgets and monthly turnovers of the company from the retailing industry is a **linear function**.

First alternative hypothesis - H_1 - the trend pattern for the monthly sustainable marketing budgets and monthly turnovers of the company from the retailing industry is a **quadratic function**.

Second alternative hypothesis - H_2 - the trend pattern for the monthly sustainable marketing budgets and monthly turnovers of the company from the retailing industry is an **exponential function**.

The testing of the three above stated hypotheses, which represents the foundation for explaining the conceptual model of the longitudinal research, included the use of the variation coefficient method, through which we can evaluate the selection criteria for the optimal trend model.

When good time-series data on revenues and marketing budgets are available, it is possible to apply multivariate measures to identify which strategic scenarios could occur and which trend patterns could be observed (Dekimpe & Hanssens, 1999).

Using trend patterns to test the usage frequency of online cyclical payments compared to other payment channels (Szopinski & Staniewski, 2014) is a good practice for developing the architecture of the current research framework.

The variation coefficient method is among the most applied statistical instruments aimed at valuing the consequences generated by group differences at an organizational level. This method is focused on comparing the internal variations of the research variables (Bedeian & Mossholder, 2000). Even if the variation coefficient is also used to determine data or samples' distributions, in the context of trend model's identification, it is generally viewed as an analytic and measurement instrument for sampled data.

The variation coefficient represents the index of the standard deviation of the average, and makes a comparison of the sample comparison, although the averages differ significantly. In our case, the sustainable marketing budgets were allocated by the company's manager in alignment with specific priorities. The primary rule of the variation coefficient method states the following: the lower value of the variation coefficient, the greater the homogenization of the data.

4. Analysis and Findings

A preliminary data analysis shows that the company assigned higher **sustainable marketing budgets** for the period of June-August and December of each year and generally, the turnovers were directly influenced by the amounts invested in sustainable development campaigns.

The monthly sustainable marketing budgets and monthly turnovers of the company analyzed in our study were synthesized from the financial reports provided by the company's manager and are provided in Table 1.

Targeting allows an enterprise to channel its sustainable development budget where there is the greatest (and fastest) possibility of return on investment (ROI). In this manner, our study provides explanations regarding the efficiency of budget assignment in terms of benefits perceived as turnover.

4.1 Analysis of the trend pattern related to monthly sustainable marketing budgets' dynamics

Using the data in Table 1, first, we presented the statistical pattern reflecting the trend of the monthly sustainable marketing budgets assigned by the analyzed company for the period 2012-2013. In this manner, we applied the coefficient of variation method as the selection criterion for the optimal trend pattern.

In the conditions of null hypothesis H_0, which proposes that the trend pattern for the X factor (the monthly sustainable marketing budgets, influencing the turnover of the company) is a **linear function** $x_{t_i} = a + b \cdot t_i$, the parameters "a" and "b" will be calculated using the following system of equations:

$$\begin{cases} n \cdot a = \sum_{i=-m}^{m} x_i \\ b \cdot \sum_{i=-m}^{m} t_i^2 = \sum_{i=-m}^{m} t_i \cdot x_i \end{cases} \qquad (1)$$

Consequently,

$$a = \frac{\sum_{i=-m}^{m} x_i}{n} \quad (2) \quad \text{and} \quad b = \frac{\sum_{i=-m}^{m} t_i \cdot x_i}{\sum_{i=-m}^{m} t_i^2} \quad (3)$$

Using the statistical data that have been calculated to fit the linear function (Table 2), we are able to determine the following values for the parameters "a" and "b" using an Excel spreadsheet as follows:

$$a = \frac{330.044}{24} = 13.751{,}83 \quad \text{and} \quad b = \frac{169.622}{1.300} = 130{,}48 \ .$$

Thus, the coefficient of variation in the case of the linear function will be:

$$v_l = \left[\frac{\sum_{i=-m}^{m} \left| x_i - x_{t_i}^l \right|}{n} : \frac{\sum_{i=-m}^{m} x_i}{n} \right] \cdot 100 \Rightarrow v_l = \frac{\sum_{i=-m}^{m} \left| x_i - x_{t_i}^l \right|}{\sum_{i=-m}^{m} x_i} \cdot 100 \quad (4)$$

$$v_l = \frac{59.770{,}36}{330.044} \cdot 100 \Rightarrow v_l = 18{,}11\%$$

Table 1. The evolution of the monthly sustainable marketing budgets and turnovers of the company, in the period 2012 - 2013

Year	Month	Average monthly sustainable marketing budgets (*EURO*)	Average monthly turnovers (*EURO*)
2012	January	11.470	78.322
	February	9.320	71.160
	March	12.850	86.468
	April	10.145	82.234
	May	14.140	107.236
	June	17.134	125.260
	July	18.460	114.207
	August	15.360	129.459
	September	12.640	104.460
	October	12.115	94.720
	November	11.430	96.236
	December	19.450	142.364
2013	January	10.840	88.260
	February	8.800	73.124
	March	10.390	78.360
	April	12.230	87.320
	May	13.200	96.240
	June	14.360	102.450
	July	16.940	123.236
	August	16.320	135.172
	September	13.210	115.576
	October	12.360	102.360
	November	15.460	106.361
	December	21.420	156.367

Source: Adapted from "Financial reports" [Internal data] by Grande Gloria (2014, November 20). Available at http://www.grandegloria.com/en/

Table 2. The pattern reflecting a linear function for the analysis of sustainable marketing budgets dynamics in the case of company

Year	Month	Monthly sustainable marketing budget (*EURO*) (*xi*)	Linear trend				
			t_i	t_i^2	$t_i x_i$	$x_{t_i} = a + bt_i$	$\lvert x_i - x_{t_i} \rvert$
2012	January	11.470	-12	144	-137.640	12.186,07	716,07
	February	9.320	-11	121	-102.520	12.316,55	2.996,55
	March	12.850	-10	100	-128.500	12.447,03	402,97
	April	10.145	-9	81	-91.305	12.577,51	2.432,51
	May	14.140	-8	64	-113.120	12.707,99	1.432,01
	June	17.134	-7	49	-119.938	12.838,47	4.295,53
	July	18.460	-6	36	-110.760	12.968,95	5.491,05
	August	15.360	-5	25	-76.800	13.099,43	2.260,57
	September	12.640	-4	16	-50.560	13.229,91	589,91
	October	12.115	-3	9	-36.345	13.360,39	1.245,39
	November	11.430	-2	4	-22.860	13.490,87	2.060,87
	December	19.450	-1	1	-19.450	13.621,35	5.828,65
2013	January	10.840	1	1	10.840	13.882,31	3.042,31
	February	8.800	2	4	17.600	14.012,79	5.212,79
	March	10.390	3	9	31.170	14.143,27	3.753,27
	April	12.230	4	16	48.920	14.273,75	2.043,75
	May	13.200	5	25	66.000	14.404,23	1.204,23
	June	14.360	6	36	86.160	14.534,71	174,71
	July	16.940	7	49	118.580	14.665,19	2.274,81
	August	16.320	8	64	130.560	14.795,67	1.524,33
	September	13.210	9	81	118.890	14.926,15	1.716,15
	October	12.360	10	100	123.600	15.056,63	2.696,63
	November	15.460	11	121	170.060	15.187,11	272,89
	December	21.420	12	144	257.040	15.317,59	6.102,41
TOTAL		**330.044**	**-**	**1.300**	**169.622**	**-**	**59770,36**

In the conditions of the alternative hypothesis H_1, which proposes that the trend pattern for the X factor (the monthly sustainable marketing budgets, influencing the turnover of the company) is a **quadratic function** $x_{t_i} = a + b \cdot t_i + ct_i^2$, the parameters "a", "b" and "c" are calculated using the following system of equations:

$$\begin{cases} n \cdot a + c\sum_{i=-m}^{m} t_i^2 = \sum_{i=-m}^{m} x_i \\ b \cdot \sum_{i=-m}^{m} t_i^2 = \sum_{i=-m}^{m} t_i \cdot x_i \\ a \cdot \sum_{i=-m}^{m} t_i^2 + c\sum_{i=-m}^{m} t_i^4 = \sum_{i=-m}^{m} t_i^2 \cdot x_i \end{cases} \quad (5)$$

Consequently,

$$a = \frac{\sum_{i=-m}^{m} t_i^4 \cdot \sum_{i=-m}^{m} x_i - \sum_{i=-m}^{m} t_i^2 \cdot \sum_{i=-m}^{m} t_i^2 \cdot x_i}{n \cdot \sum_{i=-m}^{m} t_i^4 - (\sum_{i=-m}^{m} t_i^2)^2} \quad (6),$$

$$b = \frac{\sum_{i=-m}^{m} t_i \cdot x_i}{\sum_{i=-m}^{m} t_i^2} \quad (7) \text{ and } c = \frac{n \cdot \sum_{i=-m}^{m} t_i^2 \cdot x_i - \sum_{i=-m}^{m} t_i^2 \cdot \sum_{i=-m}^{m} x_i}{n \cdot \sum_{i=-m}^{m} t_i^4 - (\sum_{i=-m}^{m} t_i^2)^2} \quad (8).$$

Using the statistical data that have been calculated to fit the quadratic function (Table 3), we are able to determine the following values for the parameters "a", "b" and "c":

$$a = \frac{121.420 \cdot 330.044 - 1.300 \cdot 18.373.556}{24 \cdot 121.420 - (1.300)^2} = 13.224{,}89$$

$$b = \frac{169.622}{1.300} = 130{,}48$$

$$c = \frac{24 \cdot 18.373.556 - 1.300 \cdot 330.044}{24 \cdot 121.420 - (1.300)^2} = 9{,}73$$

Thus, the coefficient of variation in the case of the quadratic function will be:

$$v_{II} = \left[\frac{\sum_{i=-m}^{m} \left| x_i - x_{t_i}^{II} \right|}{n} : \frac{\sum_{i=-m}^{m} x_i}{n} \right] \cdot 100 \Rightarrow v_{II} = \frac{\sum_{i=-m}^{m} \left| x_i - x_{t_i}^{II} \right|}{\sum_{i=-m}^{m} x_i} \cdot 100 \quad (9)$$

$$v_{II} = \frac{58.449{,}3}{330.044} \cdot 100 \Rightarrow v_{II} = 17{,}71\%$$

In the conditions of the alternative hypotheses H_2, which proposes that the trend pattern for the X factor (the monthly sustainable marketing budgets, influencing the turnover of the company) is an **exponential function** $x_{t_i} = ab^{t_i}$, the parameters "a" and "b" are calculated using the following system of equations:

$$\begin{cases} n \cdot \ln a = \sum_{i=-m}^{m} \ln x_i \\ \ln b \cdot \sum_{i=-m}^{m} t_i^2 = \sum_{i=-m}^{m} t_i \cdot \ln x_i \end{cases} \quad (10)$$

Consequently, $\ln a = \frac{\sum_{i=-m}^{m} \ln x_i}{n}$ (11)

and $\ln b = \frac{\sum_{i=-m}^{m} t_i \cdot \ln x_i}{\sum_{i=-m}^{m} t_i^2}$ (12)

Using the statistical data that have been calculated to fit the exponential function (Table 4), we are able to determine the values associated with "ln a" and "ln b":

$$\ln a = \frac{228{,}07}{24} = 9.50 \text{ and } \ln b = \frac{12{,}15}{1.300} = 0{,}0093$$

Thus, the coefficient of variation in the case of the exponential function will be:

$$v_{\exp} = \left[\frac{\sum_{i=-m}^{m} \left| x_i - x_{t_i}^{\exp} \right|}{n} : \frac{\sum_{i=-m}^{m} x_i}{n} \right] \cdot 100 \Rightarrow v_{\exp} = \frac{\sum_{i=-m}^{m} \left| x_i - x_{t_i}^{\exp} \right|}{\sum_{i=-m}^{m} x_i} \cdot 100 \quad (13)$$

$$v_{\exp} = \frac{58.672{,}02{,}68}{330.044} \cdot 100 \Rightarrow v_{\exp} = 17{,}78\%$$

We note the following relationships between the coefficients of variation related to the linear, quadratic and exponential functions of the sustainable marketing budgets dynamics observed in the company:

$$v_{II} = 17{,}71\% < v_{\exp} = 17{,}78\% < v_I = 18{,}11\%$$

We can conclude that the path described by the monthly sustainable marketing budgets, influencing the monthly turnovers reported by the company, is represented by a **quadratic trend** ($x_{t_i} = a + bt_i + ct_i^2$); to clarify, the first alternative hypothesis H_1 is confirmed.

Table 3. The pattern reflecting a quadratic function for the analysis of sustainable marketing budgets' dynamics in the case of company

Year	Month	Monthly sustainable marketing budget (*EURO*) (*xi*)	Quadratic trend				
			t_i^2	t_i^4	$t_i^2 \cdot x_i$	$X_t = a + bt_i + ct_i^2$	$\lvert x_i - x_{t_i} \rvert$
2012	January	11.470	144	20.736	1.651.680	13.060,25	1.590,25
	February	9.320	121	14.641	1.127.720	12.966,94	3.646,94
	March	12.850	100	10.000	1.285.000	12.893,09	43,09
	April	10.145	81	6.561	821.745	12.838,7	2.693,7
	May	14.140	64	4.096	904.960	12.803,77	1.336,23
	June	17.134	49	2.401	839.566	12.788,3	4.345,7
	July	18.460	36	1.296	664.560	12.792,29	5.667,71
	August	15.360	25	625	384.000	12.815,74	2.544,26
	September	12.640	16	256	202.240	12.858,65	218,65
	October	12.115	9	81	109.035	12.921,02	806,02
	November	11.430	4	16	45.720	13.002,85	1.572,85
	December	19.450	1	1	19.450	13.104,14	6.345,86
2013	January	10.840	1	1	10.840	13.365,1	2.525,1
	February	8.800	4	16	35.200	13.524,77	4.724,77
	March	10.390	9	81	93.510	13.703,9	3.313,9
	April	12.230	16	256	195.680	13.902,49	1.672,49
	May	13.200	25	625	330.000	14.120,54	920,54
	June	14.360	36	1.296	516.960	14.358,05	1,95
	July	16.940	49	2.401	830.060	14.615,02	2.324,98
	August	16.320	64	4.096	1.044.480	14.891,45	1.428,55
	September	13.210	81	6.561	1.070.010	15.187,34	1.977,34
	October	12.360	100	10.000	1.236.000	15.502,69	3.142,69
	November	15.460	121	14.641	1.870.660	15.837,5	377,5
	December	21.420	144	20.736	3.084.480	16.191,77	5.228,23
TOTAL		**330.044**	**1.300**	**121.420**	**18.373.556**		**58.449,3**

Table 4. The pattern reflecting an exponential function for the analysis of sustainable marketing budgets' dynamics in the case of company

Year	Month	Monthly sustainable marketing budget (*EURO*) (*xi*)	Exponential trend				
			$\ln x_i$	$t_i \ln x_i$	$\ln x_t = \ln a + t_i \cdot \ln b$	$x_{t_i} = ab^{t_i}$	$\lvert x_i - x_{t_i} \rvert$
2012	January	11.470	9,35	- 112,17	9,39	11.948,97	478,97
	February	9.320	9,14	-100,54	9,40	12.060,61	2.740,61
	March	12.850	9,46	-94,61	9,41	12.173,30	676,70
	April	10.145	9,22	-83,02	9,42	12.287,04	2.142,04
	May	14.140	9,56	-76,45	9,43	12.401,84	1.738,16
	June	17.134	9,75	-68,24	9,43	12.517,71	4.616,29
	July	18.460	9,82	-58,94	9,44	12.634,67	5.825,33
	August	15.360	9,64	-48,20	9,45	12.752,72	2.607,28
	September	12.640	9,44	-37,78	9,46	12.871,88	231,88
	October	12.115	9,40	-28,21	9,47	12.992,14	877,14
	November	11.430	9,34	-18,69	9,48	13.113,53	1.683,53
	December	19.450	9,88	-9,88	9,49	13.236,06	6.213,94
2013	January	10.840	9,29	9,29	9,51	13.484,55	2.644,55
	February	8.800	9,08	18,17	9,52	13.610,54	4.810,54
	March	10.390	9,25	27,75	9,53	13.737,71	3.347,71
	April	12.230	9,41	37,65	9,54	13.866,07	1.636,07
	May	13.200	9,49	47,44	9,55	13.995,62	795,62
	June	14.360	9,57	57,43	9,56	14.126,39	233,61
	July	16.940	9,74	68,16	9,57	14.258,38	2.681,62
	August	16.320	9,70	77,60	9,57	14.391,60	1.928,40
	September	13.210	9,49	85,40	9,58	14.526,07	1.316,07
	October	12.360	9,42	94,22	9,59	14.661,79	2.301,79
	November	15.460	9,65	106,11	9,60	14.798,78	661,22
	December	21.420	9,97	119,66	9,61	14.937,05	6.482,95
TOTAL		**330.044**	**228,07**	**12,15**	-		**58.672,02**

4.2 Analysis of the trend pattern related to monthly turnovers' dynamics

The second analysis is focused on the identification of the trend pattern reflecting monthly turnovers reported by the company during the period 2012-2013.

In the conditions of the null hypothesis H_0, which proposes that the trend pattern for the X factor (the monthly turnovers, influenced by the monthly sustainable marketing budgets) is a **linear function** ($x_{t_i} = a + b \cdot t_i$), the parameters "a" and "b" are determined using the formula described in the previous section.

Using the statistical data that have been calculated to fit the linear function (Table 5), we are able to determine the following values for the parameters "a" and "b", using an Excel spreadsheet:

$$a = \frac{2.496.952}{24} = 104.039,67$$

and $b = \frac{1.537.464}{1.300} = 1.182,66$

Thus, the coefficient of variation in the case of the linear function will be:

$$v_I = \left[\frac{\sum_{i=-m}^{m} |x_i - x_{t_i}^I|}{n} : \frac{\sum_{i=-m}^{m} x_i}{n} \right] \cdot 100 \Rightarrow v_I = \frac{\sum_{i=-m}^{m} |x_i - x_{t_i}^I|}{\sum_{i=-m}^{m} x_i} \cdot 100 \quad (4)$$

$$v_I = \frac{414.054,08}{2.496.952} \cdot 100 \Rightarrow v_I = 16,58\%$$

In the conditions of the alternative hypothesis H_1, which proposes that the trend pattern for the X factor (the monthly turnovers, influenced by the monthly sustainable marketing budgets) is a **quadratic function** ($x_{t_i} = a + b \cdot t_i + ct_i^2$), the parameters "a", "b" and "c" are calculated using the statistical data that have been calculated to fit the quadratic function (Table 6).

$$a = \frac{121.420 \cdot 2.496.952 - 1.300 \cdot 136.847.474}{24 \cdot 121.420 - (1.300)^2} = 102.344,78$$

$$b = \frac{1.537.464}{1.300} = 1.182,66$$

$$c = \frac{24 \cdot 136.847.474 - 1.300 \cdot 2.496.952}{24 \cdot 121.420 - (1.300)^2} = 31,29$$

Thus, the coefficient of variation in the case of the quadratic function will be:

$$v_{II} = \left[\frac{\sum_{i=-m}^{m} |x_i - x_{t_i}^{II}|}{n} : \frac{\sum_{i=-m}^{m} x_i}{n} \right] \cdot 100 \Rightarrow v_{II} = \frac{\sum_{i=-m}^{m} |x_i - x_{t_i}^{II}|}{\sum_{i=-m}^{m} x_i} \cdot 100 \quad (9)$$

$$v_{II} = \frac{414846,7}{2.496.952} \cdot 100 \Rightarrow v_{II} = 16,61\%$$

In the conditions of the alternative hypotheses H_2, which proposes that the trend pattern for the X factor (the monthly turnovers, influenced by the monthly sustainable marketing budgets) is an **exponential function** ($x_{t_i} = ab^{t_i}$), the parameters "a" and "b" are calculated using the statistical data that have been calculated to fit the exponential function (Table 7).

$$\ln a = \frac{276,73}{24} = 11,53 \quad \ln b = \frac{14,76}{1.300} = 0,0114$$

Thus, the coefficient of variation in the case of the exponential function will be:

$$v_{\exp} = \left[\frac{\sum_{i=-m}^{m} |x_i - x_{t_i}^{\exp}|}{n} : \frac{\sum_{i=-m}^{m} x_i}{n} \right] \cdot 100 \Rightarrow v_{\exp} = \frac{\sum_{i=-m}^{m} |x_i - x_{t_i}^{\exp}|}{\sum_{i=-m}^{m} x_i} \cdot 100 \quad (13)$$

$$v_{\exp} = \frac{406.513,21}{2.496.952} \cdot 100 \Rightarrow v_{\exp} = 16,28\%$$

We remark the following relationships between the coefficients of variation related to the linear, quadratic and exponential functions in the case of the monthly turnovers dynamics observed in the company:

$$v_{\exp} = 16,28\% < v_I = 16,58\% < v_{II} = 16,61\%$$

We can conclude that the path described by the monthly turnovers, influenced by the monthly sustainable marketing budgets assigned by the company, is represented by an **exponential trend**; to clarify, the second alternative hypothesis H_2 is confirmed.

5. Conclusions and future research agenda

This study reveals that the process of identifying a trend model by using adequate statistical and mathematical tools provides a methodological framework for the appraisal of temporal monthly sustainable marketing

Table 5. The pattern reflecting a linear function for the analysis of monthly turnovers dynamics in the case of company

Year	Month	Monthly turnovers (EURO) (xi)	Linear trend				
			t_i	t_i^2	$t_i x_i$	$x_{t_i} = a + bt_i$	$\lvert x_i - x_{t_i} \rvert$
2012	January	78.322	-12	144	-939.864	89.847,75	11.525,75
	February	71.160	-11	121	-782.760	91.030,41	19.870,41
	March	86.468	-10	100	-864.680	92.213,07	5.745,07
	April	82.234	-9	81	-740.106	93.395,73	11.161,73
	May	107.236	-8	64	-857.888	94.578,39	12.657,61
	June	125.260	-7	49	-876.820	95.761,05	29.498,95
	July	114.207	-6	36	-685.242	96.943,71	17.263,29
	August	129.459	-5	25	-647.295	98.126,37	31.332,63
	September	104.460	-4	16	-417.840	99.309,03	5.150,97
	October	94.720	-3	9	-284.160	100.491,69	5.771,69
	November	96.236	-2	4	-192.472	101.674,35	5.438,35
	December	142.364	-1	1	-142.364	102.857,01	39.506,99
2013	January	88.260	1	1	88.260	105.222,3	16.962,33
	February	73.124	2	4	146.248	106.405	33.280,99
	March	78.360	3	9	235.080	107.587,7	29.227,65
	April	87.320	4	16	349.280	108.770,3	21.450,31
	May	96.240	5	25	481.200	109.953	13.712,97
	June	102.450	6	36	614.700	111.135,6	8.685,63
	July	123.236	7	49	862.652	112.318,3	10.917,71
	August	135.172	8	64	1.081.376	113.501	21.671,05
	September	115.576	9	81	1.040.184	114.683,6	892,39
	October	102.360	10	100	1.023.600	115.866,3	13.506,27
	November	106.361	11	121	1.169.971	117.048,9	10.687,93
	December	156.367	12	144	1.876.404	118.231,6	38.135,41
TOTAL		**2.496.952**	-	**1.300**	**1.537.464**	-	**414.054,08**

Table 6. The pattern reflecting a quadratic function for the analysis of monthly turnovers dynamics in the case of company

Year	Month	Monthly turnovers (*EURO*) (*xi*)	Quadratic trend				
			t_i^2	t_i^4	$t_i^2 \cdot x_i$	$X_t = a + bt_i + ct_i^2$	$\lvert x_i - x_{t_i} \rvert$
2012	January	78.322	144	20.736	11.278.368	92.658,62	14.336,62
	February	71.160	121	14.641	8.610.360	93.121,61	21.961,61
	March	86.468	100	10.000	8.646.800	93.647,18	7.179,18
	April	82.234	81	6.561	6.660.954	94.235,33	12.001,33
	May	107.236	64	4.096	6.863.104	94.886,06	12.349,94
	June	125.260	49	2.401	6.137.740	95.599,37	29.660,63
	July	114.207	36	1.296	4.111.452	96.375,26	17.831,74
	August	129.459	25	625	3.236.475	97.213,73	32.245,27
	September	104.460	16	256	1.671.360	98.114,78	6.345,22
	October	94.720	9	81	852.480	99.078,41	4.358,41
	November	96.236	4	16	384.944	100.104,6	3.868,62
	December	142.364	1	1	142.364	101.193,4	41.170,59
2013	January	88.260	1	1	88.260	103.558,7	15.298,73
	February	73.124	4	16	292.496	104.835,3	31.711,26
	March	78.360	9	81	705.240	106.174,4	27.814,37
	April	87.320	16	256	1.397.120	107.576,1	20.256,06
	May	96.240	25	625	2.406.000	109.040,3	12.800,33
	June	102.450	36	1.296	3.688.200	110.567,2	8.117,18
	July	123.236	49	2.401	6.038.564	112.156,6	11.079,39
	August	135.172	64	4.096	8.651.008	113.808,6	21.363,38
	September	115.576	81	6.561	9.361.656	115.523,2	52,79
	October	102.360	100	10.000	10.236.000	117.300,4	14.940,38
	November	106.361	121	14.641	12.869.681	119.140,1	12.779,13
	December	156.367	144	20.736	22.516.848	121.042,5	35.324,54
TOTAL		**2.496.952**	**1.300**	**121.420**	**136.847.474**		**414846,7**

Table 7. The pattern reflecting an exponential function for the analysis of sustainable marketing budgets' dynamics in the case of company

Year	Month	Monthly sustainable marketing budget (*EURO*) (*xi*)	Exponential trend				
			$\ln x_i$	$t_i \ln x_i$	$\ln x_{t_i} = \ln a + t_i \cdot \ln b$	$x_{t_i} = ab^{t_i}$	$\lvert x_i - x_{t_i} \rvert$
2012	January	78.322	11,27	-135,22	11,39	88.716,40	10.394,40
	February	71.160	11,17	-122,90	11,40	89.733,55	18.573,55
	March	86.468	11,37	-113,68	11,42	90.762,37	4.294,37
	April	82.234	11,32	-101,86	11,43	91.802,98	9.568,98
	May	107.236	11,58	-92,66	11,44	92.855,52	14.380,48
	June	125.260	11,74	-82,17	11,45	93.920,13	31.339,87
	July	114.207	11,65	-69,87	11,46	94.996,94	19.210,06
	August	129.459	11,77	-58,86	11,47	96.086,11	33.372,89
	September	104.460	11,56	-46,23	11,48	97.187,75	7.272,25
	October	94.720	11,46	-34,38	11,50	98.302,03	3.582,03
	November	96.236	11,47	-22,95	11,51	99.429,09	3.193,09
	December	142.364	11,87	-11,87	11,52	100.569,07	41.794,93
2013	January	88.260	11,39	11,39	11,54	102.888,38	14.628,38
	February	73.124	11,20	22,40	11,55	104.068,02	30.944,02
	March	78.360	11,27	33,81	11,56	105.261,18	26.901,18
	April	87.320	11,38	45,51	11,58	106.468,03	19.148,03
	May	96.240	11,47	57,37	11,59	107.688,71	11.448,71
	June	102.450	11,54	69,22	11,60	108.923,38	6.473,38
	July	123.236	11,72	82,05	11,61	110.172,21	13.063,79
	August	135.172	11,81	94,51	11,62	111.435,36	23.736,64
	September	115.576	11,66	104,92	11,63	112.713,00	2.863,00
	October	102.360	11,54	115,36	11,64	114.005,28	11.645,28
	November	106.361	11,57	127,32	11,66	115.312,37	8.951,37
	December	156.367	11,96	143,52	11,67	116.634,45	39.732,55
TOTAL		**2.496.952**	**276,73**	**14,76**	-	-	**406.513,21**

budgets' impact on the monthly turnovers of a company. Furthermore, the use of the coefficient of variation method allows the identification of the longitudinal data homogeneity, reflecting the dynamics of the indicators, sustainable marketing budgets and turnovers.

In addition, it is important to emphasize the primary principle of the methodology employed, reflecting that when the variation coefficient has a lower value, the homogenization of the data is greater. In this context, we note lower levels of variation coefficients in the case of monthly turnovers.

This study was limited to only one company in the retailing industry. Although the results cannot be generalized, they provide interesting insights. The dynamics of the monthly sustainable marketing budgets, reflected by a quadratic trend, has a significant impact on the monthly turnover dynamics, reflected by an exponential trend. This valuable research outcome lets us argue, based on empirical results, the increasing role of sustainable marketing initiatives in supporting higher financial results in the long term. Therefore, managers should balance financial resources by investing more in sustainable activities.

In addition, the limitations of this study provide additional opportunities for research directions. We are aware that additional studies should be conducted in this area and the future research agenda includes the design of an appraisal model that will assess the results described above; the research will focus on the use of the test series analysis, the augmented Dickey-Fuller test (ADF), that allows the determination of stationary or non-stationary dynamics of a series by determining the deterministic trend indicated by the coefficient of variation method.

References

Baker, S. (2007). Sustainable development as symbolic commitment: Declaratory politics and the seductive appeal of ecological modernisation in the European Union. *Environmental Politics, 16*(2), 297-317.

Baldassarre, F., & Campo, R. (2016). Sustainability as a marketing tool: To be or to appear to be? *Business Horizons, 59*(4), 421-429.

Bansal, P. (2002). The corporate challenges of sustainable development. *The Academy of Management Executive, 16*(2), 122-131.

Bedeian, A. G., & Mossholder, K. W. (2000). On the use of the Coefficient of Variation as a measure of diversity. *Organizational Research Methods, 3*(3), 285-297.

Cairns, G., & Macdonald, L. (2016). Stakeholder insights on the planning and development of an independent benchmark standard for responsible food marketing. *Evaluation and Program Planning, 56*, 109-120.

Capron, M. (2005). Les nouvelles responsabilités sociétales des entreprises: De quelles «nouveautés» s'agit-il? [The new societal responsibilities of the organizations: What are the novelties?] *La Revue des Sciences de Gestion: Direction et Gestion [Journal of Management Science : Direction and Administration]*, 40(211/212), 47-54

Christofi, M., Leonidou, E., & Vrontis, D. (2014). Cause–related marketing, product innovation and extraordinary sustainable leadership: the root towards sustainability. *Global Business and Economics Review, 17*(1), 93-111.

De Boer, J. (2003). Sustainability labelling schemes: the logic of their claims and their functions for stakeholders. *Business Strategy and the Environment, 12*(4), 254-264.

Dekimpe, M. G., & Hanssens, D. M. (1999). Sustained spending and persistent response: A new look at long-term marketing profitability. *Journal of Marketing Research, 36*(4), 397-412.

Eccles, R. G., Ioannou, I., & Serafeim, G. (2014). The impact of corporate sustainability on organizational processes and performance. *Management Science, 60*(11), 2835-2857.

Figge, F., & Hahn, T. (2004). Sustainable value added—measuring corporate contributions to sustainability beyond eco-efficiency. *Ecological economics, 48*(2), 173-187.

Gallego-Alvarez, I., Prado-Lorenzo, J. M., Rodríguez-Domínguez, L., & García-Sánchez, I. M. (2010). Are social and environmental practices a marketing tool? Empirical evidence for the biggest European companies. *Management Decision, 48*(10), 1440-1455.

Giddings, B., Hopwood, B., & O'Brien, G. (2002). Environment, economy and society: fitting them together into sustainable development. *Sustainable Development, 10*(4), 187-196.

Grande Gloria. (2014, November 20). Financial reports [Internal data]. Available at http://www.grandegloria.com/en/

Global Reporting Initiative. (2011). GRI and ISO 26000: How to use the GRI Guidelines in conjunction with ISO 26000. Retrieved from https://www.globalreporting.org/resourcelibrary/How-To-Use-the-GRI-Guidelines-In-Conjunction-With-ISO26000.pdf

Hult, G. T. M. (2011). Market-focused sustainability: market orientation plus!. *Journal of the Academy of Marketing Science, 39*(1), 1-6.

Karna, J., Hansen, E., & Juslin, H. (2003). Social responsibility in environmental marketing planning. *European Journal of Marketing, 37*(5-6), 848-871.

Kumar, V., Rahman, Z., Kazmi, A. A., & Goyal, P. (2012). Evolution of sustainability as marketing strategy: Beginning of new era. *Procedia-Social and Behavioral Sciences, 37*, 482-489.

Lee, R. P., & Grewal, R. (2004). Strategic responses to new technologies and their impact on firm performance. *Journal of Marketing, 68*(4), 157-171.

Mitchell, R. W., Wooliscroft, B., & Higham, J. (2010). Sustainable market orientation: A new approach to managing marketing strategy. *Journal of Macromarketing, 30*(2), 160-170.

Morrow, D., &Rondinelli, D. (2002). Adopting corporate environmental management systems: Motivations and results of ISO 14001 and EMAS certification. *European Management Journal, 20*(2), 159-171.

Nkamnebe, A. D. (2011). Sustainability marketing in the emerging markets: Imperatives, challenges, and agenda setting. *International Journal of Emerging Markets, 6*(3), 217-232.

Pautard, D. (2004). Les avantages d'une approche marketing consciente des principes de responsabilité sociétale [The advantages of a sustainable marketing approach regarding CSR principles]. *Revue française du marketing [French Marketing Journal], 200*(5/5), 67-81.

Purcarea, I. (2008). The place of small and medium enterprises within the sustainable development framework. *Contemporary Economics, 2*(3), 65-69.

Redclift, M. (2005). Sustainable development (1987–2005): An oxymoron comes of age. *Sustainable development, 13*(4), 212-227.

Rondinelli, D., & Vastag, G. (2000). Panacea, common sense, or just a label?: The value of ISO 14001 environmental management systems. *European Management Journal, 18*(5), 499-510.

Sheth, J. N., & Sisodia, R. S. (2002). Marketing productivity: issues and analysis. *Journal of Business Research, 55*(5), 349-362.

Sun, Y., Garrett, T. C., & Kim, K. H. (2016). Do Confucian principles enhance sustainable marketing and customer equity?. *Journal of Business Research, 69*(9), 3772-3779.

Szopinski, T., & Staniewski, M. W. (2014). Trends in the use of cyclical payment channels by Polish households: Implications for e-banking. *Transformation in Business & Economics, 13*(3), 235-250.

Urbaniec, M. (2016). Measuring and monitoring effects of sustainable development in the European Union. *European Journal of Sustainable Development, 5*(1), 1-18.

7

Institutional gaps in managing multiple European projects co-funded by public and private institutions

Raluca Vasilache[1], Madalin Darie[1]

ABSTRACT

The purpose of this paper is to compare perceptions on drivers of managing multiple European co-funded projects among public and private institutions from Romania, and determine which dimensions of multi-project management optimization have the greatest impact on institutional financial stability and organizational learning. Data were collected using an online questionnaire administrated to two convenience samples of 100 public institutions, and 100 private organizations from Romania, involved in managing multiple European co-funded projects. Multi-project management optimization was measured using two dimensions: the relational dimension for governance of multiple projects and the regulative dimension. Data were analyzed by using confirmatory factor analysis, ANOVA and linear regression. In the private organizations sample, relational dimension was the most important predictor of organizational learning, while regulative dimension was the most important predictor of financial stability in the sample of public institutions.

KEY WORDS: multiple project management, financial stability, organizational learning, project management governance

[1] "Dunarea de Jos" University of Galati, Romania

1. Introduction

The literature on the differences in public and private management of multiple projects outlines several important gaps in what concern the managers' orientation toward financial stability versus organizational learning from past insights. Significant gaps between these sectors are identified at the managerial level and project management team level (Bretschneider, 1990). While significant expertise has been developed within the area of multiple project management, the need to manage ever more varied projects in the same time poses new and challenging issues for both public-funded and privately-owned organizations (Dooley, Lupton, & O'Sullivan, 2005).

There is a gap in the literature on Project Management when it comes to understanding the focal pain points related to simultaneous multi-project management in privately owned companies and public institutions; thus, a challenging question arises: "Which multi-project management optimization dimension (relational or regulative) is the most important predictor of financial stability and organizational learning in privately owned companies and public institutions?".

Correspondence concerning this article should be addressed to: **Madalin Darie**, "Dunarea de Jos" University of Galati, Domneasca Street, no. 47, Galati, Romania. E-mail: madalin.darie85@gmail.com

The objective of this study is twofold: to identify the factors correlating with success in managing strategic intentions through multiple projects and to find out the gaps of managing multiple European co-funded projects between public and private institutions. In comparison to previous research, we approach the phenomenon with a quantitative approach and thus aim to provide more generalizable results on how organizations can implement strategies successfully through projects.

The remainder of the paper is as follows: Section 2 focuses on the literature review regarding multiple project management peculiarities in privately owned companies and public institutions. Section 3 highlights the quantitative method's applicability to the research framework. Section 4 presents the results based on the ANOVA and regression analyses conducted on both research samples. Section 5 discusses these results and offers conclusions, which cover managerial implications, limitations of the study, and suggestions for forthcoming research.

2. Theoretical background

Multiple project management frameworks have been developed in the private sector and often blindly adapted to the public sector (Cats-Baril & Thompson, 1995). Unlike private companies, public administration institutions do not encounter the competitive pressures that drive their managers to think out of the financial stability box, while dealing with multiple projects. The public sector objectives in terms of multiple project management adoption are negatively affected by the bureaucratic structures (Holmes, 2001), due to standard operating procedures, bureaucratic culture, levels of hierarchy and many other factors (Keiser, 2011). Critical success factors identified as relevant for multiple project management optimization to the private sector must be assessed within the relational dimension, while in public institutions, regulative dimension is primordial (Rosacker & Olson, 2008).

Project managers in the public sector face team management challenges such as the incapacity to select project team members based on their expertise, due to the fact that the pool of human resources is rarely shared (Wirick, 2011). In private organizations, sharing best practices for multi-project success with the entire pool of human capital is perceived one of the biggest project management competitive advantage (Kerzner, 2013).

In the case of private organizations, the commitment to achieve multiple project objectives aligns with the strategy to share the project vision all the employees involved in simultaneous projects. In the case of public administration, the professional competencies in the area of multiproject management are influenced to a great extent by the relations with top management, which are connected with political power in many situations (Jałocha, Krane, Ekambaram, & Prawelska-Skrzypek, 2014).

At the level of public administration institutions, the projects have become increasingly complex and difficult to manage as they often require extended deadlines and contingency plans are not always appropriate (Klakegg, Williams, & Shiferaw 2016). In contrast, private company stakeholder management is based on organizational learning sense making and sense giving through effective involvement of stakeholders in the simultaneous projects (Purvis, Zagenczyk, & McCray, 2015).

In Romania, the companies from the private sector are aware that their growth is conditioned by attracting financial resources by means of EU funding instruments. Therefore, they manifest a higher propensity to implement multi-project management methodologies and technologies (Turner, Ledwith, & Kelly, 2010). There is strong evidence that the application of critical chain project planning leads to better results in multiple project management contexts, considering the evidence from several Romanian privately owned companies (Deac & Vrincut, 2013).

European Union has often requested Romanian public institutions to activate a number of specific factors to absorb more funding, strengthening administrative capacity; preparing qualified personnel and avoiding the fluctuation of employees in simultaneous projects and creating greater transparency by providing exhaustive information on project steps and milestones and the elimination of excessive bureaucracy (Zaman & Georgescu, 2009).

Even if the concept of multiple project management is still more theoretical than practical in the Romanian public administration, some new managerial ideas: strategic management and planning, performance-measurement systems, knowledge sharing, etc. were included in their managers' responsibilities (Bouckaert, Nakrošis, & Nemec, 2011).

Despite of all its problems, Romanian public management has made progress in the field of multiple project management, as it tried to replicate the best practices learnt from private companies, even if in some institutions the results were not satisfactory (Istrate & Marian, 2012). Romanian public management has improved due to the strategy regarding the acceleration of the public administration reform in order to attract more EU funding, which created a new legislative framework in providing the prerequisites for a better multi-project management, avoiding the corruption and other bad things (Ortansa, 2012).

3. Method

The fast-growing number of EU co-funded projects in Romania requires the multi-project management optimization, in order to provide the greatest impact on institutional financial stability and organizational learning in both public and private institutions.

The current research framework advances the contributions of relational and regulative dimensions for governance of multiple projects on boosting the multi-project management efficiency.

The dimensions for analysis related to the multi-project management optimization are represented by:

- **Relational dimension,** which enables a collaborative project management environment to insure a shared resource pool to the simultaneous projects;
- **Regulative dimension,** which outlines the formal processes and procedures used in monitoring, tracking and evaluating the simultaneous projects.

An empirical study was conducted to address the following research questions:

RQ1. What are the gaps between the drivers of managing multiple European co-funded projects perceived by public and private institutions?

RQ2. Which dimensions of multi-project management optimization have the greatest impact on institutional financial stability and organizational learning?

Sample, data collection and measures

The data analysed in our study are selected from an online survey which took place in the period: 1st of October 2017 – 15th of November 2017. The target was represented by 200 Project Managers divided in two groups of 100, each group belonging to public institutions, and privately-owned organizations. The aim of the online questionnaire was to identify their perceptions about multi-project management optimization, considering both relational and regulative dimensions for governance of simultaneous EU co-funded projects.

Multi-project management optimization measures were adapted from Dye and Pennypacker (2001), Engwall and Jerbrant (2003) and Tsaturyan and Muller (2015). The online questionnaire was composed of 10 items and designed as a Likert seven-point scale:

- **$MPMOPT_1$**: The organization developed a common resource pool for multiple projects management focused on best practices sharing among projects.
- **$MPMOPT_2$**: Priority assignment leads to an effective communication flow among project managers from your institution.
- **$MPMOPT_3$**: The organization introduced Project Management governance mechanisms to facilitate the interactions among the actors of the multiple projects network.
- **$MPMOPT_4$**: The organization implemented a central IT interface to make the interactions of project managers more effective and to avoid a competition between projects.
- **$MPMOPT_5$**: The organization established a balance between the freedom of project managers in the process of administrating their projects and the internal regulations and procedures to foster the collaborative learning.
- **$MPMOPT_6$**: The organization developed a standardized methodology for multiple project management, aligning the procedures for project tracking in different domains.
- **$MPMOPT_7$**: The organization established project control tools to avoid overlapping schedule.
- **$MPMOPT_8$**: The organization implemented a central IT interface to deliver standardized reporting tools for the governance of multiple projects.
- **$MPMOPT_9$**: The organization developed internal procedures to avoid additional bureaucracy in favor of accelerating the execution of simultaneous projects.
- **$MPMOPT_{10}$**: The organization implemented clear procedures to mitigate the risks of "after-the-fact prioritization" between ongoing projects.

Principal component analysis

The results achieved after the application of the Principal Component Analysis (PCA) with rotation VARIMAX

Table 1. Results of PCA application - Rotated component matrix

(KMO: 0,821; determinant: 0,008; Barlett's test of Construct sphericity (significance level : 0,003)	Dimension for analysing the governance of simultaneous EU co-funded projects	
	Relational	**Regulative**
$MPMOPT_1$	0,502	0,341
$MPMOPT_2$	0,747	0,202
$MPMOPT_3$	0,727	0,313
$MPMOPT_4$	0,758	0,186
$MPMOPT_5$	0,726	0,336
$MPMOPT_6$	0,396	0,785
$MPMOPT_7$	0,211	0,823
$MPMOPT_8$	0,283	0,868
$MPMOPT_9$	0,337	0,865
$MPMOPT_{10}$	0,365	0,795

emphasize a bi-dimensional structure of the multi-project management optimization assessment scale, considering the relational and regulative dimensions for governance of simultaneous EU co-funded projects (Table 1).

The statistical indicator Kaiser-Meyer-Olkin (KMO) enables the assessment of the factorial analysis validity; the high values (between 0.5 and 1.0) prove the necessity to apply the factorial analysis. Bartlett sphericity test is used to examine the existence of correlations among the variables included into the factorial.

In the current research design, the value of KMO (0.832) reveals the necessity to perform factorial analysis, while the significance level of Bartlett sphericity test (under 0.05) highlight the strong correlation of the variables embedded into the research framework.

After the preliminary exploratory phase, PCA results were computed into confirmatory factor analysis in view to validate the ten constructs research framework, without deleting any construct. The values associated to CFI (Comparative Fit Index), NFI (Normed Fit Index) and IFI (Incremental Fit Index) more than the critical threshold (0.9), validate the research framework. This validation is also confirmed by the very low value (0.0386) of the Root Mean Square Error of Approximation (RMSEA).

The internal consistency of the measurement scale is confirmed, as the Cronbach' Alpha coefficients assigned to all analyzed items overcome the 0.7 recommended threshold. According to Fornell and Larcker criterion, the discriminant validity is confirmed (Table 2).

The **independent variable** of the research model is the multi-project management optimization (MPMOPT), while the **dependent variables** are financial stability and organizational learning.

4. Findings

According to the results of one factor variance analysis (one-way ANOVA), we observe a significant difference between Romanian public institutions and privately owned organizations regarding their project managers' perceptions of multi-project management optimization at the level of the proposed dimensions: relational and regulative (Table 3).

The results of ANOVA analyses done on an item-by-item (Table 4) outline that the score associated to nine items from ten overcomes the threshold 5, proving

Table 2. Results of the confirmatory factor analysis

Dimension	Item	Squared multiple correlation	Standard error	Critical ratio	Cronbach' Alpha ∞>**0.7**	Composite fidelity ρ (A)>**0.7**	Convergent validity ρ_{vc}>**0.5**	Discriminant validity $\rho_{vc}>r_{ij}^2(0.728)^2$
		CFI= 0,931; NFI= 0,946; IFI=0,965; RMR=0,086; RMSEA= 0,0386						
Relational	$MPMOPT_1$	0,511	0,721	10,857	0,868	0.909	0.598	0.598>0.520
	$MPMOPT_2$	0,658	0,679	9,436				
	$MPMOPT_3$	0,509	0,634	8,022				
	$MPMOPT_4$	0,512	0,763	9,526				
	$MPMOPT_5$	0,537	0,758	8,624				
Regulative	$MPMOPT_6$	0,802	0,904	12,318	0,826	0.864	0.748	0.748>0.520
	$MPMOPT_7$	0,613	0,819	12,156				
	$MPMOPT_8$	0,625	0,736	11,185				
	$MPMOPT_9$	0,592	0,752	9,958				
	$MPMOPT_{10}$	0,654	0,682	9,825				

Table 3. Project managers' perceptions of multi-project management optimization, according to one factor variance analysis

		Sum of squares	**Degrees of freedom**	**Mean square**	**F**	**Sig. level**
MPMOPT relational dimension	Between groups	21,246	1	21,246	26,172	0,002
	Within groups	174,754	195	0,812		
	Total	196,000	196			
MPMOPT regulative dimension	Between groups	14,682	1	14,6822	16,942	0,004
	Within groups	181,318	195	0,828		
	Total	196,000	196			

a positive appreciation of the main part of the factors affecting multi-project management optimization.

In the case of public institutions, the highest score (5,92) was assigned to the item $MPMOPT_6$ (the organization developed a standardized methodology for multiple project management, aligning the procedures for project tracking in different domains), followed by the item $MPMOPT_8$ (the organization implemented a central IT interface to deliver standardized reporting tools for the governance of multiple projects: 5,32) and $MPMOPT_7$ (the organization established project control tools to avoid overlapping schedule: 5,21). We notice that these three highest score correspond to regulative dimension of multi-project management optimization. We also remark that only $MPMOPT_2$ (priority assignment leads to an effective communica-

Table 4. Results of ANOVA item-by-item application

Item	Average score Public institutions sample (n=100)	Average score Private organizations sample (n=100)	F Test (Fisher)	Sig. level
$MPMOPT_1$	**5,02**	**5,96**	21,258	0,002
$MPMOPT_2$	**4,62**	**6,23**	21,203	0,000
$MPMOPT_3$	**5,02**	**6,34**	23,106	0,001
$MPMOPT_4$	**5,10**	**5,09**	20,348	0,002
$MPMOPT_5$	**5,14**	**6,78**	26,685	0,000
$MPMOPT_6$	**5,92**	**5,29**	35,416	0,001
$MPMOPT_7$	**5,21**	**5,62**	21,221	0,003
$MPMOPT_8$	**5,32**	**5,11**	22,816	0,001
$MPMOPT_9$	**5,18**	**5,08**	21,912	0,001
$MPMOPT_{10}$	**5,12**	**5,29**	23,068	0,000

tion flow among project managers from your institution) is under the threshold 5.

In the case of private organizations, the highest score (6,78) was assigned to the item $MPMOPT_5$ (the organization established a balance between the freedom of project managers in the process of administrating their projects and the internal regulations and procedures to foster the collaborative learning), followed by the item $MPMOPT_3$ (the organization introduced Project Management governance mechanisms to facilitate the interactions among the actors of the multiple projects network) and $MPMOPT_2$ (priority assignment leads to an effective communication flow among project managers from your institution: 6,23). We notice that these three highest score correspond to relational dimension of multi-project management optimization.

It is also proved that there is no significant difference between the project managers' answers from both samples in what concerns the item 4 (the organization implemented a central IT interface to make the interactions of project managers more effective and to avoid a competition between projects: 5,10 in public institutions versus 5,09 in private organizations).

To identify the multi-project management optimization (MPMOPT) dimensions that provide the highest contributions to financial stability and organizational learning, four linear regression analyses were conducted (two in each of the public institution and privately owned companies samples) with financial stability and organizational learning as the dependent variables and the two dimensions of multi-project management optimization (relational and regulative) as the independent variables.

Tables 5 and 6 outline the results for public institutions sample. For the first regression with financial stability as the dependent variable (Table 5), the adjusted R-square was 0.768, which indicates that the two dimensions related to multi-project management optimization explained 76,8% of the variation in financial stability. The two dimensions related to multi-project management optimization (MPMOPT) highlights a significant effect on financial stability; in order of importance, these were:

- MPMOPT regulative dimension (β=0,685);
- MPMOPT relational dimension (β=0,586).

Remaining in the context of public institutions sample, for the second regression with organizational learning as the dependent variable (Table 6), the adjusted R-square was 0.396, which indicates that the two dimensions related to multi-project management

Table 5. Regression analysis with financial stability as dependent variable (public institutions sample)

	Unstandardized coefficients	Standard error	Standardized coefficients (β)	T test	Sig. level
MPMOPT relational dimension	0,529	0,042	0,586	11,282	0,001
MPMOPT regulative dimension	0,728	0,058	0,685	15,164	0,001
Adjusted R-square = 0.768; F = 142.311; Sig. = 0.001					

Table 6. Regression analysis with organizational learning as dependent variable (public institutions sample)

	Unstandardized coefficients	Standard error	Standardized coefficients (β)	T test	Sig. level
MPMOPT relational dimension	0.319	0.069	0.282	8.173	0.001
MPMOPT regulative dimension	0.293	0.073	0.341	10.182	0.001
Adjusted R-square = 0.396; F = 118,317; Sig. = 0.001					

optimization explained 39,6% of the variation in organizational learning. The two dimensions related to multi-project management optimization (MPMOPT) highlights a lower effect on organizational learning; in order of importance, these were:

- MPMOPT regulative dimension (β=0,341);
- MPMOPT relational dimension (β=0,282).

Tables 7 and 8 reveal the results for private organizations sample. For the first regression with financial stability as the dependent variable (Table 7), the adjusted R-square was 0.695, which indicates that the two dimensions related to multi-project management optimization explained 69,5% of the variation in financial stability. The two dimensions related to multi-project management optimization (MPMOPT) highlights a significant effect on financial stability; in order of importance, these were:

- MPMOPT relational dimension (β=0.711);
- MPMOPT regulative dimension (β=0.622).

The second regression in the private organizations, with organizational learning as the dependent variable (Table 8), outline the value of adjusted R-square (0.628), which indicates that the two dimensions related to multi-project management optimization explained 62,8% of the variation in organizational learning. The two dimensions related to multi-project management optimization (MPMOPT) highlights a significant effect on financial stability; in order of importance, these were:

- MPMOPT relational dimension (β=0.805);
- MPMOPT regulative dimension (β=0.583).

These results reflect clear differences between Romanian public institutions and privately owned companies regarding the issues of multi-project management optimization that provide financial stability and organizational learning. While MPMOPT relational dimension is primordial in the private organizations, being the predictor of organizational learning in the field of simultaneous projects, MPMOPT regulative dimension proved to be essential in the case of public institutions, being the predictor of financial stability.

5. Conclusions, managerial implications, limitations and further research

The objective of this research was to identify key success factors in managing multiple projects within Romanian public institutions and privately owned companies. The framework focused on the predictors financial stability, respectively organizational learning, was tested empirically. The key success factors were built upon the perceptions of project managers from both samples regarding

Table 7. Regression analysis with financial stability as dependent variable (private organizations sample)

	Unstandardized coefficients	Standard error	Standardized coefficients (β)	T test	Sig. level
MPMOPT relational dimension	0.682	0.031	0.711	14,263	0.001
MPMOPT regulative dimension	0.701	0.038	0.622	16,118	0.001
Adjusted R-square = 0.695; F = 112,962; Sig. = 0.001					

Table 8. Regression analysis with organizational learning as dependent variable (private organizations sample)

	Unstandardized coefficients	Standard error	Standardized coefficients (β)	T test	Sig. level
MPMOPT relational dimension	0.724	0.019	0.805	16.132	0.001
MPMOPT regulative dimension	0.474	0.023	0.583	14.137	0.001
Adjusted R-square = 0.628; F = 128,310; Sig. = 0.001					

the relational and regulative dimensions of multi-project management optimization.

Most of the findings of this study are aligned with prior studies representing relevant body of knowledge in managing multi-project contexts, revealing a stronger project management strategic focus of public institutions on financial stability, whilst private organizations' strategic focal point is on learning from past insights.

The theoretical contribution of this research lies primarily in the fact that the study sheds light on factors that are crucial for financial stability, respectively organizational learning, influencing the quality of decision making, specifically in a multiple project environment, being in line with the findings reported by Caniels and Bakens (2012).

The results of this study provide valuable insights into project management practices in contrasting types of organizations: public vs. private organizations, with totally different organizational cultures. Furthermore, the findings serve as grounds for further qualitative research on implementing EU projects in a multi-project context. In addition, the results of the study can be applied to the development of strategic guides, able to change public institution managers' mind-sets, while operating in multi-project environments.

The findings of this study provide a useful decision-making support for managers from both private and public organizations, in order to better understand the degree to which multiple project management practices can be optimized to better tailor to stakeholders' needs, and to identify the dimensions of MPMOPT that determine financial stability and organizational learning in each type of organization.

Finally, this research encourages practitioners from both Romanian public and private organizations to strengthen their capabilities regarding multiple project management and to strive to continue their efforts to obtain top management support, considered a key enabler of multiple project management effectiveness by Elbanna (2013).

The most significant limitation of this study is the use of a convenience sample. The results may therefore not be representative of the perceptions of the whole population of project managers from Romanian public and private organizations. Further research should be conducted to validate the results of our study by using larger samples.

Future studies, based on the current research framework, should be replicated in other countries, as different cultural, social and economic environments will certainly lead to significant gaps in what concern project managers' perceptions on the improvement of simultaneous EU funded projects practices. Another research avenue should be the application of QCA (Qualitative Comparative Analysis) method on the research samples used in this study, to explore alternative configurations of causal conditions which can lead to financial stability, respectively organizational learning.

References:

Bouckaert, G., Nakrošis, V., & Nemec, J. (2011). Public administration and management reforms in CEE: Main trajectories and results. *NISPAcee Journal of Public Administration and Policy, 4*(1), 9-29.

Bretschneider, S. (1990). Management information systems in public and private organizations: An empirical test. *Public Administration Review, 50*(5), 536-545.

Caniels, M. C., & Bakens, R. J. (2012). The effects of Project Management Information Systems on decision making in a multi project environment. *International Journal of Project Management, 30*(2), 162-175.

Cats-Baril, W., & Thompson, R. (1995). Managing information technology projects in the public sector. Public Administration Review, 55(6), 559-566.

Deac, V., & Vrincut, M. (2013). Qualitative techniques for project management. *Quality-Access to Success, 14*(133), 82-85.

Dooley, L., Lupton, G., & O'Sullivan, D. (2005). Multiple project management: A modern competitive necessity. *Journal of Manufacturing Technology Management, 16*(5), 466-482.

Dye, L. D., & Pennypacker, J. S. (2000, September). Project portfolio management and managing multiple projects: Two sides of the same coin? Paper presented at the Project Management Institute Annual Seminars & Symposium, Houston, TX.

Elbanna, A. (2013). Top management support in multiple-project environments: An in-practice view. *European Journal of Information Systems, 22*(3), 278-294.

Engwall, M., & Jerbrant, A. (2003). The resource allocation syndrome: The prime challenge of multi-project management? *International Journal of Project Management, 21*(6), 403-409.

Holmes, D. (2001). Egov: Ebusiness Strategies for Government. Naperville, IL: Nicholas Brealey.

Istrate, L., & Marian, L. (2012). Research on the use of project management in organizational culture change in public administration institutions. *Procedia Economics and Finance, 3*, 617-622.

Jałocha, B., Krane, H. P., Ekambaram, A., & Prawelska-Skrzypek, G. (2014). Key competences of public sector project managers. *Procedia-Social and Behavioral Sciences, 119*, 247-256.

Keiser, L. R. (2011). The impact of bureaucratic structure on government eligibility decisions. In Public Management Research Association Conference. Retrieved from https://pdfs.semanticscholar.org/061a/115b32213e7750551e08eb127d2fafd05fae.pdf

Kerzner, H. (2013). Project management: A systems approach to planning, scheduling, and controlling. Hoboken, NJ: John Wiley & Sons.

Klakegg, O. J., Williams, T., & Shiferaw, A. T. (2016). Taming the 'trolls': Major public projects in the making. *International Journal of Project Management, 34*(2), 282-296.

Ortansa, M. (2012). New public management elements in Romania's public services in the European context. *Annals of the University of Oradea Economic Sciences, 1*, 115-120.

Purvis, R. L., Zagenczyk, T. J., & McCray, G. E. (2015). What's in it for me? Using expectancy theory and climate to explain stakeholder participation, its direction and intensity. *International Journal of Project Management, 33*(1), 3-14.

Rosacker, K. M., & Olson, D. L. (2008). Public sector information system critical success factors. *Transforming Government: People, Process and Policy, 2*(1), 60-70.

Tsaturyan, T., & Muller, R. (2015). Integration and governance of multiple project management offices (PMOs) at large organizations. *International Journal of Project Management, 33*(5), 1098-1110.

Turner, R., Ledwith, A., & Kelly, J. (2010). Project management in small to medium-sized enterprises: Matching processes to the nature of the firm. *International Journal of Project Management, 28*(8), 744-755.

8

Can Monetary Policy drive economic growth? Empirical evidence from Tanzania

Enock Nyorekwa Twinoburyo[1], Nicholas M Odhiambo[1]

ABSTRACT The role of monetary policy in promoting economic growth remains empirically an open research question. This paper attempts to bridge the knowledge gap by investigating the impact of monetary policy on economic growth in Tanzania during the period from 1975 to 2013, using the autoregressive distributed lag (ARDL) bounds-testing approach. To our knowledge, this study may be the first of its kind to examine in detail this nexus in Tanzania. The study uses two proxies of monetary policy, namely, money supply and interest rate, to examine this linkage. The empirical results of this study reveal no impact of monetary policy on economic growth in the long term – irrespective of the proxy used to measure monetary policy. However, the short-term results confirm the existence of monetary policy neutrality – but only when the interest rate is used as a proxy for monetary policy. When money supply is used to measure monetary policy, a negative relationship between monetary policy and economic growth is found to predominate. The study findings suggest that monetary policy may not be a panacea for economic growth in Tanzania.

KEY WORDS: Monetary policy, economic growth, interest rate, money supply

[1] University of South Africa, South Africa

1. Introduction

Economic growth is traditionally believed to be driven by a wide range of factors, mainly by primary factors such as capital accumulation, growth in labor participation, advancement of knowledge, and technological progress (see, among others, Anyanwu, 2014; Barro & Sala-i-Martin, 1995; Levine & Renelt, 1992; Mankiw & Taylor, 2007). However, the primary factors are believed to be affected by other factors, including the policy environment (Smith, 2004). Economic growth is also largely attributed to real shocks that are linked to technological progress and cannot be effectively offset by monetary policy (Lucas, 2003). This postulation is supported by empirical evidence suggesting that monetary policy has a limited role in driving economic growth, particularly in the long term (Arestis, 2007; Asongu, 2014; Fontana & Palacio-Vera, 2007). The results of the both theoretical and empirical literature on the role of monetary policy instruments in stimulating economic growth are not universally generalizable and remain variant, inconsistent, and inconclusive (see, among others, Amarasekara, 2009; Dele, 2007; White, 2013).

The notion of monetary policy promoting economic growth by maintaining price stability has garnered increasing theoretical and empirical consensus particularly in the short term (Fontana & Palacio-Vera, 2007;

Correspondence concerning this article should be addressed to: **Enock Nyorekwa Twinoburyo**, University of South Africa - Department of Economics, P.O Box 392, Pretoria 0003, Pretoria, South Africa. E-mail: etwinon@gmail.com

Mester, 2015). This view is also enshrined in the Bank of Tanzania Act, 1966. In recent practice, a growing number of central banks have focused on inflation targeting to indirectly spur higher growth rates (Heintz & Ndikumana, 2010). While the literature on the linkage between monetary policy and economic growth through the promotion of price stability is wide ranging, empirical research questions continue to abound (Lacker, 2014; Papademos, 2003).

On the one hand, monetary policy yielding low and stable inflation is believed to spur economic growth, mainly in the short term (Fontana & Palacio-Vera, 2007; Papademos, 2003; Yilmazkuday, 2013). Poor monetary policies associated with high and volatile inflationary tendencies distort the allocation of productive resources, eventually harming economic growth in the long term (see, among others, Barro, 1997; Fischer, 1993; Hossain, 2014). On the other hand, some empirical studies discount the negative relationship between inflation and economic growth (Levine & Renelt, 1992; McCandless & Weber, 1995). Monetary policy actions driving steady and stable inflation tend to have a depressing effect on economic growth, resulting in a sacrifice ratio (Dornbusch, Fischer & Startz, 2012; Mankiw, 2010). Broadly, countercyclical monetary policy can be counterproductive.

Uncertainty about the effect of monetary policy on economic growth, particularly in developing economies, continues to prevail (Berg, Charry, Portillo & Vlcek, 2013; Papademos, 2003). Some studies suggest that a monetary policy impetus to spur growth is likely to be inflationary, having a countervailing effect (Issing, 2001). The recent surge of non-conventional monetary policy in the wake of the global crisis of 2008 highlights the limited role of conventional monetary policy.

The link between monetary policy, inflation and economic growth has been found to be weak, particularly in developing countries (Al-Mashat & Billmeier, 2007; Mishra, Montiel & Spilimbergo, 2010; Monteil, Adam & O'Conell, 2012). In addition, some studies confirm a weakening relationship between money supply and policy objectives (International Monetary Fund [IMF], 2014; White, 2013). In some instances, the appropriateness and relevance of monetary policy has been questioned, particularly for some developing countries with large informal sectors, a poorly integrated financial sector, and low financial development and where the fiscal policy plays the dominant role in the economy (Weeks, 2010).

Against this backdrop, the aim of this paper is to empirically investigate what monetary policy can or cannot do in relation to driving economic growth in Tanzania, in both the short and long terms – a subject that has received very limited attention in scholarly work on Tanzania. The article adopts two monetary policy variables of money supply in tandem with monetarist theory and short-term interest rates premised on the Keynesian theory. The paper also includes inflation as one of the variables in the growth equation to capture the indirect impact of monetary policy on economic growth by maintaining price stability.

This paper also makes an additional contribution by employing the superior autoregressive distributed lag (ARDL) bounds testing approach by Pesaran, Shin & Smith (2001) in an attempt to establish the effect of monetary policy on economic growth in Tanzania. The rest of the paper is organized as follows: Section 2 gives an overview of monetary policy reform and economic performance in Tanzania, while Section 3 presents the empirical literature review. The empirical model and estimation methods are presented in Section 4. Section 5 presents the empirical results and discussion, while Section 6 provides the conclusion.

2. Monetary Policy Reform and Economic Performance in Tanzania: An Overview

The Bank of Tanzania (BoT) was set up in June 1966, becoming a cornerstone for monetary policy reform in Tanzania (Bank of Tanzania [BoT], 2011). The performance of the economy has, since then, been mixed owing to the varying economic policies over the corresponding period. The most resolute macro-economic performance in the form of sound economic growth and low inflation is traced back to the 1990s and in part explained by macro-economic stabilization and economic reforms that commenced in the late 1980s (BoT, 2011; Ndulu, 1987).

The current economic structure remains consistent with the characteristics of low-income countries, characterized by high dependency on the primary sectors of agriculture and mining. The economy is largely service-sector driven – accounting for 43.5% of GDP

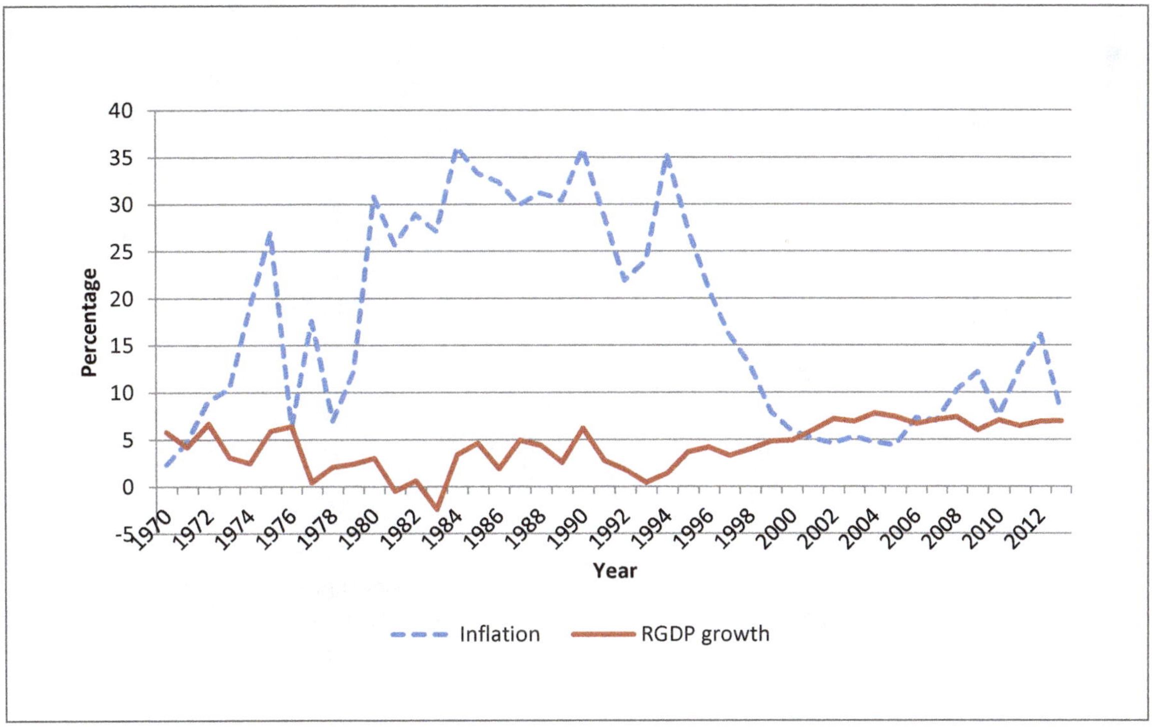

Figure 1. Inflation and economic growth performance (1970-2013)
Source: Adapted from "Publications and Statistics" by Bank of Tanzania (2014). Available at https://www.bot.go.tz/Publications/PublicationsAndStatistics.asp#Statistics

in 2014 – but also remains largely rural-based, with a rural population of 70%. Trade volumes as a share of GDP remain low at 49.4% of GDP in 2014 (World Bank, 2015).

In 1967, the Arusha Declaration was put in place, putting emphasis on state ownership, nationalization of foreign-owned enterprises, and control of production by the state (Nyerere, 1977). This laid the foundation for the subsequent administrative control of all interest and exchange rates by government throughout the 1970s. Eventually, all major economic activities, including trade and credit, were controlled by government following the establishment of the confinement policy in 1972 (Ndulu, 1987). Fiscal dominance increased, characterized by heightened government borrowing and financial repression (BoT, 2011).

While Tanzania commenced discussions of macroeconomic adjustment reforms in the 1980s, these did not reach full realization until the 1990s. Socioeconomic policies characterized by sizeable government controls and domestic borrowing prevailed until 1986, when an economic recovery program aimed at market-driven economic reforms through gradual deregulation of segments of the economy was adopted (Maehle, Teferra & Khachatryan, 2013; Ndulu, 1987). As a result, the real GDP growth rates that averaged over 6% per annum in the late 1960s decelerated in the 1970s, finally reaching negatives in the early 1980s (Maehle et al., 2013). For the corresponding period, inflation persisted in double digits but dwindled in a deflation in the early 1980s, consistent with the subdued growth and recessionary trend (BoT, 2011; Maehle et al., 2013). The associated economic performance in the form of a scissor co-movement between inflation and economic growth for the period from the mid-1970s to 2013 is also shown in Figure 1.

In 1986, Tanzania adopted the IMF- and World Bank-led economic recovery program, eventually guiding the actual transitioning from directly controlled monetary policy to indirect (market-driven) monetary

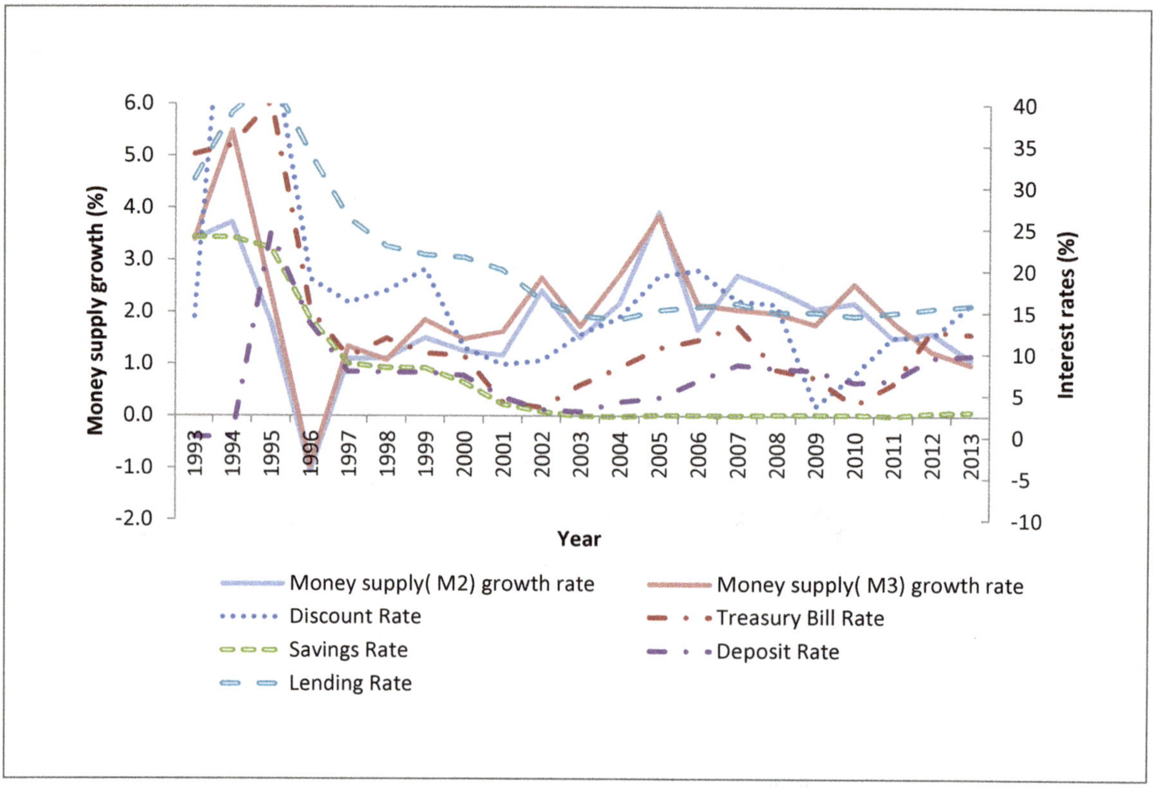

Figure 2. Monetary growth and interest rate structure (1993-2013)
Source: Adapted from "Publications and Statistics" by Bank of Tanzania (2014). Available at https://www.bot.go.tz/Publications/PublicationsAndStatistics.asp#Statistics

policy in the early 1990s (Nord et al., 2009). The mainstream economic reforms included, inter alia, the adoption of a monetary-targeting regime in 1993, the liberalization of the banking sector in 1991, the eventual change of the exchange rate to a free floating regime in 1996, and the introduction of government securities (Treasury bills and bonds) in the 1990s and longer-term bonds of five, seven and ten years in 2002 (BoT, 2011; Nord et al., 2009). These reforms were supported by legislative reforms, including the amendment of the BoT Act in 1995, making price stability its primary objective (BoT, 2011). Further amendments to the BoT Act were undertaken in 2006, enriching the Central Bank's independence (Nord et al., 2009). The Government of Tanzania only recently partially liberalized its capital account of the balance of payments, allowing only transactions to East African Community (EAC) residents, while it committed to extending the liberalization to the rest of the world (IMF, 2016). However, Tanzania will retain less restrictive prudential rules, including minimum holding periods for debt inflows and participation in short-term papers (IMF, 2016).

The post-1990 reforms arguably created a supportive environment for strong macro-economic performance in terms of reducing inflation rates and encouraging robust economic growth (also see Figure 1). The period 1993-2013 was associated with astounding nominal monetary growth per annum, as shown in Figure 2. The interest structure, also shown in Figure 2, remains characterized by relatively high rates and spreads.

3. Empirical Literature Review

Buigut (2009), using recursive vector autoregression (VAR) on annual data from 1984 to 2005, examined monetary transmission mechanisms in Uganda, Kenya, and Tanzania. The results revealed that an interest rate (monetary policy variable) shock has no effect on inflation and economic growth in all three countries.

Using structural VAR on monthly data from January 2002 to September 2010 to investigate monetary transmission mechanisms in Tanzania, Monteil et al. (2012) found that a positive shock to reserve money has no effect on output. The results are consistent with Davoodi, Dixit & Pinter (2013), who applied a structural VAR, Bayesian VAR, and factor- augmented VAR to monthly data from 2000 to 2010 for all EAC countries, namely, Uganda, Kenya, Tanzania, Rwanda, and Burundi. Their results, however, reveal that a negative shock to interest rates has a significant, positive effect on output in Kenya, Burundi, and Rwanda, while a positive shock to reserve money increases output significantly in Uganda, Rwanda, and Burundi.

Berg et al. (2013) adopted a Romer and Romer (1989) narrative approach with a focus on the contractionary monetary policy undertaken by four members of the East African Community - Kenya, Uganda, Tanzania, and Rwanda - in 2011. Their main finding is that the effect of monetary policy on output in Tanzania is limited. The effects of monetary policy on output are, however, more pronounced in Kenya and Uganda, where more forward-looking monetary policy frameworks are in place.

The limited literature that exists on Tanzania confirms no role of monetary policy in boosting economic growth (Berg et al., 2013). These results are consistent with some other country studies. Mutoti (2006), employing a cointegrated structural VAR, showed that the impact of money supply shocks on Zambia's output was minor and temporary.

Maturu et al. (2010), applying the recursive and structural VAR on Kenya's quarterly data from the first quarter of 2000 to the second quarter of 2010, indicated that an expansionary monetary policy (positive shock to M3) has no effect on output.

Lashkary and Kashani (2011), using econometric regression model analysis on annual data for Iran from 1959 to 2008, revealed no impact of monetary policy (money volume) on economic growth. Additionally, Mutuku and Koech (2014), using recursive VAR on Kenyan data from 1997 to 2010, revealed that money supply and short-term interest rates (monetary policy variables) had no effect on output.

Mugume (2011), using a non-recursive VAR on Uganda's quarterly data from the first quarter of 1999 to the first quarter of 2009, found that a positive shock to interest rates (contractionary monetary policy) only significantly drives output up to 2 quarters. A shock to money supply (M2) is found to have no effect on output.

However, there are studies that offer alternative views and results, some suggesting a positive impact of monetary policy on economic growth. Khabo and Harmse (2005) applied ordinary least squares (OLS) methodology to annual data series from 1960 to 1997 and established that money supply (M3) had a significant, positive impact on economic growth in South Africa. Similar results were obtained by Ali *et al.* (2008) using an ARDL bounds test on South Asian countries, based on annual data from 1990 to 2007.

Additionally, studies by Nouri and Samimi (2011) and Ogunmuyiwa and Ekone (2010) both using OLS methodology, respectively found a positive impact of money supply on economic growth in Nigeria and Iran. Similar results were obtained by Jawaid, Quadri & Ali (2011) and Senbet (2011), respectively for Pakistan and the United States of America. The findings are corroborated by the more recent studies of Onyeiwu (2012), Kareem, Afolabi, Raheem & Bashir (2013), Havi and Enu (2014).

Applying both recursive and non-recursive structural VAR to Kenya's monthly data from 1997 to 2005, Cheng (2006) found that a positive shock to interest rates led to a short-term rise in output, contrary to theoretical expectation. Applying recursive VAR and semi-structural VAR methodology to monthly data for Sri Lanka for the period from 1978 to 2005, Amarasekara (2009) revealed that a positive shock on interest rates reduced economic growth. Similar findings were found in the study by Vinayagathasan (2013) using a structural VAR model and monthly data for Sri Lanka covering the period from January 1978 to December 2011.

4. Empirical Model Specification and Estimation Methods

4.1 Empirical Model

The empirical growth literature is wide-ranging, buttressed by both neoclassical and endogenous growth models (Anyanwu, 2014; Levine & Renelt, 1992; Mansouri, 2005). This paper narrows the scope, drawing from the St Louis equation and McCallum (1991) on the role of monetary policy. The selected set of control variables is supported by the aggregate production empirical models used in the literature (Anyanwu, 2014). This paper specifies a modified equation for economic growth including two independent proxies for monetary policy - money supply and short-term interest rates - to capture the effect of monetary policy on economic growth. In addition, capital stock, trade openness, inflation, and exchange rate are included as control variables. The modified equation is presented in equation 1.

$$RGDP_t = C + \varphi RM2_t + \lambda IR_t + \alpha RK_t + \theta REXC_t + \gamma TO_t + + \delta INF_t + \varepsilon_t \qquad (1)$$

where RGDP is real gross domestic product, a proxy for economic growth; M2 is real money supply; IR is the interest rate; RK is capital stock; REXC is the real exchange rate; TO is trade openness; and INF is inflation. All variables are expressed in natural logarithm, except interest rates.

In this paper, real GDP is used as a proxy for economic growth, as has been extensively done in the literature (Nogueira, 2009). The monetary policy variables of money supply (measured by M2) and interest rates (proxied by the 3-month Treasury bill rate) are adopted owing to their empirical use in a wide range of studies (Christiano, Eichenbaum, & Evans, 1999; Ivrendi & Yildirim, 2013). Expansionary monetary policy (increase in money supply or reduction in interest rates) is expected to spur growth.

Capital stock, proxied by real gross fixed capital formation, is one the fundamental engines of economic growth, and its effects are expected to be positive (Fosu & Magnus, 2006; Havi & Enu, 2014; Kohpaiboon, 2003). Trade openness, measured by the sum of exports and imports to GDP, is believed to have a positive and statistically significant impact on economic growth (Fosu & Magnus, 2006; Sakyi, 2011).

Low and stable inflation is believed to create a favorable environment for economic growth, while volatile and high inflation (beyond a threshold level) deters economic growth (Khan & Senhadji, 2001; Pollin & Zhu, 2006; Yilmazkuday, 2013). Real exchange rate has garnered ground in research as a proxy for external competitiveness. While the findings are inconclusive, the majority support a positive relationship between real exchange rate and economic growth (Haddad & Pancaro, 2010; Rodrik, 2008).

4.2 Estimation Methodology

To investigate the long-term and short-term relationships between monetary policy and economic growth, this paper adopts the approach of Pesaran *et al.* (2001) to cointegration, known as autoregressive distributed lag (ARDL). This approach has distinct advantages over other cointegration procedures proposed by Engle and Granger (1987) and Johansen and Juselius (1990). Following the establishment of the order of the ARDL model, the single reduced equation can be estimated by OLS. This approach does not require the order of integration of the variables to be the same, implying that the bounds test works well whether underlying regressors are purely $I(0)$, purely $I(1)$, fractionally integrated, or mutually co-integrated. In addition, this technique is suitable for small or finite sample size and provides unbiased estimates of the long-term model even when there is endogeneity in some of the explanatory variables (see Harris & Sollis, 2003).

The ARDL bounds testing procedure involves two stages. First, the ARDL model of interest, specified in equation 2, is estimated by using the OLS to test for the existence of a long-term relationship among the relevant variables. An F-test for the joint significance of the lagged levels of the variables is performed to test the null hypothesis of no long-term relationship among the variables in the equation. If the F-statistic is above the upper critical value, the null hypothesis of no long-term relationship can be rejected, irrespective of the orders of integration of the time series. Conversely, if the test statistic falls below the lower critical value, then the null hypothesis cannot be rejected. However, if the statistic falls between the upper and the lower critical values, then the result is inconclusive.

The second stage involves the estimation of the long-term and short-term coefficients once the long-term relationship or cointegration has been established. The optimal order of the variables is obtained using the Schwarz-Bayesian criterion (SBC) or the Akaike information criterion (AIC).

Based on equation 1, the ARDL-bounds model used in this study can be expressed as follows:

$$\Delta RGDP_t = \delta_0 + \sum_{i=1}^{n}\delta_{1i}\,\Delta RGDP_{t-i} + \sum_{i=0}^{n}\delta_{2i}\,\Delta M2_{t-i} +$$
$$+\sum_{i=0}^{n}\delta_{3i}\,\Delta IR_{t-i} + \sum_{i=0}^{n}\delta_{4i}\,\Delta RK_{t-i} + \sum_{i=0}^{n}\delta_{5i}\,\Delta REXC_{t-i} +$$
$$+\sum_{i=0}^{n}\delta_{6i}\,\Delta TO_{t-i} + \sum_{i=0}^{n}\delta_{7i}\,\Delta INF_{t-i} + \alpha_1 RGDP_{t-i} + \alpha_2 M2_{t-i} +$$
$$+\ \alpha_3 IR_{t-i} + \alpha_2 RK_{t-i} + \alpha_5 REXC_{t-i} + \alpha_6 TO_{t-i} +$$
$$+\ \alpha_7 INF_{t-i} + \vartheta_t \qquad (2)$$

where Δ denotes the first difference operator; δ_0 is the drift component; n is the lag length; ϑ_t is the white noise residuals; δ_{1i} - δ_{7i} are the coefficients of short-term dynamics; and $\alpha_1 - \alpha_6$ represent the long-term relationship. The variables are as defined in equation 1. All variables except interest rates are expressed in natural logarithm.

The corresponding general error-correction model (ECM) is formulated as follows:

$$\Delta RGDP_t = \delta_0 + \sum_{i=1}^{n}\delta_{1i}\,\Delta RGDP_{t-i} + \sum_{i=0}^{n}\delta_{2i}\,\Delta M2_{t-i} +$$
$$+\sum_{i=0}^{n}\delta_{3i}\,\Delta IR_{t-i} + \sum_{i=0}^{n}\delta_{4i}\,\Delta RK_{t-i} + \sum_{i=0}^{n}\delta_{5i}\,\Delta REXC_{t-i} +$$
$$+\sum_{i=0}^{n}\delta_{6i}\,\Delta TO_{t-i} + \sum_{i=0}^{n}\delta_{7i}\,\Delta INF_{t-i} + \gamma_1 ECM_{t-1} + \tau_t \qquad (3)$$

where ECM is the error correction term, which captures the correction of the long-term economic growth model to its steady state position in case of any short term disturbances. The ECM is expected to be negative and statistically significant. τ_t is the white noise error term.

4.2.1 Data Sources

The Tanzania dataset used in this study covers the period, 1975-2013. The real values of GDP, gross fixed capital formation, and money supply (M2) were obtained by dividing them by the Tanzania Consumer Price Index (CPI). The Tanzania CPI and the US CPI were obtained from the International Financial Statistics (IFS). Nominal values of GDP and money supply (M2) were obtained from the Bank of Tanzania.

The nominal exchange rate obtained from the Bank of Tanzania is multiplied by the ratio of the US CPI to the domestic CPI to obtain the real exchange rate. Nominal values of M2, inflation rate, nominal Treasury bill rate for Tanzania (1993 to 2013), and export and import values were sourced from the Bank of Tanzania. The 1975-1993 set of Treasury bill rate series was obtained from the BoT annual publications and IFS books (various issues). Nominal gross fixed capital formation was obtained from the World Bank (2015).

4.3 Empirical Analysis

4.3.1 Unit root tests

Owing to the weaknesses of the traditional augmented Dickey-Fuller (ADF) test (Dickey and Fuller, 1979), particularly for small samples, this paper adopts the Dickey-Fuller - generalized least squares (DF-GLS) de-trending test proposed by Elliot, Rothenberg & Stock (1996). In addition, the Phillips-Perron (PP) unit root test by Phillips and Perron (1988) is also used.

The graphical representation of the data series suggests that the variables real GDP, real gross fixed capital formation, and consumer price index are trend stationary, while trade openness, real Treasury bill rate, and real exchange rate are difference stationary. The DF-GLS and the Phillips-Perron unit root tests presented in Table 1 include the constant and trend for the trend stationary variables and only the constant for the difference stationary variables. Both tests confirm the absence of $I(2)$ and beyond. Both tests confirm that only the Treasury bill rate is an $I(0)$, while the rest are $I(1)$.

4.3.2 ARDL-Bounds Testing Approach

Table 2 presents the bounds test for the existence of a long-term relationship among real GDP, money supply, interest rates (Treasury bill rate), capital (investment), real exchange rate, trade openness, and inflation.

The computed F-statistic is 4.63, as shown in Table 2, and is statistically significant at the 1% significance level, implying that these variables have a long-term relationship among themselves. Following the confirmation of the existence of a long-term relationship between the variables in the model, the long-term and short-term models were derived using SBC due to the superior results relative to the AIC. The selected

Table 1. Stationarity (unit root) tests

Variable	Dickey-Fuller Generalized Least Square (DF-GLS)				Phillips-Perron test			
	Stationarity of Variables in levels		Stationarity of Variables in difference		Stationarity of Variables in levels		Stationarity of Variables in difference	
	Constant	with trend	Constant	with trend	Constant	with trend	Constant	with trend
RGDP	-	-1.653	-	-4.343***	-	-1.955	-	-4.642***
RM2	-	-2.591	-	-3.995**	-	-1.311	-	-4.218**
IR	-2.140**	-	-	-	-2.674*	-	-	-
RK	-	-2.174	-	-4.148***	-	-1.626	-	-4.423***
REXC	-1.303	-	-5.132***	-	-1.573	-	-5.083***	-
TO	-1.497	-	-4.337***	-	-1.964	-	-4.783***	-
INF	-	-1.065	-	-3.194**	-	-0.223		-3.571**

Note: Note: for all p-values: *** 1% significance level; ** 5% significance level; * 10% significance level.

Table 2. ARDL bounds test results

Dependent Variable	**Function**					**F-test Statistics**
LRGDP	F(RGDP|RM2,IR,RK,REXC,TOP,INF)					4.63***
Asymptotic Critical Values						
Pesaran *et al.* (2001), p.300. Table CI(III)	1%		5%		10%	
	I(0)	I(1)	I(0)	I(1)	I(0)	I(1)
	2.12	3.23	2.45	3.61	3.15	4.43

Note: *** denotes significance at the 1% level

ARDL model, based on the SBC criteria, is an ARDL model (1, 0, 1, 0, 2, 1, 2).

The long-term results reported in Panel A of Table 3 indicate that the coefficients of both monetary policy variables, i.e., interest rate and money supply, are statistically insignificant, suggesting long-term monetary policy neutrality. The long-term neutrality of monetary policy is backed by a wide range of empirical findings (see, among others, Bullard, 1999; Nogueira, 2009; Monteil *et al.* 2012). The coefficient of capital is positive in the long term, consistent with the previous studies of Havi and Enu (2014) and Fosu and Magnus (2006). Additionally, the long-term effect of inflation is found to be positive, which is contrary to the *a priori* expectation of a negative sign. The long-term positive effect of inflation on economic growth is supported by empirical evidence from Malik and Chowdhury (2001).

As seen in Panel B of Table 3, the short-term effect of the interest rate monetary policy variable is insignifi-

Table 3. Results of ARDL model (1, 0,1,0,2,1,2)

Panel A: Long-term Coefficients - Dependent Variable is RGDP				
Regressor	Coefficient	Standard Error	T-Ratio	Probability
C	6.453***	2.219	2.908	0.008
RM2	-0.679	0.447	-1.518	0.143
IR	-0.002	0.003	-0.745	0.464
RK	0.640***	0.224	2.845	0.009
REXC	-0.308	0.312	-0.987	0.334
TO	0.512	0.355	1.442	0.163
INF	0.202***	0.072	2.806	0.010
Panel B: Short-term Coefficients - Dependent Variable is ΔRGDP				
ΔRM2	-0.205***	0.069	-2.940	0.007
ΔIR	0.001	0.781	1.507	0.143
ΔRK	0.193***	0.055	3.527	0.002
ΔREXC	0.163***	0.488	3.339	0.002
ΔREXC1	0.083*	0.041	2.036	0.052
ΔTO	-0.060	0.066	-0.900	0.376
ΔINF	-0.216	0.266	-0.811	0.424
ΔINF1	-0.513**	0.241	-2.130	0.042
ECM (-1)	-0.301**	0.117	-2.572	0.016

R-Squared	0.911	**R-Bar-Squared**	0.861
SE of Regression	0.017	**F-Stat F(9,27)**	26.155 (0.000)
Residual Sum of Squares	0.007	**DW statistic**	2.172
Akaike Info. Criterion	92.542	**Schwarz Bayesian Criterion**	81.266

Note: *** denotes significance at the 1% level

Table 4. ARDL-VECM model diagnostic tests

Test Statistics	**Results**
Serial Correlation	0.514 (0.473)
Functional Form	2.308 (0.129)
Normality	2.362 (0.307)
Heteroscedasticity	0.486 (0.486)

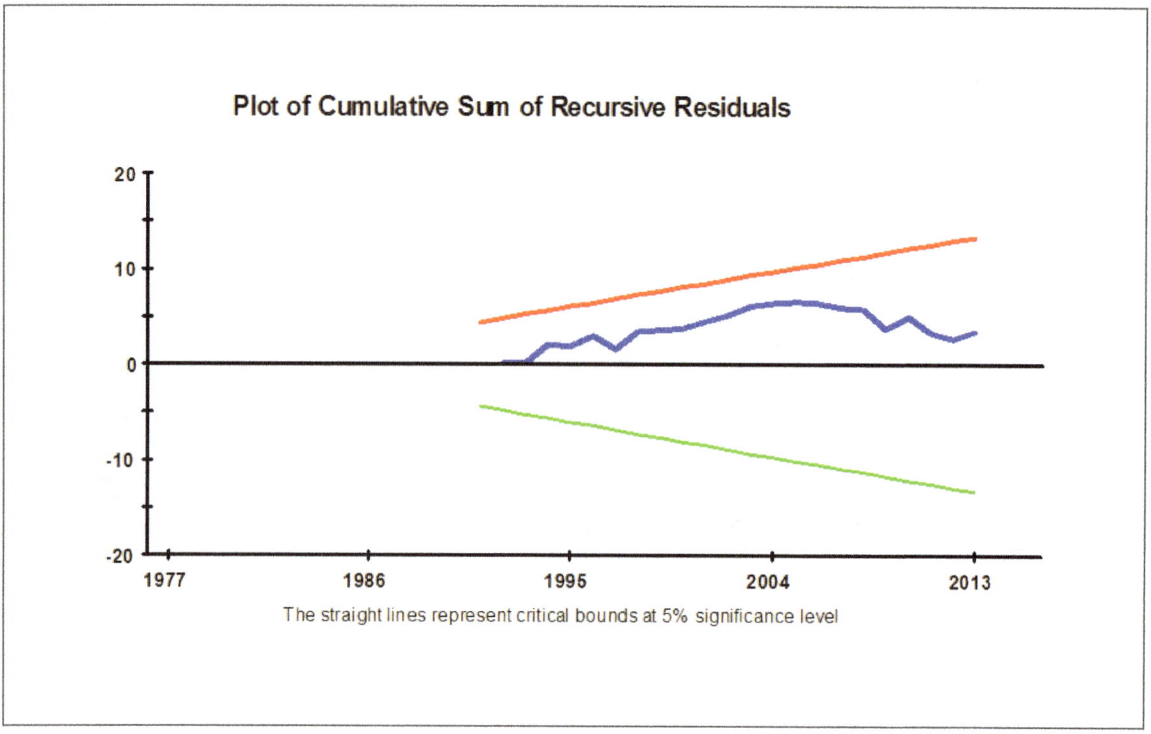

Figure 3. CUSUM

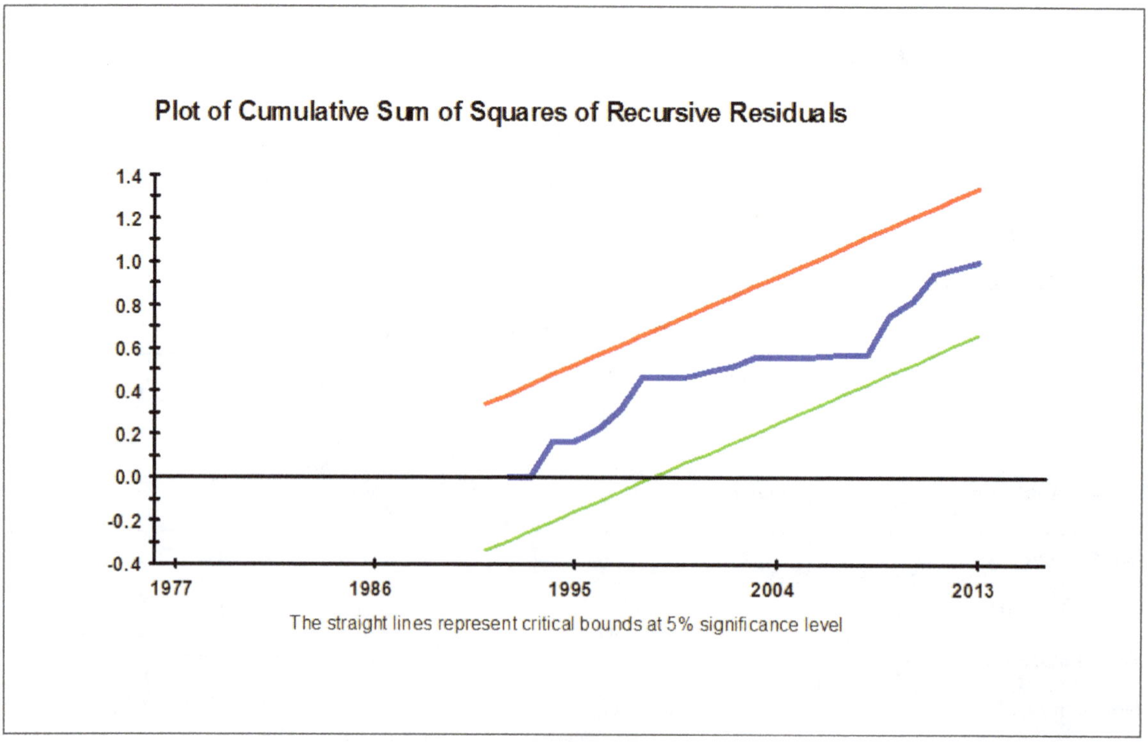

Figure 4. CUSUMQ

cant, while the coefficient of money supply is found to be negative and statistically significant, contrary to *a priori* expectation. While the short-term money supply's negative effect on economic growth was unexpected, a few studies have similar findings (Jawaid et al., 2011).

Additionally, in the short term, the coefficient of capital, real exchange rate and its lag are found to be positive and statistically significant. Unlike the long-term results, the coefficient of inflation is statistically insignificant, but its lag is found to have a negative and significant impact on economic growth. The coefficient of the ECM (-1) is -0.301 and is statistically significant at the 5% level. This implies that the disequilibrium occurring due to a shock is totally corrected in approximately 3 years and 4 months at a rate of approximately 30.1% per annum.

The regression for the underlying ARDL model fits well, as indicated by an R-squared of 91.1%. The results displayed in Table 4 show that the model passes the diagnostic tests of serial correlation, normality, functional form, and heteroscedasticity. The plots of the cumulative sum of recursive residuals (CUSUM) and the cumulative sum of squares of recursive residuals (CUSUMQ), reported respectively in Figures 3 and 4, are within the 5% critical lines, revealing that the model is stable and confirming the stability of the long-term coefficients of the regressors.

5. Conclusion

The role of monetary policy in promoting economic growth, both directly and indirectly, through maintenance of price stability, remains mixed and inconclusive. This paper empirically investigates what monetary policy can or cannot do in relation to driving economic growth in Tanzania, in both the short and long terms, a subject that has received very limited attention in scholarly work on Tanzania. Unlike the empirical studies on Tanzania that have relied mainly on VAR methodology, this paper uses the autoregressive distributed lag (ARDL) to examine this nexus. The results confirm long-term monetary policy neutrality – irrespectively of whether money supply or interest rate is used as a proxy for monetary policy. The short-term results, on the other hand, confirm the neutrality of monetary policy only when interest rate is used as a proxy for monetary policy. When money supply is used as a proxy for monetary policy, a negative effect of monetary policy on economic growth is found to prevail. There was no established impact of inflation on economic growth in the short term, discounting the conventional notion that monetary policy by attaining price stability would spur economic growth. The study findings also suggest that monetary policy may not be a panacea for economic growth in Tanzania. Overall, the results of the impact of monetary policy on economic growth in Tanzania may be explained by the nature of the financial structure, characterized by a low level of development, the banking sector dominance of the financial sector and the oligopolistic nature of the banking industry. Furthermore, investment is found to have a positive impact on economic growth both in the short term and in the long term. Therefore, the study recommends that measures to further promote both public and private investments should be put in place to stimulate economic growth.

References

Al-Mashat, R., & Billmeier, A. (2007, December). The monetary transmission mechanism in Egypt *(Working Paper* No. 07/285). International Monetary Fund. Retrieved from https://www.imf.org/external/pubs/ft/wp/2007/wp07285.pdf

Amarasekara, C. (2009). The impact of monetary policy on economic growth & inflation in Sri Lanka. *Staff Studies, 38,* 1-44. http://doi.org/10.4038/ss.v38i1.1220

Anyanwu, J. C. (2014). Factors affecting economic growth in Africa: Are there any lessons from China? *African Development Review, 26*(3), 468-493. https://doi.org/10.1111/1467-8268.12105

Arestis, P. (2007). What is the new consensus in macroeconomics? In P. Arestis (Ed.), Is there a new consensus in macroeconomics? (pp. 22-42). New York, NY: Palgrave Macmillan.

Asongu, S. A. (2014). A note on the long-run neutrality of monetary policy: New empirics. *European Economics Letters, 3*(1), 1-6. http://dx.doi.org/10.2139/ssrn.2493400

Bank of Tanzania. (2011, June). Tanzania mainland's 50 years of independence: A review of the role & functions of the Bank of Tanzania (1961-2011). Retrieved from https://www.bot.go.tz/Adverts/PressRelease/2011-Nov-04-PressRelease.pdf

Bank of Tanzania (2014). Publications and Statistics. Available at https://www.bot.go.tz/Publications/PublicationsAndStatistics.asp#Statistics

Barro, R. & Sala-i-Martin, X. (1995). *Economic growth.* New York, NY: McGraw-Hill.

Barro, R. J. (1997). *Determinants of economic growth: A cross-country empirical study.* Cambridge, MA: The MIT Press.

Berg, A., Charry, L., Portillo, R., & Vlcek, J. (2013, September). The monetary transmission mechanism in the Tropics: A Narrative approach (Working Paper No. 13/197). International Monetary Fund. Retrieved from https://www.imf.org/external/pubs/ft/wp/2013/wp13197.pdf

Buigut, S. (2009). Monetary policy transmission mechanism: Implications for the proposed East African Community (EAC) Monetary Union. Retrieved from https://pdfs.semanticscholar.org/7ad8/5292c2f547b0b75aff3dd639c3537646c0d7.pdf

Bullard, J. (1999). Testing long-run neutrality propositions: Lessons from the recent research. *Federal Reserve Bank of St. Louis Review, 81*(6), 57-78.

Cheng, K. C. (2006, December). A VAR analysis of Kenya's monetary policy transmission mechanism: How does the central bank's REPO rate affect the economy (Working Paper No. 06/300). International Monetary Fund. Retrieved from www.imf.org/external/pubs/ft/wp/2006/wp06300.pdf

Christiano, L., Eichenbaum, M., & Evans, C. (1999). Monetary policy shocks: What have we learned and to what end? In J. Taylor & M. Woodfoord (Ed.), Handbook of Macroeconomics (Vol. 1, pp. 65-148). Amsterdam: North Holland.

Davoodi, H., Dixit, S., & Pinter, G. (2013, February). Monetary transmission mechanism in the East African Community: An empirical investigation (Working Paper No. 13/39). International Monetary Fund. Retrieved from http://www.imf.org/external/pubs/ft/wp/2013/wp1339.pdf

Dele, B. E. (2007). Monetary policy & economic performance of West African Monetary zone countries. (MPRA Working Paper No. 4308). University Library of Munich, Germany. Retrieved from https://mpra.ub.uni-muenchen.de/4308/1/MPRA_paper_4308.pdf

Dickey, D. A., & Fuller, W. A. (1979). Distribution of the estimators for autoregressive time series with a unit root. *Journal of the American Statistical Association, 74*(366), 427–431. http://doi.org/10.2307/2286348

Dornbusch, R., Fischer, S. & Startz, R. (2012). *Macroeconomics* (10th ed.). New Delhi, Mcgraw Hill Education (India) Pvt. Ltd.

Elliot, G., Rothenberg, T., & Stock, J. (1996). Efficient tests for an autoregressive unit root. Econometrica, 64(4), 813-836. http://dx.doi.org/10.2307/2171846

Engle, R. F. & Granger, C. J. (1987). Cointegration and error-correction: Representation, estimation and testing. *Econometrica, 55*(2), 251-276. http://doi.org/10.2307/1913236

Fischer, S. (1993, December). The role of macroeconomic factors in growth (Working Paper No. 4565). National Bureau of Economic Research. Available at https://ssrn.com/abstract=227969

Fontana, G., & Palacio-Vera, A. (2007). Are long-run price stability and short-run output stabilisation all that monetary policy can aim for? *Metroeconomica, 58*(2), 269-298. https://doi.org/10.1111/j.1467-999X.2007.00268.x

Fosu, O. A. E., & Magnus, F. J. (2006). Bounds testing approach to cointegration: An examination of foreign direct investment trade and growth relationships. *American Journal of Applied Sciences, 3*(11), 2079-2085. https://doi.org/10.3844/ajassp.2006.2079.2085

Haddad, M. & Pancaro, M. (2010, June). Can real exchange rate undervaluation boost exports and growth in developing countries? Yes, but not for long. Washington, DC: The World Bank. Retrieved from http://siteresources.worldbank.org/INTPREMNET/Resources/EP20.pdf

Harris, R., & Sollis, R. (2003). *Applied time series modelling and forecasting.* West Sussex, UK: Wiley.

Havi, E. D. K., & Enu, P. (2014). The effect of fiscal policy and monetary policy on Ghana's economic growth: Which policy is more potent? *International Journal of Empirical Finance, 3*(2), 61-75.

Heintz, J., & Ndikumana, L. (2010). Is there a case for formal inflation targeting in Sub-Saharan Africa? *Journal of African Economies, 20*(2), 67–103. https://doi.org/10.1093/jae/ejq027

Hossain, A. A. (2014). Monetary policy, inflation and inflation volatility in Australia. *Journal of Post*

Keynesian Economics, 36(4), 745-780. http://doi.org/10.2753/PKE0160-3477360408

International Monetary Fund. (2014, April). Regional Economic Outlook. Sub-Saharian Africa. Fostering durable and inclusive growth. Washington, DC. Available at https://www.imf.org/en/Publications/REO/SSA/Issues/2017/02/01/Fostering-Durable-and-Inclusive-Growth

International Monetary Fund. (2016, February). Third review under the policy support instrument—press release; staff report; and statement by the executive director for United Republic of Tanzania. International Monetary Fund Country Report, No. 29. Washington, DC. Retrieved from https://www.imf.org/external/pubs/ft/scr/2016/cr1629.pdf

Issing, O. (2001). Why price stability. In A. Garcia-Herrero, V. Gaspar, L. Hoogduin, J. Morgan & B. Winkler (Eds.), Why price stability? (pp. 179-202). Frankfurt am Main: European Central Bank.

Ivrendi, M., & Yildirim, Z. (2013, December 9). Monetary policy shocks and macroeconomic variables: Evidence from fast growing emerging economies (Discussion Papers No. 2013-61), Kiel Institute for the World Economy. Retrieved from http://www.economics-ejournal.org/economics/discussion-papers/2013-61/file

Jawaid, S. T., Quadri, F. S., & Ali, N. (2011). Monetary-fiscal-trade policy and economic growth in Pakistan: Time series empirical investigation. *International Journal of Economics and Financial Issues, 1*(3), 133-138. Available at http://dergipark.gov.tr/download/article-file/362645

Johansen, S., & Juselius, K. (1990). Maximum likelihood estimation and inference on cointegration with applications to the demand for money. *Oxford Bulletin of Economics and Statistics, 52*(2), 169-210. http://dx.doi.org/10.1111/j.1468-0084.1990.mp52002003.x

Kareem, R. O., Afolabi, A. J., Raheem, K. A., & Bashir, N. O. (2013). Analysis of fiscal and monetary policies on economic growth: Evidence from Nigerian democracy. *Current Research Journal of Economic Theory, 5*(1), 11-19. Retrieved from http://www.maxwellsci.com/print/crjet/v5-11-19.pdf

Khabo, V., & Harmse, C. (2005). The impact of monetary policy on economic growth of a small open economy: The case of South Africa. *South African Journal of Economic and Management Sciences, 8*(3). https://doi.org/10.4102/sajems.v8i3.1201

Khan, M. S., & Senhadji, A. S. (2001). Threshold effects in the relationship between inflation and growth. *International Monetary Fund Staff Papers, 48*(1), 1–21. Retrieved from http://www.imf.org/External/Pubs/FT/staffp/2001/01a/pdf/khan.pdf

Kohpaiboon, A. (2003). Foreign trade regime and FDI-growth nexus: A case study of Thailand. *The Journal of Development Studies, 40*(2), 55-69. https://doi.org/10.1080/00220380412331293767

Lacker, M. J. (2014, February 24). Can monetary policy affect economic growth? [Podcast]. Retrieved from https://www.richmondfed.org/press_room/speeches/jeffrey_m_lacker/2016/lacker_speech_20160224

Lashkary, M., & Kashani, H. B. (2011). The impact of monetary variables on economic growth in Iran: A Monetarists' Approach. *World Applied Sciences Journal, 15*(3), 449-456. Retrieved from https://pdfs.semanticscholar.org/ec51/5675d6573c4405a5e858976275cf433b867f.pdf

Levine, R., & Renelt, D. (1992). A sensitivity analysis of cross-country growth regressions. *American Economic Review, 82*(4), 942–963. Retrieved from http://www.jstor.org/stable/2117352

Lucas, R. E. (2003). Macroeconomic priorities. *American Economic Review, 93*(1), 1-14. Retrieved from http://www.jstor.org/stable/3132159

Maehle, N., Teferra, H., & Khachatryan, A. (2013, January). Exchange rate liberalization in selected Sub-Saharan African countries. Successes, failures, and lessons (Working Paper, No. 13/32). International Monetary Fund. Retrieved from http://www.imf.org/external/pubs/ft/wp/2013/wp1332.pdf

Malik, G., & Chowdhury, A. (2001). Inflation and economic growth: Evidence from four South Asian Countries. *Asia-Pacific Development Journal, 8*(1), 123-135. Retrieved from http://citeseerx.ist.psu.edu/viewdoc/download?doi=10.1.1.516.9478&rep=rep1&type=pdf

Mankiw, G. N., & Taylor, M. P. (2007). *Macroeconomics*. (European Edition). Basingstoke: Palgrave Macmillan.

Mankiw, N. G. (2010). *Macroeconomics.* (7th ed.). New York, NY: Worth Publishers.

Mansouri, B. (2005, December). *The interactive impact of FDI & trade openness on economic growth: Evidence from Morocco.* Paper presented at the 12th Economic Research Forum (ERF) Conference, Cairo.

Maturu, B., Maana, I. & Kisinguh, K. (2010). Monetary policy transmission mechanism in Kenya: A VAR Approach (Working Paper). Central Bank of Kenya.

McCallum, J. (1991). Credit rationing and the monetary transmission mechanism. *American Economic Review, 81*(4), 946-951. Retrieved from http://www.jstor.org/stable/2006654

McCandless, G. T., & Weber, W. E. (1995). Some monetary facts. *Federal Reserve Bank of Minneapolis. Quarterly Review, 19*(3), 2-11. Retrieved from https://www.minneapolisfed.org/research/qr/qr1931.pdf

Mester, L. J. (2015, October 15). Long-run economic growth. Federal Reserve Bank of Cleveland. Retrieved from https://www.clevelandfed.org/en/newsroom-and-events/speeches/sp-20151015-long-run-economic-growth.aspx

Mishra, P., Montiel, P. J., & Spilimbergo, A. (2010). Monetary transmission in low income countries. (Working Paper No. 10/223). International Monetary Fund. Retrieved from https://www.imf.org/external/pubs/ft/wp/2010/wp10223.pdf

Monteil, P., Adam, C., & O'Conell, S. (2012). Financial architecture and the monetary transmission mechanism in Tanzania *(Working Paper* No 03). Centre for the Study of African Economies. Retrieved from http://www.csae.ox.ac.uk/materials/papers/csae-wps-2012-3.pdf

Mugume, A. (2011). Monetary transmission mechanisms in Uganda (Working Paper). Bank of Uganda. Retrieved from https://www.bou.or.ug/bou/bou-downloads/research/BouWorkingPapers/2011/All/Monetary_Transmission_Mechanisms_in_Uganda_BOU_version.pdf

Mutoti, N. (2006, June). Monetary policy transmission in Zambia *(Working Paper* No. 06). Bank of Zambia.

Mutuku, C., & Koech, E. (2014). Monetary and fiscal policy shocks and economic growth in Kenya: VAR econometric approach. *Journal of World Economic Research, 3*(6), 95-108.

Ndulu, B. (1987). Structural adjustment policies and programmes: A case study of Tanzania. Helsinki: World Institute for development economics research for the United Nations University.

Nogueira, R. P. (2009). Is monetary policy really neutral in the long-run? Evidence for some emerging and developed economies. *Economics Bulletin, 29*(3), 2432- 2437.

Nord, R., Sobolev, Y., Dunn, D., Hajdenberg, A., Hobdari, N., Maziad, S., & Roudet, S. (2009). Tanzania: The Story of an African Transition. Washington, DC: International Monetary Fund. Retrieved from https://www.imf.org/external/pubs/ft/books/2009/tanzania/tanzania.pdf

Nouri, M. and Samimi, A. (2011). The Impact of Monetary Policy on Economic Growth in Iran. *Middle-East Journal of Scientific Research, 9*(6): 740-743. Retrieved from https://pdfs.semanticscholar.org/6c36/124e81b3731868b0417afb5bd66f796c1536.pdf

Nyerere, J. K. (1977). The Arusha Declaration. Ten years after. Dar es Salaam: Government Printer.

Ogunmuyiwa, M. S., & Ekone, A. F. (2010). Money supply - economic growth nexus in Nigeria. *Journal of Social Sciences, 22*(3), 199 - 204. https://doi.org/10.1080/09718923.2010.11892802

Onyeiwu, C. (2012). Monetary policy and economic growth of Nigeria. *Journal of Economics and Sustainable Development, 3*(7), 62-70. Retrieved from http://www.iiste.org/Journals/index.php/JEDS/article/viewFile/2046/2025

Papademos, L. (2003, March). Economic cycles and monetary policy: Paper presented at the International Symposium of the Banque de France, Monetary Policy, Economic Cycle & Financial Dynamics, Paris.

Phillips, P. C. B., & Perron, P. (1988). Testing for a unit root in time series regression. *Biometrica, 75*(2), 335-446. https://doi.org/10.1093/biomet/75.2.335

Pesaran, M. H., Shin, Y. & Smith, R. J. (2001). Bounds testing approaches to the analysis of level relationships. Journal of Applied Econometrics, 16(3), 289–326. Retrieved from http://www.jstor.org/stable/2678547

Pollin, R., & Zhu, A. (2006). Inflation and economic growth: A cross-country nonlinear analysis. *Journal of Post Keynesian Economics, 28*(4), 593-614.

http://www.tandfonline.com/doi/abs/10.2753/PKE0160-3477280404

Rodrik, D. (2008). The real exchange rate and economic growth. Brookings Papers on Economic Activity, 39(2), 365-439. Retrieved from https://www.brookings.edu/wp-content/uploads/2008/09/2008b_bpea_rodrik.pdf

Romer, C. D., & Romer, D. H. (1989). Does monetary policy matter? A new test in the Spirit of Friedman and Schwartz. In O. Blanchard, & S. Fisher (Eds.), NBER Macroecononomics Annual 1984 (Vol. 4, pp. 121-184). National Bureau of Economic Research. Cambridge, MA: The MIT Press. Retrieved from http://www.nber.org/chapters/c10964

Sakyi, D. (2011). Trade openness, foreign aid and economic growth in post-liberalization Ghana: An application of ARDL Bounds Test. *Journal of Economics and International Finance, 3*(3), 146-156. Retrieved from http://www.academicjournals.org/article/article1379672933_Sakyi.pdf

Senbet, D. (2011). The relative impact of fiscal versus monetary actions on output: A Vector Autoregressive (VAR) approach. *Business and Economics Journal*, 1-11. Retrieved from http://astonjournals.com/manuscripts/Vol2011/BEJ-25_Vol2011.pdf

Smith, C. (2004). The long-run effects of monetary policy on output growth. *Reserve Bank of New Zealand Bulletin, 67*(3), 6-18. Retrieved from https://www.rbnz.govt.nz/-/media/ReserveBank/Files/Publications/Bulletins/2004/2004sept67-3smith.pdf

Vinayagathasan, T. (2013, July). Monetary policy and the real economy: A structural VAR approach for Sri Lanka (Discussion Paper No. 13-13). *National Graduate Institute for Policy Studies.* Retrieved from http://www.grips.ac.jp/r-center/wp-content/uploads/13-13.pdf

Weeks, J. (2010, June). Why monetary policy is irrelevant in Africa South of the Sahara. London, UK: *Centre for Development Policy and Research. School of Oriental and African Studies, University of London.* Retrieved from https://www.soas.ac.uk/cdpr/publications/dv/file59766.pdf

White, W. R. (2013, September). Is monetary policy a science? The interaction of theory and practice over the last 50 years (Working Paper No. 155). Globalization and Monetary Policy Institute Federal Reserve Bank of Dallas. Retrieved from http://www.dallasfed.org/assets/documents/institute/wpapers/2013/0155.pdf

World Bank. (2015). World Development Indicators 2015. Available at http://databank.worldbank.org/data/reports.aspx?source=2&country=TZA

Yilmazkuday, H. (2013). Inflation thresholds and growth. *International Economic Journal, 27*(1), 1-10. http://dx.doi.org/10.1080/10168737.2012.658831

9

The Paris Agreement and electricity markets outside the EU

João Estevão[1], Clara Raposo[1], José Dias Lopes[1]

ABSTRACT

Climate change has been at the center of economic and social discussion for some years. The passage of time has intensified this debate and reflection. A well-known relevant event in this domain was the signature of the Paris Agreement in 2014, and its subsequent enforcement by European Union (EU) member countries.

This study examines if the climate change measures adopted by the Agreement had an impact on the electricity sector outside the EU28, seeking to assess whether there is international diversity in these markets or if they work uniformly at global level.

The goal of this work is to study the behavior of spot electricity prices before and after the Agreement was signed by EU members, analyze its effect in terms of spot prices, and determine the conditions that lead to stability and non-stability. We examine the behavior of spot electricity prices in two different electricity markets: the US and Brazil.

The study applies both qualitative methodologies, namely fsQCA, and quantitative methodology, in order to identify changes in the pattern of electricity price behavior with the advent of the Agreement.

Arguably, regulatory theory still incorporates the effects of the emergence of global dynamics in the regulation process. However, what this article suggests is that changes in regulatory frameworks with global impact, even if exogenous to a specific market, can profoundly alter the dynamics of that market.

KEY WORDS: electricity markets, spot price, Paris Agreement, fsQCA

[1] Advance/CSG-ISEG, Universidade de Lisboa, Portugal

1. Introduction

Climate change has been at the center of economic and social discussion for some years. The passage of time has intensified this debate and reflection. A well-known relevant event in this domain was the signature of the Paris Agreement in 2014, and its subsequent enforcement by European Union (EU) member countries. Previous work (Estevão & Raposo, 2018) identifies the impact of the signature of the Paris Agreement by EU countries in 2014 in the Iberian electricity market MIBEL. This Agreement brought more stability to the spot price in MIBEL market, a reduction of volatility in the two markets and a larger number of paths that are associated with price stability.

Correspondence concerning this article should be addressed to: **Clara Raposo**, Advance/CSG-ISEG, Universidade de Lisboa, Rua Miguel Lupi, 20 - 1249-078 Lisboa, Portugal. E-mail: clararaposo@iseg.ulisboa.pt

This study examines if the climate change measures expected after the signing of the Agreement had an impact on different markets in the electricity sector outside the EU28, seeking to assess whether there is international diversity in these markets or if they work uniformly at global level. The goal of this work is to study the behavior of spot electricity prices before and after the Agreement was signed by EU members, and to analyze its impact. We propose to examine the behavior of spot electricity prices in two different electricity markets.

In particular, we examine the Pennsylvania, Maryland and New Jersey market (PJM) and the Brazilian market (Bra), having chosen these two markets because they are from a continent different than Europe, and because one of them is the largest developed country in the world while the other is one of the largest emerging economies in the world. By doing so, we want to test if the legislation had an impact beyond the countries where it was imposed. The globalization of the markets is present in the negotiations of the same futures contracts in different parts of the globe at the same time (Scholte, 2008). For that reason, it is expectable that an important measure could influence other markets besides those of the countries that directly sign the Agreements, as happened with the study of Estevão and Raposo (2018) were the volatility decreased, but having more configurations for stability of the spot prices. For that reason, similar results are expected for these two American countries.

The study applies both qualitative methodologies, namely fsQCA, and quantitative methodology in order to identify changes in the pattern of electricity price behavior with the advent of the Agreement. The econometric approach aims to model the behavior of spot prices before and after the Agreement and the qualitative approach seeks to show the configurations that lead to the presence of stability in the spot price of electricity. We use daily data collected from several markets for a period of 6 years – 3 years prior to the Paris Agreement being signed, and 3 years after.

This paper is organized as follows: section 2 presents a brief survey of the literature, section 3 presents the traditional time-series quantitative methodology results. In section 4 the qualitative analysis fsQCA is presented and section 5 discusses the results. Finally, section 6 concludes.

2. Literature review: electricity prices behavior

Electricity markets have three main distinctive features: limited possibility of transmission, seasonality, and impossibility of storage (Janczura, Trück, Weron, & Wolff, 2013; Pietz, 2009; Pirrong & Jermakyan, 2008). Weron and Misiorek (2008) add that electricity is also a special commodity since demand depends on the weather and on the business cycle, but in the sort-term the elasticity is very reduced (Redl, Haas, Huber, & Böhm, 2009). Hence, these commodities present high volatility, and peaks in prices (Janczura & Weron, 2010), features that can be harmful to consumers (Newbery, 1998). The impossibility of storage makes electricity prices more volatile than other commodities, such as oil, gas or coal, due to the need for immediate consumption (Shawky, Marathe, & Barrett, 2003).

The Paris Agreement addresses the concerns of the world community regarding climate change "Recognizing the need for an effective and progressive response to the urgent threat of climate change" (United Nations, 2015, p. 1). Large externalities are associated with the production and the consumption of energy often in the form of emissions of greenhouse gases (Jacobsen, 2015). The European Council (2014) defined three main objectives in this field: growth of renewable energy to a minimum of 27% of the energy consumption, target of 40% in greenhouse gas emissions relative to 1990 levels, and energy efficiency through possible modifications to the energy efficiency directive. In view of the imposition of these measures it is to be expected that spot prices will increase because the cost of producing renewable energy is higher than the cost of producing fossil fuels, and also market instability, due to a change of legislation. The Paris Agreement does not clearly mention fossil fuels, but it is implicit that there is a strong commitment towards a low-carbon energy shift, providing arguments to increase the speed for fossil fuel subsidies reform (Rentschler & Bazilian, 2017). Climate change affects consumer behavior and consequently the consumption and price of electricity (Véliz, Kaufmann, Cleveland, & Stoner, 2017). In addition, modern electrical power systems face the inherent uncertainty and variability of renewable energy resources (Chakraborty, Baeyens, & Khargonekar, 2018). Paraschiv, Erni, & Pietsch (2014) brought to scrutiny the formation of prices in the German market from renewable energies photovoltaic and wind. Ketterer (2014) and Cardella, Ewing, & Williams (2017) emphasize the significance of this kind of research given the increasing production of renewable energy in recent years. Still, guaranties given to producers of energy from renewable sources affects the prices to the final consumer (Ketterer, 2014).

Nevertheless, additional analyse is required in this area, not only the necessity of subsidies in the carbon price, but also factors like surplus of generation or solid energy efficiency (International Energy Agency, 2016). In developed and developing countries, many electricity systems are not completely liberalized, "so the textbook model in which the carbon price is passed through to marginal electricity prices, driving dispatch decisions, does not directly apply" (International Energy Agency, 2016, p. 48).

The introdution of open markets for electricity and the liberalization of the power industry has split activities into generation, transmission and distribuion. Policy makers have the goal of reducing the volatility because they see it as a risk to economies and wish to avoid energy price shocks (Atalla, Blazquez, Hunt, & Manzano, 2017). One of the goals of deregulation is to bring competition between generation units to deliver consistent electricity supply to consumers. The liberalization of energy markets brought about a switch from coal to natural gas, but with increased macroeconomic volatility (Atalla et al., 2017), with the Scandinavian market and the German market being the main electricity markets in Europe.

Gummer et al. (2017) show that electricity prices increase 61% between 2004 and 2016 in the UK, and defends the main causes of the increase is a rise in wholesale and network costs, and the impact of the climate policies. Similar results are obtained in Australia where the retail electricity prices also increased between 2006 and 2013 but the increase almost stagnated (Climate Change Authority, 2016). The report of the Committee on Climate Change by Gummer et al. (2017) estimates a growth in electricity prices of 33% between 2016 and 2030, due to climate policy costs and the increase of network costs and wholesale. In the same direction, the study (International Energy Agency, 2016) predicts that as the production of energy through fossil fuels decreases, this will be directly reflected in a reduction of carbon prices on electricity. If consumption of reweable energy is expected to increase, importance must be given to the plants already in place because following Ziegler, Gonzalez, Rubert, Smolka, and Melero (2018, p. 1261) "in 2016, 12% of the installed wind turbine capacity in Europe was older than 15 years. This share increases to 28% by 2020".

Estevão & Raposo (2018) provided evidence of lower volatility and higher price stability – in terms of a larger number of configurations leading to stability – in Portugal and Spain after the introduction of the Paris Agreement in 2014. It is an open question if other markets reacted in a similar fashion. This study provides evidence from two very different markets: Brazil and the PJM US energy market. The current study has the goal of assessing supposing both markets reacted similarly to the Paris Agreement. It is expected that the markets have the same behavior because, being liberalized, the different types of agents can take positions on this commodity, regardless of where they are from and of the type of development that the country has.

To measure the reaction of these markets, we adopt a mixed-methodologies approach: a quantitative approach to identify the time series model that better describes the behavior of spot prices, i.e., determine how prices have been behaving, and not determine which factors (variables) lead to price formation and validate the presence of price peaks, and a qualitative fsQCA approach to find the paths to stability and non-stability in these markets, i.e., which variables are important to achieve stability of spot electricity prices.

3. Time series econometric method

Financial markets are characterized by higher volatility and, for that reason (Wooldridge, 2006; 2013), spot electricity prices are extremely more volatile than any other commodities' (Girish, Rath, & Akram, 2018).

3.1 Sample description

To analyze the existence of stability in spot electricity prices in the PJM and Brazilian markets, we collect data from Datastream for the day after market (spot price) for the period between October 24, 2011 and October 24, 2017. From now on, the term spot price refers to the electricity price for next day delivery.

The sample is divided in two sub samples, the first one the data are between October 24, 2011 and October 24, 2014 (the date of signature of the Paris Agreement), and the second is the period after the signature. The first period has 785 observations and the second

Table 1. Summary Statistics

PJM before 10/24/2014		Bra before 10/24/2014	
Mean	31.88894	Mean	112.0846
Standard Error	0.893534	Standard Error	2.63879
Median	27.11	Median	90.55
Mode	27.78	Mode	27.51
Standard Deviation	25.03491	Standard Deviation	73.93322
Sample Variance	626.7469	Sample Variance	5466.121
Kurtosis	160.9855	Kurtosis	-0.59126
Skewness	10.32071	Skewness	0.798545
Range	481.41	Range	253.04
Minimum	15.32	Minimum	17.19
Maximum	496.73	Maximum	270.23
Sum	25032.82	Sum	87986.4
Count	785	Count	785
PJM after 10/24/2014		**Bra after 10/24/2014**	
Mean	27.24383	Mean	71.5873
Standard Error	0.362403	Standard Error	1.957379
Median	25.86	Median	53.875
Mode	19.73	Mode	36.12
Standard Deviation	10.14727	Standard Deviation	54.80661
Sample Variance	102.9671	Sample Variance	3003.764
Kurtosis	39.70085	Kurtosis	2.075204
Skewness	4.688827	Skewness	1.354166
Range	140.77	Range	248.56
Minimum	2.33	Minimum	8.09
Maximum	143.1	Maximum	256.65
Sum	21359.16	Sum	56124.45
Count	784	Count	784

period has 784 observations. Data are for the 5 days of the working week. The unit of measure in the spot price contracts is euros for a megawatt per hour (€/Mwh). Each contract guarantees the supply of one Mwh of electricity. Table 1 presents the summary statistics for the data.

Table 2. Summary models

	R^2	Standard deviation	Volatility market	Type Model	Average
Brazil before	0.016583	73.88€/Mwh	151%	GARCH (1,1)	MA(1) MA(15) MA(23)
Brazil after	0.099424	73.88€/Mwh	102%	GARCH (1,1)	AR(1) AR(2) AR(3) MA(1)
PJM before	0.131543	25.02€/Mwh	431%	GARCH (1,1)	AR(1) MA(1) MA(2)
PJM after	0.252881	10.14€/Mwh	469%	GARCH (1,1)	AR(1) MA(1)

3.2. Results for the econometric method

The descriptive statistics show that in the PJM market before 2014, spot price has a standard deviation of 25.02€/Mwh and the mean of price is 31.92€/Mwh, with the minimum price of 15.32€/Mwh and a maximum spot price of 496.73€/Mwh. In the case of Brazil, the average spot price was 112.48€/Mwh with a standard deviation of 74.21€/Mwh. The maximum value of electricity was 270.23€/Mwh and the minimum 17.19€/Mwh.

After the Agreement, the descriptive statistics reveal a decrease of the mean price to 27.27€/Mwh and a standard deviation of 10.14€/Mwh with the maximum and minimum prices decreasing to 134.10€/Mwh and 2.33€/Mwh. In turn, the Brazilian market after the Agreement, presented an average price of 71.58€/Mwh (decrease) with a decrease of the maximum of the spot price to 256.65€/Mwh and also a decrease of the minimum to 8.09€/Mwh

The PJM market before the Paris Agreement is defined by a GARCH model (1,1) where the volatility is according to AR(1) MA(1) MA(2). After the Agreement, in this market, the better model to describe the spot price is GARCH (1,1). The model also explains the errors, and the mean behaves according to AR(1), MA(1).

The same exercise was performed for the Brazilian market. Results before the Paris Agreement confirm that the GARCH model (1,1) better describes the volatility where the mean behaves according to MA(1) MA(15) MA(23). After 2014, in the Latin American country the GARCH(1,1) model also explains the errors, and the mean behaves according to AR(1) AR(2) AR(3) MA(1). (Table 2)

Following Bierbrauer, Trück, and Weron (2004), who define a price peak when the volatility is higher than 30% of the mean, there are several cases when this happens, with the consequence of large annual volatility in both markets, but, in particular, in PJM with volatility around 430% before, and 470% after the Agreement. In Brazil the existence of price peaks is less noted, with volatility near to 150% and 100%, respectively, before and after 2014.

4. Qualitative comparative analysis method

With the goal of analyzing which conditions lead to lower volatility in the spot price of electricity (i.e., conditions for stability in electricity prices) we use the qualitative methodology qualitative fuzzy-set QCA. We interpret a possible increase in the number of paths that lead to stability as a signal of more stability in the market.

The fsQCA analysis requires that the cases be scaled into significant clusters that reflect the degree of price stability. The degree ranges from one (price stability) to zero (absence of price stability). A score of 0.5 refers to the crossover point (Ragin, 2008a). Following the rationale of Bierbrauer et al. (2004), stability in electricity spot prices is assumed to correspond to situations in which prices are within a 30% variation of the mean for the observed period. For the crossover point, an area of 30% is divided into two bands of 15% (one above and one below the central band of stability). The remaining area corresponds to the values of instability, that is, the two bands farther away from the mean, 15% each, such as in Estevão & Raposo (2018). Table 3 summarizes the statistics and calibration values of the outcomes and antecedent conditions.

Table 3. Descriptive statistics and calibration values of the outcomes and antecedent conditions

	Descriptive statistics				Calibration		
Outcomes and Conditions	Mean	Std dev	Max	Min	Stability	Ambiguity	Absence of stability
Spot PJM before	31.92	25.02	496.73	15.32	]27.30 ; 36.67[	]24.11, 27.73[U]36.67 , 42.17[	< 24.11 U > 42.17
Spot Bra before	112.49	74.22	270.23	17.19	]97.46 ; 128.89[	]84.75 , 97.46[U]128.89 , 148.22[	< 84.75 U > 148.22
Spot PJM after	27.28	10.15	143.10	2.33	]23.71 ; 31.36[	]20.62 , 23.71[U]31.36 , 36.06[	< 20.62 U > 36.06
Spot Bra after	71.58	54.91	256.65	8.09	]62.27 ; 82.35[	]54.15 , 62.27[U]82.35 , 94.70[	< 54.15 U > 94.70
dax before	8,001.70	1,252.45	10,029.43	5428.11		(9760; 7950; 6000)*	
dax after	10,982.57	1,047.12	13,043.03	8,752.87		(12700; 10800; 9450)*	
oil before	78.74	3.72	89.34	72.37		(86; 78; 73.5)*	
oil after	45.02	8.25	74.22	28.10		(60; 43; 29)*	
nordpool before	34.50	9.01	96.13	7.94		(48; 34; 24)*	
nordpool after	26.55	7.24	81.67	6.31		(37.5; 27; 12)*	
eex before	42.46	9.85	98.98	8.40		(58; 42; 28)*	
eex after	34.46	9.43	101.92	1.52		(49.5; 33.5; 21.5)*	
gas before	2.70	0.60	5.84	1.38		(3.45; 2.7; 1.73)*	
gas after	2.44	0.44	3.56	1.35		(3.2; 2.5; 1.6)*	
sre before	15.00	11.00	40.23	3.23		(35.6; 10; 3.8)*	
sre after	58.76	15.22	84.31	25.46		(82; 60.5; 31)*	
coal before	64.85	9.19	84.18	52.79		(80; 63.5; 53)*	
coal after	59.56	11.99	83.05	44.48		(81; 56; 46)*	

*Cuts: 95%; 50% and 5%

Label: Max=maximum; Min = minimum; Std dev = standard deviation; (dax) daily DAX index, (oil) average price of oil barrel in euros, (nordpool) average price of electricity in the Scandinavian market, (eex) electricty price in the German market/ Megawatt Hour, (gas) natural gas price - per Million British Thermal Units, (sre) renewable energies index - Total Market Renewable Energy Equipment, (coal) average spot price of coal in euros per metric ton

The advantages of the fsQCA methodology, in comparison to other methodologies, is providing a better understanding of the conditions to achieve the stability in spot price, in an application in finance similar to what has been performed in different contexts (Wu, Yeh, Huan, & Woodside, 2014). Another advantage of this methodology is the fact the usual problems of correlation of variables in a regression technique (multicollinearity) are not of concern here – it is one of the assumptions of the fsQCA (Rihoux & Ragin, 2009).

4.1 Sample description

We use the same data as in the previous section where the econometric methodology results were discussed. For the application of fsQCA, we choose a set of conditions that are important to explain the electricity price behavior in these two markets. We use the daily DAX index (variable dax), which is the main reference European stock market index (Oberndorfer, 2009), to consider the relation between electricity prices and other forms of investments. The average spot price of electricity in the Scandinavian market (variable nordpool) and the electricity price in the German market per Mwh (variable eex), the most important electric markets in Europe (European Commission, 2016), are also included. The most important energy sources for the production of electricity, oil, coal and gas, are also included – the price of a barrel of oil in euros (variable oil), price of coal in euros per metric tonne (variable coal) and the price of natural gas per million BTUs (variable gas) (Paraschiv et al., 2014). We also consider the renewable energies index—Total Market Renewable Energy Equipment (variable sre).

4.2 Analysis of the necessary condition

We test the markets of Pennsylvania, New Jersey and Maryland (PJM) and Brazil (Bra) and the variables dax, oil, nordpool, eex, gas, sre and coal to assess if necessary conditions exist for the outcome in the sub periods before and after the Paris Agreement. Usually, a condition or a combination of configurations is necessary if the consistency score exceeds 0.8 (Ragin, 2000; Ragin, 2008a; Schneider, Schulze-Bentrop, & Paunescu, 2010). Based in (Ragin, 2008b), you define the cut of necessary conditions in 0.8. The output shows that for the PJM market before the Agreement, there exists only one condition necessary for stability in this market (in this case, stability in gas prices); and after the Agreement there is still one condition for the stability in spot electricity prices, this time oil. The same procedure was followed for non-stability and no necessary conditions were found (table 4).

The same analysis was conducted for the Brazilian market and the results are different. In the case of the necessary conditions for stability, before October 2014, three conditions exist, dax, gas and non-coal; whereas after the Agreement, oil is the sole necessary condition. Examining the necessary conditions for non-stability in this market we find that before the Agreement there are two conditions (variables coal and non-dax.); and after the Agreement, there are no necessary conditions for the non-stability in the spot prices in the Brazilian market.

4.3. Analysis of the sufficient conditions sets

After the study of necessary conditions, the next procedure is to analyze the sufficient conditions. For that, following the recommendations of (Ragin, 2008b) for a large sample, we accept a minimum of 4 observations of configurations that lead to stability or non-stability of the spot prices in these markets. Following (Ragin, 2008a), (Woodside, Prentice, & Larsen, 2015), we adjust the cut-values depending on the number of items in each variable and its statistics.

Based on the table 5, the results show that the PJM market has two configurations for stability in spot prices, with a coverage solution of 0.38 and a solution consistency of 0.90. In the Brazilian case, there are more configurations (five) for the period before the Agreement, with a solution consistency of 0.88 and a coverage solution of 0.71. After the Agreement (table 6), the North American market presents two different configurations and the Latin American market has only one configuration, and respectively, presented a solution coverage of 0.31 and a solution consistency of 0.86 in the first case, whereas in the second case, 0.32 and 0.94 in terms of coverage and consistency.

In both cases – PJM and Brazilian markets, and also before and after the Agreement – the individual and overall consistency are higher than 0.8. In terms of coverage, the recommendations of (Fiss, 2011; Ragin, 2008b; Woodside, 2013) is more than 0.25 and the results, individual and overall, are aligned. For example, in the configurations number 2 of PJM market, the individual consistency is 0.89. Such score means that in 89 per cent of cases where this configuration of conditions is present stability occurs. The coverage level of the causal configuration number 2 is 0.28. Such score means that 28 per cent of stability occurrences took place precisely due to this configuration.

In the table 7, for the PJM market, before 2014, following the recommendations of (Prentice & Woodside, 2013) for the analysis of the negation conditions, there are three sufficient condition for non-stability.

Table 4. Results of analysis of the necessary conditions

Analysis of Necessary Conditions																
Outcome variable	fsPJM before		~fsPJM before		fsBrasil before		~fsBrasil before		fsPJM after		~fsPJM after		fsBrasil after		~fsBrasil after	
Conditions tested	Consistency	Coverage	Consistency	Coverage	Consistency	Coverage	Consistency	Coverage	Consistency	Coverage	Consistency	Coverage	Consistency	Coverage	Consistency	Coverage
fsdax	0.743028	0.630377	0.596012	0.644610	0.862688	0.801068	0.480808	0.481460	0.726511	0.523978	0.612734	0.756774	0.782916	0.733479	0.541267	0.551793
~fsdax	0.581100	0.530148	0.658242	0.765560	0.441573	0.440929	0.801336	0.862888	0.662759	0.499842	0.614580	0.793739	0.521582	0.510975	0.738564	0.787332
fsoil	0.617744	0.552550	0.702888	0.801488	0.574334	0.562275	0.712295	0.751998	0.835916	0.563528	0.669288	0.772660	0.881594	0.772009	0.600295	0.572019
~fsoil	0.778065	0.672585	0.607593	0.669563	0.746676	0.706456	0.585383	0.597263	0.662770	0.539230	0.621921	0.866500	0.511269	0.540333	0.760741	0.874865
fsnordpool	0.648723	0.588790	0.665208	0.769672	0.623959	0.619837	0.639520	0.685092	0.767142	0.554801	0.639128	0.791537	0.712574	0.669410	0.610397	0.623974
~fsnordpool	0.746227	0.636156	0.644601	0.700537	0.682999	0.637284	0.645125	0.649128	0.711752	0.535259	0.640523	0.824884	0.599727	0.585855	0.676605	0.719224
fseex	0.643432	0.569698	0.658128	0.742848	0.532169	0.515718	0.724086	0.756704	0.774203	0.578571	0.599221	0.766852	0.721282	0.700177	0.593441	0.626863
~fseex	0.709566	0.619498	0.618774	0.688693	0.748943	0.715676	0.536593	0.552950	0.688017	0.500617	0.670692	0.835705	0.615614	0.581857	0.716162	0.736565
fsgas	0.820178	0.694099	0.593212	0.639986	0.851956	0.789135	0.504888	0.504315	0.797046	0.600269	0.596359	0.769117	0.769955	0.753232	0.556020	0.591897
~fsgas	0.574590	0.525617	0.716456	0.835504	0.464853	0.465423	0.788894	0.851774	0.693429	0.500796	0.690055	0.853425	0.582834	0.546770	0.768190	0.784190
fssre	0.676903	0.628264	0.550622	0.651504	0.727857	0.739406	0.449447	0.492366	0.645420	0.472617	0.650817	0.816109	0.591768	0.562884	0.684617	0.708611
~fssre	0.624525	0.521568	0.685825	0.730167	0.500295	0.457308	0.762121	0.751241	0.748873	0.556024	0.579430	0.736731	0.693658	0.669008	0.577685	0.606275
fscoal	0.591031	0.535153	0.664974	0.767573	0.478348	0.474059	0.800608	0.855621	0.683437	0.526598	0.586075	0.773315	0.705971	0.706592	0.499756	0.544293
~fscoal	0.743304	0.635086	0.597286	0.650572	0.854313	0.798921	0.507873	0.512171	0.705802	0.498931	0.641220	0.776223	0.544693	0.500161	0.730601	0.730013

But in the Brazilian market the number of sufficient conditions found is two. In the case of non-stability, for the sufficient conditions after 2014 (table 8), the opposite is found – this means that the PJM market has just two sufficient condition and the Brazilian market has 3 sufficient conditions. The results obtained for the non-stability in both markets and periods present individual and overall consistency in agreement with (Ragin, 2008a) and (Fiss, 2011). The same results are achieved in terms of coverage (tables 7 and 8).

5. Discussion of the results

This Agreement brought to the PJM American market different configurations that lead to stability in the prices of electricity, but the number of configurations is the same as previously. The highlight is that the variables nordpool, sre and coal have the same behavior in one configuration, before and after. This means that when we are in the presence of stability in these three variables, there also exists stability in this market. It should be noted that the variables in one configuration before de Agreement, the same variables (nordpool, sre and coal) have opposite behavior in the two periods. For the Brazilian market, it is more difficulty to obtain a condition to have stability in spot prices of electricity (the number changes from 5 combinations to 1 combination), it being important to mention that, after the Agreement, variables eex and gas are no longer significant in explaining the electricity price in Brazil as before. Previous to the Agreement, the variable gas was always present in the conditions for stability in a positive way, i.e., when there was stability in the spot electricity

Table 5. Results of the intermediate solutions before the Paris Agreement (outcome: PJM and Bra)

	Intermediate solution PJM before 10/24/2014		**Intermediate solution Brasil before 10/24/2014**				
	Model: 2014PJM = f(oil_ before, gas_before, eex_ before, nordpool_before, dax_before, sre_before, coal_before)		**Model: 2014Bra = f(oil_ before, gas_before, eex_ before, nordpool_before, dax_before, sre_before, coal_before)**				
	1	2	1	2	3	4	5
fsdax_before	●	○	●	●	●	●	o
fsoil_before	o	●	o	o			•
fsnordpool_before	○	●		•	o	•	•
fseex_before	●	○		○	○	•	○
fsgas_before	●	●	●	●	●	●	●
fssre_before	●	○	●		●	●	o
fscoal_before	o	●	○	○	○	○	•
Consistency	0.92	0.82	0.91	0.92	0.91	0.88	0.90
Raw coverage	0.27	0.21	0.04	0.008	0.03	0.01	0.02
Unique coverage	0.14	0.08	0.57	0.37	0.50	0.28	0.21
Overall solution consistency	0.90				0.88		
Overall solution coverage	0.38				0.71		

Label: Max=maximum; Min = minimum; Std dev = standard deviation; (dax) daily DAX index, (oil) average price of oil barrel in euros, (nordpool) average price of electricity in the Scandinavian market, (eex) electricty price in the German market/ Megawatt Hour, (gas) natural gas price - per Million British Thermal Units, (sre) renewable energies index - Total Market Renewable Energy Equipment, (coal) average spot price of coal in euros per metric tonne; full black circles (●) indicate the presence of a condition, and center white circles (o) indicate its absence. Large circles indicate core conditions; small ones, peripheral conditions. Blank spaces indicate "does not contribute to configuration".

price, the Brazilian market stability also existed in the prices of gas. After the Agreement, the variable gas is no longer necessary to explain the stability in the electricity market. It is also relevant to mention the behavior of variable coal before the Agreement: out of the 5 configurations obtained, 4 configurations have non-stability in the price of coal (has the opposite behavior). After the Agreement the variables dax, oil and coal, when they are stable, and nordpool and sre (when these are instable) are the condition for stability in the Brazilian market.

Regarding the configurations to non-stability in these markets, it is noticeable that the PJM market reduces the number of configurations from three to two. Before 2014 when we are in the presence of non-stability in the American market, in the Scandinavian market (variable nordpool) the prices are stable. In the opposite side is the case of the variable gas which has always (in the three conditions) the same behavior of non-stability. After the Agreement, for the existence of non-stability, the variables dax,

Table 6. Results of the intermediate solutions after the Paris Agreement (outcome: PJM and Bra)

	Intermediate solution PJM after 10/24/2014		**Intermediate solution Bra after 10/24/2014**
	Model: 2014PJM = f(oil_ before, gas_before, eex_ before, nordpool_before, dax_before, sre_before, coal_before)		**Model: 2014Bra = f(oil_ before, gas_before, eex_ before, nordpool_before, dax_before, sre_before, coal_before)**
	1	2	1
fsdax_after	◦	•	●
fsoil_after	•	◦	●
fsnordpool_after	●	●	○
fseex_after	•	•	
fsgas_after	◦	•	
fssre_after	○	○	○
fscoal_after	●	●	●
Consistency	0.86	0.89	0.94
Raw coverage	0.24	0.28	0.31
Unique coverage	0.03	0.06	0.31
Overall solution consistency	0.86		0.94
Overall solution coverage	0.31		0.32

Label: Max=maximum; Min = minimum; Std dev = standard deviation, (dax) daily DAX index, (oil) average price of oil barrel in euros, (nordpool) average price of electricity in the Scandinavian market, (eex) electricty price in the German market/ Megawatt Hour, (gas) natural gas price - per Million British Thermal Units, (sre) renewable energies index - Total Market Renewable Energy Equipment, (coal) average spot price of coal in euros per metric tonne; full black circles (●) indicate the presence of a condition, and center white circles (o) indicate its absence. Large circles indicate core conditions; small ones, peripheral conditions. Blank spaces indicate "does not contribute to configuration".

oil, nordpool, sre and coal must have stability in their prices. When the variable eex presents not stability in its prices it can lead to no stability in the market PJM. The Latin American market shows that the Agreement increases the number of configurations for the non-stability of the prices, from two to three. It is a common denominator for both periods the fact that, in order to achieve non-stability, the variable dax has non-stability. In the period before 2014, the necessary conditions sre and coal are present in both solutions as core conditions, which means that when we are in presence of stability in the prices of index of energy renewables and the prices of coal, there are indications that there may be non-stability in the prices of the Brazilian market. After the Agreement, the variable sre as necessary condition is a core conditions in the three solutions presented and we have indications of non-stability when the prices of index energy renewable are stable. In the opposite direction, dax and oil variables are negatively correlated with the Brazil-

Table 7. Results of the intermediate solutions before the Paris 2030Agreement (outcome: ~PJM and ~Bra)

	Intermediate solution ~PJM before 10/24/2014			**Intermediate solution ~Brasil before 10/24/2014**	
	Model: ~2014PJM = f(oil_ before, gas_before, eex_ before, nordpool_before, dax_before, sre_before, coal_before)			**Model: ~2014Bra = f(oil_ before, gas_before, eex_ before, nordpool_before, dax_before, sre_before, coal_before)**	
	1	2	3	1	2
fsdax_before	•	o	o	O	O
fsoil_before	•	•	o		O
fsnordpool_before	●	●	●	O	•
fseex_before		O	•	●	●
fsgas_before	O	O	O	O	O
fssre_before	●	o	●	o	●
fscoal_before	o	•	•	●	●
Consistency	0.95	0.96	0.95	0.98	0.99
Raw coverage	0.22	0.21	0.01	0.39	0.19
Unique coverage	0.10	0.07	0.03	0.24	0.04
Overall solution consistency	0.95			0.98	
Overall solution coverage	0.36			0.43	

Label: Max=maximum; Min = minimum; Std dev = standard deviation; (dax) daily DAX index, (oil) average price of oil barrel in euros, (nordpool) average price of electricity in the Scandinavian market, (eex) electricty price in the German market/ Megawatt Hour, (gas) natural gas price - per Million British Thermal Units, (sre) renewable energies index - Total Market Renewable Energy Equipment, (coal) average spot price of coal in euros per metric tonne; full black circles (●) indicate the presence of a condition, and center white circles (o) indicate its absence. Large circles indicate core conditions; small ones, peripheral conditions. Blank spaces indicate "does not contribute to configuration".

ian spot prices of electricity. The other variables do not have a defined pattern of behavior, varying from configuration to configuration.

In what concerns the quantitative methodology, a reduction of volatility after the Paris Agreement is identified, decreasing price peaks in both markets; the Brazilian market has a different behavior than the PJM market, which is confirmed with lower volatility. Although the Brazilian market presents lower volatility than the PJM market, it is more difficult to model the behavior of spot prices, as can be observed by the R squared of the models, that is, the model has a lower explanatory power.

6. Conclusions

Summarizing, the Paris Agreement brought to the PJM market more stability, since the volatility decreased after the signature of the Agreement, despite the number of configurations leading to stability remaining the same as before the Agreement. Analyzing conditions for non-stability, the number of configurations de-

Table 8. Results of the intermediate solutions after the Paris 2030Agreement (outcome: ~PJM and ~Bra)

	Intermediate solution ~PJM after 10/24/2014		**Intermediate solution ~Bra after 10/24/2014**		
	Model: ~2014PJM = f(oil_ before, gas_ before, eex_ before, nordpool_before, dax_before, sre_before, coal_before)		**Model: ~2014Bra = f(oil_ before, gas_before, eex_ before, nordpool_before, dax_before, sre_before, coal_before)**		
	1	2	1	2	3
fsdax_after	●	●	○	○	○
fsoil_after	●	●	◦	◦	◦
fsnordpool_after	●	○	◦	◦	•
fseex_after	○	○	◦	◦	•
fsgas_after	○	•	◦		•
fssre_after	●	●	●	●	●
fscoal_after	●	●		•	•
Consistency	0.97	0.96	0.99	0.99	0.98
Raw coverage	0.22	0.23	0.37	0.21	0.21
Unique coverage	0.03	0.04	0.17	0.008	0.05
Overall solution consistency	0.96			0.99	
Overall solution coverage	0.26			0.44	

Label: Max=maximum; Min = minimum; Std dev = standard deviation; (dax) daily DAX index, (oil) average price of oil barrel in euros, (nordpool) average price of electricity in the Scandinavian market, (eex) electricty price in the German market/ Megawatt Hour, (gas) natural gas price - per Million British Thermal Units, (sre) renewable energies index - Total Market Renewable Energy Equipment, (coal) average spot price of coal in euros per metric tonne; full black circles (●) indicate the presence of a condition, and center white circles (o) indicate its absence. Large circles indicate core conditions; small ones, peripheral conditions. Blank spaces indicate "does not contribute to configuration".

crease from three to one, meaning that it is more difficult to have non-stability in the prices. In sum, the PJM market price stability benefited from the Agreement. These results are similar to those found by (Estevão & Raposo, 2018) for the MIBEL market.

In what concerns the Brazilian market, the situation got worse after the Agreement, in terms of price stability, when considering the number of configurations for price stability that decreased from 5 to 1. Regarding non-stability, there are more configurations after the signature of the Agreement. It will be interesting to further examine in the future which legislative initiatives or policy measures took place in this country to justify the difference in results compared to developed countries such as Spain or the US. In fact, the different results found for Brazil could be explained by some change in legislation in 2015, or can be due to the fact that it is a developing country. Future studies conducted for emerging economies like China, India or Russia can further clarify this matter.

References

Atalla, T., Blazquez, J., Hunt, L. C., & Manzano, B. (2017). Prices versus policy: An analysis of the drivers of the primary fossil fuel mix. *Energy Policy, 106*, 536–546. https://doi.org/10.1016/j.enpol.2017.03.060

Bierbrauer, M., Trück, S., & Weron, R. (2004). Modeling electricity prices with regime switching models. *Lecture Notes in Computer Science (Including Subseries Lecture Notes in Artificial Intelligence and Lecture Notes in Bioinformatics), 3039*, 859–867.

Cardella, E., Ewing, B. T., & Williams, R. B. (2017). Price volatility and residential electricity decisions: Experimental evidence on the convergence of energy generating source. *Energy Economics, 62*, 428–437. https://doi.org/10.1016/j.eneco.2016.07.012

Chakraborty, P., Baeyens, E., & Khargonekar, P. P. (2018). Cost Causation Based Allocations of Costs for Market Integration of Renewable Energy. *IEEE Transactions on Power Systems, 33*(1), 70–83. https://doi.org/10.1109/TPWRS.2017.2690404

Climate Change Authority. (2016, August). Policy Options for Australia's electricity supply sector. Special review research report.

Estevão, J., & Raposo, C. (2018). The impact of the 2030 Climate and Energy Framework Agreement on electricity prices in MIBEL: A mixed-methods approach. *Journal of Business Research, 89*, 411–417. https://doi.org/10.1016/j.jbusres.2017.12.037

European Commission. (2016). Energy prices and costs in Europe. Commission Staff Working Document, SWD(2016) 420.

European Council. (2014). 2030 Climate and Energy Policy Framework, Conclusions, EUCO 169/14. Available at http://www.consilium.europa.eu/en/policies/climate-change/2030-climate-and-energy-framework/

Fiss, P. C. (2011). Building Better Causal Theories: A Fuzzy Set Approach to Typologies in Organizational Research. *Academy of Management Journal, 54*(2), 393–420. https://doi.org/10.5465/AMJ.2011.60263120

Girish, G. P., Rath, B. N., & Akram, V. (2018). Spot electricity price discovery in Indian electricity market. *Renewable and Sustainable Energy Reviews, 82*, 73–79. https://doi.org/10.1016/j.rser.2017.09.009

Gummer, H., Chater, N., Hoskins, B., Johnson, P., King, J., Le Quéré, C., & Skea, J. (2017). *Energy Prices and Bills - impacts of meeting carbonn budgets. Committee on Climate Change.* Retrieved from https://www.theccc.org.uk/wp-content/uploads/2017/03/Energy-Prices-and-Bills-Committee-on-Climate-Change-March-2017.pdf

International Energy Agency. (2016). *Energy, Climate Change and Enviroment 2016 Insights*. https://doi.org/10.1787/9789264266834-en

Jacobsen, G. D. (2015). Do energy prices influence investment in energy efficiency? Evidence from energy star appliances. *Journal of Environmental Economics and Management, 74*, 94–106. https://doi.org/10.1016/j.jeem.2015.09.004

Janczura, J. & Weron, R. (2010). An empirical comparison of alternate regime-switching models for electricity spot prices. Energy Economics, 32, 1059–1073.

Janczura, J., Trück, S., Weron, R., & Wolff, R. C. (2013). Identifying spikes and seasonal components in electricity spot price data: A guide to robust modeling. *Energy Economics, 38*, 96–110. https://doi.org/10.1016/j.eneco.2013.03.013

Ketterer, J. C. (2014). The impact of wind power generation on the electricity price in Germany. *Energy Economics, 44*, 270–280. https://doi.org/10.1016/j.eneco.2014.04.003

Newbery, D. (1998). Competition, contracts, and entry in the electricity spot market. RAND Journal of Economics, 29(4), 726–74.

Oberndorfer, U. (2009). Energy prices, volatility, and the stock market: Evidence from the Eurozone. Energy Policy, 37(12), 5787–5795. https://doi.org/10.1016/j.enpol.2009.08.043

Paraschiv, F., Erni, D., & Pietsch, R. (2014). The impact of renewable energies on EEX day-ahead electricity prices. *Energy Policy, 73*, 196–210. https://doi.org/10.1016/j.enpol.2014.05.004

Pietz, M. (2009). Risk premia in the German electricity futures market Working Paper No. 2009-07). Center for Entrepreneurial and Financial Studies.

Pirrong, C., & Jermakyan, M. (2008). The price of power: The valuation of power and weather derivatives. *Journal of Banking and Finance, 32*(12), 2520–2529. https://doi.org/10.1016/j.jbankfin.2008.04.007

Prentice, C., & Woodside, A. G. (2013). Problem Gamblers' Harsh Gaze on Casino Services. *Psychol-*

ogy & Marketing, 30(12), 1108–1123. https://doi.org/10.1002/mar

Ragin, C. (2000). Fuzzy-set social science. Chicago, IL: University of Chicago Press.

Ragin, C. C. (2008a). Measurement Versus Calibration: A Set-Theoretic Approach. In J. M. Box-Steffensmeier, H. E. Brady, & D. Collier (Eds.), *The Oxford Handbook of Political Methodology* (pp. 174-198). Oxford, UK: Oxford University Press.

Ragin, C. C. (2008b). Redesigning Social Inquiry. Fuzzy Sents and Beyong. Chicago, IL: University of Chicago Press.

Redl, C., Haas, R., Huber, C., & Böhm, B. (2009). Price formation in electricity forward markets and the relevance of systematic forecast errors. *Energy Economics, 31*(3), 356–364. https://doi.org/10.1016/j.eneco.2008.12.001

Rentschler, J., & Bazilian, M. (2017). Reforming fossil fuel subsidies: drivers, barriers and the state of progress. *Climate Policy, 17*(7), 891–914. https://doi.org/10.1080/14693062.2016.1169393

Rihoux, B., & Ragin, C. (Eds.). (2009). *Configurational Comparative Methods: Qualitative comparative analysis (QCA) and related techniques*. Los Angeles, CA: SAGE.

Schneider, M. R., Schulze-Bentrop, C., & Paunescu, M. (2010). Mapping the institutional capital of high-tech firms: A fuzzy-set analysis of capitalist variety and export performance. *Journal of International Business Studies, 41*(2), 246–266. https://doi.org/10.1057/jibs.2009.36

Scholte, J. A. (2008). Defining globalisation. *World Economy, 31*(11), 1471–1502. https://doi.org/10.1111/j.1467-9701.2007.01019.x

Shawky, H. A., Marathe, A., & Barrett, C. L. (2003). A first look at the empirical relation between spot and futures electricity prices in the United States. *Journal of Futures Markets, 23*(10), 931–955. https://doi.org/10.1002/fut.10093

United Nations. (2015). United Nations Framework Convention on Climate Change. Retrieved from https://unfccc.int/resource/docs/2015/cop21/eng/l09r01.pdf

Véliz, K. D., Kaufmann, R. K., Cleveland, C. J., & Stoner, A. M. K. (2017). The effect of climate change on electricity expenditures in Massachusetts. *Energy Policy, 106*, 1–11. https://doi.org/10.1016/j.enpol.2017.03.016

Weron, R., & Misiorek, A. (2008). Forecasting spot electricity prices: A comparison of parametric and semiparametric time series models. *International Journal of Forecasting, 24*(4), 744–763. https://doi.org/10.1016/j.ijforecast.2008.08.004

Woodside, A. G. (2013). Moving beyond multiple regression analysis to algorithms: Calling for adoption of a paradigm shift from symmetric to asymmetric thinking in data analysis and crafting theory. *Journal of Business Research, 66*(4), 463–472. https://doi.org/10.1016/j.jbusres.2012.12.021

Woodside, A. G., Prentice, C., & Larsen, A. (2015). Revisiting problem gamblers' Harsh Gaze on Casino services: Applying complexity theory to identify exceptional customers. *Psychology & Marketing, 32*(1), 64–77. https://doi.org/10.1002/mar

Wooldridge, J. (2006). Introductory econometrics—A modern Approach (3rd ed.). Andover, UK: Cengage EMEA.

Wooldridge, J. M. (2013). *Introductory Econometrics: A Modern Approach* (5th ed.). Andover, UK: Cengage EMEA.

Wu, P. L., Yeh, S. S., Huan, T. C., & Woodside, A. G. (2014). Applying complexity theory to deepen service dominant logic: Configural analysis of customer experience-and-outcome assessments of professional services for personal transformations. *Journal of Business Research, 67*(8), 1647–1670. https://doi.org/10.1016/j.jbusres.2014.03.012

Ziegler, L., Gonzalez, E., Rubert, T., Smolka, U., & Melero, J. J. (2018). Lifetime extension of onshore wind turbines: A review covering Germany, Spain, Denmark, and the UK. *Renewable and Sustainable Energy Reviews, 82*, 1261–1271. https://doi.org/10.1016/j.rser.2017.09.100

Acknowledgements

The authors acknowledge financial support from FCT-Fundação para a Ciência e Tecnologia (Portugal), national funding through research grant (UID/SOC/04521/2013). We thank comments from Carla Curado and Ricardo Rodrigues.

10

Statistical Properties of Rates of Return on Shares Listed on the German, French, and Polish Markets

Wiesław Dębski[1], Ewa Feder-Sempach[2], Szymon Wójcik[2]

ABSTRACT The financial market and its instruments are subject to numerous studies all over the world. Special attention is duly earned by the multifaceted research and analysis of the behavior of rates of return on shares, as well as shares' other statistical properties including the beta parameter. Stock stability is considered by dividing the whole market into the bull and bear categories, and the rate of return is studied according to different frequencies of measurement.

The purpose of this article is to examine the statistical properties of monthly rates of return for the biggest companies in terms of capitalization and turnover, which were listed on the stock exchange in Frankfurt, Paris, and Warsaw between 2005 and 2015. The basic descriptive statistics of the rates of return as well as the normality and stationarity of their time series undergo analysis. Moreover, hypotheses about equality of the expected value of the rate of return and its variance are subject to verification. This study is also conducted considering the division of the whole market into the bull and bear categories according to two definitions. The obtained results serve to conduct a comparative analysis of the three stock markets enumerated above. The results constitute an introduction to further and more advanced research on the beta parameter and its properties.

KEY WORDS: rates of return of shares; statistical properties; normality and stationarity; equality of mean and variance; German, French and Polish markets

[1] University of Finance and Management in Warsaw, Poland; [2] University of Lodz, Poland

1. Introduction

The mechanisms of the functioning of the financial market and investments have been subject to multifaceted research all over the world for many years. Special attention is duly earned by numerous studies on investment in shares of companies listed on the applicable stock exchange, whether taking into consideration a single country or comparing many countries. In countries where the financial market is highly developed, advanced research has been conducted since the middle of the previous century. In other countries, however, especially countries where political transformation occurred at the end of the previous century, such research may only be conducted in the present day. In certain countries, the present situation includes a quite well-developed financial market and the availability of ample time series for conducting advanced statistical or econometric research, allowing the ob-

Correspondence concerning this article should be addressed to: **Wiesław Dębski**, University of Finance and Management in Warsaw, Pawia 55 Str., 01-030 Warsaw, Poland. E-mail: wdebski@vizja.pl

tained results to be generalized. Poland is an example of such a country where the financial market started to emerge at the beginning of the 1990s.

As far as investment in shares is concerned, research and analysis chiefly focus on the mechanisms shaping prices, rates of return, and the beta parameter. Time series characterized by a varied frequency of measurement, e.g., a month, week or day, are most commonly used in studies. Because the share market is subject to large fluctuations in time, the whole sample period in many studies is divided into a bull and a bear market for which it is verified whether, for example, the rates of return have similar statistical properties in these markets or whether the beta parameters are stable. Numerous studies on rates of return on shares also examine their statistical properties, such as the mean value, dispersion, asymmetry or concentration, and verify hypotheses on the normality of distribution and stationarity of the time series of the rates of return. Hypotheses on the equality of the mean and variance undergo verification as well. Such research is most commonly employed in various comparative analyses, mainly in the international context, or serves as an introduction to further, more advanced studies, e.g., studies concerning the beta parameter and its properties.

For the purposes of the latter, the basic statistical properties of the rates of return on the shares under examination need to be known in order to select the method of estimation of the beta parameter so that it will meet the requirements for the best estimator (i.e., unbiased, consistent, and the most effective). It is also significant when the stability of the beta parameter is tested in the case of division of the whole market under analysis into the bull and bear subperiods and when the Sharpe's model (Sharpe, 1963) is estimated separately for each of these two subperiods.

Studies regarding statistical properties of rates of return are mostly concerned with the developed markets and, in the past two decades, emerging markets, as well. These studies point to certain statistical properties shown by time series of the rates of return on shares and the correlations existing between them, as well as their differences in distribution. For example, a basic characteristic is the existence of fat-tails in distributions, which signifies a lack of normality. Other such characteristics are the existence of autocorrelation and asymmetry and leptokurtosis of distribution (Jajuga, 2000). The characteristic fat-tailed distribution of the rate of return was already described in 1972 by Officer (1972), who analyzed monthly distributions of rates of return of 39 shares listed on the American stock exchange between 1926 and 1968. The authors of numerous studies on rates of return, which have been carried out on emerging markets, find that the distributions of rates of return on shares listed on these markets are different, sometimes considerably so, from the distributions observable on the well-developed markets. For instance, in a study conducted on BRICS countries, it turned out that the distributions of rates of return on shares at different frequencies of measurement have fatter and longer tails than on the developed markets (Adu, Alagidede, & Karimu, 2015). Such findings mean that atypical values of the rates of return on the emerging markets appeared more commonly than on the developed markets and did not depend on the frequency of measurement.

In contrast, in a study concerning rates of return on shares listed on 5 developed European markets, Corhay and Tourani Rad (1994) concluded that time series of daily rates of return are characterized by the lack of autocorrelation and that daily rates of return on the indices of these markets are marked with heteroscedasticity. The authors of the study also indicated that GARCH-type models are the most suitable in statistical terms for analyzing daily rates of return on shares on these markets.

Another study examining the statistical properties of rates of return tested the stationarity of the rates of return on stock indices on ten markets in Central and Eastern Europe between 1994 and 2006. Its authors (Harrison, Lupu, & Lupu, 2010) concluded that these time series at daily measurement of the rates of return are stationary and that there is a significant cross-correlation among the rates of return on indices in these countries. Examination of a cross-correlation among companies was also carried out for the rates of return on shares listed on the Chinese stock exchange between 1999 and 2011. It was observed that the correlations increased significantly during the crashes of the market in China in 2001 and 2008 (Ren & Zhou, 2014).

Other examples of studies of the statistical properties of rates of return on shares at various frequencies of measurement of the rate of return may be, among others, (Poon & Taylor, 1992; Ren, Guo, & Zhou, 2009; Zumbach, Fernandez, & Weber, 2014). Research studies on the statistical properties of the rates of return on shares listed on the German and French market were based, however, on data collected at a high frequency of measurement (daily and minute-based data) and were conducted, among others, by (Kramer & Runde, 1996; Qiua, Zhenga, Rena, & Trimper, 2007; Teiletche, 1998).

In Poland the statistical properties of rates of return on shares were also examined in numerous studies. For instance, based on a sample of data collected from the biggest companies listed on the Warsaw stock exchange between 2000 and 2006, Kompa and Matuszewska-Janica (2008) concluded that for the majority of shares under analysis, the distributions of the rates of return are asymmetric, that kurtosis is significantly different form the normal distribution and that the estimated variances for the bull and bear subperiods are significantly different in statistical terms. In another study, Piontek (2007) also stated that the majority of distributions of the rates of return on shares of several dozen companies listed on the Warsaw stock exchange were fat-tailed and asymmetric.

The main objective of the article is examination of the statistical properties of monthly rates of return of companies listed on the stock exchange in Frankfurt, Paris, and Warsaw between 2005 and 2015, which were the biggest in terms of capitalization and turnover. This analysis covers the descriptive statistics of the rates of return as well as normality of distribution and stationarity of their time series. Moreover, hypotheses about the equality of the expected value of the rate of return and equality of its variance undergo examination. This study is also conducted for a division of the whole market into the bull and the bear segments according to two definitions used in the relevant literature. The results that have been obtained serve to carry out a comparative analysis of the largest companies on the German, French, and Polish markets. We want to compare the Polish market with the two largest markets in the EU.

The study may be particularly useful for Poland, whose stock market has operated for 26 years and is considered to be relatively large and well-developed in Europe (although has been little diagnosed so far), and where an important role is played by international institutional investors. Knowledge acquired from the comparative analysis that is part of this study will carry cognitive value not only for Poland but for investors from the European Union as well, who may use it in the course of making investment decisions on these three stock markets under examination. Such comprehensive research comparing the properties of the rates of return on shares listed on the abovementioned stock markets has not been conducted before.

2. Research sample and methodology

The study examines logarithmic monthly rates of return on shares (measured in %) of the biggest companies listed on stock markets in Frankfurt (28 companies included in the DAX index portfolio), Paris (36 companies included in the CAC40 index portfolio), and Warsaw (37 companies included in the WIG20 and mWIG40 index portfolio) between 2005 and 2015 (132 observations) and calculated according to the closing rates on the last day of the month. Data were obtained from the Thomson Reuters service. The rates of return were calculated without taking into account income from dividends.

For the rates of return defined in such a way, the basic descriptive statistics are estimated, and the normality and stationarity of their time series are analyzed in statistical terms. The following questions are examined as well: a) Is the expected value of the rate of return on a share of a company under analysis significantly different from zero? b) Does a statistically significant difference exist between the rate of return on a share of a company and the rate of return of a portfolio of the stock index the company belongs to? c) Is there a statistically significant difference between volatility of the rate of return on a share of a company and the volatility of the rate of return of the portfolio of the relevant stock index? This study was also carried out considering the division of the whole market into the bull and bear segments, which was done according to the behavior of the STOXX Europe 600 Index (containing companies from 17 European states) throughout the period of the sample and taking into consideration the recommendations proposed in the contemporary relevant literature, e.g., by Pagan and Sossounov (2003). This division was made according to the following two

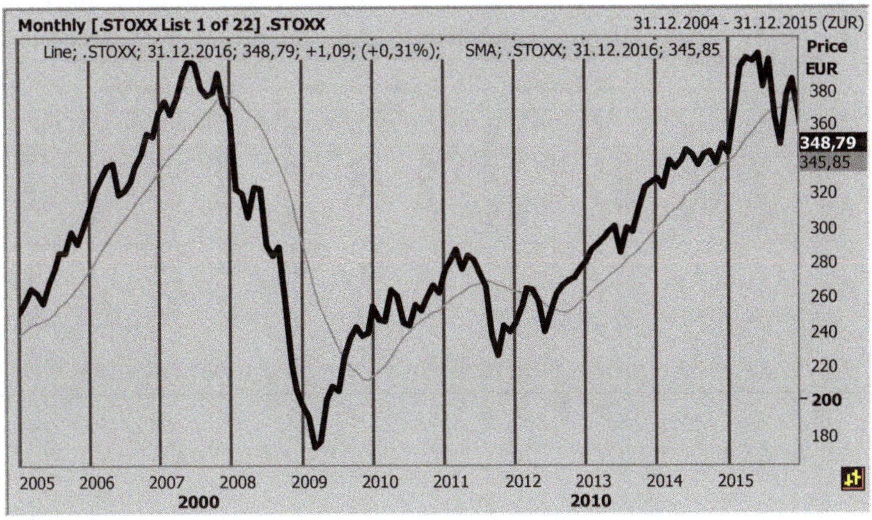

Figure 1. STOXX Europe 600 Index in 2005-2015

definitions that are most often used in the literature (Dębski & Feder-Sempach, 2012):

1. Definition 1 is based on the crossover of a 14-day moving average with the index, which is illustrated below in Figure 1 presenting the STOXX Europe 600 Index, where the index is marked with a line in bold and the thin line indicates the moving average (the average from a longer period was a straight line, and the bull and bear markets were difficult to indicate).
2. Definition 2 – the period of the STOXX Europe 600 Index from the bottom (the smallest value of the index) to the top (the highest value of the index) is the bull market, and the period between the top and the bottom is the bear market.

According to definition 1, there are three periods of bull market (101 observations) and two periods of bear market (31 observations), whereas according to definition 2, there are three periods of bull market (97 observations) and three periods of bear market (35 observations).

3. Discussion of the results

During analysis of the basic statistical properties of monthly rates of return enjoyed by the largest companies on the German, French, and Polish markets, their basic descriptive statistics were estimated first, which are the arithmetic mean ($\bar{R}$), standard deviation (S), standard semideviation (SS), skewness (A), and kurtosis (K). The results are presented in Table 1 as a percentages for the distinguished ranges of these statistics for the whole sample and taking into account the division into the bull and bear markets according to the definitions provided above.

These results demonstrate that the mean of the largest number of companies from all the three markets (from 54% to 64%), considering the whole sample, fits within the range [0; 1]; that is, it is not very high. The mean of the biggest number of companies that are to be found on the Polish market (35%) is above 1, and that on the French market is negative (25%). On the bull market, the overwhelming majority of companies achieve a mean of above 1 (from 67% to 76% accord-

Table 1. Consolidated information about descriptive statistics of CAC40, DAX and WIG20+40 companies

Value of statistic form a given range		Share of the companies (in %)														
		Whole sample			Definition 1						Definition 2					
					Bull market			Bear market			Bull market			Bear market		
		CAC40	DAX	WIG20+40	CAC40	DAX	WIG20+40	CAC40	DAX	WIG20+40	CAC40	DAX	WIG20+40	CAC40	DAX	WIG20+40
	$(-\infty;0)$	25	14	11	3	7	3	94	96	87	3	0	3	100	100	100
$\bar{R}$	$[0;1]$	64	64	54	30	18	21	6	4	8	8	11	5	0	0	0
	$(1;+\infty)$	11	22	35	67	75	76	0	0	5	89	89	92	0	0	0
	$[0;10)$	78	72	46	94	96	76	39	36	11	89	89	62	61	50	27
S	$[10;15]$	22	21	49	6	4	21	39	36	51	11	11	35	33	32	62
	$(15;+\infty)$	0	7	5	0	0	3	22	28	38	0	0	3	6	18	11
	$[0;7)$	72	64	38	100	96	92	97	86	92	100	100	92	100	82	100
SS	$[7;10]$	28	18	57	0	4	5	3	14	8	0	0	5	0	18	0
	$(10;+\infty)$	0	18	5	0	0	3	0	0	0	0	0	3	0	0	0
	$(-\infty;-0,5)$	42	61	33	3	14	3	28	43	24	8	4	3	44	68	57
A	$[-0.5;0.5]$	58	39	62	94	82	84	69	50	68	75	79	57	53	32	43
	$(0.5;+\infty)$	0	0	5	3	4	13	3	7	8	17	18	41	3	0	0
	$(-\infty;-1)$	0	0	0	0	0	0	0	0	0	0	0	0	0	0	0
K	$[-1;1]$	50	25	32	81	79	54	83	68	65	75	71	51	83	61	49
	$(1;+\infty)$	50	75	68	19	21	46	17	32	35	25	29	49	17	39	51

ing to definition 1 and approximately 90% according to definition 2), whereas on the bear market, a substantial majority of companies (from 87% to 96% according to definition 1) or all of them (according to definition 2) have a negative mean. On the Polish bear market according to definition 1, 5% of the companies have a mean higher than 1, and 8% of companies have a mean within the range [0; 1]. Companies listed on the French (78%) and German (72%) markets pose the smallest investment risk measured by standard deviation, and the biggest risk is posed by companies on the Polish market in which only 46% of companies pose risk lower than 10, and 49% ranged from [10; 15].

Similar relations are observed on the bull market where the overwhelming majority of companies pose risk smaller than 10, and the fewest companies with such risk are found on the Polish market. On the bear market, there are relatively high fractions of companies with risk ranging [10; 15] or even exceeding 15. In terms of risk measured by standard semideviation for the whole sample, companies on the French market have the best scores, and companies on the Polish market, where 57% have a semideviation within the range [7; 10], have the worst scores. It is noteworthy that 18% of companies on the German market have a semideviation higher than 10, which is relatively high. On the bull market, 92% or more of the companies have a standard semideviation within the range [0; 7), and on the bear market, these fractions are slightly smaller; there are at least 14% companies with a semideviation ranging from [7; 10] on the German market.

For the whole sample, the largest number of companies with low asymmetry (range [-0.5; 0.5]) is found on the Polish market (62%); on the French market, it is 58%, and on the German market, it is 39%. A relatively large number of companies have negative asymmetry lower than -0.5; on the German market, it is as much as 61% (on the French market it is 42%), and only 5% of companies exclusively on the Polish market have positive asymmetry higher than 0.5. This could signify that the distribution of rates of return on the markets that are more developed than the Polish one have the so-called fat tails. Admittedly, approximately 60% of companies on the Polish and French market are characterized by very low asymmetry (or show no asymmetry at all). On the bull market, the vast majority of companies from all the markets show asymmetry within the range [-0.5; 0.5], and the fractions of companies are larger when using definition 1 rather than definition 2. On the Polish market, (according to definition 2) 41% of companies show right-sided asymmetry higher than 0.5. In contrast, on the bear market, relatively high fractions of companies with left-sided asymmetry below -0.5 may be observed, and these fractions are higher for definition 2 than for definition 1.

The results obtained for kurtosis (estimated as excess kurtosis, which is equal to 0 for a normal distribution) indicate that on all the markets under examination for the whole research sample and a relatively large number of companies, the values of kurtosis exceed 1 (75% of companies on the German market, 68% on the Polish market, and 50% on the French market), which testifies to the fact that the empirical distribution of logarithmic monthly rates of return of these companies is thinner than normal, that is, leptokurtic. There is, however, a relatively wide group of companies (on the French market amounting to as much as 50%) whose kurtosis takes the values from the range [-1; 1], which may signify that their empirical distribution of the rate of return coincides with the normal rate. On the French and German bull markets, there are substantially more companies whose kurtosis ranges [-1; 1] than companies whose kurtosis exceeds 1. On the Polish market, the fractions of kurtosis from these ranges fluctuate around 50%. On the bear market, the situation is similar, and according to definition 2, 49% of companies on the Polish market show kurtosis ranging from [-1; 1], and 51% of companies have kurtosis higher than 1. Altogether, this means that there are a relatively high number of companies (and this is mainly true for the French and German markets – the ones that are more developed than the Polish market) whose empirical distributions of the rates of return may be convergent with the normal distribution. This may confirm a thesis often encountered in the relevant literature, which states that on the developed markets, empirical distributions of monthly rates of return display a tendency to coincide with a normal distribution.

One of the fundamental statistical properties of the rates of return on shares, in particular in analyses based on time series, is an answer to the question of whether an empirical distribution of a rate of return under examination is a normal distribution. The study may be carried out on the basis of several tests, and the most commonly used are the Jarque-Bera test and the Shapiro-Wilk test. The values of these statistics are presented in Table 2 (as p-values) for the rates of return on shares of companies on the German, French, and Polish markets.

The table demonstrates that for the whole sample, fractions rejecting the null hypothesis in both tests that have been performed are relatively high, which means that empirical distributions of the rates of return from all the three markets are not normal (at the level of significance of 0.05 in line with the Jarque-Bera test, it is true in the case of over 78% companies on the German market, over 64% companies on the Polish market, and over 63% on the French market). Everything changes completely when the market is divided into the bull and bear segments because fractions rejecting the null hypothesis are considerably smaller for definition 1 and slightly higher for definition 2. For example, when the Jarque-Bera test is applied at significance level of 0.05, this fraction does not exceed 30% according to definition 1 and 55% according to definition 2 (and the highest fractions are found on the Polish market). This signifies that there is no basis to reject the null hypothesis for the remaining companies, that is, the empirical distributions of the rates of return on shares

Table 2. Fraction of rejections of the null hypothesis in the normality tests of returns of CAC40, DAX and WIG20+40 companies (in %)

		Index	Jarque-Bera test			Shapiro-Wilk test		
			pval<0.01	pval<0.05	pval<0.1	pval<0.01	pval<0.05	pval<0.1
Whole sample		CAC40	41.67	63.89	77.78	41.67	55.56	72.22
		DAX	67.86	78.57	85.71	64.29	78.57	82.14
		WIG20+40	51.35	64.86	70.27	59.46	62.16	75.68
Definition 1	Bull market	CAC40	2.78	13.89	22.22	5.56	16.67	22.22
		DAX	17.86	21.43	28.57	17.86	25.00	25.00
		WIG20+40	16.22	29.73	45.95	18.92	32.43	45.95
	Bear market	CAC40	5.56	11.11	19.44	2.78	13.89	16.67
		DAX	10.71	25.00	32.14	3.57	14.29	28.57
		WIG20+40	8.11	24.32	29.73	8.11	13.51	27.03
Definition 2	Bull market	CAC40	19.44	30.56	36.11	13.89	25.00	38.89
		DAX	25.00	28.57	35.71	21.43	28.57	32.14
		WIG20+40	29.73	54.05	64.86	32.43	51.35	62.16
	Bear market	CAC40	11.11	22.22	30.56	13.89	25.00	25.00
		DAX	25.00	39.29	46.43	25.00	35.71	42.86
		WIG20+40	24.32	48.65	59.46	37.84	54.05	62.16

of the companies under examination are normal. The conclusion is that a relatively large number of companies on the bull and the bear markets (which might be over 70% on the French market, more than 60% on the German market, and over 45% on the Polish market) may have distributions of rates of return that are convergent with the normal distribution. It is also observable that on the better-developed markets, these fractions are higher than on the Polish market.

Another desirable property, which is particularly important in analyses and modeling of financial time-series, is that their stationarity is confirmed. An Augmented Dickey-Fuller test (ADF) was adopted in order to examine the stationarity of time series of rates of return of companies from the markets under analysis (Charemza & Deadman, 1997, pp. 110-122). The study was performed for a case in which there was so-called drift observed in a time series of a rate of return on shares, which in the random walk testifies to the existence of a steady trend, as well as for a case in which a deterministic trend was additionally taken into account. The results of this study are presented in Table 3.

The outcome of the first test indicated that at all three significance levels, the time series of all the companies in all the segments of the markets under analysis are stationary. In the second test, at the significance level of 0.05, there are three cases (one of which is encountered on the French market and two on the German market) where the number of stationary time series of the rates of return reaches over 96%. These results indicate that there should be no major complications in the process of correct – in terms of properties – estimation of the beta parameter and its fundamental characteristics, e.g., dispersion.

Table 3. Fraction of rejections of the null hypothesis in the unit root tests of returns of CAC40, DAX and WIG20+40 companies (in %)

		Index	ADF test with drift (p-value)			ADF test with drift and trend (p-value)		
			pval<0.01	pval<0.05	pval<0.1	pval<0.01	pval<0.05	pval<0.1
Whole sample		CAC40	100.00	100.00	100.00	100.00	100.00	100.00
		DAX	100.00	100.00	100.00	100.00	100.00	100.00
		WIG20+40	100.00	100.00	100.00	100.00	100.00	100.00
Definition 1	Bull market	CAC40	100.00	100.00	100.00	100.00	100.00	100.00
		DAX	100.00	100.00	100.00	100.00	100.00	100.00
		WIG20+40	100.00	100.00	100.00	100.00	100.00	100.00
	Bear market	CAC40	100.00	100.00	100.00	88.89	97.22	100.00
		DAX	100.00	100.00	100.00	89.29	96.43	100.00
		WIG20+40	100.00	100.00	100.00	91.89	100.00	100.00
Definition 2	Bull market	CAC40	100.00	100.00	100.00	100.00	100.00	100.00
		DAX	100.00	100.00	100.00	100.00	100.00	100.00
		WIG20+40	100.00	100.00	100.00	100.00	100.00	100.00
	Bear market	CAC40	100.00	100.00	100.00	94.44	100.00	100.00
		DAX	100.00	100.00	100.00	92.86	96.43	100.00
		WIG20+40	100.00	100.00	100.00	97.30	100.00	100.00

Next, the study proceeds to statistically verify the hypotheses regarding whether the expected rate of return on shares of a company under analysis is significantly different from zero and whether this expected rate of return is significantly different from the expected rate of return on the stock index that the company belongs to. In other words, the null hypothesis in the former case was formulated as follows: $H_0 : E(R_i) = 0$, and that in the latter case was $H_0 : E(R_i) = E(R_{index})$. The values of the statistics (as p-values) for both hypotheses that undergo verification are provided in Table 4.

The presented estimations demonstrate that in the majority of cases (for the whole sample), there is no basis to reject the null hypothesis regarding the equality of the expected rate of return on shares of companies being tested neither with zero nor with the expected rate of return on the index that the company is included in. For instance, the fractions rejecting the null hypothesis (at $\alpha = 0.05$) are 14.29% on the German market, 8.11% or 0% on the Polish market, and 5.56% on the French market. The results obtained for a division of the whole market into the bull and bear segments are very diversified and allow no general conclusion to be drawn. For example, on the bull market according to definition 1, at the significance level of 0.05, the fractions rejecting the null hypothesis of equality of the rate of return of a company being tested with zero are as follows: 67.86% (the German market), 45.95% (the Polish market), and 41.67% (the French market), whereas on the same market according to definition 2, the fractions are considerably higher. Moreover, a very broad difference between the obtained fractions reject-

Table 4. Fraction of rejections of the null hypothesis of equality to zero of returns and of equality of index return and company return of CAC40, DAX and WIG20+40 companies (in %)

		Index	$H_0: E(R_i)=0$			$H_0: E(R_i)=E(R_{index})$		
			pval<0.01	pval<0.05	pval<0.1	pval<0.01	pval<0.05	pval<0.1
Whole sample		CAC40	0.00	5.56	8.33	0.00	5.56	11.11
		DAX	3.57	14.29	17.86	7.14	14.29	17.86
		WIG20+40	2.70	8.11	16.22	0.00	0.00	8.11
Definition 1	Bull market	CAC40	11.11	41.67	66.67	0.00	2.78	2.78
		DAX	28.57	67.86	75.00	7.14	17.86	17.86
		WIG20+40	13.51	45.95	56.76	21.62	56.76	72.97
	Bear market	CAC40	2.78	5.56	11.11	0.00	8.33	16.67
		DAX	0.00	0.00	10.71	0.00	0.00	7.14
		WIG20+40	0.00	0.00	8.11	0.00	0.00	5.41
Definition 2	Bull market	CAC40	55.56	77.78	88.89	2.78	11.11	16.67
		DAX	64.29	78.57	85.71	14.29	17.86	28.57
		WIG20+40	62.16	86.49	86.49	89.19	94.59	94.59
	Bear market	CAC40	30.56	63.89	69.44	0.00	22.22	25.00
		DAX	21.43	42.86	67.86	10.71	25.00	32.14
		WIG20+40	29.73	70.27	81.08	89.19	100.00	100.00

ing the null hypothesis emerges between the bear market segments distinguished according to definitions 1 and 2. Regarding verification of the null hypothesis about equality of a rate of return on a share of a company being tested with the rate of return on the index portfolio the company is part of, the fractions rejecting this hypothesis both on the bull and the bear markets are significantly varied. In particular, such differences occur between the Polish market and the French German markets and between the adopted definitions that divide the market into the bull and bear segments.

The last hypothesis that undergoes verification concerns the equality of variance of a rate of return on a share of a company with variance of a rate of return on the stock index in which the company is included. Verification of the hypothesis formulated in such a way is carried out based on the Fisher-Snedecor test statistic. The values of this statistic are provided as p-values in Table 5.

The table shows that for the whole sample, in the majority of cases and on all the markets (e.g., at significance level of 0.05), variance of the rate of return of a company is significantly different from variance of the rate of return of the whole stock index portfolio (on the Polish market, the fraction rejecting the null hypothesis is approximately 97%). On the Polish bull market (according to both definitions), the fraction rejecting the null hypothesis even amounts to 100% (this is also true for the German bull market distinguished in line with definition 1). On the French market, the fraction is slightly smaller and reaches 89%. On the bear market, the fractions rejecting the null hypothesis

Table 5. Fraction of rejections of the null hypothesis of equality of variances of returns of CAC40, DAX and WIG20+40 companies (in %)

		Index	$H_0 : S^2_i = S^2_{index}$		
			pval<0.01	pval<0.05	pval<0.1
Whole sample		CAC40	77.78	80.56	83.33
		DAX	67.86	71.43	78.57
		WIG20+40	91.89	97.30	100.00
Definition 1	Bull market	CAC40	83.33	88.89	88.89
		DAX	89.29	100.00	100.00
		WIG20+40	97.30	100.00	100.00
	Bear market	CAC40	52.78	61.11	66.67
		DAX	42.86	46.43	53.57
		WIG20+40	40.54	64.86	72.97
Definition 2	Bull market	CAC40	77.78	83.33	88.89
		DAX	85.71	96.43	96.43
		WIG20+40	97.30	100.00	100.00
	Bear market	CAC40	47.22	63.89	63.89
		DAX	46.43	50.00	60.71
		WIG20+40	64.86	75.68	83.78

are slightly smaller and range from 61%-65% according to definition 1 and 50%-76% according to definition 2. This means that on the bull and bear market segments of all the three markets under examination, there are also differences in the volatility of the rates of return of a company and the rates of return on an index portfolio the company is included in for the majority of companies.

4. Conclusions

To summarize the findings of the study and the comparative analysis of the biggest companies listed on two developed (German and French) markets and a third emerging (Polish) market, it may be concluded that they are interesting in cognitive terms. The obtained results indicate that there are quite significant differences in the statistical properties of the rates of return on shares of companies between both types of markets as well as between the distinguished bull and bear market segments. In contrast, their common characteristics are low asymmetry and kurtosis in the case of a relatively large number of companies, especially when the division into the bull and bear markets is adopted, which could suggest convergence between the empirical distributions of the rates of return under examination and normal distribution. This has also been confirmed by tests that were adopted to verify the hypothesis concerning the normality of empirical distributions of the rates of return of companies under analysis; however, for the whole sample, there are definitely more cases in which the rates of return have no normal distribution. An undoubtedly positive – from the point of view of statistics – property of nearly all time series under examination is their stationarity. Verification of the hypothesis concerning equality of the expected rate of return on shares of a company being tested with zero or the expected rate of return on the index portfolio to which the company belongs has demonstrated that for the vast majority of companies (for the whole sample), the equality is present, whereas for the bull and bear segments, the outcome is highly equivocal, especially with the division made according to the adopted definitions. Verification of the hypothesis concerning equality of investment risk of the rate of return on shares of a company being tested with the risk posed by the stock index portfolio to which the company belongs reveals that the risks are predominantly different. The study also demonstrated that the market has rightly been divided into the bull and bear segments since the results obtained for these segments are occasionally significantly different from the results for the whole sample.

References

Adu, G., Alagidede, P., & Karimu, A. (2015). Stock return distribution in the BRICS. *Review of Development Finance, 5*(2), 98-109.

Charemza, W., Deadman, D. F. (1997). *Nowa ekonometria [New econometrics].* Warsaw: PWE.

Corhay, A., Tourani Rad, A. (1994). Statistical Properties of Daily Returns: Evidence from European Stock Markets. *Journal of Business Finance and Accounting, 21*(2), 271-282.

Dębski W., Feder-Sempach E. (2012). Beta Coefficients of Polish Blue Chip Companies in the Period of 2005-2011. *Folia Oeconomica Stetinensia, 12*(20), 90 - 102.

Harrison, B., Lupu, R., & Lupu, I. (2010). Statistical Properties of the CEE Stock Market Dynamics. A Panel Data Analysis. *The Romanian Economic Journal, 13*(37), 41-54.

Jajuga, K. (2000). *Metody ekonometryczne i statystyczne a analizie rynku kapitałowego (Econometric and statistical methods in the analysis of the capital market).* Wrocław: Wydawnictwo Akademii Ekonomicznej we Wrocławiu..

Kompa, K., Matuszewska-Janica, A. (2008). Charakterystyki opisowe i efektywność informacyjna wybranych instrumentów notowanych na GPW [The characteristics of descriptive and informational efficiency of selected instruments listed on Warsaw Stock Exchange]. In W. Tarczyński (Ed.), Rynek kapitałowy. Skuteczne inwestowanie [The capital market. Successful investing] (pp. 614-629). Szczecin: Studia i prace Wydziału Nauk Ekonomicznych i Zarządzania, Uniwersytet Szczeciński.

Kramer W., Runde, R. (1996). Stochastic properties of German stock returns. *Empirical Economics, 21*(2), 281-306.

Officer, R. (1972). The Distribution of Stock Returns. *Journal of American Statistical Association, 67*(340), 807-812.

Pagan, A. R., Sossounov, K. A. (2003). A Simple Framework for Analyzing Bull and Bear Markets. *Journal of Applied Econometrics, 18*(1), 23-46.

Piontek, K. (2007). Pomiar i testowanie skośności rozkładów stóp zwrotu instrumentów finansowych [Measuring and Testing of Skewness for Financial Return Distributions]. *Prace Naukowe Akademii Ekonomicznej we Wrocławiu. Taksonomia, 14*(1169), 122-130.

Poon, S. H., Taylor, S. J.(1992). Stock returns and volatility: An empirical study of the UK stock market. *Journal of Banking & Finance*, 16(1), 37-59.

Qiua, T., Zhenga, B., Rena, F., & Trimper, S., (2007). Statistical properties of German Dax and Chinese indices. *Physica A* 378, 387–398.

Ren, F., Guo, L., & Zhou, W. X. (2009). Statistical properties of volatility return intervals of Chinese stocks. *Physica A: Statistical Mechanics and its Applications, 388*(6), 881-890.

Ren, F., Zhou, W. X. (2014). Dynamic Evolution of Cross-Correlations in the Chinese Stock Market. *PLOS One, 9*(5), https://doi.org/10.1371/journal.pone.0097711.

Sharpe, W. F. (1963). A Simplified Model of Portfolio Analysis. *Management Science, 9*(2), 277-293.

Teiletche, J. (1998). La dynamique à treès haute fréquence de l'indice **CAC 40,** (The High Frequency Dynamic of the CAC40 Market). *Finance, 19*(2), 197-220.

Zumbach, G., Fernández, L., & Weber, C. (2014). Processes for stocks capturing their statistical properties from one day to one year. *Quantitative Finance, 14*(5), 849-861.

11

Measuring economic spatial evolutional trend of Central and Eastern Europe by SDE method

Xiaoxin Yang[1], Adriana Grigorescu[2]

ABSTRACT The economic crisis affected the Central and Eastern European economic spatial structure and reshaped perspectives at the European Union and international levels. Whereas Western Europe's stable economic system has entered maturity, Eastern Europe's economic landscape is still constantly evolving and improving. From a geographical perspective, based on standard distance and the standard deviational ellipse method, we examine the space-time evolution of the Central and Eastern European economy from 1995-2015. During this period, the Central and Eastern European economic spatial barycenter moves northeastward, and the economic distribution scale extends north-south in space. At the same time, the demographic barycenter moves northwestward, with an intense contraction in space. By comparing the economic and demographic standard deviation ellipses, we found a large degree of spatial differentiation, which gradually decreases. This trend shows that in Central and Eastern Europe, the economic development and demographic distribution is not symmetrical, and there still is large potential for the internal market. We propose that Eastern European countries such as Romania and Bulgaria, which have an abundant population, can increase investment in their home market by linking up with Asian countries. This connection can enable them to make full use of external capital, mine demographic advantages and exploit the benefits of being the hub of both Europe and Asia.

KEY WORDS: economic landscape; evolution of space time, spatial difference; the standard deviation ellipse; economic development

[1] Ocean University of China, China; [2] National University of Political Studies and Public Administration - Public Management, Romania

1. Introduction

In the late 1980s, Central and Eastern Europe (CEE) entered an era of transformation. On the economic front, Central and Eastern Europe transitioned from being an inefficiently operated planned economy system to establishing a market economy system. In May 2004, countries in Central and Eastern Europe started to join the European Union, ushering in new opportunities and challenges. With the 2008 financial crisis, Central and Eastern European countries suffered severely. Therefore, in the current steady development period of the global economy, it is of vital importance to stimulate both production and consumption in the

Correspondence concerning this article should be addressed to: **Adriana Grigorescu**, National University of Political Studies and Public Administration - Public Management, 6, Povernei Street, Bucharest 010643, Romania. E-mail: adriana.grigorescu@snspa.ro

CEE region in order to promote coordinated development of regional endogenous growth. Central and Eastern Europe is not only an economic region but also a densely populated region. Therefore, after a series of changes and transformations, how has the economic development of at national spatial level in Central and Eastern Europe changed? What kind of influence do Central and Eastern European markets have on the economic landscape? The answer to these questions can provide a quantitative basis for an investment and development strategy to promote the balanced growth of economic space and provide important references for optimizing spatial development patterns.

In PricewaterhouseCoopers' study "Central and Eastern Europe. Economic scorecard: A sustainable future in a great region" (2013), based on a scorecard comparison, the top four countries in terms of growth conditions are the Czech Republic, Slovakia, Poland and the Baltic States. In terms of the size of the economy, Poland outperforms the others.

Studying the potential economic growth in CEE countries, Dombi (2013) uses a growth accounting model that highlights the accumulation of capital. Baltic States, such as Romania and Bulgaria, are better positioned than other countries in terms of the differences between investing and saving rates. The study, which references the German economy (considered the leading economy in Europe), concludes that the CEE countries possess "considerable potential", even if there will continue to be a gap between them and Western European countries. These findings support our theory and confirm the instability between European member states.

Economic convergence is of great interest in the European Union, but some achievements are incomplete. For example, countries such as Slovenia and Hungary have limited results (Dąbrowski, 2014; Forgó & Jevcák, 2015), but the GDP per capita increased in Baltic countries, Poland, Romania and Slovakia and even Bulgaria. Forgó and Jevcák (2015) found that the share of gross fixed capital formation (GFCF) in the GDP was 25% in the Czech Republic, Estonia and Romania in 2014, followed by Poland and Lithuania with 20%. Another difference between EU countries is export accounting, which has very large distribution rates, from 90% of the GDP for Hungary to less than 50% for Poland and Romania.

Monastiriotis (2011) used theoretical and empirical models of regional growth, focusing on three models: neoclassical convergence, cumulative causation and the regional Kuznets Curve. The findings revealed that "this process is not applicable with the same force and in the same manner to the case of the older member states of the EU". The efforts of convergence have side effects, as there is evidence that the more developed Western countries have a more robust process of growth than the CEE countries. The CEE countries made efforts to address the convergence requirements, and even they have had growth in the cumulative force, while polarization is still produced. The polarization and disparities of the development in the EU will probably have a chance to be reduced if the development model of the CEE influences the process in the more advanced EU member states.

The economic crisis caused an important recession in CEE countries due to their transitional fragile economies, as confirmed by the negative rates of economic growth. This heterogeneous recovery process was started at the end of 2009 by Poland, the Czech Republic and Estonia. Hungary and Latvia followed in the beginning of 2010, while Romania and Bulgaria were the last and consequently the weakest (European Central Bank [ECB], 2010). The latest figures turned expectations upside down by showing that Romania has had the highest rate of economic growth in Europe in the last few years—Economic Growth (GDP, annual variation in %) 2011 – 1.1%; 2012 – 0.6%; 2013 – 3.5%; 2014 – 3.0%; 2015 – 3.8%, according to Eurostat—while the Bloomberg analysis reveals a higher regional growth (Iordan,http://www.sciencedirect.com/science/article/pii/S2212567115002749 - cor0005 Chilian, & Grigorescu, 2015; Kluvánková-Oravská, Chobotová, Banaszak, Slavikova, Trifunovova, 2009). It must be considered that this growth is based on consumption and does not show any Western influences or structural changes. Ultimately, due to its fragility, the economy could be blown away at the slightest gust of wind.

The CEE region is a fascinating area in terms of economic growth after the last recession. This growth was supported by competitive advantages such as a highly educated workforce, a stable macroeconomic environment, favorable business environments and strategic locations (Labaye et al., 2013; Thies, 2016). This region also has weaknesses, highlighted by its interdependence with Western European countries; for instance, foreign investment and exports comprise more than 2/3 of the economy, and it depends on older developed economies.

To accurately reveal the spatial evolution of Central and Eastern Europe's economy, driven by both the labor and consumer markets, we used the spatial statistics method of standard distance and standard deviational ellipse. Using ArcGIS10.2 software, we were able to analyze the economic elements of space and time changing processes from multiple angles, depict quantitative identification and the overall characteristics of the pattern of economic evolution in the form of visual space-time and space processes in order to inform decision-making in the development of economic policy and strategy.

This article comprehensively reveals the overall trend of space-time evolution for Central and Eastern Europe's economy. It ware considered previous spatial studies as Chang, Hu, and Chou (2012); Li and Wei (2010); Visser (1980; 1999); Yeung, He and Liu (2012) for Chinese economy or banking and finance studies. The spatial characteristics of CEE economic evolution have not aroused the concern of academia (Kluvánková-Oravská et al., 2009). Previous researchers have conducted related work from the angle of regions and adopted a non-spatial view to analyze the economic development of Central and Eastern Europe. Part 1 of this article introduces the main research methods and data. Part 2 focuses on analyzing the evolution trend of economic space. Finally, Part 3 summarizes this paper, and we draw the main conclusions and discuss relevant policy recommendations.

2. Research methods and data

Standard deviational ellipse (SDE) is a spatial statistics method that can accurately reveal the economic characteristics of spatial distribution. SDE was first introduced by Lefever in 1926 to reveal the geographical characteristics of spatial distribution elements (Burt & Barber, 1996; Yuill, 1971). At present, the SDE method is widely accepted in the spatial statistical field. With the development of GIS technology, the SDE method based on geographic information has become a conventional module of ArcGIS spatial statistical tools (Furfey, 1927; Gong, 2002; Li, Wei, 2010; Tellier, 1995; Wong, 1999). SDE from multiple perspectives reflects the characteristics of the integrity of the spatial distribution of economic elements. For example, the SDE barycenter reflects the relative position of the overall center using two-dimensional geographic coordinates with the weight of the economic elements in the spatial distribution. The long axis direction reflects its main trend orientation using the azimuth angle, which is the measure of the clockwise rotation angle from the arctic direction to the standard deviation ellipse's vertex. The long axis length is the characterization of the spatial distribution of elements in the main direction, while the short axis length describes the secondary direction of the spatial distribution. The length ratio of the long and short axes can reflect the element's shape of the spatial distribution. Therefore, the barycenter, long axis, short axis and azimuth angle are the basic parameters of standard deviation ellipses. The computation formulas viewed below are explained as follows, with geographic coordinate data longitude X_i, latitude Y_i and the corresponding economic or demographic weight W_i:

Mean Center:

$$\overline{X_W} = \frac{\sum_{i=1}^{n} W_i X_i}{\sum_{i=1}^{n} W_i}, \quad \overline{Y_W} = \frac{\sum_{i=1}^{n} W_i Y_i}{\sum_{i=1}^{n} W_i} \tag{1}$$

Azimuth Angle:

$$\tan\theta = \frac{(\sum_{i=1}^{n} W_i^2 X_i^2 - \sum_{i=1}^{n} W_i^2 \widetilde{Y_i^2}) +}{\sum_{i=1}^{11} W_i^2 \widetilde{X_i^2} \widetilde{Y_i^2}}$$

$$\frac{+\sqrt{(\sum_{i-1}^{n} W_i^2 \widetilde{X_i^2} - \sum_{i=1}^{n} W_i^2 \widetilde{Y_i^2})^2 + 4\sum_{i=1}^{n} W_i^2 \widetilde{X_i^2} \widetilde{Y_i^2}}}{\sum_{i=1}^{11} W_i^2 \widetilde{X_i^2} \widetilde{Y_i^2}} \tag{2}$$

Standard Deviation Distance of X:

$$\sigma_x = \sqrt{\frac{\sum_{i=1}^{n} (W_i X_i - W_i X_i)}{\sum_{i=1}^{n} W_i X_i}} \tag{3}$$

Standard Deviation Distance of Y:

$$\sigma_y = \sqrt{\frac{\sum_{i=1}^{n} (W_i \tilde{X}_i \cos\theta - W_i \tilde{Y}_i \sin\theta)^2}{\sum_{i=1}^{n} W^2{}_i}} \tag{4}$$

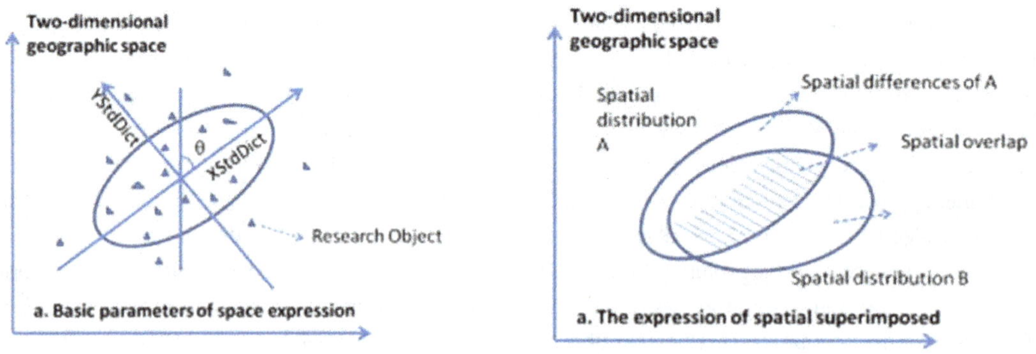

Figure 1. The pictorial view of standard deviational ellipse

A balanced economic spatial distribution should have the same spatial characteristics as a demographic distribution, and its spatial distribution should show the same standard deviational ellipse. Otherwise, the spatial distribution of both standard deviation ellipses will vary (Tellier, 1995). The spatial unconformity of economic factors and the demographic distribution can reflect the imbalance of economic space directly. It will be defined as the space difference index, and the specific calculation method is as follows:

Space difference index:

$$SDI_{j,p} = 1 - \frac{Area(SDE_j \cap SDE_p)}{Area(SDE_j \cup SDE_p)} \quad (5)$$

SDEj and SDEp, respectively, represent the SDE area of economic elements and the demographic spatial distribution. $SDI_{j,p}$ is the spatial difference index for economic factors and the demographic distribution, between 0 and 1, which reflects a greater discrepancy with a greater value.

This study uses the weighted standard deviational ellipse method based on the space and location of 11 countries, and it calculates the standard deviation of the spatial distribution ellipse. The 11 countries included are Estonia, Latvia, Lithuania, Poland, the Czech Republic, Slovakia, Hungary, Slovenia, Croatia, Romania and Bulgaria (which joined the EU after the system transformation). We used national geographic location data including territory, a national economic factor (GDP) and a social factor (population). We obtained the national geographic latitude and longitude data from the GISCO database and other data from the Eurostat website.

The spatial calculation is performed using the ArcGIS10.2 platform and the spatial reference for Albers' projected coordinate system. Under the given plane coordinates, we calculated the standard deviational ellipse of the spatial distribution of economic factors. The maps of the 11 countries display the nations' location, GDP and demographic value. The different colors, from light to dark, represent the quantity, from low to high, in 2015.

Table 1a. The population of the studied countries

Population (unit: thousand persons)					
Country	**1995**	**2000**	**2005**	**2010**	**2015**
Estonia	1448.1	1401.3	1358.9	1333.3	1313.3
Latvia	2485.1	2367.6	2238.8	2097.3	1977.3
Lithuania	3629.1	3499.5	3322.5	3097.3	2904.9
Poland	38275.0	38256.0	38161.0	38517.0	38455.0
Czech Republic	10330.8	10272.5	10234.1	10517.3	10542.9
Slovakia	5363.4	5400.7	5387.1	5430.0	5422.3
Hungary	10329.0	10211.0	10087.1	10000.0	9839.3
Slovenia	1988.7	1989.4	2000.8	2048.8	2063.3
Croatia	4658.9	4425.7	4311.7	4296.0	4201.5
Romania	22681.0	22435.2	21319.7	20246.8	19819.7
Bulgaria	8406.1	8170.2	7659.0	7395.6	7197.5

Source: "Eurostat-Data Explorer: Population and employment" by Eurostat (2016).

Table 1b. The GDP of the studied countries

Country	**1995**	**2000**	**2005**	**2010**	**2015**
Estonia	2902.3	6170.8	11262.3	14718.5	20460.9
Latvia	4134.5	8606.2	13710.6	17772.4	24377.7
Lithuania	5124.1	12491.3	21002.4	28027.7	37123.6
Poland	108715.7	186375.9	246201.3	361744.3	427737.4
Czech Republic	45541.7	66648.8	109394.0	156369.7	166964.1
Slovakia	15259.4	22346.8	39219.9	67387.1	78070.8
Hungary	35296.2	51185.8	90543.0	98198.4	108747.9
Slovenia	16279.8	21923.5	29235.4	36252.4	38570.0
Croatia	17326.6	23582.0	36508.4	45004.3	43897.0
Romania	28763.0	40796.8	80225.6	126746.4	160352.8
Bulgaria	11029.9	14300.5	24001.6	37723.8	44162.3

Source: "Eurostat - Data Explorer: GDP and main components (output, expenditure and income" by Eurostat (2016).

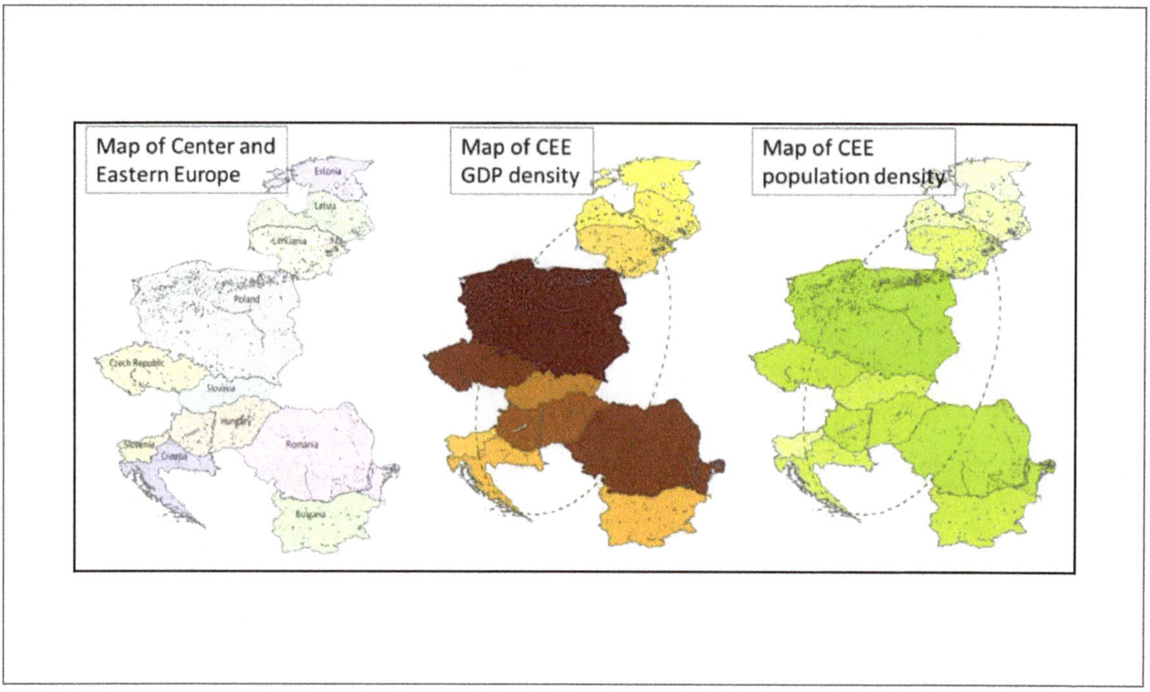

Figure 2. The map of CEE, GDP density and demographic density in 2015

3. Central and Eastern European economic spatial evolution trend

By means of a comparative analysis of the above economic factors from 1995 to 2015, we drew a standard deviational ellipse to find the distribution of the weighted parameters. The Central and Eastern European economic spatial ellipses can be observed in Figure 3, and detailed information is provided in table 2-3, which summarizes the evolution trend in four aspects.

3.1 The barycenter of the economy moving northeast

By comparing the standard deviation ellipses in different years, we found that the GDP spatial distribution ellipses barycenter has a northeastward moving track from 1995 to 2015. The detailed movement record of the GDP ellipses' barycenter for Central and Eastern Europe is shown in Figure 4. The total displacement of the GDP barycenter is 42.71 km, including a move eastward of 10.6 km and northward of 40.7 km, of which the movement has a small southeast callback in 2000-2005 and from 2005 to 2015, a smooth move to the northeast. The GDP barycenter moves from Slovakia in 1995 to Poland in 2015. In the picture, we can see the ellipses' moving track clearly pressing closer to the demographic ellipse.

The demographic spatial distribution ellipses barycenter (Figure 4) has a southwestward moving trend overall. The barycenter moves 13 km in total, including 11 km westward and 7 km southward. The demographic barycenter's moving direction is clear and stable. There is no back folding during the whole route, which reflects the Central and Eastern European migration direction within the last long period and a definite moving tendency in the future. The moving distance between 2000 and 2005 is the largest (22 km); after that, the moving distance is reduced, but there is no change in the direction. From the moving trace, we can conclude that the dynamic of a northward-moving tendency is weaker now, but the westward moving momentum is still strong. These days, the demographic ellipses' barycenter of gravity is located in Slovakia.

As observed from the space, shown in figure 5, economic ellipses' barycenter (represented by GDP and the total demographic ellipses barycenter) are con-

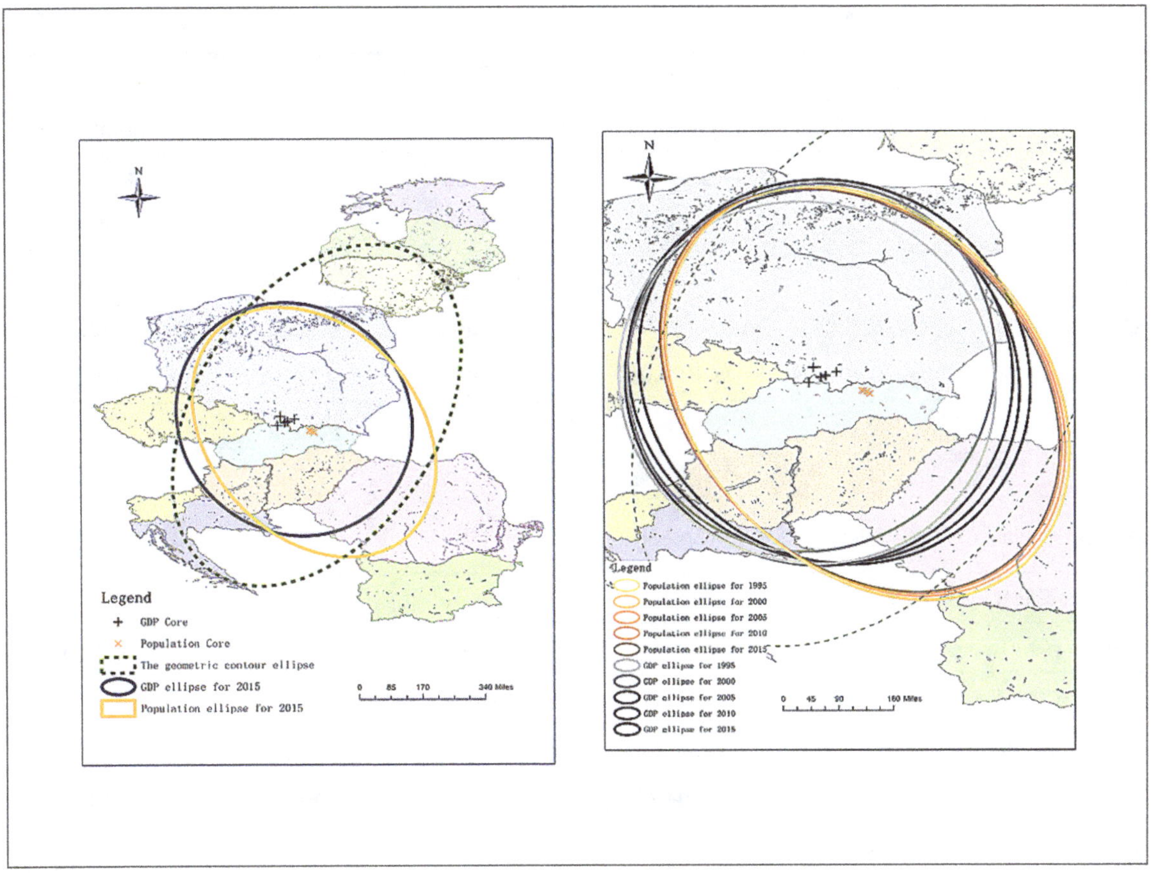

Figure 3. The contrast between GDP and demographic ellipse of CEE in 2015 and the variation tendency of double ellipses of CEE from 1995 to 2015

stantly approaching each other in space. The regional economic development and demographic distribution incline towards an equilibrium.

3.2 Economic spatial orientation

The Central and Eastern European demographic spatial distribution trend during the 1995-2015 period is shown in Figure 6. The standard deviational ellipse length of the X axis and the Y axis are reduced year after year, which means that the whole ellipse area is shrinking, moving gradually towards the center. Compared with the change in the economic spatial distribution, the demographic tendency is so unremarkable that to the naked eye, it is virtually microscopic. However, we are able to quantify it using numerical digits, where we can always find a smooth, stable variation towards one target. This variation indicates a partiality that can conduct the demographic movement

For the Central and Eastern European GDP spatial distribution, we can see a directionally stretched ellipse with small fluctuations. As shown in Figure 6, the standard deviation ellipse X axis in GDP increased every year after 2000, which indicates that the CEE economy remained along the north-south longitudinal extension from 2000 to 2015 and continued the trend of elongation. Among the process of shape-changing ellipses, the countries in the south of CEE play a bigger role than those in the central region and will stabilize the momentum. Although the GDP standard deviational ellipse is volatile, the length of the Y axis relatively stable, which indicates there is not much change in the east-west direction, as the economy has become stable. During the growth process for the length of the

Table 2. Standard deviation ellipse data of GDP

GDP Barycenter					
Feature	**centerX**	**centerY**	**XStdDist**	**YStdDist**	**Rotation**
ellipseGDP2015	19.969308	49.688798	4.933588	4.504663	150.648344
ellipseGDP2010	19.713476	49.59088	4.829346	4.468308	142.178839
ellipseGDP2005	19.603397	49.549298	4.727685	4.559695	178.303605
ellipseGDP2000	19.42821	49.795691	4.296936	4.655131	17.912925
ellipseGDP1995	19.325826	49.417404	4.596867	4.380448	151.444012

Table 3. Standard deviation ellipse data of demographic

Demographic Barycenter					
Feature	**centerX**	**centerY**	**XStdDist**	**YStdDist**	**Rotation**
ellipsePop2015	20.56432	49.223501	5.549827	4.119539	142.45571
ellipsePop2010	20.605509	49.215271	5.569524	4.14771	143.064694
ellipsePop2005	20.687748	49.19087	5.609377	4.151724	143.491456
ellipsePop2000	20.749103	49.143508	5.655776	4.169084	143.612027
ellipsePop1995	20.764892	49.142754	5.667183	4.195824	144.145527

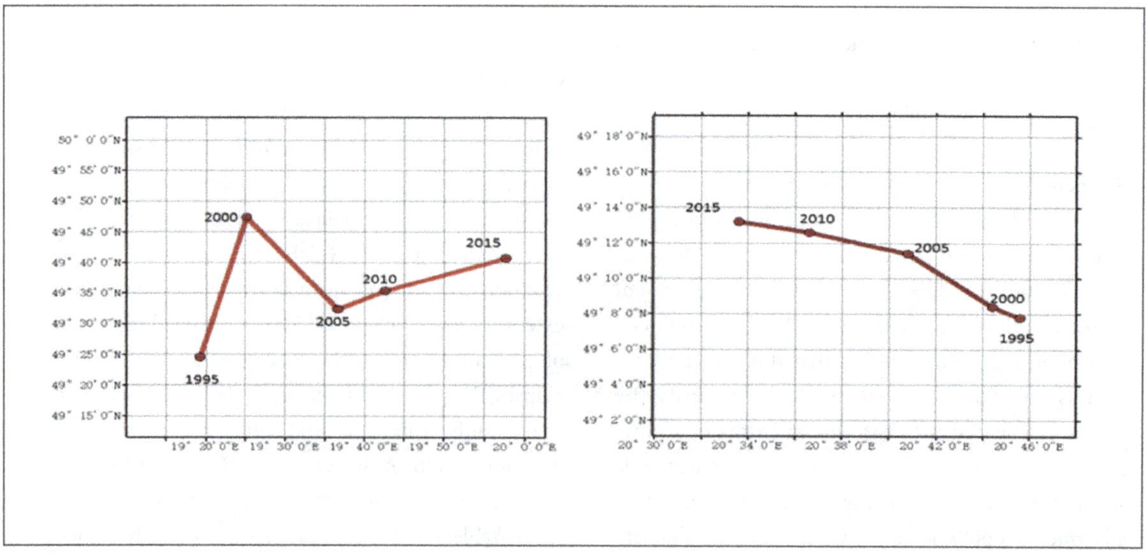

Figure 4. The moving tendency of GDP and demographic barycenter

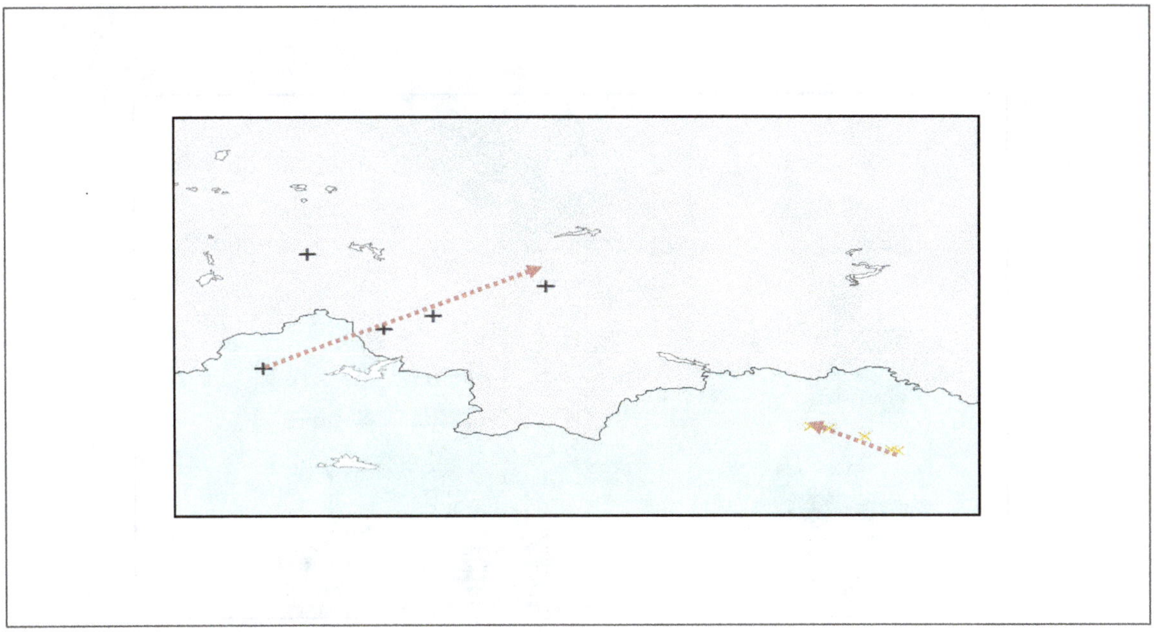

Figure 5. The tendency of approaching for barycenter

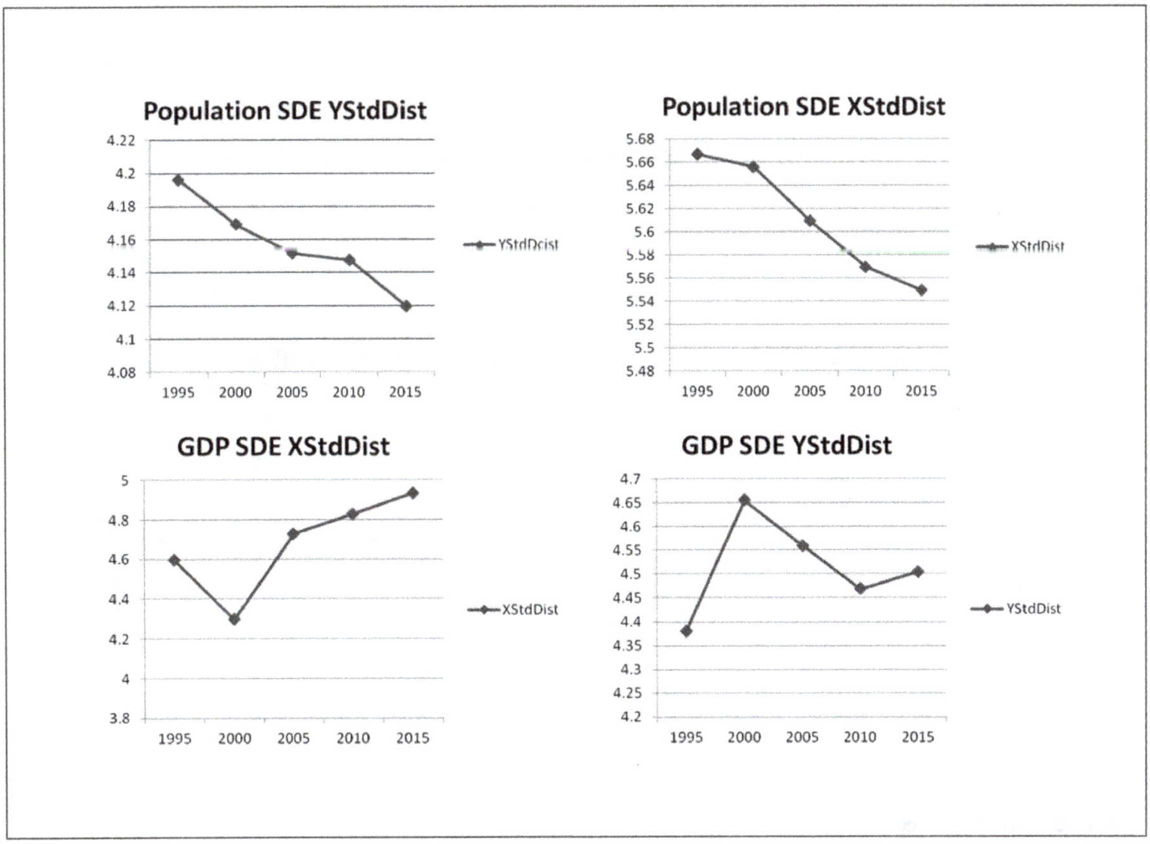

Figure 6. The change in spatial distribution range for demographic and GDP

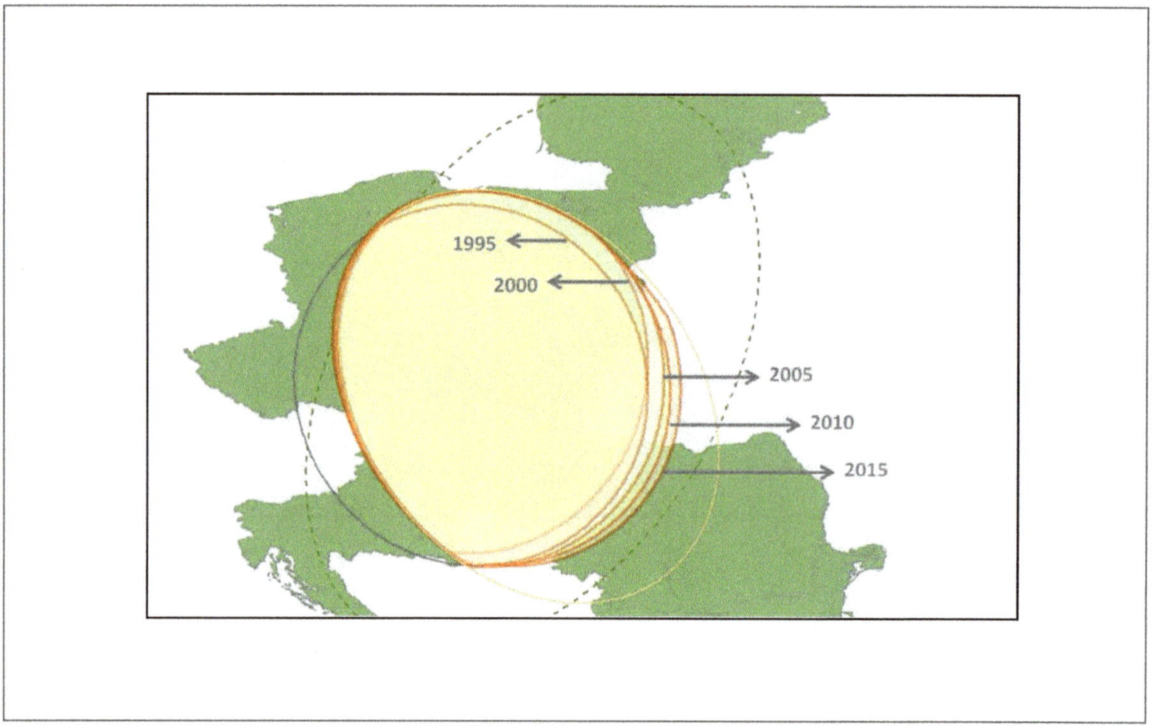

Figure 7. Ellipses intersect area from 1995 to 2015

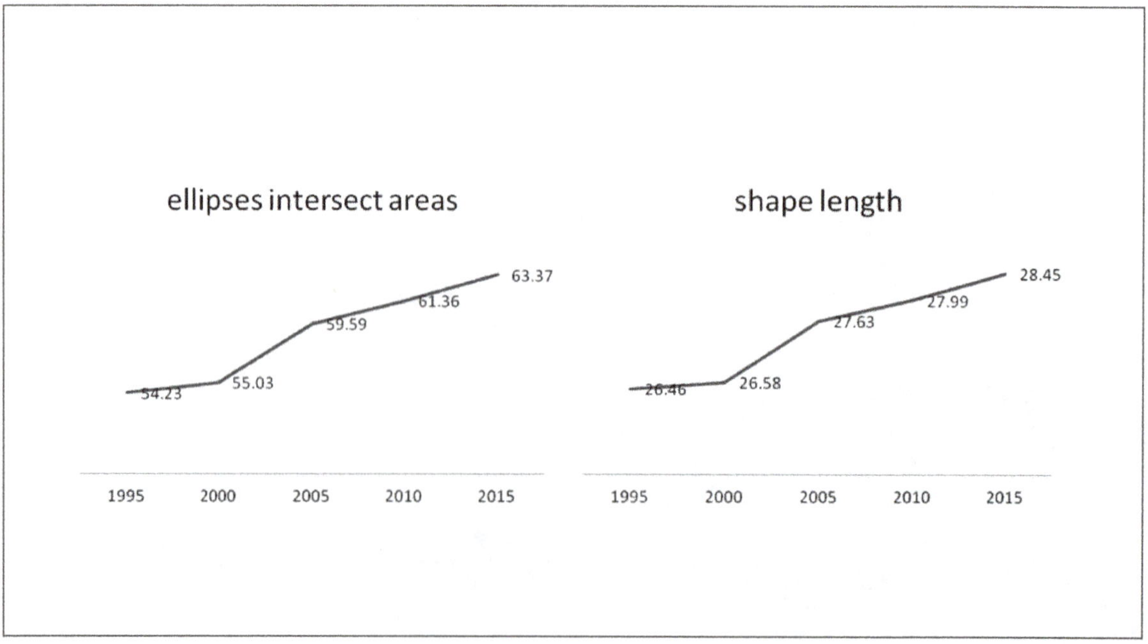

Figure 7a. Ellipses intersection area from 1995 to 2015

Table 4. The area and length of ellipses intersection

	1995	2000	2005	2010	2015
ellipses intersect areas /km^2	54.23	55.03	59.59	61.36	63.37
shape length /km	26.46	26.58	27.63	27.99	28.45
SDI	0.29	0.27	0.21	0.18	0.14

Y axis, the largest growth was registered from 2000-2005. From 2005-2010 and from 2010- 2015, the economic crisis caused the growth trend to significantly decrease.

For GDP ellipses, the current standard deviational ellipse X axis distribution ranges between 4.30 and 4.93. The Y axis distribution ranges between 4.38 and 4.65. The X axis and Y axis have similar lengths, so the standard deviation ellipses have a similar "round" shape, different from the Central and Eastern European geography distributional ellipses and demographic distributional ellipses. The larger the value of the discrepancy between the two axes, the more obvious the direction indicated by the ellipses. From the data, we can conclude that the land and population ellipses have a distinct orientation, while the economic ellipses do not and are consequently not reasonable for a mature economic system. It is sensible to note the different spatial discrepancies of the economy and the population. Considering the length of both the X and Y axes and the ratio of both standard deviational ellipses, the length of the Y axis of the GDP standard deviational ellipse still shows a larger growing trend.

3.3 Axis of rotation

The long axis of the Central and Eastern Europe GDP standard deviation ellipses move in a clockwise motion and fluctuate between 150.65° and 179.13°. They are located on a small scale and travel back and forth with no clear trend. There appears to be no structural change for the whole CEE. The corresponding azimuth of the demographic standard deviational ellipses decreases from 144.15° in 1995 to 142.46° in 2015. The demographic distribution rotation has a continuous change that is obviously north-westward; the GDP standard deviational ellipse center is located in the north-west of the demographic, as the demographic moving trace continues to travel in that direction. This illustrates the attraction controlled by the demographic distribution given by a certain economic situation. Economic factors are especially important for migrant workers in the process of labor migration.

3.4 Economic spatial differentiation is on the decline

There is a contrast in the overlap area formed by the economic output SDE and the demographic distribution SDE, where an economic spatial differentiation evolution tendency can be observed. As shown in Figure 6, from 1995-2000 in Central and Eastern Europe, the standard deviational ellipse GDP and the demographic standard deviation ellipse created a larger and larger overlap area. As shown in Figure 7, during this same period, the distance between the economic ellipse barycenter and the demographic ellipse barycenter (shortened in waves), the spatial differentiation of GDP and the population distribution show an overall downward trend. This can be explained in terms of shortened distances. The demographic ellipse barycenter is moving towards the economic ellipse barycenter, which shows the natural law of population flowing to the intensive capital place. The GDP barycenter moving towards the population indicates that population migration provides abundant labor and a larger consumer market, which can stimulate economic vitality. After a series of measures, the economic and demographic ellipses of the reforming European Union system gradually converge, but so far, there still exists a large degree of differentiation for the standard deviation ellipse, denoting a clear mobile trend in economic and demographic distributions.

The economy and demographic standard deviation ellipses indicate that the northwest boundary of the GDP ellipses is close to the boundary of population ellipses but still generates large differentiation in the southeast direction. The results show that the southeast countries in Central and Eastern Europe, including Romania and Bulgaria, have a high population and a large consumer market, which are unfortunately are not able to fulfil that role. As a result, there is considerable economic potential in these areas.

4. The main conclusions and policy recommendations

After institutional reforms, Central and Eastern European economic patterns suffered complex and diverse changes. The standard deviation ellipse method can reveal and visualize the changes in different ways. The Central and Eastern European economic spatial evolution mechanism provides a quantitative basis for the future, for both economic development as well as strategies for native land development, ensuring the effectiveness of the development strategy and target.

In comparing the standard deviation ellipses, the change in Central and Eastern Europe's demographic center is not so obvious. The lack of cash flow directly reflects the European labor migration feature, and to a large extent, it can also reflect the European nations' emotional dependence on their birthplace because of the language and cultural differences among European Union countries. It can also become one of the barriers for labor mobility. The demographic standard deviation ellipse moves only a short distance but with a strong regularity, shrinkage and direction to the west while year after year remaining close to the economic ellipse barycenter. Although labor mobility is influenced by social psychological factors, the drive of economic variables is also an important factor in the change in the labor force spatial distribution. In view of the present trend of population migration, countries at different stages of development need to adjust the corresponding policy according to their developing circumstances. Southeast countries, such as Romania and Bulgaria, should be particularly aware of their demographic surplus situation in the Central and Eastern European area, taking into account that "labor outflow impact on regional economic performance has a significant nonlinear relationship with a 'U' shape", before reaching the peak. By studying a stimulated labor outflow, we can utilize new technology and new ideas, which can result in an active domestic market.

The Central and Eastern European economic barycenter moves towards the northeast, with an elongated distribution scale towards the north-south direction. The distance stretches larger and has obvious trends of getting close to the demographic distribution standard deviation ellipse. According to this trend, the future economy will continue to stretch along the north-south direction; therefore, more investments in southeastern European countries, such as Romania and Bulgaria, can be the most effective way to improve efficiency and development universally. Promoting the use of southeast surplus labor can reduce the unemployment rate and decrease the degree of economy and the demographic spatial differentiation. Countries such as Romania and Bulgaria, which are neighboring Asian countries and have a central location between Asia and Europe, should be able to make full use of capital investments from Asia. For example, they could actively participate in the "One belt and One Road" project, which is driven by China's government and taps into the existing potential of the transportation industry, processing industry, service industry and other labor-intensive industries to promote economic development with endogenous power. The project can make the area of Central and Eastern Europe a connection "between developed countries in the west and connect developing countries in the east" and promote a two-way drive development pattern.

There are two main policy recommendations that could be considered by the Romanian and Bulgarian governments and by other CEE countries. One is to access foreign investments from Western European countries, to develop strategies to determine the employment of the existing workforce and to stop its migration to the West. European Union funds should also be considered for the development of infrastructure. A second option, as we mentioned, is to access investments from other regions, such as the Asian market, especially China, to reindustrialize and create sufficient jobs and economic growth. Romania could look for investments from the US as well because of its strategic position, long-term cooperation and contribution as part of the NATO.

References

Burt, J. E., & Barber, G. M. (1996). *Elementary statistics for geographers* (2nd ed.). New York and London: The Guilford Press.

Chang, T. P., Hu, J. L., Chou, R. Y., Sun, L. (2012). The sources of bank productivity growth in China during 2002 - 2009: A disaggregation view. *Journal of Banking & Finance, 36*(7), 1997-2006.

Dąbrowski, M. (2014, December 10). Central and Eastern Europe: Uncertain prospects of economic convergence [Blog post]. Retrieved from http://bruegel.org/2014/12/central-and-eastern-europe-uncertain-prospects-of-economic-convergence/

Dombi, Á. (2013). Economic growth and development in Central and Eastern Europe after the transformation. *Public Finance Quarterly, 58*(4), 452-468.

Forgó, B., & Jevcák, A. (2015). Economic convergence of Central and

Eastern European EU member states over the last decade (2004-2014) (Discussion Paper No. 001). European Commission's Directorate-General for Economic and Financial Affairs. Retrieved from https://ec.europa.eu/info/sites/info/files/file_import/dp001_en_2.pdf

European Central Bank. (2010, December). *Economic and Monetary Developments.* Monthly Bulletin. Retrieved from https://www.ecb.europa.eu/pub/pdf/other/mb201012_focus01.en.pdf?09cd03707c24ebc4c25731f56b9ee74e

Furfey, P. H. (1927). A note on Lefever's "standard deviational ellipse". *The American Journal of Sociology, 33*(1), 94-98.

Gong, J. (2002). Clarifying the standard deviational ellipse. *Geographical Analysis, 34*(2), 155-167.

Iordan, M.,http://www.sciencedirect.com/science/article/pii/S2212567115002749 - cor0005 Chilian, M. N., Grigorescu, A. (2015). Regional resilience in Romania – between realism and aspirations. *Procedia Economics and Finance, 22*, 627–635.

Kluvánková-Oravská, T., Chobotová, V., Banaszak, I., Slavikova, L., Trifunovova, S. (2009). From government to governance for biodiversity: The perspective of Central and Eastern European transition countries. *Environmental Policy and Governance, 19*(3), 186–196.

Labaye, E., Sjatil, P. E., Bogdan, W., Novak, J., Mischke, J., Fruk, M., & Ionutiu, O. (2013, December). *A new dawn: Reigniting growth in Central and Eastern Europe.* McKinsey Global Institute. Available from http://www.mckinsey.com/~/media/McKinsey/Global%20Themes/Europe/A%20new%20dawn%20Reigniting%20growth%20in%20Central%20and%20Eastern%20Europe/MGI_CEE_A_new_dawn_Full_report_Dec_2013.ashx

Lefever, D. W. (1926). Measuring geographic concentration by means of the standard deviational ellipse. *The American Journal of Sociology, 32*(1), 88-94.

Li, Y., & Wei, Y. H. D. (2010). The spatial-temporal hierarchy of regional inequality of China. *Applied Geography, 30*(3), 303-316.

Monastiriotis, V. (2011). *Regional growth dynamics in Central and Eastern Europe* (Discussion Paper No. 33). The London School of Economics and Political Science. Retrieved from http://www.lse.ac.uk/europeanInstitute/LEQS%20Discussion%20Paper%20Series/LEQSPaper33.pdf

PricewaterhouseCoopers. (2013). Central and Eastern Europe. Economic Scorecard. A sustainable future in a great region. Retrieved from http://www.business.edu.pl/upload/files/CEE%20Economic%20Scorecard%202013.pdf

Tellier, L. N. (1995). Projecting the evolution of the North American urban system and laying the foundations of a topodynamic theory of spatial polarization. *Environment and Planning A, 27*(7), 1109-1131.

Thies, R. (2016). Romania poised to be Europe's fastest growing economy in 2016. Driehaus Capital Management. Available from https://www.driehaus.com/ EM-Commentary-Romania-Poised-to-be-Europes-Fastest-Growing-Economy-in-2016.php

Yuill, R. (1971). The standard deviational ellipse: An updated tool for spatial description. *Geografiska Annaler. Series B, Human Geography, 53*(1), 28-39.

Yeung, G., He, C., & Liu, H. (2012). Centralization and marginalization: The Chinese banking industry in reform. *Applied Geography, 32*(2), 854-867.

Visser, S. (1980). Technological change and the spatial structure of agriculture. *Economic Geography*, *56*(4), 311-319.

Visser, S. (1999). Scale-economy conditions for spatial variation in farm size. *Geographical Analysis*, *31*(1), 27-44.

Wong, D. W. S. (1999). Several fundamentals in implementing spatial statistics in GIS: Using centrographic measures as examples. *Geographic Information Sciences*, *5*(2), 163-174.

12

The evolution of the tax burden for EU companies

Elisabeth Bustos Contell[1], Salvador Climent-Serrano[2], Gregorio Labatut-Serer[1]

ABSTRACT Since its creation, the EU has targeted tax harmonization to protect the single market and avoid capital outflow to regions that have lower tax rates. However, despite repeated attempts, complete convergence has not yet been achieved. Using the effective tax rate, the statutory tax rate, and the absolute difference between these two rates, this study explored the trends of the tax burden in 15 EU member states. The study period of 2006 to 2014 enabled analysis of the tax burden before and after the financial crisis. Analysis was conducted using an econometric model. The results suggest that during periods of economic stability, the tax burden tends to converge. In contrast, during periods of crisis, countries apply their own tax policies to protect themselves from the adverse effects of the crisis.

KEY WORDS: tax harmonization, effective tax rate, tax burden, European Union

[1] Department of Accounting, University of Valencia, Spain
[2] Department of Financial and Actuarial Economics, University of Valencia, Spain

1. Introduction

Since the creation of the EU, tax harmonization across member states has been a priority for successive governments (Osterloh & Heinemann, 2013). However, corporate income tax harmonization has never been fully achieved. Several scholars have provided evidence of significant differences between the tax rates of different EU member states (Buijink, Janssen, & Schols 2002; Giannini & Maggiulli, 2002; Marques & Pinho, 2014).

The 2008 financial crisis forced each member state to address its own problems by designing and applying its own tax policy to mitigate the adverse effects of the crisis (Bustos, Climent, & Labatut, 2017). Accordingly, the tax gap grew during the height of the financial crisis. However, tax harmonization remains a target for most EU member states. It is hoped that tax harmonization will avoid the relocation of companies to regions that have lower tax rates. Thus, the goal is to avoid capital outflow and the consequent reduction in tax income and wealth.

In light of this situation, this study examined the differences between the tax burdens in different EU member states and investigated the tax harmonization trend over the period 2006 to 2014. The goal was to predict whether the trend of the tax burdens in 15 EU member states was convergent or, conversely, divergent.

To achieve our goals, we studied the effective tax rate (ETR) and the difference between the ETR and the statutory tax rate (STR). The STR is equivalent to the percentage of corporate income tax. For the EU member states, this percentage ranges from 12.5% for

Correspondence concerning this article should be addressed to: **Elisabeth Bustos Contell**, Department of Accounting, Faculty of Economics, University of Valencia, Av. dels Tarongers, s/n, 46022, València, Spain. E-mail: elisabeth.bustos@uv.es

Ireland to 34% for Belgium. The ETR is the most commonly used variable to determine the tax burden that businesses actually face (Armstrong, Blouin, & Larcker 2012) after applying the tax deductions that are applicable under each country's tax policy.

This study contributes to the literature by adding to the few studies that have examined the trend of tax harmonization since the 2008 financial crisis. This study's scope covers political, economic, and social issues. In section 2, we present the theoretical framework and review the literature. In section 3, we describe the research design, including descriptions of the variables and sample. We then state our hypotheses. In section 4, we describe the method that we used to analyze the data. In sections 5 to 7, we present the results of our analysis. Finally, in section 8, we draw conclusions from our findings.

2. Literature review

The goal of tax harmonization across the EU is to eliminate tax avoidance and protect the European single market. Daly and Weiner (1993) explored the primary characteristics of corporate taxation in three federations: Canada, Switzerland, and the United States. The goal was to provide a guide to the member states of the recently created EU to tackle tax policy issues and achieve tax harmonization.

Tax harmonization of corporate tax is a research stream that has elicited considerable interest from the scientific community, as demonstrated by the extensive literature on the topic (Bettendorf, Devereux, van der Horst, Loretz, & de Mooij, 2010; Itaya, Okamura, & Yamaguchi, 2016; Mintz, 2004; Schindler & Schjelderup, 2009; Surugiu & Surugiu, 2012; Szabo & Condea, 2012). However, the alignment of tax policies is a complex issue because of the reluctance of countries that have low tax rates and the accession of Central and Eastern European countries, whose economic growth is comparatively slow (Wasserfallen, 2014). Sosnowski (2011) concluded that tax harmonization through an increase in tax rates would be a considerable encumbrance for the countries that recently joined the EU.

To resolve these issues, Conconi, Perroni, and Riezman (2008) proposed three possible tax harmonization scenarios: no tax harmonization, global tax harmonization, and partial tax harmonization. Conconi, Perroni, and Riezman (2008) argue that if capital is sufficiently mobile, partial tax harmonization is the best course of action because it benefits all countries.

Osterloh and Heinemann (2013) conducted surveys of Members of the European Parliament and Members of the German Bundestag. Both surveys revealed support for tax harmonization and a minimum corporate tax. Similarly, Ohsawa (2003) created a multi-country model over a one-dimensional space, where each country seeks to maximize its tax income, subject to the constraint that its tax rate lies within a given common band. The results show that tax harmonization with very high minimum or very low maximum standard rates produces flat tax structures. Finally, Fernandez-de-Cordoba and Torres (2012) suggest that tax harmonization may be achieved through small changes in tax revenues and output for most countries.

3. Research design

3.1. Variable specification and research hypotheses

To study the evolution of the tax convergence across 15 EU member states for the period 2006 to 2014, we used the variables that are shown in Table 1.

ETR is the standard indicator to measure the tax burden (Armstrong et al., 2012; Buijink et al., 2002; Chang, Chen, & Chen, 2017). We compared the ETR with the STR, as in other studies (Chen, Cuestas, & Regis, 2016). While the ETR depends on the STR, it also depends on other tax mechanisms that are independent of the STR. These mechanisms are displayed in Table 2.

The variable DISAB was used to calibrate the deductions and permanent differences between accounting regulations and tax regulations. Thus, the DISAB was used to measure non-STR tax mechanisms (Buijink et al., 2002). Interpreting the sign of the variable DISAB is important because it indicates incentives or disincentives, as shown in Table 3.

We formulated and tested the following hypotheses regarding ETR:

$$H_0\text{: } ETR_i = ETR_j \text{ for all i,j} = 2006, 2007, 2008, \ldots, 2014$$

$$H_1\text{: } ETR_{2006} > ETR_{2007} > ETR_{2008} > \ldots > ETR_{2014}$$

Table 1. Description of variables

Variable name	Label	Description
Effective tax rate	ETR	$\frac{\text{Total income tax expense}}{\text{Financial accounting income before tax}}$
Statutory tax rate	STR	Percentage value of the nominal rate (provided by the European Commission)
Absolute difference between ETR and STR	DISAB	ETR – STR (absolute value)
Country	COUNTRY	EU15 member states
Year	YEAR	(2006–2014)

Table 2. Tax mechanisms that affect the ETR

Mechanisms that worsen the tax burden	- Reduction of deductions - Reduction of negative permanent differences - Increase in positive permanent differences
Mechanisms that ease the tax burden	- Increase in deductions - Increase in negative permanent differences - Reduction of positive permanent differences

Table 3. Interpretation of the sign of DISAB

Sign DISAB	Interpretation	Cause
DISAB (-)	Tax mechanisms that offer net incentives	Permanent differences (+) < Deductions + Permanent differences (-)
DISAB (+)	Tax mechanisms that offer net disincentives	Permanent differences (+) > Deductions + Permanent differences (-)

To avoid the problems that derive from negative values for DISAB, we considered DISAB in terms of net independent tax incentives. We formulated and tested the following hypotheses regarding DISAB:

H_0: $DISAB_i = DISAB_j$ for all i,j = = 2006, 2007, 2008, …, 2014

H_1: $DISAB_{2006} < DISAB_{2007} < DISAB_{2008} < \ldots < DISAB_{2014}$

3.2. *Sample*

We drew our sample from the population of companies located in 15 EU member states that have similar economic characteristics. We excluded the 13 EU

Table 4. Number of observations by country and year

EU member state	2006	2007	2008	2009	2010	2011	2012	2013	2014	Total obs.	%
Germany	158	156	150	145	158	150	148	144	145	1354	21.7%
Austria	28	27	25	25	27	27	27	26	27	239	3.8%
Belgium	21	22	21	21	20	22	22	22	20	191	3.1%
Denmark	34	33	29	30	35	34	35	34	30	294	4.7%
Spain	26	26	25	27	26	24	22	19	25	220	3.5%
Finland	41	41	40	35	38	38	36	32	37	338	5.4%
France	87	91	87	82	90	87	88	84	87	783	12.5%
Greece	22	23	20	18	17	20	17	10	21	168	2.7%
Netherlands	28	28	24	25	28	27	24	27	24	235	3.8%
Ireland	18	20	20	18	20	19	20	19	18	172	2.8%
Italy	18	18	17	14	19	16	16	14	14	146	2.3%
Luxembourg	6	8	8	8	8	6	8	8	8	68	1.1%
Portugal	3	3	3	3	3	3	3	2	3	26	0.4%
UK	161	163	147	146	152	159	155	153	154	1390	22.2%
Sweden	70	70	69	66	69	72	64	70	75	625	10.0%
Total obs.	721	729	685	663	710	704	685	664	688	6249	100.0%
%	11.5%	11.7%	11.0%	10.6%	11.4%	11.3%	11.0%	10.6%	11.0%	100.0%	

Note: Total obs. – Total number of observations.

member states that joined after 2003. The sample comprised 777 listed companies from different sectors. We excluded companies from the financial sector, as in other studies (Crabbe & Vandenbussche, 2009; Lisowsky, 2010). The period that we considered in this study was 2006 to 2014. This interval was chosen because it ranges from the period right before the crisis to the beginning of the economic recovery. Table 4 provides details of the sample.

4. Method

After performing descriptive analysis, we used the Jonckheere-Terpstra test to identify significant differences. We applied this test because our hypotheses predict a specific order, namely the year-on-year decrease of ETR and the year-on-year increase of DISAB. Finally, we performed econometric analysis to estimate several multiple linear regression equations using the minimum least squares method. These models are defined as follows:

$$ETR = \beta_0 + \sum_{i=1}^{8} \beta_i \text{ Years } + \varepsilon_i \qquad \text{Model 1}$$

$$DISAB = \beta_0 + \sum_{i=1}^{8} \beta_i \text{ Years } + \varepsilon_i \qquad \text{Model 2}$$

We used a dummy variable to indicate the year. This variable took the value 1 if it corresponded to the year that was under study, and 0 otherwise. To avoid prob-

Table 5. Interpretation of the sign of the coefficient

	Sign in reference year 2006	Sign of coefficient in a given year that is not the reference year	
		+	-
Model ETR	+	Same sign as in reference year Increase in ETR	Different sign from in reference year Reduction in ETR
		+	-
Model DISAB	+ Net tax disincentives	Same sign as in reference year Increase in disincentives (Aggravating tax conditions)	Different sign from in reference year Reduction in disincentives (Easing tax conditions)
		+	-
Model DISAB	- Net tax incentives	Different sign from in reference year Reduction in incentives (Aggravating tax conditions)	Same sign as in reference year Increase in incentives (Easing tax conditions)

lems of perfect multicollinearity, we excluded the year 2006 from the model. This year was taken as a reference year and was represented by β_0. Thus, for each variable, the results of the coefficients represent the difference for each year with respect to the reference year of 2006.

Table 5 displays the interpretations of the sign of the coefficient for a given year for each model. Gray shading reflects the results that lead to the rejection of H_0 and the acceptance of H_1.

The Levin–Lin–Chu unit-root test did not reveal stationarity in the dependent variable. We estimated the model using the White method with robust standard errors to avoid heteroskedasticity through cross-sectional weighting. The model's goodness of fit was measured using the adjusted R^2 coefficient of determination. Finally, the Durbin–Watson statistic did not detect autocorrelation of the residuals in the overall EU models by year. Autocorrelation in the individual country models by year was detected only for Greece.

5. Descriptive analysis

5.1. Evolution of the statutory tax rate

Table 6 shows the statistics for the STR across all EU member states that were considered in this study. The cells that are shaded in gray display the means at the start and the end of the period as well as the overall variation across the whole period. Figure 1 shows the mean STR across all EU member states that were considered in this study.

Table 6 illustrates a decreasing trend of the mean STR for the EU, which fell from 32% in 2006 to 27% in 2014. Thus, the mean STR decreased by 5 percentage points over the study period. Notably, the STR decreased much faster in the two years prior to the crisis. Over these two years, the mean STR for the EU fell by 2.5 percentage points. Over the next six years, the mean STR for the EU fell by the same amount but at a much slower rate.

5.2. Evolution of the effective tax rate

Table 7 presents the statistics for the ETR across all EU member states that were considered in this study. Gray shading indicates the EU-wide mean at the start and end of the study period as well as the overall variation across the study period. Figure 2 illustrates the mean ETR for the 15 EU member states that were considered in this study.

The descriptive analysis shows that the mean ETR for the EU also decreased in all years except 2010 and 2014. However, the ETR decreased less than the STR did. The ETR fell by 1.7 percentage points from 27.4% to 25.7%, whereas the STR fell by 5 percentage points. This smaller drop was a consequence of a restriction in tax incentives.

Table 6. STR statistics

	Obs.	Mean	Variation	Median	SD	Maximum	Minimum
2006	721	0.317		0.300	0.054	0.387	0.125
2007	729	0.311	-0.006	0.300	0.057	0.387	0.125
2008	685	0.291	-0.021	0.300	0.040	0.344	0.125
2009	663	0.285	-0.006	0.280	0.040	0.344	0.125
2010	710	0.285	-0.000	0.280	0.040	0.344	0.125
2011	704	0.279	-0.006	0.263	0.043	0.344	0.125
2012	685	0.276	-0.003	0.263	0.050	0.361	0.125
2013	664	0.270	-0.006	0.250	0.053	0.361	0.125
2014	688	0.266	-0.005	0.250	0.063	0.380	0.125
2006–2014	6249	0.287	-0.051	0.300	0.052	0.387	0.125

Note: Obs. – Number of observations.

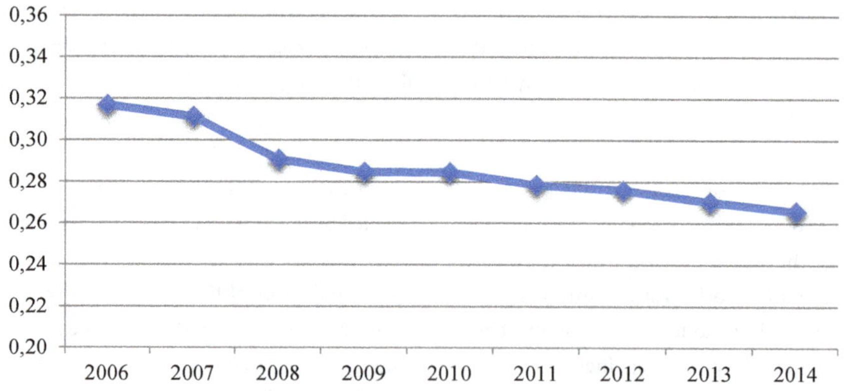

Figure 1. Mean STR across EU15 member states 2006–2014

5.3. Evolution of the difference between the effective tax rate and the statutory tax rate

Table 8 presents the statistics for the variable DISAB across all EU member states that were considered in this study. Gray shading indicates the EU-wide mean at the start and end of the study period as well as the overall difference across the whole period. Figure 3 shows the mean DISAB across the 15 EU member states that were considered in this study.

Table 7. ETR statistics

	Obs.	Mean	Variation	Median	SD	Maximum	Minimum
2006	721	0.274		0.283	0.103	0.585	0.000
2007	729	0.269	-0.005	0.278	0.100	0.582	0.000
2008	685	0.268	-0.001	0.278	0.096	0.598	0.000
2009	663	0.260	-0.008	0.271	0.104	0.589	0.000
2010	710	0.266	0.006	0.271	0.098	0.595	0.003
2011	704	0.260	-0.007	0.270	0.101	0.583	0.000
2012	685	0.259	-0.001	0.263	0.105	0.599	0.000
2013	664	0.253	-0.006	0.255	0.100	0.575	0.000
2014	688	0.257	0.004	0.255	0.108	0.597	0.000
2006–2014	6249	0.263	-0.017	0.271	0.102	0.599	0.0000

Note: Obs. – Number of observations.

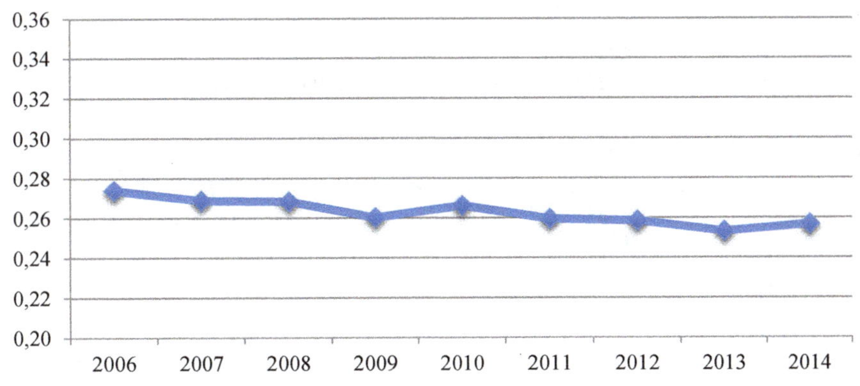

Figure 2. Mean ETR across EU15 member states 2006–2014

The sign of the variable DISAB was negative for all years in the study period. This result implies that there were net tax incentives across the EU over the entire study period. However, the DISAB increased (i.e., the tax incentives decreased) over the study period, with the only exception being the year 2009. Although the net tax incentives did not disappear completely, in 2014, the ETR and ETR were very close, so the DISAB was less than 1 percentage point.

Table 8. DISAB statistics

	Obs.	Mean	Variation	Median	SD	Maximum	Minimum
2006	721	-0.043		-0.024	0.104	0.286	-0.380
2007	729	-0.043	0.001	-0.028	0.101	0.311	-0.384
2008	685	-0.023	0.020	-0.014	0.097	0.343	-0.340
2009	663	-0.025	-0.002	-0.010	0.105	0.335	-0.340
2010	710	-0.019	0.006	-0.012	0.099	0.322	-0.328
2011	704	-0.019	-0.000	-0.011	0.100	0.320	-0.340
2012	685	-0.017	0.001	-0.011	0.104	0.474	-0.340
2013	664	-0.017	0.001	-0.009	0.098	0.300	-0.340
2014	688	-0.009	0.008	-0.007	0.109	0.364	-0.344
2006–2014	6249	-0.024	0.034	-0.014	0.102	0.474	-0.384

Note: Obs. – Number of observations.

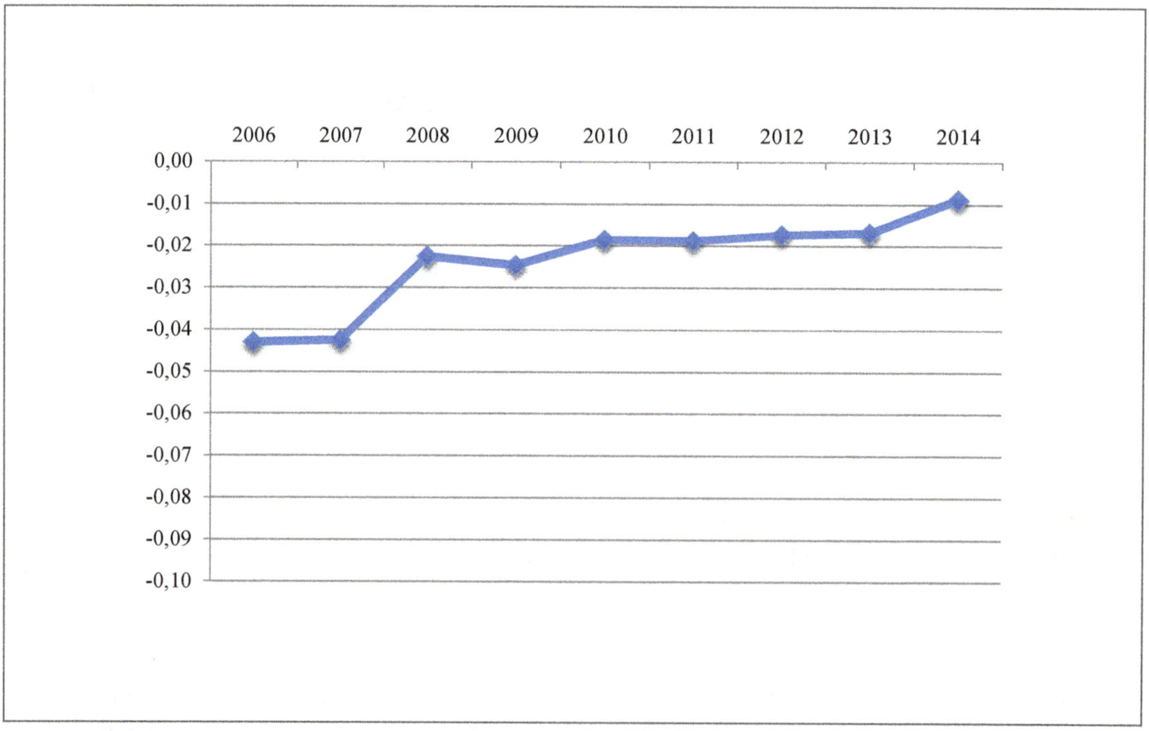

Figure 3. Mean DISAB across EU15 member states 2006–2014

Table 9. Econometric model: Estimated coefficients for the ETR

Year	Estimated coefficients
C	0.274046*** (0.002936)
2007	-0.004693 (0.004068)
2008	-0.006223 (0.004076)
2009	-0.012400*** (0.004325)
2010	-0.009077** (0.003911)
2011	-0.013670*** (0.003955)
2012	-0.016220*** (0.004061)
2013	-0.021053*** (0.004065)
2014	-0.016779*** (0.004302)
Adjusted R^2	0.375681
Durbin-Watson	1.674827
F-statistic	5.801662
Akaike	-2.086601
Significance ***,**,* at 1%, 5%, and 10%, respectively	
Robust standard errors in parentheses	

6. Results for the effective tax rate

6.1. Jonckheere-Terpstra test for the effective tax rate

The Jonckheere-Terpstra test, which tests the significance of the results of the descriptive analysis, was asymptotically significant at the 1% level. Therefore, we reject H_0, which proposes that the mean EU-wide ETR was the same in all years, and accept H_1, which proposes a year-on-year decrease in the mean EU-wide ETR.

6.2. Econometric analysis of the effective tax rate

We conducted econometric analysis of the ETR to identify convergence or divergence of the tax burden

Table 10. Econometric model: Estimated coefficients for the DISAB

Year	Estimated coefficients
C	-0.042582*** (0.003001)
2007	0.000415 (0.004146)
2008	0.020384*** (0.004112)
2009	0.019247*** (0.004401)
2010	0.022918*** (0.003980)
2011	0.023932*** (0.004033)
2012	0.024705*** (0.004134)
2013	0.024774*** (0.004153)
2014	0.033675*** (0.004421)
Adjusted R^2	0.363496
Durbin-Watson	1.680945
F-statistic	5.554072
Akaike	-2.055147
Significance ***,**,* at 1%, 5%, and 10%, respectively	
Robust standard errors in parentheses	

among the EU member states that were considered in this study. Table 9 shows the estimated coefficients for the ETR in EU member states.

The model explains 38% of the variance of the ETR. The residuals were not correlated (Durbin–Watson was between 1.5 and 2.5). The ETR fell by just under 2 percentage points, from 27.4% in 2006 to 25.7% in 2014. The model once again confirms the results of the descriptive analysis. The negative sign of the coefficients indicates a reduction in the ETR of the EU member states. The ETR decreased year on year except in 2010 and 2014. Although the coefficients were still negative in 2010 and 2014, the coefficient rose with respect the previous year in both cases.

7. Results for the DISAB

7.1. Jonckheere-Terpstra test for the DISAB

The Jonckheere-Terpstra test, which tests the significance of the results of the descriptive analysis, was asymptotically significant at the 1% level. Therefore, we reject H_0, which proposes that the mean EU-wide DISAB was the same in all years, and accept H_1, which proposes a year-on-year increase in the mean EU-wide DISAB (i.e., year-on-year decreases in net tax incentives).

7.2. Econometric analysis for the DISAB

We conducted econometric analysis of the DISAB to identify whether the gap between the ETR and STR closed or widened for the EU member states that were considered in this study. The estimated coefficients for the DISAB in the EU member states are shown in Table 10.

The model explains 36% of the variance of the net tax incentives. The residuals were not correlated (Durbin–Watson was between 1.5 and 2.5). The DISAB rose by approximately 3.4 percentage points, from -4.3 percentage points in 2006 to -0.9 percentage points in 2014. The model once again confirms the results of the descriptive analysis. The model thus shows that the difference between the ETR and the STR, which in 2006 was 4.3 percentage points, decreased significantly by approximately 3 percentage points in absolute terms.

8. Conclusions

Since the creation of the EU, successive governments have strived to achieve tax harmonization to avoid capital outflow to regions with low tax rates. This study explored the convergence of the tax burden. In this study, the tax burden was measured in terms of the ETR and the DISAB, which was calculated as the absolute difference between the ETR and STR.

Our results show that between 2006 and 2014, the STR and ETR decreased. This decrease reflects a relaxing of the tax burden in EU member states. Notably, the reduction in the ETR was smaller than the reduction in the STR, reflecting a decrease in the net tax incentives over this period. Nevertheless, there was general tax convergence in the EU over this period.

The results also show that in 2010, there was a slight increase in the ETR as well as a slight drop in the DISAB with respect to the values for 2009. At this time, Europe was in the midst of the financial crisis. Therefore, despite government goals of achieving tax harmonization, each country applied its own tax strategy during the crisis to protect its tax income. After 2010, the tax convergence trend returned, but in 2014, the ETR rose again, while the DISAB decreased. Thus, against the backdrop of the sovereign debt crisis, each country once again applied its own tax policy to address its individual needs.

Thus, in times of economic stability, the tax rates of EU member states tend to converge. However, in times of crisis, each country applies its own tax policy to address its individual problems and mitigate the negative impact of the crisis. Further study is nonetheless required to analyze the years posterior to 2014 and thus corroborate our conclusions.

References

Armstrong, C. S., Blouin, J. L., & Larcker, D. F. (2012). The incentives for tax planning. *Journal of Accounting and Economics*, 53(1), 391–411.

Bettendorf, L., Devereux, M. P., van der Horst, A., Loretz, S., & de Mooij, R. A. (2010). Corporate tax harmonization in the EU. *Economic Policy*, 63, 537–590.

Buijink, W., Janssen, B., & Schols, Y. (2002). Evidence of the effect of domicile on corporate average effective tax rates in the European Union. *Journal of International Accounting, Auditing & Taxation*, 11, 115–130.

Bustos-Contell, E., Climent-Serrano, S., & Labatut-Serer, G. (2017). Offshoring in the European Union: a study of the evolution of the tax burden. *Contemporary Economics*, 11(2), 235–247.

Chang C. W, Chen M. C., & Chen V. Y. S. (2017). Are Corporate Tax Reductions Real Benefits under Imputation Systems? *European Accounting Review*, 26(2), 215–237.

Chen, Y., Cuestas, J. C., & Regis, P. (2016). Convergence in Corporate Statutory Tax Rates in the Asian and Pacific Economies. *International Journal of Finance & Economics*, 21(3), 266–278.

Conconi, P., Perroni, C., & Riezman, R. (2008). Is partial tax harmonization desirable? *Journal of Public Economics*, 92(1–2), 254–267.

Crabbe, K., & Vandenbussche, H. (2009). Are your firm's taxes set in Warsaw? Spatial tax competition in Europe (Discussion Paper No. 7159). Centre for Economic Policy Research.

Daly, M., & Weiner, J. (1993). Corporate-tax harmonization and competition in federal countries - some lessons for the European community. *National Tax Journal*, 46(4), 441–461.

Fernandez-de-Cordoba, G., & Torres, J. L. (2012). Fiscal harmonization in the European Union with public inputs. *Economic Modelling*, 29(5), 2024–2034.

Giannini, S., & Maggiulli, C. (2002). The Effective Tax Rates in the EU Commission Study on Corporate Taxation: Methodological Aspects, Main Results and Policy Implications (Working Paper No. 666). The CESifo Group.

Itaya, J., Okamura, M., & Yamaguchi, C. (2016). Implementing partial tax harmonization in an asymmetric tax competition game with repeated interaction. *Canadian Journal of Economics-Revue canadienne d'économique*, 49(4), 1599–1630.

Lisowsky, P. (2010). Seeking shelter: Empirically modeling tax shelters using financial statement information. *Accounting Review*, 85(5), 1693–1720.

Marques, M., & Pinho, C. (2014). Tax-Treaty Effects on Foreign Investment: Evidence from European Multinationals. *Finanzarchiv*, 70(4), 527–555.

Mintz, J. (2004). Corporate tax harmonization in Europe: It's all about compliance. *International Tax and Public Finance*, 11(2), 221–234.

Ohsawa, Y. (2003). A spatial tax harmonization model. *European Economic Review*, 47(3), 443–459.

Osterloh, S., & Heinemann, F. (2013). The political economy of corporate tax harmonization - Why do European politicians (dis)like minimum tax rates? *European Journal of Political Economy*, 29, 18–37.

Schindler, D., & Schjelderup, G. (2009). Harmonization of corporate tax systems and its effect on collusive behavior. *Journal of Public Economic Theory*, 11(4), 599–621.

Sosnowski, M. (2011). Tax competition and harmonization of direct taxation within the European Unión. *Transformations in Business & Economics*, 10(2A), 401–411.

Surugiu, M., & Surugiu, C. (2012). Tax competition, harmonization and development: challenges and consequences. *Argumenta Oeconomica*, 28(1), 139–154.

Szabo, I. A., & Condea, B. (2012). Tax harmonization process in the European Community. *Metalurgia International*, 17(8), 122–126.

Wasserfallen, F. (2014). Political and economic integration in the EU: the case of failed tax harmonization. *JCMS-Journal of Common Market Studies*, 52(2), 420–435.

13

On the Cyclical Behavior of Fiscal Policy in Egypt

Israa A. El Husseiny[1]

ABSTRACT Optimal fiscal policy is expected to behave in a countercyclical manner to stabilize economies during business cycles. In particular, the public expenditure-to-GDP ratio should go up during recessions and down during expansions, while the public revenues-to-GDP ratio should move in the opposite direction. As a result, the budget deficit-to-GDP ratio should rise during recessions and decline during expansions. While this behavior of fiscal policy is common in most developed countries, the situation is different in developing nations where, due to several financial and institutional factors, a procyclical policy is more common. Using a time series dataset for the Egyptian economy during the period (1981/1982-2013/2014), this study provides empirical evidence that Egypt has not been able to conduct a countercyclical fiscal policy. In addition, the analysis provided by this study indicates that while several financial and credit factors might contribute to this behavior of fiscal policy in Egypt, the institutional and political economy factors seem to have the dominant role in this regard.

KEY WORDS: fiscal policy, cyclical properties, business cycles, output gap, Egypt state's general budget

[1] Economics Department, Faculty of Economics and Political Science, Cairo University, Egypt

1. Introduction

It is widely accepted as a normative prescription that fiscal policy should be used to stabilize the economy during business cycles, aiming at keeping the output close to its potential. This implies that optimal fiscal policy ought to be 'countercyclical'. Namely, during a boom, (i) government spending as a share of GDP should go down; (ii) government revenues as a share of GDP should go up; and (iii) as a result, budget deficit (surplus) as a share of GDP should decrease (increase). The opposite should be true in recession times. Nevertheless, in practice, governments in many developing countries tend to run procyclical, rather than countercyclical, fiscal policies. This suboptimal fiscal policy that might add to macroeconomic instability is usually attributed to two groups of factors, namely, limited access to domestic or external funds and poor institutions associated with widespread corruption.

The main goal of this study is to empirically test the cyclical properties of the main fiscal aggregates in Egypt. While many studies have addressed the cyclical behavior of fiscal policy empirically using panel data techniques applied to different samples of both developing and industrial countries, poor data availability (especially in developing countries) has constrained the ability to use time series datasets to investigate this issue. Accordingly, this study is expected to fill a gap

Correspondence concerning this article should be addressed to: **Israa A. El Husseiny**, Economics Department, Faculty of Economics and Political Science, Cairo University, Giza, Egypt.
E-mail: israa_adel_feps@feps.edu.eg

in the relevant literature by utilizing time series data for the Egyptian economy during the time period (1981/1982-2013/2014).

The study is organized as follows: section 2 focuses on reviewing theoretical and empirical literature on the cyclical behavior of fiscal policy and its determinants. Section 3 analyzes the stance and composition of Egypt's fiscal policy during the time period from fiscal year 1981/1982 to fiscal year 2013/2014. Section 4 discusses the methodology and findings of the empirical analysis of the study. Finally, section 5 concludes with some relevant policy implications.

2. Cyclicality of fiscal policy: Theoretical arguments and empirical evidence

Fiscal policy has always been one of the most important tools for combating business cycles. Given that national income shocks associated with international markets are much more severe in developing countries than in wealthy countries, studying the cyclicality of fiscal policy would have a special relevance for developing countries, which are characterized by relatively high poverty rates, low accessibility to international capital markets, narrow tax bases and weak institutions. Such factors together might lower the capacity of governments in such countries to use fiscal policy countercyclically. Instead, governments in those countries might be forced to spend and tax procyclically in a way that would exacerbate the fluctuations induced by business cycles (Wibbels, 2006). The relatively weak quality of data and their frequency, however, has limited the research on the cyclical behavior of fiscal aggregates in developing countries (Agenor, McDermott, & Prasad, 2000).

In light of the conventional wisdom, most economists agree with the normative Keynesian prescription that optimal fiscal policy is countercyclical, aiming at keeping output close to its potential (Calderón, Duncan, & Schmidt-Hebbel, 2004; Talvi & Végh, 2005). This would require tax rates and discretionary spending to remain constant over the business cycle. As a result, during bad times (recessions), i) government spending as a share of GDP should go up because of automatic stabilizers; ii) government revenues as a share of GDP should go down since tax rates are assumed to remain constant and exhibit some degree of progressivity (the effects would be reinforced by tax cuts during recessions and tax increases in booms); and iii) as a result, budget surplus as a share of GDP should decrease. The opposite should occur during a boom (Alesina & Tabellini, 2005). This behavior would give the fiscal policy a very important stabilizing role since it would dampen business cycle fluctuations and the excessive cyclical unemployment and inflationary pressure (Alberola, Montero, Braun, & Cordella, 2006; Manasse, 2006).

Even if the Keynesian notion of demand management was rejected, one should not reject the neoclassical notion of tax smoothing, according to which tax policy should be used to smooth expenditure and tax distortions over business cycles, given that shocks to tax bases or spending are temporary (Manasse, 2006). Moreover, according to the *permanent income hypothesis*, the government would set its consumption levels according to long-term income expectations rather than according to the current fluctuating levels, which would minimize the distortions associated with frequent changes in taxation and expenditure (Wibbels, 2006).

A large body of literature has argued that governments in wealthy countries, whatever their motivations, behave in this optimal fashion by borrowing and spending on social programs in bad times and saving in good times to smooth the short-term shocks of the business cycles. The evidence for developing countries, however, is different (Ben Slimane & Ben Tahar, 2009).

Developing countries encounter many problems in seeking to manage their economies. Their increased exposure to international markets makes them more vulnerable to external shocks and exacerbates swings in the business cycle through either trade or finance channels. More specifically, fluctuations in the terms of trade and/or the international price of capital can introduce an additional source of output volatility in developing countries compared to the situation in industrial nations (Wibbels, 2006). As a result, the governments in many – though not all – emerging and developing economies tend to run procyclical fiscal policies, according to which the budget deficit goes up during expansions and down during recessions (Alesina & Tabellini, 2005; Ben Slimane & Ben Tahar, 2009; Calderón et al., 2004). This situation hurts social policy and introduces an additional source of volatility into the economy, which in turn reduces investment and growth (Alberola et al., 2006).

In fact, income smoothing (through countercyclical fiscal policy) would require either significant borrowing during economic downturns or large surpluses during good times. However, this is usually not the case in the real world. Governments in developing countries might face strong political pressures to increase public spending or decrease tax rates in a way that makes budget surpluses unlikely to exist during good times. At the same time, heavy borrowing during bad times might also be problematic given that developing nations would have limited access to financial markets. Moreover, the automatic stabilizers that explain countercyclical spending in the developed countries are impossible in most developing nations (Wibbels, 2006). Accordingly, the procyclical nature of fiscal policies in developing countries is usually attributed to two broad groups of potential factors, namely, '*financial or credit*' factors and '*political economy and institutional*' factors (Ben Slimane & Ben Tahar, 2009; Calderón et al., 2004).

According to the financial or credit arguments, procyclical behavior of fiscal policy in developing countries can be explained by the procyclical nature of their capital inflows and the cost of capital. In contrast to OECD countries, developing countries would have limited access to domestic or international financial markets during downturns compared to the access during periods of expansion. Accordingly, many developing countries cannot borrow in bad times, or they can do so only at relatively higher interest rates. As a result, they are forced to cut spending instead of expanding it as might be suggested. In booms, however, governments in developing countries can borrow more easily with relatively lower cost, and thus, they tend to increase public spending and fiscal deficit, as well (Alesina & Tabellini, 2005; Ben Slimane & Ben Tahar, 2009; Wibbels, 2006).

Although such arguments have their own merits in explaining fiscal procyclicality in developing countries, many economists note that they are incomplete and problematic. More specifically, such arguments provide no answers to the following two questions. First, why would a government not self-insure by accumulating reserves in good times to prevent the borrowing (credit) constraints from being binding in bad times? Second, why would lenders not provide funds to countries in recessions if they know that the borrowing would smooth out the cycle? In addition, the fact that procyclical fiscal policy is also present in some OECD countries that have full access to capital markets suggests that financial or credit factors do not represent the whole story (Alesina & Tabellini, 2005; Talvi & Végh, 2005).

The institutional and political economy factors are concerned with the role of voters in shaping fiscal policy decision making through their demand for a greater level of public spending, especially in good times. This situation might result from weak institutions as represented in the widespread corruption and lack of fiscal transparency (Ben Slimane & Ben Tahar, 2009). According to this view, the ability to run large budget surpluses is severely hampered by political pressures, which are always present but are exacerbated in good times (Alberola et al., 2006; Talvi & Végh, 2005).

One such political pressure can be best represented by the *voracity effect*. This was first introduced by Tornell and Lane (1998) to explain the overspending of transitory increases in fiscal revenues. This effect arises in the presence of various powerful groups involved in the fiscal system working in a weak institutional framework and treating the country's revenues as a common pool[1]. Thus, during good times, when there is a positive shock to the country's resources, each group knows that if it moderates its claims on the increased resources, other groups will appropriate them. This leads fiscal resources to be wasted rather than saved for bad times or even used for debt repayment (Alberola et al., 2006; Alesina & Tabellini, 2005; Ben Slimane & Ben Tahar, 2009; Talvi & Végh, 2005).

Another potential political explanation for the fiscal policy procyclicality can be represented by what is called the *political agency problem*. Alesina and Tabellini (2005) and Alesina, Tabellini, and Campante (2008) argue that in countries with corrupt governments that can appropriate part of tax revenues for unproductive public activities, voters demand higher utility for themselves during booms in the form of lower taxes or higher productive public spending. Given that voters do not trust their governments and do not have complete information about their actions, they demand (through a re-election mechanism) a level of government debt that forces the government to use resources to pay interest rather than to steal them. In this context, Talvi and Végh (2005) argue that procyclical behavior of fiscal policy during good times is mainly derived from tax reductions that the governments in developing countries might be forced to introduce to avoid pressures of the demands for higher public spending. Based on this model, however, procyclical fiscal policy is expected to be less observed in countries where the government is unaccountable to the voters, as in a stable dictatorship, even if corruption is high (Alesina & Tabellini, 2005).

Woo (2009) developed a simple model that links social polarization of preferences to the procyclicality of fiscal policy. According to the author's intuition, a high degree of polarization of preferences may make it hard for heterogeneous policymakers to agree on ideal government policies. Accordingly, policymakers may have greater incentives to insist on their individual preferred policies which might be inefficient for the whole economy. Such incentives may become stronger during good times with the rising government revenues and resources especially when institutional constraints are insufficient or absent. As a result, procyclical fiscal policies would arise.

Applying the previous theoretical arguments of fiscal procyclicality to the Egyptian case, it can be argued that if Egypt could not conduct a countercyclical fiscal policy (a hypothesis that will be tested in the empirical section), both the 'financial/credit' factors and the 'political economy/institutional' factors are expected to have their own significance in this regard.

On one hand, during recession times, the Egyptian economy might be unable to access international capital markets (borrow from abroad) due to its weakened creditworthiness. This limited access to capital markets is expected to hinder the government's ability to respond countercyclically to the recession through increasing its spending. However, if this is the case with the external capital markets, the situation seems different with regard to the domestic capital market, where the Egyptian government has a relatively easy access through the issuance of treasury bills, bonds, and similar financing tools (domestic borrowing). Such tools represent an attractive investment option for both individuals and institutions in Egypt because they are fully guaranteed by the government and at the same time offer relatively higher interest rates. The fact that Egypt's public debt is approaching 100% of GDP, approximately 90% of which is represented by domestic borrowing, indicates that the 'financial/credit' factors (in the form of the limited access to capital markets and/or the relatively high cost of borrowing) are not expected to act as the main contributor to the non-optimal behavior of fiscal policy in Egypt. However, as long as fiscal sustainability has been taken into consideration by the government (given the recent deterioration in the fiscal stance of the Egyptian economy within the last few years starting from 2011/2012), financial/credit factors might be a significant parameter in the Egyptian fiscal decision making.

During expansion times, on the other hand, there is a strong reason to expect that the Egyptian economy will be unable to accumulate surpluses due to its poor budgetary institutions that govern the whole budget cycle and thus distribute the power among the key relevant players involved in the process. El Husseiny (2016a) has provided theoretical insights on how poor budget institutions in Egypt may contribute to the country's weak fiscal performance.

For example, during the budget 'formulation' phase, the absence of numerical fiscal rules and budget ceilings are expected to reinforce the incentives of the key players to act according to the 'common pool' phenomenon. This means that during a boom, there will always be incentives for the various budget authorities to compete for extracting more resources for projects that might be useful for their own constituencies, neglecting the true social costs that might result from such behavior. Moreover, no group will be willing to reduce its share in the increased resources since it knows that the saved resources will be exploited in one way or another. This behavior is expected to be reinforced by the lack of fiscal transparency that may lead to the 'political agency' problem, according to which people are expected to have incentives to ask for more spending and/or lower tax levels to avoid the waste of public resources in unproductive activities by the corrupt government and politicians.

During the 'approval' and 'implementation' phases of the budget cycle, poor budgetary institutions in Egypt are represented by the absence of a top-down procedure for the approval of the budget by the legislature; the lack of discussion or dissemination of budget documents outside the legislature; the lack of effective systems for financial controls, internal audit, and external audit; the poor credibility and sustainability of the budget due to the lack of data on expenditure arrears, quasi-fiscal activities, and contingent liabilities; and the lack of public accessibility to external audit reports.

Egypt's weak budgetary institutions as presented above are expected not only to lead to higher levels of public expenditure and budget deficit but also to constrain the government's ability to utilize its fiscal policy effectively in a countercyclical manner.

It can then be argued that although the 'political economy/institutional' arguments seem to be more significant in explaining how Egypt's fiscal decision making has always been taken, 'credit/financial' factors are expected to be much more significant during the current period compared to the situation previously. This is because the current deterioration of Egypt's fiscal stance as measured by the unpreceded ratios of budget deficit and public debt to GDP should limit the government's ability to use its fiscal policy countercyclically in the future. This should be a valid expectation as long as the government values the long-term fiscal sustainability more than the short-term macroeconomic stability.

At the empirical level, many researchers have been interested in improving the comprehension of the abovementioned theoretical arguments through assessing the cyclicality of the main fiscal indicators. Alberola et al. (2006) found strong evidence confirming that fiscal policy is procyclical in a sample of Latin American countries during the time period (1981-2004). In a similar context, Alesina and Tabellini (2005) confirmed the previous evidence on the widespread fiscal procyclicality in developing countries and presented some suggestive evidence that corruption and political agency problem in democracies, rather than credit market imperfections, are what explain fiscal procyclicality. Such findings were supported by Talvi and Végh (2005), who explained fiscal procyclicality behavior in developing countries by a political distortion that makes it costly to run budget surpluses due to the pressures that abundant fiscal resources create to increase public spending. While Sabir and Zahid (2012) provided empirical evidence that poor institutions are the main determinant of fiscal procyclicality in developing countries, Woo (2009) presented strong econometric evidence in support of the theoretical prediction that social polarization (as measured by inequality in income and education distribution across the population) is robustly and positively associated with procyclicality of fiscal policy in a large sample of countries for the period (1960-2003).

According to Gali and Perotti (2003), while the adoption of the fiscal rules might constrain the ability of policymakers to run discretionary policy, the countercyclical fiscal policy became stronger after the adoption of the Maastricht Treaty and the Stability and Growth Pact by the EU members. This seems to be logical since such fiscal rules ensure that the fiscal decision making will no longer be based on the preferences of the various interest groups and relevant players who are seeking to maximize their own benefit at the expense of the country's fiscal stance. This ensures that fiscal surpluses can be accumulated during good times to finance the expansionary fiscal policy during recessions without the fear of exceeding the official limits of budget deficit and public debt-to-GDP ratios. Moreover, Lane (2003) provided empirical support for political economy factors as determinants of fiscal policy stance in OECD countries.

Aghion, Marinescu, Caballero and Kashyap (2007) found evidence that the budget deficit has become increasingly countercyclical in most OECD countries and that the countercyclical behavior of budgetary policy is positively associated with a higher level of financial development, a lower level of openness, and the adoption of an inflation-targeting regime. Using a sample of emerging and industrial countries for the period (1970-2004), Manasse (2006) found that fiscal rules and fiscal responsibility laws tend to enhance countercyclical policy and that the effects of fiscal institutions on procyclicality are different in good and bad times. Kaminsky, Reinhart, and Végh (2004) recognized that net capital inflows are procyclical in most OECD and developing countries and that fiscal policy is procyclical for the majority of developing countries during the period (1960-2003). Using a panel dataset for eleven emerging countries over the period (1996-2002) and an annual time series sample for Chile covering the period (1991-2003), Calderón et al. (2004) provided empirical support to the hypothesis that countries exhibiting higher policy credibility levels (as reflected in a lower country risk spread on sovereign debt) are able to conduct countercyclical macroeconomic policies. Lee and Sung (2007) provided empirical evidence that government's recurrent expenditures and subsidies move countercyclically, while capital expenditures move procyclically in a sample of industrial and developing countries. This sounds logical since most of the automatic stabilizers (such as subsidies) are related to the recurrent component of government expenditure, which by nature tends to act countercyclically. In this case, the overall behavior of the government expenditure in response to business cycles is expected to depend on the relative individual responses of the recurrent and the capital components of government expenditure.

Contrasting with the results from most empirical studies on emerging markets and developing economies, Thornton (2007) concluded that public spending and budget deficit in South Africa were countercyclical during the period (1972-2001). Moreover, Jaimovich and Panizza (2007) suggested that there is no statistical difference between the cyclicality of fiscal policy in developing and industrial countries over the period (1970-2003). Ben Slimane and Ben Tahar (2009) found that, while budget balance in the MENA region is countercyclical, both total expenditure and total revenues are procyclical. This study, however, did not provide any justification for the contradiction observed in the behavior of total expenditure and total revenues, which proved to act in a procyclical manner, on one hand, and the behavior of the overall fiscal balance (the difference between total revenues and total expenditures), which proved to act countercyclically, from the other hand. More specifically, the study showed that during expansion times, total expenditure increases, while total revenues decrease. While this should result into a decrease in the overall fiscal balance indicating a procyclical behavior, the study's findings have indicated the opposite.

3. Stance and composition of Egypt's fiscal policy (1981/1982-2013/2014)

This section is devoted to analysis of the stance of Egypt's fiscal policy and its composition during the period from fiscal year 1981/1982 to fiscal year 2013/2014. The main objective of such analysis is to provide a deep understanding of the structural features of the fiscal policy in Egypt and to determine whether such features would enable or hinder the government's optimal use of the fiscal policy in stabilizing the economy and combating business cycle fluctuations. The analysis of this section covers the three pillars of the fiscal policy, namely, public expenditure, public revenues and taxation, and budget deficit.

It is worth mentioning that the classification of the state's general budget has changed since fiscal year 2005/2006. Starting from this year, the Ministry of Finance adopted the IMF Government Finance Statistics Manual (GFSM) for preparation and presentation of the government's budget. The adoption of the new classification system resulted in different classification of the budget chapters and different concepts of the budget deficit, as well. Accordingly, some amendments were introduced to the fiscal data by the author to ensure consistency over the time series under study (*see* appendix 1).

Public expenditure in Egypt (1981/1982-2013/2014)

Figure 1 presents data on average ratios of total public expenditure and total public utilization to GDP. Total public expenditure is defined as the sum of the first six chapters on the expenditure side of the state's general budget, namely, wages and salaries; goods and services; interest payments; subsidies, grants and social benefits; other expenditures; and investments. Total public utilization includes total public expenditure in addition to the 7th chapter 'acquisition of financial assets' and the 8th chapter 'loans repayment'. The data show that total public expenditure as a share of GDP reached its maximum, approximately 40% on average, during the time period (1981/1982-1985/1986). This reflects the major role that the government used to play in the Egyptian economy during this period before shifting to a more market-based and private sector-oriented economy with the implementation of the Economic Reform and Structural Adjustment Program (ERSAP) in 1991. As indicated by Figure 1, the ratio of total public utilization to GDP exceeded the ratio of total public expenditure to GDP by approximately five percentage points on average during the whole period of analysis. This approximately reflects the relative share of loans repayment in GDP.

As for the structure of public expenditure, the data in table 1 and figure 2 show that recurrent public ex-

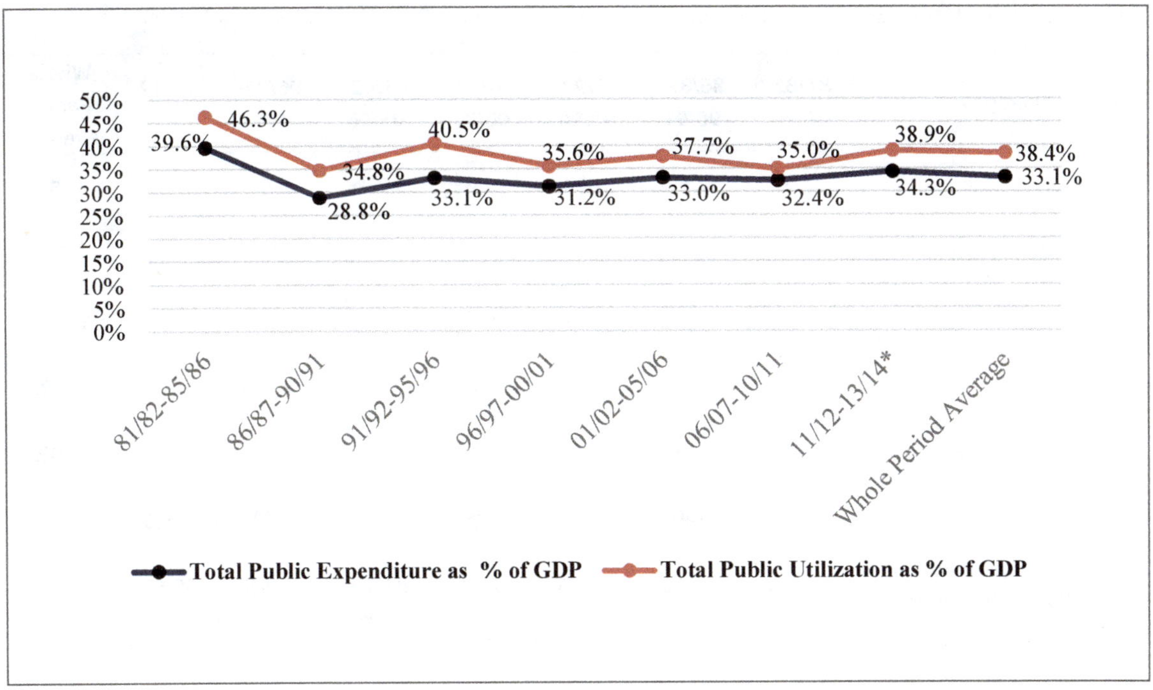

Figure 1. Public Expenditure-to-GDP Ratios in Egypt: Five-Year Averages for the Period (1981/1982-2013/2014)
Source: Made by the author based on the final accounts of the state's general budget provided by the Ministry of Finance and data on GDP at market prices provided by the Ministry of Planning.
*Represents three-year average.

penditure (the first five chapters) constituted almost 85% of total public expenditure, on average, during the whole period of analysis, compared to an average share of 15% for investments. In fact, this pattern is very common in most developing countries, where the recurrent expenditure (mainly dominated by relatively high wages, interest payments and subsidies) constitutes the major part of the budget.

As a share of total public expenditure, figure 2 indicates that the first chapter 'wages and salaries' came first, with an average share of 23.8% during the whole period of analysis. The fourth chapter 'subsidies, grants and social benefits' and the third chapter 'interest payments' accounted for 20.5% and 18.9% , respectively, on average.

The relatively high share of wages and salaries in Egypt's budget is expected to hinder the fiscal authority from using fiscal policy optimally (countercyclically) in stabilizing the economy during business cycles. Since wages and salaries result from previous hiring decisions, the expenditure on this chapter is not expected to be reduced in response to positive economic shocks as would be recommended by full tax smoothing theory. The political pressures that exist in Egypt will make it difficult to behave in the optimum way during booms.

On the other side, social spending on subsidies should at least theoretically enable the government to conduct a countercyclical fiscal policy since this kind of expenditure, especially when linked to unemployment and income levels, is often assumed to act as an automatic stabilizer by expanding during recessions and shrinking during booms. At the practical level, however, this kind of expenditure in Egypt has always been disconnected from the economic activity. More specifically, public expenditure on 'subsidies, grants and social benefits' in Egypt has been dominated mainly by energy and food subsidies, which represented on average almost 60% and 20%, respectively, during the fiscal years from 2008/2009 to 2012/2013. The share of public expenditure on social benefits (including social security benefits, social pensions

Table 1. Structure of Public Expenditure in Egypt: Five-Year Averages for the Period (1981/1982-2013/2014)

Five-Year Averages	**81/82-85/86**	**86/87-90/91**	**91/92-95/96**	**96/97-00/01**	**01/02-05/06**	**06/07-10/11**	**11/12-13/14***	**Whole Period Average**
1) Wages and Salaries	22.3%	24.7%	21.1%	25.3%	25.3%	22.9%	25.3%	**23.8%**
2) Goods and Services	5.4%	5.0%	5.5%	7.1%	6.9%	5.8%	4.0%	**5.8%**
3) Interest Payments	9.2%	15.4%	24.1%	18.3%	19.5%	19.0%	23.9%	**18.9%**
4) Subsidies, Grants and Social Benefits	23.1%	17.3%	14.5%	11.9%	18.5%	30.7%	32.6%	**20.5%**
5) Other Expenditures	28.3%	21.7%	16.2%	16.6%	15.1%	9.8%	6.9%	**16.0%**
6) Investments	12.1%	15.4%	18.6%	21%	14.7%	11.8%	7.3%	**14.8%**
Total Public Expenditure as % of Total Public Utilization	**85.4%**	**82.9%**	**82.3%**	**87.6%**	**87.5%**	**92.6%**	**88.5%**	**86.6%**

Source: Made by the author based on the final accounts of the state's general budget provided by the Ministry of Finance.
*Represents three-year average.

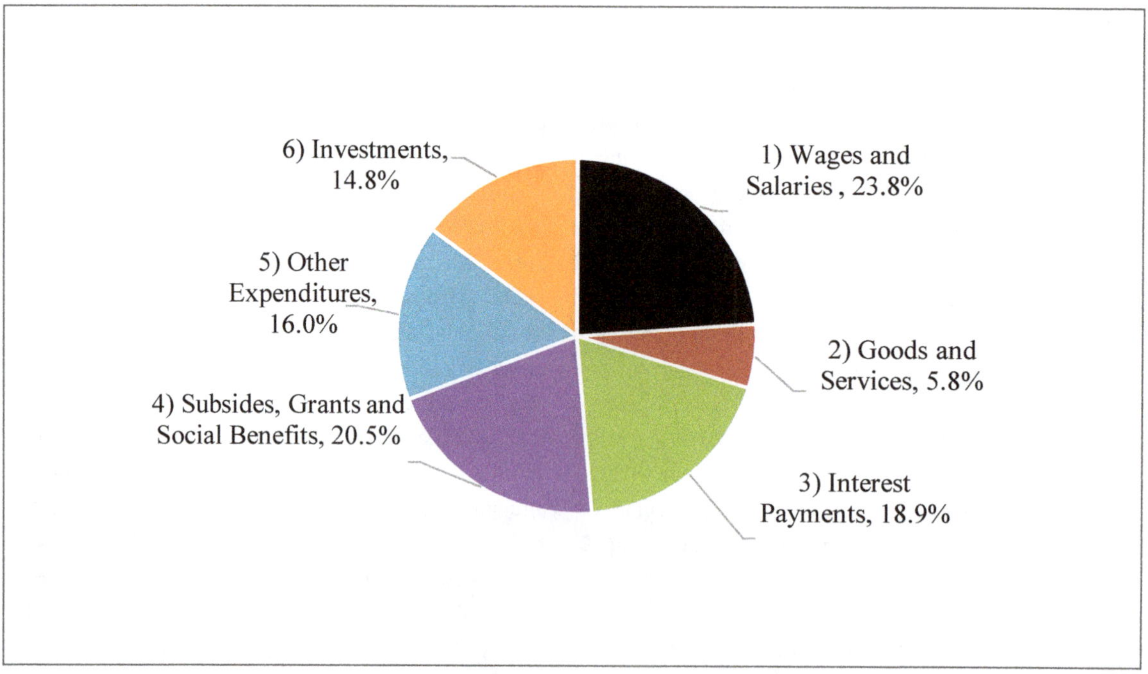

Figure 2. Structure of Public Expenditure in Egypt: Average for the Period (1981/1982-2013/2014)
Source: Made by the author based on the final accounts of the state's general budget provided by the Ministry of Finance.

and social aids), however, did not exceed 10% during the same period, on average. This pattern is expected to constraint the government's power to use subsidies countercyclically to stabilize the economy, especially during boom times. The reason is that people in Egypt have become accustomed to benefiting from such subsidies whatever their income levels or the status of the economy, and thus, subsidy reductions have not been politically welcomed. It should be noted, however, that the government of Egypt has started recently (in year 2015) to reform its subsidy system. Such reforms included the replacement of in-kind subsidies by cash subsidies as well as the gradual reduction of the energy subsidy as reflected in higher prices of oil, gas, electricity, etc. Such reforms are expected to bring social and economic benefits in terms of achieving more social justice and freeing more budget resources to be spent on those items that are expected to contribute to sustainable development including social services (health and education), transportation, infrastructure, and environment protection.

The fact that Egypt's total expenditure is mainly dominated by wages and subsidies indicates that the government will have a very limited fiscal space that would allow it to respond countercyclically to the business cycle. Moreover, the political and institutional constraints described in the previous section can be easily applied to the Egyptian case, especially during expansion times. More specifically, since people do not trust their government due to the presence of corruption and lack of transparency, and given that there exist a large number of interest groups that may compete in the budgeting process to maximize their own benefits, wages and subsides are not expected to decline during booms. In recessions, however, there is good reason to predict that the same factors may lead to pressure to raise such expenditure items, causing countercyclical behavior.

The interest payments, which represent the third major chapter in Egypt's budget, are expected to act countercyclically as a result of the countercyclical behavior of interest rates, which tend to increase during recessions (reflecting a higher cost of capital) and decrease during booms.[2]

Given the structure of Egypt's total expenditure as described above, one would expect that the cyclical behavior of public expenditure would depend on the individual cyclical responses to business cycles of wages and subsidies, on one hand, and interest payments, on the other hand. Furthermore, it is expected that the optimal behavior of public expenditure, if any, may tend to prevail during recessions rather than during expansions. During expansions, the government might find it difficult to cut its public spending due to either the lack of automatic stabilizers and the limited fiscal space that it can freely manage or the political pressures to increase public spending to avoid the case of wasting public resources through corrupt government practices. During recessions, however, there might be greater opportunity for the government to increase public spending as long as it can easily access the capital markets through public borrowing.

Public revenues in Egypt (1981/1982-2013/2014)

Figure 3 provides data on the ratios of total public revenues and total public resources to GDP. Total public revenues are defined as the sum of the first three chapters in the revenue side of the state's general budget, namely, taxes, grants, and other non-tax revenues. Total public resources include total public revenues in addition to the 4th revenue chapter 'lending proceeds and sales of financial assets' and the 5th revenue chapter 'borrowing'[3].

As indicated by figure 3, total public revenues represented approximately 25% of GDP during the whole period under analysis, while the share of total public resources averaged approximately 38%. Moreover, the data indicate the declining trend of both public revenues and public resources as shares of GDP during the analyzed period.

As for the structure of public revenues, table 2 indicates that the share of tax revenues has been increasing from 62% during the first sub-period to 67% during the last sub-period, on average. This was at the expense of the other revenues including grants and other non-tax revenues. This has important implications for the cyclicality of fiscal policy since non-tax revenues are often outside the control of the government, and thus, high reliance on non-tax revenues is usually expected to limit the government's ability to implement countercyclical fiscal policy.

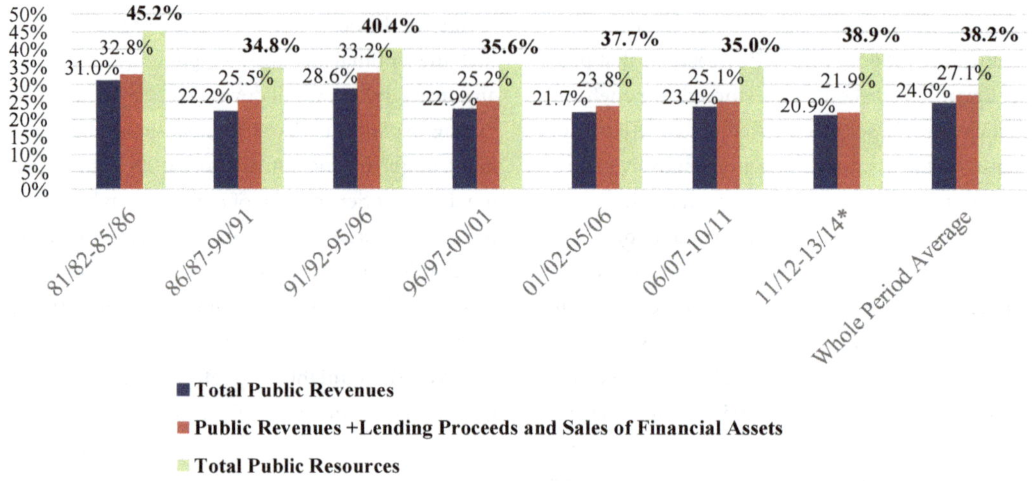

Figure 3. Public Revenues-to-GDP Ratios: Five-Year Averages for the Period (1981/1982-2013/2014)
Source: Made by the author based on the final accounts of the state's general budget provided by the Ministry of Finance and data on GDP at market prices provided by the Ministry of Planning.
*Represents three-year average.

Table 2. Structure of Public Revenues in Egypt: Five-Year Averages for the Period (1981/1982-2013/2014)

Five-Year Averages	81/82-85/86	86/87-90/91	91/92-95/96	96/97-00/01	01/02-05/06	06/07-10/11	11/12-13/14*	Whole Period Average
1) Taxes (% of Total Public Revenues)	62.2%	63.9%	66.3%	71.8%	70.5%	67.1%	67.0%	**67.1%**
2) Grants + 3) Other Non-Tax Revenues (% of Total Public Revenues)	37.8%	36.1%	33.7%	28.2%	29.5%	32.9%	33.0%	**32.9%**
Total Public Revenues (% of Total Public Resources)	**68.1%**	**64.1%**	**70.9%**	**64.3%**	**57.6%**	**66.8%**	**53.6%**	**64.3%**
4) Lending Proceeds and Sales of Financial Assets (% of Total Public Resources)	4.2%	9.4%	10.9%	6.5%	5.5%	4.8%	2.6%	**6.5%**
5) Borrowing (% of Total Public Resources)	27.7%	26.6%	18.2%	29.2%	36.8%	28.4%	43.8%	**29.2%**

Source: Made by the author based on the final accounts of the state's general budget provided by the Ministry of Finance.
*Represents three-year average.

According to the capital or financial constraints that were introduced in the previous section, the inability of an economy to access domestic or external capital markets during recessions, or the ability to do so only at relatively higher cost of borrowing, represent the main impediments on the government to act countercyclically by raising public spending and/or reducing taxes. The data shown in table 2 indicate that the average relative share of government borrowing in total public resources has been increasing from 28% in the first sub-period to 44% during the last sub-period, on average. This relatively high reliance on borrowing, compared to on other public resources, may indicate that credit constraints are not binding for the Egyptian government. In fact, the government of Egypt has always relied on borrowing to finance its budget deficit, and this has been reflected in the increasing ratio of public debt to GDP that approximately approaches 100%. Moreover, it can be concluded from the presented data measures that the government could expand its borrowing during the period that followed the economic downturn resulting from the 25th of January Revolution in 2011. In this context, it should be noted that the majority of the government borrowing is derived from domestic rather than external sources. According to the official data of the Ministry of Finance, domestic debt represented approximately 84% of the total public debt, on average, during the time period from June 2009 to June 2015. Regarding the composition of the government debt service, data for the period from fiscal year 2008/2009 to fiscal year 2014/2015 show that domestic interest payments represented approximately 96.3% of the total interest payments on the government debt, while principal payments of domestic debt constituted approximately 73.2% of the total principal payments of government debt, on average.

Since different types of tax revenues might behave differently following shocks to economic activity, the issue of tax structure should be considered. Tax revenues result from both tax rates and tax bases. Thus, it is not only the tax base response to business cycle that matters, but the changes in tax rates are also important in explaining the cyclicality of tax revenues. Taxes whose rates are more progressive (usually direct personal and corporate income taxes) are expected to act countercyclically, as automatic stabilizers, since their revenues would be more elastic with respect to income changes induced by the business cycles compared to those whose rates are flat (constant). Taxes on goods and services, as they depend on the volume of sales, which tends to fall during recessions and expand during booms, are expected to behave in the same manner to dampen fluctuations in real GDP. Other forms of taxation, however, might not exhibit such effects if they bear no relation to income (e.g., poll taxes, export tariffs or property taxes).

As for the tax structure in Egypt, data presented in table 3 confirm one of the major features of tax policies in developing countries, namely, the relatively high dependence on indirect taxes as the main source of public revenues[4]. This pattern is usually derived by the narrow income tax bases and widespread tax evasion and tax avoidance practices in most developing countries (Alm, Bahl, & Murray, 1991). Indirect taxes, on the other side, are characterized by relatively low administrative costs, which makes them more attractive. The relative importance of direct taxes in Egypt, however, has been increasing from 38% to approximately 45% between the first and last sub-periods, on average.

In particular, within the direct taxes, personal income tax revenues represented approximately 20% compared to approximately 80% for taxes on corporate profits during the period (2005/2006-2010/2011), on average[5]. For the structure of indirect taxes, data indicate that the relative share of international trade tax revenues has been decreasing during the time period of analysis due to several trade liberalization measures and the implementation of revenue-neutral reforms that reduced the customs tariffs[6].

Given that Egypt's tax structure is biased towards indirect rather than direct taxes, on one hand, and that the direct taxes are mainly dominated by corporate income taxes rather than by personal income taxes which proved to be more progressive [7], on the other hand, one may expect that the tax system in Egypt lacks the sufficient automatic stabilizers that would allow the economy to respond countercyclically to the business cycles.

Since the budget deficit represents the difference between public expenditure and public revenues, the expected cyclical behavior of budget deficit should be derived from the expectations regarding the cyclical behavior of public expenditure and of public revenues.

Table 3. Structure of Tax Revenues in Egypt: Five-Year Averages for the Period (1981/1982-2013/2014)

Five-Year Averages	81/82-85/86	86/87-90/91	91/92-95/96	96/97-00/01	01/02-05/06	06/07-10/11	11/12-13/14*	Whole Period Average
Direct Taxes								
Taxes on Incomes, Profits, and Capital Gains	37.7%	42.8%	45.0%	42.3%	46.1%	47.2%	44.7%	**44.1%**
Indirect Taxes								
Taxes on International Trade	31.9%	24.9%	19.9%	19.7%	14.7%	8.8%	6.9%	**17.7%**
Taxes on Goods and Services	23.0%	23.1%	25.8%	30.4%	31.1%	31.1%	32.5%	**28.4%**
Other Taxes**	7.3%	9.1%	9.4%	7.7%	8.1%	12.9%	16%	**9.9%**

Source: Made by the author based on the final accounts of the state's general budget provided by the Ministry of Finance.
*Represents three-year average.
* *Property tax revenues are included within this group.

In other words, the budget deficit is expected to act countercyclically (procyclically) if both public expenditure and public revenues behave in a countercyclical (procyclical) manner, while it is expected to act a-cyclically if the behavior of public expenditure and public revenues leads to no change in the budget deficit.

Budget deficit in Egypt (1981/1982-2013/2014)

Based on the GFS classification system, two concepts of budget deficit emerge, namely, cash deficit and overall deficit. While cash deficit measures the difference between total public expenditure and total public revenues, overall deficit adds to the cash deficit the value of net acquisition of financial assets. In addition, primary deficit that excludes interest payments from the deficit measure can be used to reflect the ability of government revenues to cover expenditure items that result from current rather than previous decisions.

As indicated by figure 4, the three measures of fiscal deficit had their lowest average ratios to GDP during the five-year period (1991/1992-1995/1996) [8]. This came as a result of implementing the ERSAP starting from 1991. By contrast, budget deficit measures had their highest average ratios to GDP during the last sub-period (2011/2012-2013/2014), which was mainly derived by the expansionary fiscal policy that the government had to adopt in response to the economic downturn that followed the Egyptian revolution in 2011. Since Egypt's overall budget deficit is mainly financed by net borrowing (the difference between borrowing and loans repayment), the trend of the budget deficit measures as shown by figure 4 is consistent with that of the public borrowing as indicated by figure 3 (the difference between the second and third bars for each sub-period). More specifically, public borrowing had its lowest average ratio to GDP of approximately 7.2% during the sub-period (1991/1992-1995/1996), while it had its greatest average ratio of approximately 17% during the last sub-period of the entire sample.

Before concluding this section, it should be emphasized that although the analysis provided above does not show significant changes in terms of the structure of Egypt's fiscal policy during the whole period under analysis, this does not imply that the Egyptian economy has been stable during that relatively long period or that there have not been major shocks that could affect the overall macroeconomic policy in general and the fiscal policy in particular. In fact, three main shocks that have affected the Egyptian economy during the analyzed period can be mentioned, namely, the implementation of the ERSAP at the beginnings of the 1990s, the global financial and economic crisis in 2008, and the political uprisings in 2011 that led to the 25th of January Revolution. Each of these three shocks

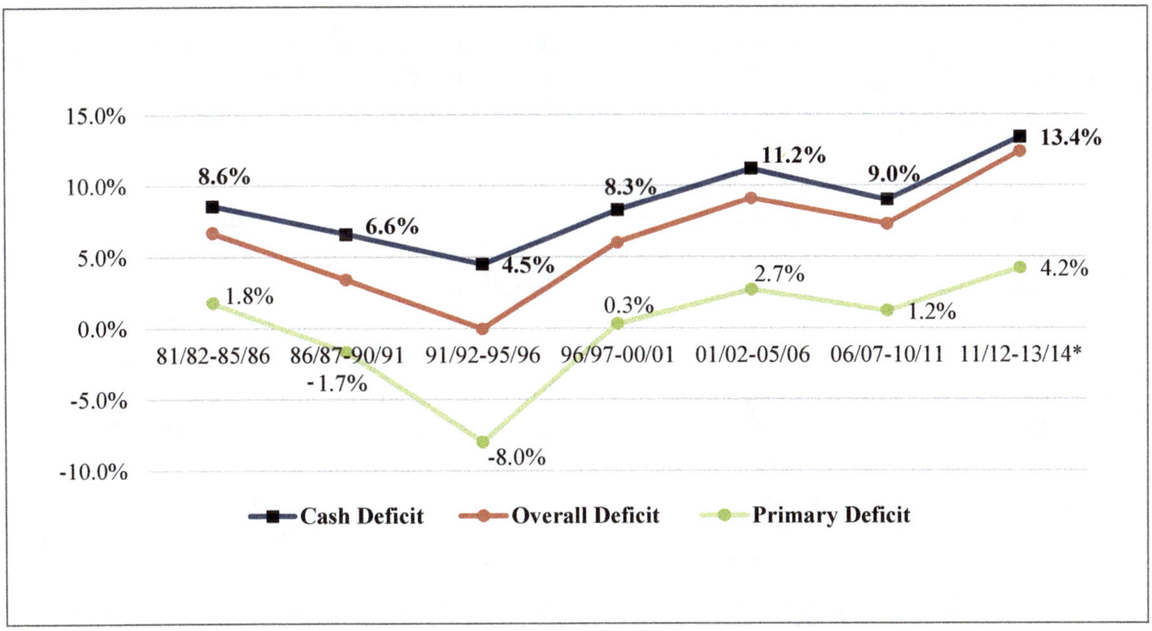

Figure 4. Budget Deficit Measures as Ratios of GDP: Five-Year Averages for the Period (1981/1982-2013/2014)
Source: Made by the author based on the final accounts of the state's general budget provided by the Ministry of Finance and data on GDP at market prices provided by the Ministry of Planning.
*Represents three-year average.

had its own social, economic, and fiscal impact on the country. It seems, however, that such impact was not strong enough to derive significant changes in the structure of Egypt's state budget or its fiscal policy.

4. The cyclical behavior of fiscal policy in Egypt: An empirical investigation

This section empirically tests the cyclical properties of Egypt's fiscal policy during the time period (1981/1982-2013/2014). For this aim, a regression is estimated to assess the response of each of the key fiscal aggregates (public expenditure, public revenues, and budget deficit) to economic business cycles as measured by the output gap. As far as the available literature is concerned, this issue has not been examined for the Egyptian economy in a similar manner. Two relevant studies can be referred to in this regard, namely, Ben Slimane and Ben Tahar (2009), and Panizza (2001). While the former discussed the fiscal cyclicality in a sample of 16 countries in the MENA region during the period (1975-2008) using a panel data set, the latter focused on the cyclicality of the fiscal policy (as one of the macroeconomic policies) in Egypt using the real GDP growth rate as a measure of the business cycle. Accordingly, the current study contributes to the existing literature as it focuses thoroughly on the Egyptian economy using time series data sets. This focus as reflected by the qualitative analysis (section 3) and the empirical analysis (section 4) is expected to allow for a better understanding of the particularities of Egypt's fiscal policy and how it behaves in response to business cycles. Moreover, the current study uses the 'output gap' instead of the real GDP growth rate as a measure of the business cycle. This is expected to lead to more precise conclusions regarding the question under study. The reason is that the growth rate of real GDP can fluctuate within the same period of recession or expansion making it a relatively poor measure for the business cycle.

Model specification, data sources and estimation methodology

The cyclical properties of fiscal aggregates in Egypt during the period under analysis are examined using the following equation:

$$F_t = \alpha_0 + \alpha_1 F_{t-1} + \alpha_2\, output\_gap_t + \\ + \alpha_3\, (output\_gap_t{*}institut_t) + \alpha_4 (output\_gap_t{*}cycle_t) + \\ + \alpha_5\, (output\_gap_t{*}credit\_gdp_t) + \\ + \alpha_6\, (output\_gap_t{*}exchange_t) + e_t \quad (1)$$

where F_t is the ratio of the fiscal variable (public expenditure, public revenues, tax revenues, or budget deficit) to GDP at year t; F_{t-1} is the lagged value of the dependent variable; $output\_gap_t$ is a measure of the business cycle at year t; $institut_t$ is a dummy variable for the budgetary institutions' reforms that were introduced since fiscal year 2005/2006; $cycle_t$ is a dummy variable for the business cycle (expansion versus recession); $credit\_gdp_t$ is the domestic credit to private sector as a ratio of GDP at year t; $exchange_t$ is the official exchange rate (local currency per one US dollar) at year t; and e_t is the error term at year t.

This specification follows the empirical literature on the cyclical properties of fiscal policy, in which the fiscal variable (usually measured as a percentage of GDP) is regressed on its lagged value, some measure of the business cycle (or the output gap), and a group of control variables (usually dummies) that account for different institutional, economic and political factors within a country (Alesina & Tabellini, 2005; Ben Slimane & Ben Tahar, 2009; Calderón et al., 2004; Jaimovich & Panizza, 2007; Manasse, 2006; Wibbels, 2006).

Economic fluctuations induced by business cycles are usually measured using the concept of output gap as the deviation of actual output from its potential level[9]. Measuring the output gap, however, is not an easy task. Different sets of assumptions can be used in combination with various econometric techniques to provide different measures of the output gap. One common assumption is that the output gap is some part of the transitory (cyclical) component of real output (St-Amant & van Norden, 1997). More specifically, the definition of the output gap is mainly derived from an assumption of pure statistical methods that GDP time series can be decomposed into two parts: *trend* (potential or long-run) component and *cyclical* component. That is,

$$Y_t = Trend_t + Cyclical_t \quad (2)$$

where Y_t is the actual level of output at time t; $Trend_t$ is the trend component of the output at time t; and $Cyclical_t$ is the cyclical component of the output at time t. The trend component reflects a broad long-term output around which actual levels of output fluctuate. It is often regarded as a measure of the potential output. Accordingly, the cyclical component of the GDP series ($Cyclical_t$) can be simply viewed as the output gap since it measures the difference between actual level of output (Y_t) and its trend (or potential) level in the long-term ($Trend_t$).

Two main methods have been used in the literature to estimate the trend (or potential) component of a time series, namely, statistical approaches (including polynomial trend extrapolation and Hodrick-Prescott filters) and the estimation of production function usually using the Cobb-Douglas specification. Following the approach used in the relevant literature (Alberola et al., 2006; Alesina & Tabellini, 2005; Calderón et al., 2004), trend (or potential) output in this study is calculated by applying a Hodrick Prescott (HP) filter to the real GDP time series[10]. Then, the output gap is estimated as follows:

$$output\ gap = \frac{y - y^*}{y^*} \quad (3)$$

where y is the actual output (real GDP), and y^* is the trend output. Thus, positive output gaps are expected to occur in good times (economic expansions), while negative ones are associated with recessions.

In addition to the output gap measure, four interaction terms are added to the model specification to provide clues to the relationship under study. 1) The interaction term *output_gap*institut* is added to test whether the cyclical behavior of fiscal aggregates has changed starting from fiscal year 2005/2006, in which the government of Egypt introduced significant institutional reforms regarding its budgetary system. The most important of such reforms were the creation of the Treasury Single Account (TSA) at the Central Bank of Egypt that replaced the large number of different bank accounts used previously by the government entities, as well as the adoption of the IMF's GFS manual for the economic and functional classifications of the state's budget[11]. 2) The interaction term *output_gap*cycle* is included to test whether the cyclical behavior of Egypt's fiscal aggregates depends on the nature of the business cycle itself (expansions vs. recessions). 3) The interaction term *output_gap*credit_gdp* is pro-

Table 4. ADF Test Results of the Variables' Time Series

Variable Name/ Symbol	Test Statistic	AIC Automatic Specified Lag Length
Output Gap (output_gap)	-3.615**	(2)
Public Expenditure-to-GDP Ratio (exp_gdp)	-4.645***	(8)
Public Revenues-to-GDP Ratio (rev_gdp)	-3.646**	(3)
Taxes-to-GDP Ratio (tax_gdp)	-4.010**	(7)
Primary Cash Deficit-to-GDP Ratio (pri_cash_def_gdp)	-4.949***	(8)
Primary Deficit-to-GDP Ratio (pri_def_gdp)	-3.436*	(7)
Credit-to-GDP Ratio (credit_gdp)	-4.017**	(4)
Official Exchange Rate (exchange)	-3.731**	(7)

(*), (**) and (***) indicate the rejection of the null hypothesis of the ADF test at the 10%, 5% and 1% levels of significance, respectively.

posed to measure the change in the cyclical behavior of fiscal policy associated with changes in the credit-to-GDP ratio as a proxy for the financial depth[12]. 4) Finally, the interaction term *output_gap*exchange* is included to capture whether there would be any effect of the official exchange rate on the cyclical behavior of the fiscal variables[13].

Appendix 2 provides a description of the variables used in this study, the way each was measured, and the source of the collected data.

According to the model specification, a countercyclical policy would imply a negative coefficient for the output gap variable (α_2) in both public expenditure and budget deficit models and a positive coefficient in the public revenues model. The opposite should be expected in case of procyclical behavior. A non-significant coefficient of the output gap represents the case of a-cyclical behavior of the relevant fiscal variable. Given the structure of Egypt's state budget (characterized by a narrow fiscal space and the absence of real automatic stabilizers on both the expenditure and revenue sides) as discussed in the previous section and in light of understanding the nature of the financial and institutional constraints that exist in Egypt, one has no reason to expect that Egypt's fiscal policy acts in a countercyclical manner in response to business cycles. The procyclical behavior or the a-cyclical behavior are much more expected to be preserved in Egypt. Moreover, since the structure of Egypt's public expenditure is dominated by wages, subsidies, and interest payments, which are not expected to decrease in response to expansionary business cycles, one can argue that the role of fiscal policy in stabilizing the economy in Egypt would be much weaker during expansion times than during recessions. In other words, the political and institutional setup of the Egyptian economy would make it relatively hard for the government to cut the major expenditure items in the state's budget during boom times, while it would allow it to raise such items easily during recessions.

The stationarity of the variables' time series is tested using the Augmented Dickey-Fuller (ADF) test (with an intercept and trend specification) to ensure that the estimation results are not derived from a spurious regression. The test results, as shown in table 4, indicate that all variables used in estimation are stationary at the five percent significance level except for the primary deficit-to-GDP ratio which is stationary at the ten percent level of significance only. Accordingly, OLS could be used to estimate the relationship under analysis.

Model findings and discussion

The specified model is estimated separately for each of public expenditure, public revenues and taxes, and budget deficit. The estimation results are presented in table 5 with the standard errors in parentheses.

The cyclical behavior of public expenditure: In model (1), total public expenditure as a ratio of GDP is regressed on its lagged value, the output gap, and the four interaction terms mentioned above. The results show that the explanatory variables explain approximately 70% of total variation of the dependent variable and that the whole model is significant at the 1% level. The coefficient of the business cycle measure '*output gap*' is negative and significant at the one percent level. An increase in the percentage deviation of real GDP from its HP filter is associated with a decline in the public expenditure-to-GDP ratio, holding other things equal[14]. This may indicate that public expenditure behaves in a countercyclical manner; that is, it increases during recessions or when output gaps are smaller and shrinks during expansions or when output gaps are larger. However, as mentioned earlier, public expenditure in Egypt lacks the automatic stabilizers in the form of subsidies and social transfers since such expenditure is mainly dominated by energy and food subsidies, which do not respond to income changes. Thus, the countercyclical behavior of public expenditure that is inferred from the negative coefficient of the output gap variable should be questionable. According to Kaminsky et al. (2004), for example, a negative correlation between the output gap and the public expenditure-to-GDP ratio might simply result from the fact that GDP expands during expansions and shrinks in recessions; thus, even if public expenditure is kept constant over business cycles, its ratio to GDP should move in the opposite direction of the cycle.

The coefficient of the lagged value of public expenditure-to-GDP ratio '*exp_gdp(-1)*' is positive and significant. This is mainly derived from the incremental approach adopted in the formulation of Egypt's state budget, according to which the public expenditure level for a given year is largely estimated based on the previous year's level plus incremental adjustments at the margin.

The coefficient of the interaction term '*output_gap*cycle*' is positive and significant at the 1% level. This might indicate that the cyclical behavior of public expenditure differs between expansion and recession times. More specifically, since the coefficient of this interaction term is positive, while the coefficient of the output gap is negative, one would expect that public expenditure becomes less countercyclical during expansion periods than during recessions. A one percentage point increase in the output gap is associated with a decrease of 4.3 percentage points in the public expenditure ratio during recessions (when the cycle dummy = 0) compared to a 1.3 percentage point decrease during expansions (when the cycle dummy =1). This finding, in fact, is consistent with what has been expected from the structure of Egypt's public expenditure, which limits the government's ability to reduce public spending during periods of expansion.

There is also empirical evidence that supports the idea that the cyclical behavior of public expenditure in Egypt has been significantly improving since the introduction of the budget reforms in fiscal year 2005/2006. This is reflected by the negative and significant coefficient of the interaction term '*output_gap*institut*', which implies that the countercyclical behavior of public expenditure has been stronger for the years since 2005/2006 compared to the preceding period.

The coefficient of the interaction term '*output_gap*exchange*' is positive and significant at the 10% level. Given that the 'output_gap' coefficient is negative, this indicates that the higher the official exchange rate is (as measured by the value of one US dollar in terms of local currency), the lower the countercyclical response of public expenditure to business cycles. This seems logical in the sense that higher exchange rates (which reflect the deterioration of the value of the local currency versus the US dollar) indicate a deteriorated macroeconomic and fiscal environment of the economy. On one hand, the deterioration of the value of local currency reflects structural economic imbalances and institutional factors that might weaken the overall economic performance of the country. On the other hand, the decreasing value of the local currency against the US dollar means that the cost of external borrowing (as represented by the debt service paid in the foreign currency) becomes higher. This is expected to constrain the government's ability to conduct a countercyclical expenditure policy.

Finally, the coefficient of the interaction term '*output_gap*credit_gdp*' tends to be insignificant. This indicates that the cyclicality of public expenditure in Egypt might not significantly differ with different levels of financial depth, measured by domestic credit

Table 5. Results of Estimated Models (Basic Specification)

	Dependent Variables				
	Model (1)	Model (2)		Model (3)	
	exp_gdp	rev_gdp	tax_gdp	pri_cash_def_gdp	pri_def_gdp
C	11.25*** (3.01)	7.73** (3.74)	6.10*** (1.92)	0.20 (0.81)	-0.08 (1.01)
exp_gdp(-1)	0.61*** (0.09)	-	-	-	-
rev_gdp (-1)	-	0.67*** (0.13)	-	-	-
tax_gdp (-1)	-	-	0.61*** (0.11)	-	-
pri_cash_def_gdp (-1)	-	-	-	0.78*** (0.14)	-
pri_def_gdp (-1)	-	-	-	-	0.83*** (0.15)
output_gap	-4.32*** (1.07)	-4.45** (1.83)	-1.39* (0.72)	0.46 (1.31)	0.35 (1.76)
output_gap*institut	-1.82** (0.86)	-2.43 (1.46)	-0.20 (0.53)	0.69 (1.01)	1.23 (1.39)
output_gap*cycle	2.99*** (1.02)	2.91* (1.69)	0.34 (0.63)	-0.06 (1.13)	-0.54 (1.54)
output_gap*credit_ gdp	0.03 (0.03)	0.03 (0.05)	0.02 (0.02)	0.005 (0.04)	0.02 (0.05)
output_gap*exchange	0.41* (0.23)	0.51 (0.40)	0.08 (0.15)	-0.16 (0.27)	-0.26 (0.38)
Adjusted R-squared	0.70	0.59	0.65	0.61	0.60
F-statistic prob.	0.000	0.000	0.000	0.000	0.000
Durbin-Watson Stat.	2.2	1.7	1.5	1.4	1.7
Jarque-Bera prob.	0.83	0.26	0.00	0.09	0.67
Breusch-Godfrey LM test (F-statistic prob.)	0.58	0.50	0.31	0.13	0.55
RAMSEY test (F-statistic prob.)	0.79	0.98	0.46	0.27	0.84
ARCH test (F-statistic prob.)	0.25	0.12	0.83	0.1	0.17

(*), (**) and (***) indicate the significance of the coefficient at the 10%, 5% and 1% levels of significance, respectively.

to private sector as a percentage of GDP. If domestic credit to the private sector as a ratio of GDP is considered as a valid proxy for financial depth, this finding would not support the financial or credit arguments in the literature, according to which fiscal countercyclicality is expected to be more observed in economies with mature and well-developed financial markets at the domestic level. In other words, the domestic financial constraints seem insignificant for the cyclicality of government expenditure according to this model.

The cyclical behavior of public revenues and tax revenues: In model (2), total public revenues as a ratio of GDP is regressed on its lagged value, the output gap, as well as on the other four interaction terms. The results, as presented in the second column of table 5, show that the explanatory variables explain approximately 59% of the total variation of the dependent variable and that the whole model is significant at the one percent level. The results indicate that the output gap (as a measure of the business cycle) is negatively correlated to the ratio of public revenues to GDP. Thus, public revenues behave procyclically. This finding may indicate that even the automatic stabilizer (cyclical/non-discretionary) component of the public revenues is not strong enough to derive the optimal countercyclical behavior of the overall public revenues. Moreover, the fact that the Egyptian economy used to receive more grants during bad times compared to during the periods of expansion might provide a partial explanation for the procyclical behavior of public revenues. To exclude the latter effect, the cyclicality of public revenues is tested using the ratio of tax revenues (instead of total public revenues) to GDP as the dependent variable.

Estimation results, as shown in the third column of table 5, indicate a procyclical behavior, according to which higher ratios of tax revenues to GDP are correlated to lower output gaps. Since tax revenues represent the product of both tax 'bases' and tax 'rates', such procyclical behavior of tax policy should be derived by the behavior of the tax rates relative to that of the tax bases. More specifically, given that tax bases should expand during economic expansions and shrink during recessions, a decline in the tax revenues-to-GDP ratio during expansions should be derived by one of the three following scenarios: a) a fall in tax rates that is sufficient to offset the increase in tax bases, which would lead to lower tax revenues; b) a fall in tax rates that is proportional to the tax bases' increase, which would keep overall tax revenues unaffected; and c) a constant or a marginal increase in tax rates that goes in parallel with the tax base increases. Since GDP increases during expansions, scenarios (a) and (b) should automatically result in a lower ratio of tax revenues to GDP during such periods. Scenario (c), however, should lead to the same result only under the condition that the increase in tax revenues during expansion periods is less than proportional to that of GDP. This third scenario was what led Kaminsky et al. (2004) to argue that a negative correlation between the tax revenues-to-GDP ratio and the output gap should not necessarily indicate a procyclical behavior. Such negative correlation might also result from increases in tax rates, as described by scenario (c).

Regarding the other control variables in the models of public revenues and tax revenues, the results are almost similar. The lagged value of the dependent variable is positive and significant at the one percent level in both models. The insignificant coefficients of the interaction terms *'output_gap*institut'*, *'output_gap*credit_GDP'*, and *'output_gap*exchange'* support the idea that the cyclical behavior of public revenues and tax revenues in the Egyptian economy does not seem to be affected by either the institutional budget reforms that were implemented since 2005/2006 or the changing levels of financial development (as measured by the domestic credit to the private sector as a percentage of GDP) and the official exchange rate. However, the results indicate that public revenues (but not tax revenues) tend to act less procyclically during expansions than during recessions.

The cyclical behavior of budget deficit: In this model, the primary budget deficit as a ratio of GDP is used as the dependent variable, which is regressed on its lagged value, the output gap, as well as on the four developed interaction terms. Two measures of primary budget deficit are utilized, namely, cash deficit (excluding interest payments) as a ratio of GDP *'pri_cash_def_gdp'* and overall deficit (excluding interest payments) as a ratio of GDP *'pri_def_gdp'*. The estimation results are shown in the fourth and fifth columns of table 5. The business cycle measure is found to be insignificantly correlated to the two measures of primary deficit. This implies that the overall fiscal policy in Egypt, as measured by the budget deficit-to-GDP ratio, tends to behave a-cyclically; that is, it does not significantly respond to output gaps. This finding seems to be consistent with the results reached above. More specifically, since both public expenditure and public revenues as ratios of GDP decrease with economic expansions and increase with recessions, the resulting budget deficit should simply act a-cyclically by being constant over the cycle. Thus, the procyclical behavior of public revenues tends to offset the countercyclical behavior of public expenditure. As a result, the overall behavior of fiscal policy neither stabilizes nor exacerbates business cycle fluctuations.

Reliability and robustness checks

The results of the diagnostic tests, namely, the Breusch-Godfrey LM test for serial correlation in residuals; the RAMSEY test for regression specification error; and the ARCH test for Heteroskedasticity, as presented in table 5 indicate that the null hypothesis of these tests cannot be rejected and thus the estimated coefficients can be considered reliable. In addition, the Jarque-Bera test results imply the non-rejection of the null hypothesis of normal distribution of residuals in the estimated equations except for that of the tax revenues model.

As a robustness check, the cyclical behavior of public expenditure, public revenues and tax revenues is tested using different measures of fiscal aggregates as dependent variables. The budget deficit model, however, could not be estimated using the new specification since the time series of the relevant dependent variables in this case are non-stationary. Instead of using the fiscal variable's ratio to GDP as the dependent variable, the relationships under study are re-estimated using the deviation of the fiscal variable (as a ratio of GDP) from its potential value measured by the HP filter. Such a method was used by Calderón, Duncan, and Schmidt-Hebbel (2004). Thus, the new specification takes the following form:

$$F\_gap_t = \alpha_0 + \alpha_1 F\_gap_{t-1} + \alpha_2\, output\_gap_t + \\ + \alpha_3 (output\_gap_t {}^* institut_t) + \alpha_4 (output\_gap_t {}^* cycle_t) + \\ + \alpha_5 (output\_gap_t {}^* credit\_gdp_t) + \\ + \alpha_6 (output\_gap_t {}^* exchange_t) + e_t \quad (4)$$

where F_gap_t is the percentage deviation of the fiscal variable as ratio of GDP from its HP filter at year t.

The findings of the public expenditure model in the new specification almost confirm those reached by the basic one. The output gap is negatively correlated to gaps in the public expenditure-to-GDP ratio, indicating a countercyclical behavior. The coefficient of the interaction term (*output_gap*cycle*) encounters similar sign and significance compared to the case in the basic specification. The findings indicate that the official exchange rate loses its significance under the new specification, while the domestic credit to the private sector as a ratio of GDP becomes significant. For the public revenues and the tax revenues models, the findings confirm the procyclical behavior that was concluded by the basic model specification. The four interaction terms have results under the new specification that are similar to those derived from the basic specification except for '*output_gap*credit_gdp*', which shows a positive and significant relationship with the dependent variable under the new specification. This indicates that public revenues and tax revenues tend to be less procyclical with higher levels of financial development.

As another robustness check, the basic models are re-estimated using a different value of the smoothing parameter (lambda) in the HP filter applied to the real output time series. More specifically, lambda is set according to the frequency rule of Ravn and Uhlig (2002) to equal 6.25 instead of the value of 100 suggested by Hodrick and Prescott (1997) for annual data[15]. This procedure, although it results in different values for the output gap measure, does not affect the main findings of the estimated models.

In general, the findings reached by this study confirm that fiscal policy in Egypt has not been conducted in a countercyclical manner to dampen business cycle fluctuations. One possible explanation might be the fact that automatic stabilizers that are built into the fiscal system itself (such as income taxes and transfer programs) are too small to have a significant smoothing effect on aggregate fluctuations. Such a finding supports the results of previous empirical studies in this regard. For example, Panizza (2001) found evidence that supports the idea that budget deficit is insignificantly correlated to GDP growth changes in Egypt during the period (1981/2000). Moreover, Ben Slimane and Ben Tahar (2009) found evidence that total government expenditure and total government revenues measured as ratios of GDP tend to act procyclically in a sample of 16 MENA region countries over the period (1975-2008).

Study's limitations

This study provides theoretical and empirical insights on the cyclical behavior of fiscal policy aggregates in Egypt during the time period (1981/1982-2013/2014). The findings of the study, however, should be analyzed taking into account certain methodological issues that might affect their accuracy. *First*, while there is a wide agreement in the literature on the validity of using the output gap (deviation of actual real output from its potential level) as a measure of business cycles, no consensus has yet been reached on the best way to estimate the potential level of output. Different approaches to estimate the trend component of real GDP time series might yield different outcomes[16]. Accordingly, different findings might result from this study if other measures were used to estimate the potential output instead of the HP filter.

Second, the amendments introduced to the classification system of the state's general budget in fiscal year 2005/2006 forced the author to introduce some changes to the fiscal data of the period (2005/2006-2013/2014) to ensure its consistency with data of the preceding period. While the introduced changes were based on a delicate approach according to which the author compared each budget item in the two classification systems, some errors that result from such a process might challenge the qualitative and quantitative analysis provided by this paper. Related to this point is the relatively short time series data (33 years) that the author could get for Egypt's fiscal variables, which in turn has limited the potential use of more explanatory variables in the estimated models.

5. Concluding remarks and policy implications

This study uses a time series dataset for the Egyptian economy during the time period from fiscal year 1981/1982 to fiscal year 2013/2014. The study finds evidence for a countercyclical behavior of public expenditure and a procyclical behavior of public revenues and tax revenues. As a result, the overall fiscal policy, as measured by the primary budget deficit-to-GDP ratio, is found to act 'a-cyclically'; that is, it neither stabilizes nor intensifies the business cycle induced fluctuations. This main finding proved to be robust with the changes in the measurement of the dependent variables and the output gap.

Moreover, the study findings indicate that the countercyclical behavior of public expenditure and the procyclical behavior of public revenues tend to get stronger during recessions than during expansions. This finding is proved to be robust and supports the author's expectation that if the Egyptian government can raise its spending during recessions easily, expenditure contraction during expansion times might be much more difficult due to political economy and institutional factors. At the same time, this finding indicates that during recession times, the government tends to raise its public and tax revenues heavily to finance the higher level of its spending, leading to a negligible change in its budget deficit.

Regarding the factors that might explain the observed cyclical behavior of fiscal policy in Egypt, there is empirical evidence that both the credit/financial factors and the institutional factors have some role to play in this regard. The effect of such factors was observed in the models of public expenditure and public revenues separately but not in the model of budget deficit. For example, the budget institutional reforms that were introduced since 2005/2006 seem to be correlated to improvements in the cyclical behavior of public expenditure (in the form of greater countercyclicality) under the basic specification. In addition, the deterioration in the value of the local currency versus the US dollar (which reflects a higher cost of external borrowing) seems to negatively affect the performance of public expenditure during the cycles. That is, the higher the foreign exchange rate, the less the government would be able to spend countercyclically. The financial development (as measured by the domestic credit to the private sector as a percentage of GDP) may affect the cyclical behavior of both of public revenues and public expenditure only when such variables are measured in terms of their deviations from the potential (HP filter) values.

If Egypt has not been able to run an optimal fiscal policy so far, the situation is not expected to change at least in the short and medium terms. The country has been suffering from several imbalances since the political uprisings of 2011, which have been negatively reflected in almost all the fiscal and economic variables, leading to a deteriorated fiscal stance and weakened economy. The fact that Egypt has always relied on domestic rather than external borrowing to finance its budget deficit may reflect the lower accessibility of the government to international capital markets due to its weak fiscal position and deteriorated creditworthiness, which in turn result in a higher cost of capital. The current situation in Egypt is expected to reinforce this trend. On one hand, the political and economic environment have not yet stabilized since the revolution of 2011. The indicators reflect that the measures of public debt and budget deficit are approaching unpreceded levels. On the other hand, the floatation of the Egyptian pound enacted on November 2016 is expected to reinforce the existing barriers to access the international capital markets and raise the cost of external borrowing in terms of the debt service payments. This implies significant structural and credible (economic and political) reforms in the country to improve the economy's rating according to the international financial institutions and thus to facilitate its accessibility to external financial markets with reasonable costs. At the same time, those reforms should be reflected in a better fiscal stance of the country that finally allows optimal behavior of the fiscal policy.

At the institutional and political economy front, efforts are needed to focus on reforming the fiscal institutional environment in Egypt to lower corruption and enhance fiscal transparency and accountability in a way that would facilitate the use of fiscal policy as a tool to stabilize the economy during business cycles[17]. This should include (but not be limited to) the introduction of binding or indicative fiscal rules and budget ceilings (on total public expenditure and its allocation), a better coordination between the recurrent and the investment components of the state's budget, the strengthening of the existing systems of internal and financial controls, the introduction of an effective system of internal audit, and the improvement of the external audit system's role in increasing the government's responsiveness, accountability, and transparency.

In terms of the budget structure, Egypt's state budget has a structure that not only reduces the fiscal space of the government and hinders its ability to use fiscal policy in a countercyclical fashion to stabilize its economy but also reinforces the social inequalities through favoring the interests of the high-income groups and businessmen at the expense of the poor. Accordingly, reforming the structure of the state's budget itself in a way that enables more automatic stabilizers to work through social spending and tax progressivity would necessarily improve the government's ability to conduct a countercyclical fiscal policy. This in turn is expected to benefit the poorest and most vulnerable citizens, who usually suffer from business cycle fluctuations, especially when social spending and public investments are cut in times they are most needed.

Finally, it should be emphasized that the economic downturn Egypt has been passing through since 2011 should not be dealt with using austerity measures that are based on spending cuts and/or tax increases. Such measures, especially in a demand-constrained economy that works below its full employment level, would reinforce the situation and worsen it[18]. The government instead needs to seek other more effective policy options. Increasing public spending mainly on social welfare programs and investments, expanding the tax bases, and eliminating the tax evasion and tax avoidance practices through a well-designed system of tax administration might be useful.

References

Agenor, P. R., McDermott, C. J., & Prasad, E. S. (2000). Macroeconomic fluctuations in developing countries: Some stylized facts. *The World Bank Economic Review*, *14*(2), 251-285.

Aghion, P., Marinescu, I., Caballero, R. J., & Kashyap, A. K. (2007). Cyclical budgetary policy and economic growth: What do we learn from OECD panel data? [with comments and discussion]. *NBER Macroeconomic Annual*, *22*, 251-278.

Alberola, E., Montero, J. M., Braun, M., & Cordella, T. (2006). Debt sustainability and pro-cyclical fiscal policies in Latin America [with comments]. *Economia*, *7*(1), 157-193.

Alesina, A., & Tabellini, G. (2005). Why fiscal policy often procyclical? (Working Paper No. 11600). National Bureau of Economic Research. Retrieved from http://www.nber.org/papers/w11600.pdf

Alesina, A., Tabellini, G., & Campante, F. R. (2008). Why is fiscal policy often procyclical? *Journal of the European Economic Association*, 6(5), 1006-1036.

Alm, J., Bahl, R., & Murray, M. N. (1991). Tax base erosion in developing countries. *Economic Development and Cultural Change, 39*(4), 849-872.

Ben Slimane, S., & Ben Tahar, M. (2009, November). Why is fiscal policy procyclical in MENA Countries? Paper presented at the ERF 16th Annual Council Conference. Cairo, Egypt.

Bird, G. (2001). Conducting macroeconomic policy in developing countries: Piece of cake or mission impossible? Third World Quarterly, *22*(1), 37-49.

Calderón, C., Duncan, R., & Schmidt-Hebbel, K. (2004). The role of credibility in the cyclical properties of macroeconomic policies in emerging economies. *Review of World Economics, 140*(4), 613-633.

Central Bank of Iceland. (2005). Monetary Bulletin. A Quarterly Publication of the Central Bank of Iceland, 7(1). Retrieved from https://www.cb.is/lisalib/getfile.aspx?itemid=2529

Choudhary, A., Hanif, N., & Iqbal, J. (2013). On smoothing macroeconomic time series using HP and Modified HP Filter (MPRA Working Paper No. 45630). University Library of Munich, Germany. Retrieved from https://mpra.ub.uni-muenchen.de/45630/1/MPRA_paper_45630.pdf

El Husseiny, I. A. (2016a). Budgetary institutions and fiscal performance in Egypt: Is there a link? *Public Budgeting and Finance*, 36(1), 85-105.

El Husseiny, I. A. (2016b). On bringing down Egypt's budget deficit to GDP ratio: Are expenditure cuts required? *International Journal of Economics and Business Research*, 12(2), 91-102.

Gali, J., & Perotti, R. (2003). Fiscal policy and monetary integration in Europe (Working Paper No. 9773). National Bureau of Economics Research. Retrieved from http://www.nber.org/papers/w9773

Hodrick, R. J., & Prescott, E. C. (1997). Postwar U.S. business cycles: An empirical investigation. *Journal of Money, Credit and Banking, 29*(1), 1-16.

Jaimovich, D., & Panizza, U. (2007, March). Procyclicality or reverse causality? (Working Paper No. 599). Inter-American Development Bank. Retrieved from https://publications.iadb.org/bitstream/handle/11319/1949/Procyclicality%20or%20Reverse%20Causality%3F%20.pdf?sequence=1

Kaminsky, G. L., Reinhart, C. M., & Végh, C. A. (2004). When it rains, it pours: Procyclical capital flows and macroeconomic policies (Working Paper No. 10780). National Bureau of Economic Research. Retrieved from http://www.nber.org/papers/w10780.pdf

Lane, P. R. (2003). The cyclical behaviour of fiscal policy: Evidence from the OECD. *Journal of Public Economics*, 87(12), 2661-2675.

Lee, Y., & Sung, T. (2007). Fiscal policy, business cycles and economic stabilization: Evidence from industrialised and developing countries. *Fiscal Studies, 28*(4), 437-462.

Manasse, P. (2006). Procyclical fiscal policy: Shocks, rules, and institutions- A view from MARS (Working Paper No. 06/27). International Monetary Fund. Retrieved from https://www.imf.org/external/pubs/ft/wp/2006/wp0627.pdf

Norris, E. D, Allen, R., Zanna, L., Prakash, T., Kvintradze, E., Lledo, V., ... Gollwitzer, S. (2010). Budget institutions and fiscal performance in low-income countries (Working Paper No. 10/80). International Monetary Fund. Retrieved from https://www.imf.org/~/media/Websites/IMF/imported-full-text-pdf/external/pubs/ft/wp/2010/_wp1080.ashx

Panizza, U. (2001, October). Macroeconomic policies in Egypt: An interpretation of the past and options for the future (Working Paper No. 61). The Egyptian Center for Economic Studies (ECES). Retrieved from http://www.eces.org.eg/MediaFiles/Uploaded_Files/%7BEA853B45-7859-4B86-8281-9877B386B4CC%7D_ECESWP61e.pdf

Ravn, M. O., & Uhlig, H. (2002). On adjusting the Hodrick-Prescott Filter for the frequency of observations. *The Review of Economics and Statistics, 84*(2), 371-376.

Sabir, S., & Zahid, K. (2012). Macroeconomic policies and business cycle: The role of institutions in selected SAARC countries. *The Pakistan Development Review, 51*(4), 147-158.

St-Amant, P., & van Norden, S. (1997, August). Measurement of the output gap: A discussion of recent research at the Bank of Canada (Technical Report No. 79). Bank of Canada. Retrieved from https://www.bankofcanada.ca/wp-content/uploads/2010/01/tr79.pdf

Talvi, E., & Végh, C. A. (2005). Tax base variability and procyclical fiscal policy in developing countries. *Journal of Development Economics, 78*(1), 156-190.

The Ministry of Finance. (2016). State's General Budget Classification Manual in Arab Republic of Egypt. Available from http://www.mof.gov.eg/english/pages/statistics.aspx

Thornton, J. (2007). On the cyclicality of South African fiscal policy. *South African Journal of Economics,* 75(2), 258-264.

Tornell, A., & Lane, P. R. (1998, April). Voracity and growth (Working Paper No. 6498). National Bureau of Economic Research. Retrieved from http://www.nber.org/papers/w6498.pdf

Vazquez, J. M., Vulovic, V., & Liu, Y. (2011). Direct versus indirect taxation: Trends, theory and economic significance. In E. Albi, J. Martinez-Vazquez (Eds.), The Elgar Guide to Tax Systems (pp. 37-92). Cheltenham, UK: Edward Elgar Publishing.

Wibbels, E. (2006). Dependency revisited: International markets, business cycles, and social spending in the developing world. *International Organization,* 60(2), 433-468.

Woo, J. (2009). Why do more polarized countries run more procyclical fiscal policy? *The Review of Economics and Statistics,* 91(4), 850-870.

Endnotes

1 *The 'common pool phenomenon' usually arises when the various decision makers involved in the budgetary process (legislators, the Minister of Finance, line ministers, etc.) compete for public resources and fail to internalize the current and future costs of their choices (Norris et al., 2010).*

2 *According to Lane (2003), governments may attempt to induce a procyclical pattern in interest payments since they can better afford high debt payments during boom periods.*

3 *It is worth mentioning that data on total public revenues that are presented in this analysis exclude all capital revenues from the second chapter 'grants' and the third chapter 'other non-tax revenues'. Such capital revenues were classified, instead, within the fourth chapter 'lending proceeds and sales of financial assets'. This amendment was necessary to ensure that fiscal data since fiscal year 2005/2006 are consistent with those of the preceding period during which the old budget classification system was used. Thus, one would expect that total public revenues are underestimated in this analysis by the amount of the excluded capital revenues.*

4 *Using a sample of 116 developed and developing countries over the period (1972-2005), Vazquez, Vulovic, and Liu (2011) showed that the average ratio of direct to indirect taxes in developing countries is approximately one-third of the value in developed countries.*

5 *It is worth mentioning that the General Authority of Petroleum and the Suez Canal together finance more than two-thirds of the revenues from corporate income tax in Egypt.*

6 *The relatively high reliance on trade tax revenues such as taxes on exports, in many developing countries, makes such countries more vulnerable to external economic shocks. Tax revenues may fluctuate heavily based on the volume of exports, which in turn is affected by the economic conditions in the countries that comprise the markets for their exports, and based on the natural factors that might affect the supply of exports by the developing country itself (Bird, 2001).*

7 *It is worth mentioning that labor incomes finance the greatest share (almost 65%) of personal income taxes in Egypt, an issue that has implications from the perspective of social justice.*

8 *It is noteworthy that the cash deficit as calculated in this analysis is overestimated. This is because total public revenues are underestimated by the amount of capital revenues, which are excluded for data consistency reasons. Overall deficit, however, is underestimated in this analysis by the amount of the acquisition of financial assets, which could not be added to the expenditure side. The reason is that the old classification system of the budget does not allow for the separation of 'loans repayment' from the 'acquisition of financial assets', as both are aggregated in one chapter named 'capital transfers'.*

9 *The potential output of an economy is defined as the level of GDP that is consistent with full utilization of all factors of production (capital stock, labor use, and available technology). Since potential output cannot be observed directly from data, it has to be estimated using statistical methods; thus,*

it is subject to a high degree of uncertainty (Central Bank of Iceland, 2005).

10 *According to Hodrick and Prescott (1997), the smoothing parameter (lambda) in the filter should be set equal to 100 for annual data and 1600 for quarterly data.*

11 *While other variables that capture the institutional and political economy factors, such as political regime characteristics (executive recruitment, executive constraints, political participations), democracy, corruption, etc., might be much more relevant, the non-availability of data on such measures for Egypt during the time series under study is the main reason for not being able to use any of them in the analysis. Moreover, if such data were available, they would not be expected to exert significant variability during the examined period. The reason is that institutional and political factors in Egypt, at least before January 2011, have always been static or involved trivial changes.*

12 *Ben Slimane and Ben Tahar (2009) used an interaction term that involves both the output gap and the financial depth measure to test for the following hypothesis: the higher the financial depth of a given economy is, measured by the credit provided to private sector as a percentage of GDP, the greater will be the government's ability to borrow in bad times to finance its higher level of spending, and the more countercyclical its fiscal policy should be.*

13 *The author believes that the 'exchange rate' variable can account for many economic, fiscal and financial factors. A deterioration in the country's local currency versus the foreign currency reflects a weakened position of the balance of payment as well as of the state's budget. It also may reflect the lack of foreign direct investment that can be caused by the lack of credibility of government policies in general and policies related to investment in particular. Moreover, the exchange rate may be used as a proxy for the accessibility to international capital markets in the sense that higher exchange rates will constrain the government's ability to borrow from abroad since the debt service payments should be made in foreign currency, which increases the burden on the government.*

14 *Here, the interpretation of the estimated coefficient should take into consideration the fact that output gap is included in four interaction terms in this model.*

15 *For more technical details on the HP and adjusted HP filters, see Choudhary, Hanif, and Iqbal (2013).*

16 *See St-Amant and van Norden (1997) for more details on the different measures of potential output and output gap.*

17 *For more details on how poor budgetary institutions in Egypt might affect the country's fiscal performance, refer to El Husseiny (2016a).*

18 *See El Husseiny (2016b) for more details on the effect of government expenditure cuts on the budget deficit-to-GDP ratio in Egypt.*

Appendix (1)

Amendments Introduced by the Author regarding the Expenditure Side of the Budget

Name of Budget Chapter According to the New Classification System	Amendments introduced to the data of the period (2005/2006-2013/2014) which is based on the new classification system to comply with the data of the period (1981/1982-2004/2005) that is based on the old system of classification	Notes
Chapter 1: Wages and Salaries	No amendments were introduced to this chapter.	This chapter included the same items in both the old and new classification systems of the budget.
Chapter 2: Goods and Services	The following items were excluded from this chapter: - Purchases for resale - Lamp sum allocations and general reserves - Excluded goods and services.	
Chapter 3: Interest Payments	The following items were excluded from this chapter: - Lamp sum allocations and general reserves - Excluded interest payments.	
Chapter 4: Subsidies, Grants and Social Benefits	The following items were excluded from this chapter: - Lamp sum allocations and general reserves - Excluded subsidies, grants and social benefits.	
Chapter 5: Other Expenditures	The following items were added to this chapter: - Lamp sum allocations, general reserves, and all other items that were excluded from the second, third, and fourth chapters. - Purchases for resale that was excluded from the second chapter.	
Chapter 6: Investments	No amendments were introduced to this chapter.	This chapter included the same items in both the old and new classification systems of the budget.

Amendments Introduced by the Author regarding the Expenditure Side of the Budget (Continued)

Name of Budget Chapter According to the New Classification System	Amendments introduced to the data of the period (2005/2006-2013/2014) which is based on the new classification system to comply with the data of the period (1981/1982-2004/2005) that is based on the old system of classification	Notes
Total Public Expenditure	Total public expenditure is given by the sum of the first 6 expenditure chapters in the budget after introducing the abovementioned amendments to the individual chapters.	Using terminologies of the old classification system, total public expenditure represents the sum of the first 3 chapters in the expenditure side, namely, 'wages', 'recurrent expenses and recurrent transfers', and 'investment expenditure'.
Chapter 7: 'Acquisition of Financial Assets' & Chapter 8: 'Loans Repayment'	These two chapters are added together.	The summation value of Chapters 7 & 8 in the new classification correspond to the value of Chapter 4 in the old classification 'capital transfers'.
Total Public Utilization	Total public utilization is given by the sum of the 8 expenditure chapters in the budget after introducing the abovementioned amendments to the individual chapters.	Using terminologies of the old classification system, total public utilization represents the sum of the 4 expenditure chapters, namely, 'wages', 'recurrent expenses and recurrent transfers', 'investment expenditure', and 'capital transfers'.

Source: Made by the author based on "State's General Budget Classification Manual in Arab Republic of Egypt" by the Ministry of Finance (2016). Available from http://www.mof.gov.eg/english/pages/statistics.aspx

Amendments Introduced by the Author regarding the Revenues Side of the Budget

Name of Budget Chapter According to the New Classification System	Amendments introduced to the data of the period (2005/2006-2013/2014) which is based on the new classification system to comply with the data of the period (1981/1982-2004/2005) that is based on the old system of classification	Notes
Chapter 1: Taxes	The main groups of this chapter were amended as follows:	
Taxes on Incomes, Profits and Capital Gains	The following items were excluded from this group: - State's resources development fees - Stamp taxes on salaries - Localities' share in any kind of income taxes.	
Property Taxes	This group was transferred to the 'other taxes' group.	
Taxes on Goods and Services	The following items were excluded from this group: - Stamp taxes - Resources development fees - Fees and royalties.	
International Trade Tax	The following item was excluded from this group: - Localities' share in the tax on imports, exports, and movable capital.	
Other Taxes	The following items (which were excluded from the previous tax groups) are added to this group: - All types of stamp taxes - Resources development fees - Localities' share in all kinds of taxes - Fees and royalties - Property tax.	
Chapter 2: 'Grants' & Chapter 3: 'Other Non-Tax Revenues'	The following item was excluded from the 'grants' chapter: - Capital grants The following items were excluded from the 'non-tax revenues' chapter: - Optional capital transfers - Miscellaneous capital revenues.	

Amendments Introduced by the Author regarding the Revenues Side of the Budget (Continued)

Name of Budget Chapter According to the New Classification System	Amendments introduced to the data of the period (2005/2006-2013/2014) which is based on the new classification system to comply with the data of the period (1981/1982-2004/2005) that is based on the old system of classification	Notes
Total Public Revenues	Total public revenues are given by the sum of the first 3 revenue chapters in the budget after introducing the abovementioned amendments to the individual chapters.	Using the terminologies of the old classification system, total public revenues represents the sum of the first two revenues chapters, namely, 'taxes' and 'recurrent revenues and recurrent transfers'.
Chapter 4: Lending Proceeds and Sales of Financial Assets	The following items were added to this chapter: - Capital grants (excluded from chapter 2) - Optional capital transfers (excluded from chapter 3) - Miscellaneous capital revenues (excluded from chapter 3).	
Chapter 5: Borrowing	Borrowing is represented by the difference between total public utilization, on one hand, and the first 4 chapters in the resources side (after introducing the abovementioned amendments to the individual chapters), on the other hand.	Using terminologies of the old classification system, public borrowing represents the difference between the four expenditure chapters, namely, 'wages', 'recurrent expenses and recurrent transfers', 'investment expenditure', and 'capital transfers', on one hand, and the first three revenue chapters, namely, 'taxes', 'recurrent revenues and recurrent transfers', and 'capital revenues', on the other hand.
Total Public Resources	Total public resources are given by the sum of the 5 revenue chapters of the budget after introducing the abovementioned amendments to the individual chapters.	Using terminologies of the old classification system, total public resources represent the sum of the four chapters on the revenue side, namely, 'taxes', 'recurrent revenues and recurrent transfers', 'capital revenues' and 'loans and credit facilities'.

Source: Made by the author based on "State's General Budget Classification Manual in Arab Republic of Egypt" by the Ministry of Finance (2016). Available from http://www.mof.gov.eg/english/pages/statistics.aspx

Appendix (2)

Description and Measurement of the Study's Variables

Variable Name/ Symbol	Variable Description and Measurement	Data Sources
Output Gap (output_gap)	Calculated by the author as the percentage deviation of actual real GDP from its trend level as measured by the HP filter. Smoothing parameter (Lambda) = 100.	Data on real GDP obtained from the Ministry of Planning.
Public Expenditure-to-GDP Ratio (exp_gdp)	Calculated by the author as the ratio of total public expenditure to GDP at current prices.	
Public Revenues-to-GDP Ratio (rev_gdp)	Calculated by the author as the ratio of total public revenues (defined as the sum of taxes; grants; non-tax revenues; and lending proceeds and sales of financial assets) to GDP at current prices.	
Taxes-to-GDP Ratio (tax_gdp)	Calculated by the author as the ratio of taxes to GDP at current prices.	Data on fiscal variables obtained from the Ministry of Finance.
Primary Cash Deficit-to-GDP Ratio (pri _cash_ def_gdp)	Calculated by the author as the ratio of cash budget deficit, excluding interest payments, to GDP at current prices. Cash deficit here is defined as the difference between total public expenditure and total public (recurrent) revenues.	Data on GDP at current prices obtained from the Ministry of Planning.
Primary Deficit-to-GDP Ratio (pri_def_gdp)	Calculated by the author as the ratio of overall budget deficit, excluding interest payments, to GDP at current prices. Overall deficit here is defined as the difference between total public expenditure and total public revenues, with the latter including recurrent and capital revenues, lending proceeds and sales of financial assets.	
Budget Institutions Dummy (institut)	This dummy variable takes the value '1' for fiscal years from 2005/2006 to 2013/2014 and the value '0' otherwise.	
Business Cycle Dummy (cycle)	This dummy variable takes the value '1' when output gap is positive (expansion periods) and the value '0' otherwise (recession periods).	

Description and Measurement of the Study's Variables (Continued)

Variable Name/ Symbol	Variable Description and Measurement	Data Sources
Credit-to-GDP Ratio (credit_gdp)	This variable measures the domestic credit to the private sector as a percentage of GDP.	World Development Indicators (WDI) Database- 2013.
Official Exchange Rate (exchange)	This variable reflects the foreign exchange rate. It is measured by the amount of local currency (Egyptian pound) that can be purchased by one US dollar.	

14

Commodity Price Fluctuations and Unemployment in a Dependent Economy

Jonaki Sengupta[1], Ranjanendra Narayan Nag[2], Bhaskar Goswami[3]

ABSTRACT The interconnected issues of commodity price fluctuation, unemployment and balance of trade developments are of critical importance in times of globalization. The present paper addresses these issues in terms of a monetary dependent economy macro model that applies to a large class of emerging market economies that export their primary products. However, there exists a manufacturing sector that produces non-traded goods using imported capital goods as an input. Moreover, in such an emerging economy, the stocks of primary commodities constitute a widely used financial asset, among other assets. Thus, the price of these primary commodities behaves as an asset price, which has significant implications for the nature of the interlinkage between the real sector and the financial sector of the economy. In an absence of any capital account transactions, and under a fixed exchange rate regime, the paper examines the effects of supply shock, devaluation, capital flow and fiscal policy on major macro variables, including terms of trade, the stock of primary commodities and real money balances. The result points to the contractionary implications of devaluation, while an exogenous increase in food production produces favorable macroeconomic outcomes.

KEY WORDS: Commodity price fluctuation; unemployment; emerging market Economies; globalization; dependent economy

[1] Charuchandra College, Kolkata - Economics, India; [2] St. Xavier's College (Autonomous), Kolkata - Economics, India; [3] The University of Burdwan - Economics, India

1. Introduction

Commodity price fluctuations, inflation, unemployment and change in the composition of national output are topics that have recently re-surfaced in the discussion on macroeconomic development in an emerging market economy. The following questions are posed in this paper:

1) Which variable holds the key to explaining the dynamics of commodity price, inflation and terms of trade adjustment in a dependent economy?
2) What is the nature of the linkage between the financial sector and the real sector in the presence of unemployment and inflation?
3) What are different policy instruments to mitigate not only commodity price volatility but also unemployment?

In the present paper, we attempt to address these questions using a dependent economy framework. In so doing, we have examined complex interactions

Correspondence concerning this article should be addressed to: **Bhaskar Goswami**, The University of Burdwan - Economics, Golapbag Campus Burdwan, Burdwan, West Bengal 713104, India. E-mail: mailbhaskar08@gmail.com

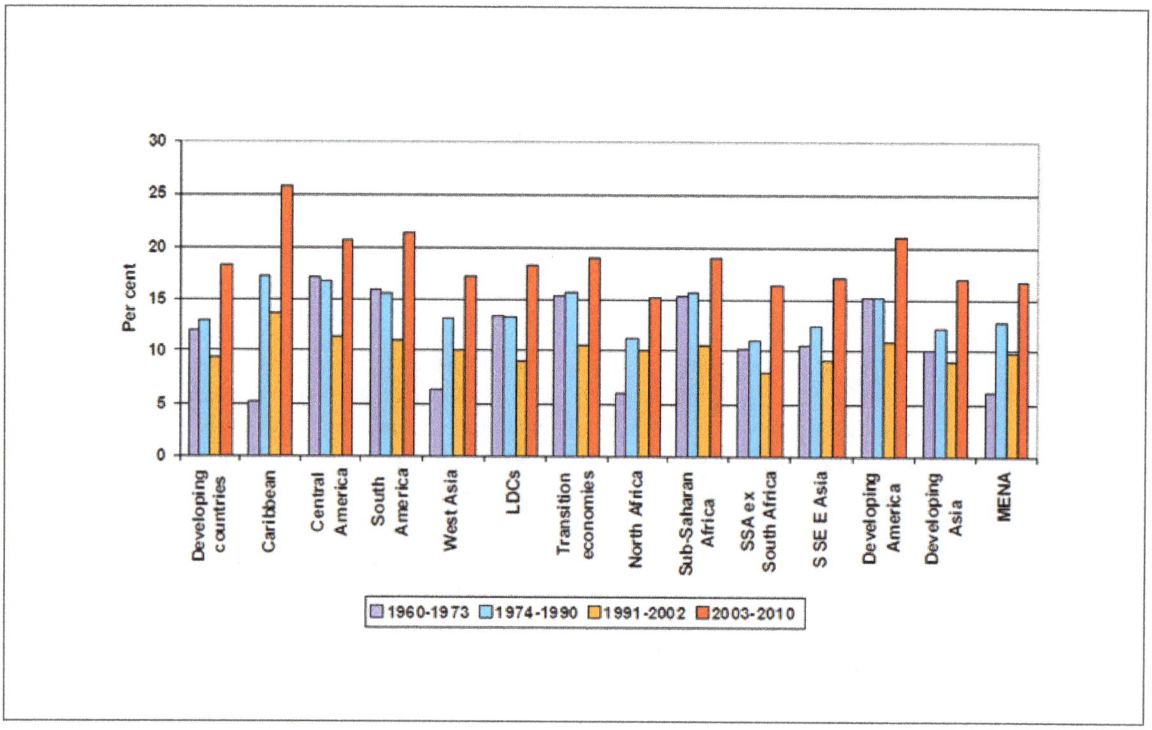

Figure 1. Volatility of commodity export baskets, selected country groups. 1960-2010
Source: From "Volatility of commodity export baskets, selected country groups. 1960–2010" by United Nations Conference on Trade and Development 2012, April 30, Excessive commodity price volatility: Macroeconomic effects on growth and policy options Contribution from the UNCTAD secretariat to the G20 Commodity Markets Working Group, p. 8.

among different macroeconomic variables, the analysis of which is seriously amiss in the existing literature.

Now, a few comments on commodity price (agricultural market) are in order.

The resurgence in interest in the commodity price volatility is backed by the empirical evidence that the volatility of commodity price indices has increased over the past 50 years. In the 2003–2010 period, it was significantly higher than in earlier decades. This is true for a dependent developing economy (figure 1).

Different theoretical models have been employed to formulate policy guidelines to reduce these fluctuations. The basic thrust of these models lies in explaining the overshooting of commodity prices as an outcome of unanticipated monetary expansion. The point is obvious. If the stock of primary commodity is an asset, and its price adjusts instantaneously compared with the industrial price, then commodity prices overshoot in response to monetary expansion. Frankel (1986) authored the seminal contribution to the analysis of the overshooting of agricultural prices. Subsequently, extensive literature emerged on the causes and effects of commodity price fluctuations. Notable studies include the works of

Bakucs and Ferto (2005), Cashin, Liang, and McDermott (2000), Gordon (1987), Goswami, and Nag (2012), Jacks, O'Rourke, and Williamson (2009), Lence and Hayes (2002), Morrison Paul and MacDonald (2003).

Lai, Hu, and Wang (1996) extended Frankel's model to investigate the effects of both anticipated and unanticipated monetary shocks on commodity prices. Moutos and Vines (1992) performed a similar exercise in a more detailed framework in which industrial output is demand determined and industrial inflation follows Phillips' curve relation. Saghaian, Hasan, & Reed, (2002) explained the overshooting of agricultural prices under monetary impacts in an open economy framework under flexible exchange rates. There are plenty of empirical works on the issue of commodity price volatility. Notable among them are Belke, Bordon, and Hendricks (2009), Belke, Bordon, and Volz (2013), Orden and Fackler (1989).

The contributions of the model in this paper are threefold. First, we expand the theoretical specification of the overshooting of agricultural prices by incorporating more macroeconomic variables. Second, the theoretical models are closed economy models, and hence, these models need to be extended to incorporate certain aspects of openness that are relevant to an emerging economy. Finally, the existing literature assumes full employment of labor, and accordingly, long-run neutrality of money exists. In this paper, we incorporate unemployment through wage indexation, and hence, money is not neutral in the long run. The relevance of this research extends far beyond the usual academic interest, and it can hopefully provide policy direction to mitigate commodity price fluctuations and unemployment.

This paper uses a dependent economy framework. Now, a few remarks on the nature of a dependent economy are in order. A dependent economy consists of both traded and non-traded sectors. We can aggregate both exportable and importable goods into a composite commodity called traded goods. Determination of the price of traded goods depends on conditions in the world market. However, domestic demand and supply conditions determine the price and output of non-traded goods.

Within the structure of a dependent economy used in this paper, the agricultural sector is the traded sector. The output from this sector is sold in both the domestic market and foreign markets. It is clear from the following figure that the share of exports of the primary commodities in their total exports has registered impressive growth for developing countries.

The industrial sector is the non-traded sector. However, the industrial sector imports capital goods. The ratio of price of exportable goods (that is, commodity price) to that of industrial goods is an economy's terms of trade, which are driven by both internal and external factors. The verbal upshot of the model is as follows. Agricultural production is fixed, and given the wage indexation, industrial production is obtained from the profit maximization exercise. The industrial price does not jump to clear the market, and industrial price inflation responds to the demand-supply gap. The asset market determines the agricultural price as a return on the stock of primary commodities. Over time, the state variables, namely the terms of trade, the stock of primary commodity and the real money balance, begin to change. The terms of trade dynamics are determined by the difference between agricultural price inflation and industrial price inflation. The change in the stock of primary commodities is governed by excess supply in the market for primary goods, while the change in the money supply is driven by the balance of payments disequilibrium under the fixed exchange rate regime. At the steady state, agricultural price inflation and industrial price inflation are equal, the market for agricultural goods clears, and trade is balanced. The system works under perfect foresight, and the macroeconomic variables of the model respond to a variety of shocks, including changes in agricultural production and policy-induced shocks, such as devaluation.

The rest of the paper is organized as follows. The model is set out in section 2, and the comparative static analysis is described in section 3. Section 4 contains the concluding remarks.

2. The Model

The nature of sectoral interlinkage in this paper is as follows. Agricultural and manufacturing are the two sectors. The agricultural sector produces primary commodities for domestic consumption and export, and agricultural production is fixed. On the other hand, the industrial sector produces non-traded goods using imported capital goods (Nag & Goswami, 2005; 2008; Rattsø & Torvik, 2003). In the spirit of the structuralist models (Buffie, 1986; Taylor, 1991), investment is a composite output produced by combining domestic and imported components. The exchange rate is fixed (Lizondo & Montiel, 1989), and the paper ignores capital account transactions (Edwards, 2001). We assume that the money wage is determined by a bargaining process, which protects the real consumption wage. Industrial price does not adjust instantaneously to clear the industrial goods market. Given any disequilibrium, the three adjustment variables are the terms of trade, the stock of primary commodities and the real money balance. Terms of trade is a jump variable, while the stock of primary commodities and the real money balance evolve continuously. The structure of the model is as follows.

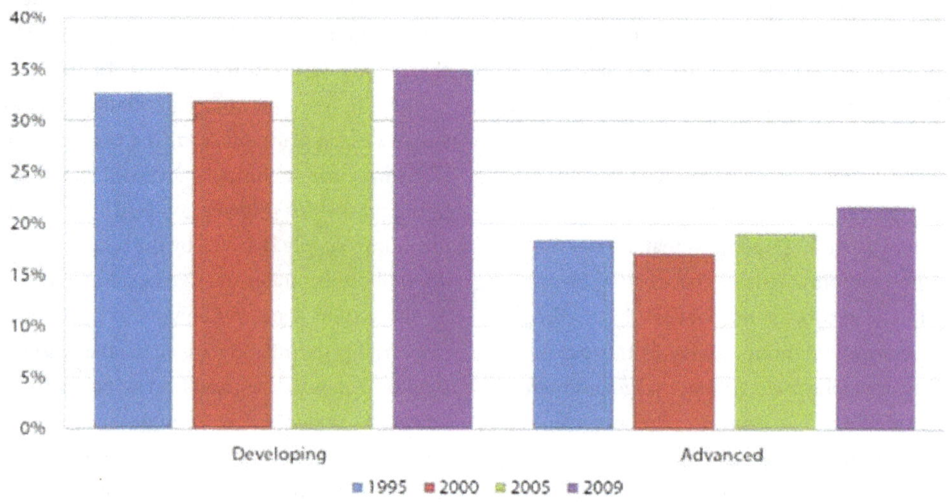

Figure 2. Share of primary commodity exports to total exports, 1995-2009
Source: From "Share of primary commodity exports in total exports, 1995-2009" by Bureau for Development Policy, 2011, September, Poverty reduction. Towards human resilience: Sustaining MDG progress in an age of economic uncertainty, p. 60.

2.1. Supply Side of the Economy:

Agricultural output (F) is exogenously given, and thus, the agricultural sector imposes a supply constraint on the economy. Relaxing supply constraints by making agricultural output dependent upon terms of trade will hardly make a major qualitative change.

The supply function of the agricultural output is

$$F = \overline{F} \tag{1}$$

Labor (L) and capital (K) are used to produce industrial output (Y). The production function for industrial output takes the following form:

$$Y = f(L, K) \tag{2}$$

Employment in the industrial sector is derived from the condition of profit maximization, that is, equality between the marginal product of labor and real product wage with an assumption that the stock of capital is a fixed factor. Thus, we get the following labor demand function:

$$L = L\left(\frac{W}{P_Y}\right), L' < 0 \tag{3}$$

where W is money wage, and P_Y is the price of industrial output.

Next, we consider the determination of money wage. Instead of assuming flexible adjustment, we take money wage to be determined as an outcome of a bargaining process. Money wage is linked to the consumer price index as

$$W = P_Y^{\alpha} P_F^{1-\alpha} \text{ with } 0 < \alpha < 1 \tag{4}$$

where α and $1-\alpha$ are the constant expenditure shares of industrial goods and agricultural goods, respectively, and P_F is the price of agricultural output.

Now, the real wage in the unit of industrial goods is

$$\frac{W}{P_Y} = \theta^{1-\alpha} \tag{5}$$

where $\theta = \frac{P_F}{P_Y}$.

From equations (2), (3) and (5), we get the supply function of industrial goods:

$$Y_s = Y_s(\theta),\ with\ Y_s' < 0$$

In linear form, the supply function is given by

$$Y_s = -x_1\theta,\ with\ x_1 > 0 \tag{6}$$

The aggregate output is the sum total of the agricultural and industrial output. Let Z denote aggregate output (or real income), measured in the unit of industrial goods. That is,

$$Z = \theta F - x_1\theta \tag{7}$$

with $\frac{dZ}{d\theta} = F - x_1$. We assume that $F > x_1$ such that $\frac{dZ}{d\theta} > 0$.

2.2. Financial Sector:

In an emerging economy, the stocks of food grains constitute a widely used financial asset. Accordingly, the financial sector is represented in terms of an asset structure that includes money (M) and stock of food grains (H). The modeling of demand for money is based on Tobin's portfolio choice. We consider a risk averter who chooses an optimum portfolio mix of money and stock of primary goods based on their respective returns.

Thus, the total value of assets (A) is given by

$$A = M + P_F H$$

The value of assets in terms of industrial goods is given by

$$a = A/P_Y = m + \left(P_F/P_Y\right)H = m + \theta H\ with\ m = \frac{M}{P_y} \tag{8}$$

The desired ratio of money to the stock of primary goods depends on the expected return of the assets, that is, on the expected percentage change in the price of food grains. Under perfect foresight, expected change in food price is equal to actual change in food price, that is, $\left(\frac{\dot{P}_F}{P_F}\right)^e = \frac{\dot{P}_F}{P_F}$, and hence, we can write

$$\frac{m}{\theta H} = h\left(\frac{\dot{P}_F}{P_F} + k\right),\ with\ h' < 0 \tag{9}$$

The term $\frac{\dot{P}_F}{P_F}$ represents the expected change (and actual change based on the assumption of perfect foresight) in food price. The term k is the difference between the convenience yield and the storage cost of holding primary commodities. Hence, the return on stocks of primary commodities is $\left(\frac{\dot{P}_F}{P_F} + k\right)$.

It will be useful to express equation (9) as

$$\left(\frac{\dot{P}_F}{P_F} + k\right) = L\left(\frac{m}{\theta H}\right),\ with\ L' < 0.$$

In a linear form, we get

$$\left(\frac{\dot{P}_F}{P_F} + k\right) = -x_2 m + x_3\theta + x_4 H + k\ with\ x_2, x_3, x_4 > 0 \tag{10}$$

2.3. Demand Side and Inflation Mechanism for the Industrial Sector:

Aggregate demand for industrial goods consists of private consumption expenditure, private investment, government expenditure and imports. Shares of expenditure on industrial goods and primary commodities are fixed, viz. α and $(1-\alpha)$, respectively. Total consumption is a function of aggregate output $(Z = \theta F - x_1\theta)$ and financial assets $(a = m + \theta H)$. We choose a linear consumption function, $C = x_5\theta + x_6 H + x_7 m + x_8 F$. Thus, consumption expenditure on industrial goods is $\alpha(x_5\theta + x_6 H + x_7 m + x_8 F)$.

Investment expenditure is assumed to be exogenously given, that is, $I = \bar{I}$. The industrial sector also imports capital goods, which are taken to be some fraction $(1-\beta)$ of total investment. Therefore, import demand for industrial goods is $(1-\beta)I$. Government expenditure (G) is parametrically given.

Thus, the aggregate demand for industrial goods is $\alpha C + \beta \overline{I} + G$. Although the industrial price is assumed to be sticky, the inflation rate can change in response to excess demand for industrial goods. Therefore, the rate of industrial price inflation can be written as

$$\frac{\dot{P}_Y}{P_Y} = \pi_Y = \delta\{\alpha C + \beta \overline{\mathrm{I}} + \mathrm{G} - \mathrm{Y_s}\} \quad with\ \delta > 0$$

Substituting the value of C and $\mathrm{Y_s}$, we get

$$\Rightarrow \frac{\dot{P}_Y}{P_Y} = \delta\left\{\alpha(x_5\theta + x_6\mathrm{H} + x_7\mathrm{m} + x_8\mathrm{F}) + \beta\overline{\mathrm{I}} + \mathrm{G} + x_1\theta\right\},\ \delta>0$$

In a linear form, we get

$$\pi_Y = b_1\theta + b_2 H + b_4 m + b_3 F + b_5 \tag{11}$$

with $b_1 = (\delta\alpha x_5 + x_1) > 0,\ b_2 = \delta x_6 > 0,\ b_3 = \delta x_8 > 0,$
$b_4 = \delta x_7 > 0\ \ and\ \ b_5 = \beta\overline{I} + G > 0$

2.4. External Sector and Adjustment in Money Supply:

Any difference between the value of export and that of import involves quantity adjustment through change in foreign exchange reserves, the stock of high-powered money and money supply under the fixed exchange rate regime. Thus, we get the following equation:

$\dot{M} = P_F X\left(\frac{s}{P_Y}\frac{1}{\theta}\right) - (1-\gamma)s\overline{I}$, where s is the nominal exchange rate.

In a linear form, we get

$$\dot{M} = P_F(\alpha_4 s - x_{10}\theta - x_{11}P_y) - (1\text{-}\lambda)\,\mathrm{s}\overline{\mathrm{I}}\ ;\alpha_4, x_{10}, x_{11} > 0 \tag{12}$$

2.5. Steady State Analysis:

The steady state analysis centers around the adjustment in terms of trade, the stock of primary commodities and the real money balance. Now, comments on adjustment in each variable are in order.

2.5.1. Terms of Trade Adjustment:

Equations (10) and (11) can be combined to produce the dynamic adjustment in the terms of trade. Noting that $\theta = \frac{P_F}{P_Y}$, we get

$$\frac{\dot{\theta}}{\theta} = \frac{\dot{P}_F}{P_F} - \frac{\dot{P}_Y}{P_Y}$$

$$\frac{\dot{\theta}}{\theta} = \text{-}x_2 m + x_3\theta + x_4 H\ \text{-}k\text{-}b_1\theta - b_2 H - b_4 m - b_3 F - b_5$$

$$\frac{\dot{\theta}}{\theta} = -am + b\theta + \gamma H - b_3 F - b_6 \tag{13}$$

$where\ a = x_2 + b_4 > 0,\ b = x_3 - b_1 > 0,\ \gamma = x_4 - b_2 > 0,$
$b_6 = b_5 + k$

In the long run, $\dot{\theta} = 0$, and the stationary values of θ, m, and H are assumed; that is, $\theta = \overline{\theta}$, $H = \overline{H}$, and $m = \overline{m}$. Thus, the long-run version of equation (13) becomes

$$b\overline{\theta} - a\overline{m} + \gamma\overline{H} - b_3 F - b_6 = 0 \tag{14}$$

Explanations of the sign restrictions of the coefficient of $\theta, m\ H$ of equation (13) are as follows:

First, an increase in θ leads to a rise in real income, which subsequently raises the consumption demand. As a result, there will be an increase in industrial price inflation. On the other hand, an increase in θ also results in food price inflation, which follows from equation (10). However, we assume that food price inflation exceeds industrial price inflation in response to an increase in θ such that $\dot{\theta} > 0$. Next, we consider an increase in H, which pushes up food price inflation from the asset market, and hence, we get $\dot{\theta} > 0$. However, an increase in H raises total financial assets, and hence, consumption demand also increases. As a result, there will be an increase in industrial price inflation. However, based on the assumption that food price inflation exceeds industrial price inflation in response to increase in θ, we get $\dot{\theta} > 0$. Again, from the asset market, an increase in m reduces food price inflation and simultaneously increases the industrial price inflation through a rise in consumption demand; hence, $\dot{\theta} < 0$.

2.5.2. Adjustment in the Stock of Primary Commodities:

Any excess supply of agricultural output over domestic absorption (D_F) generates adjustment in the stock of primary commodities. That is,

$$\dot{H} = \bar{F} - D_F$$

$$\dot{H} = \bar{F} - \frac{(1-\beta)C(Z, m+\theta H)}{\theta} - \frac{X\left(\frac{s}{P_Y}\frac{1}{\theta}\right)}{\theta} - \frac{\bar{P}}{P_Y}\left(\frac{G_w}{\theta}\right) \quad (15)$$

where G_w is the amount of government expenditure on agricultural goods at a procurement price, $\bar{P}$.

Substituting the value of C and X from equations (11) and (12), we get

$$\dot{H} = \bar{F} - (1-\alpha)(x_5\theta + x_6 H + x_7 m + x_8 F) - d_1\theta -$$

$$+(\alpha_4 s - x_{10}\theta - x_{11}P_Y) - \frac{\bar{P}}{P_Y}G_w - d_2\theta$$

$$\dot{H} = \bar{F} - \alpha_1\theta - \alpha_2 m - \alpha_3 H - x_8 F - \alpha_4 s - \frac{\bar{P}}{P_Y}G_w + x_{11}P_Y \quad (16)$$

where $\alpha_1 = (1-\alpha)x_5 - x_{10} + d_1 + d_2 > 0$, $\alpha_2 = (1-\alpha)x_7 > 0$, $\alpha_3 = (1-\alpha)x_6 > 0$

In the long run, the stationary values of θ, m and H are assumed as $\theta = \bar{\theta}$, $H = \bar{H}$ and $m = \bar{m}$. Additionally, in the long run, $\dot{H} = 0$. Thus, the long-run version of equation (16) becomes

$$\bar{F} - \alpha_1\bar{\theta} - \alpha_2\bar{m} - \alpha_3\bar{H} - x_8 F - \alpha_4 s - \frac{\bar{P}}{P_y}G_W + x_{11}P_y = 0 \quad (17)$$

Explanations of the sign restrictions of the coefficients of θ, m and H of equation (16) are as follows:

To begin with, we consider an increase in H, which raises the total financial assets. It follows from the asset market equilibrium that the food price increases. A rise in both total assets and food price inflation increases the consumption demand, and consequently, we get $\dot{H} < 0$. Again, an increase in m leads to a rise in total assets, which eventually increases the consumption demand. However, there is a counteractive force on the consumption demand originating from the asset market itself. It follows from the asset market equilibrium that a rise in total assets results in a decline in food price and thus a fall in terms of trade, which ultimately leads to a fall in consumption demand. Assuming that the asset effect dominates the terms of trade effect and that the consumption elasticity is greater than one, we get $\dot{H} < 0$.

2.5.3. Adjustment in Real Money Supply:

Equations (9) and (10) can be combined to produce the adjustment in the real money supply ($m = \frac{M}{P_Y}$)

$$\dot{m} = \theta X\left(\frac{s}{P_Y}\frac{1}{\theta}\right) - (1-\gamma)\frac{s}{P_Y}\bar{I} - \pi_Y m + J \quad (18)$$

where J denotes the capital flow.

Substituting the values of X and π_Y from equations (10) and (11), we get

$$\dot{m} = -\alpha_5\theta - \alpha_8 m - b_3 F + s\left[\alpha_4 - \frac{(1-\gamma)}{P_y}\bar{I}\right] + \theta + J$$

$$\dot{m} = -\alpha_5\theta - \alpha_8 m - b_3 F + \alpha_9 s - x_{11}P_y - b_5 + J \quad (19)$$

where $\alpha_5 = (d_3 - x_{10} - b_1) > 0, \alpha_8 = (b_4 - d_4) > 0,$

$$\alpha_9 = \alpha_4 - \frac{(1-\gamma)}{P_y}\bar{I} > 0.$$

In the long run, the stationary values of θ and m are assumed to be $\theta = \bar{\theta}$ and $m = \bar{m}$. Additionally, in the long run, $\dot{m} = 0$. Thus, the long-run form of equation (18) becomes

$$-\alpha_5\bar{\theta} - \alpha_8\bar{m} - b_3 F + \alpha_9 s - x_{11}P_y - b_5 + J = 0 \quad (20)$$

The sign restrictions of the coefficients of θ and m of equation (19) can be explained as follows:

An increase in θ causes a fall in industrial output, and accordingly, there will be a rise in industrial price inflation. Again, as θ increases, the physical volume of exports decreases. Since we assume that export elasticity is greater than one, the real value of export demand decreases. The increase in industrial price inflation and the decrease in the real value of exports makes $\dot{m} < 0$. On the other hand, an increase in m directly makes $\dot{m} < 0$.

2.6. Saddle Path Stability:

State variables in this model are terms of trade, the stock of primary commodities and the real money balance, the dynamics of which are obtained as follows.

Subtracting equation (14) from equation (13) and solving for $\tilde{\dot{\theta}}$, we get

$$\tilde{\dot{\theta}} = -a(m - \bar{m}) + b(\theta - \bar{\theta}) + \gamma(H - \bar{H})$$

$$\textit{where } \tilde{\dot{\theta}} = \frac{\dot{\theta}}{\theta} \quad (21)$$

Subtracting equation (17) from equation (16) and solving for $\dot{H}$, we get

$$\dot{H} = \alpha_1(\theta - \bar{\theta}) - \alpha_2(m - \bar{m}) - \alpha_3(H - \bar{H}) \tag{22}$$

Subtracting equation (20) from equation (19) and solving for $\dot{m}$, we get

$$\dot{m} = \alpha_5(\theta - \bar{\theta}) - \alpha_8(m - \bar{m}) \tag{23}$$

Thus, the dynamic system about its initial equilibrium is made up of equations (21), (22) and (23).

$$\begin{bmatrix} \dot{\tilde{\theta}} \\ \dot{H} \\ \dot{m} \end{bmatrix} = \begin{bmatrix} b & \gamma & -a \\ -\alpha_1 & -\alpha_3 & -\alpha_2 \\ -\alpha_5 & 0 & -\alpha_8 \end{bmatrix} \begin{bmatrix} (\theta - \bar{\theta}) \\ (H - \bar{H}) \\ (m - \bar{m}) \end{bmatrix} \tag{24}$$

The characteristic roots for equation (24) are the solutions, $\beta_1, \beta_2, \beta_3$, to the characteristic polynomial $|\beta - \alpha I| = 0$, where β is the matrix in the system equation $dX/dt = BX$ of (24). In the presence of perfect foresight, the existence of the unique convergent saddle path requires that there be one positive and two negative characteristic roots. Hence, the determinants are as follows:

$$\Delta = \begin{vmatrix} b & \gamma & -a \\ -\alpha_1 & -\alpha_3 & -\alpha_2 \\ -\alpha_5 & 0 & -\alpha_8 \end{vmatrix} > 0$$

In what follows, we explore the comparative static analysis in terms of a parametric rise in agricultural production and devaluation.

3. Comparative Static Analysis:

3.1. Increase in Agricultural Output:

The rise in agricultural production has prime significance in the context of economic development. Agricultural output can increase over time due to technical progress. The increase in agricultural output raises aggregate real income, which in turn leads to an increase in consumption demand. This, in turn, raises industrial price inflation, and as a result, $\dot{\theta} < 0$. On the other hand, an increase in agricultural output tends to increase the stock of primary goods. Again, it tends to reduce the stock of the real money balance by increasing seigniorage through industrial price inflation. Both the rise in the stock of primary goods and fall in the real money balance leads to $\dot{\theta} > 0$, and hence, θ tends to fall through the portfolio balance effect. Thus, the final effect on θ is ambiguous. In the case of a fall in θ, the industrial production rises since real wage measured in the unit of industrial goods falls. Ambiguity also exists regarding the nature of m and H. Since multiple cross effects exist, one cannot theoretically ascertain the direction of change in state variables. Overshooting or undershooting of terms of trade depends on the adjustment of the stock of primary commodity and real money supply. Next, we consider the long-run effects, short-run effects and transitional dynamics.

Long-run Effects:

Considering long-run equilibrium equations (14), (17) and (20), differentiating them with respect to F and arranging them in matrix form, we get

$$\begin{bmatrix} b & \gamma & -a \\ -\alpha_1 & -\alpha_3 & -\alpha_2 \\ -\alpha_5 & 0 & -\alpha_8 \end{bmatrix} \begin{bmatrix} \frac{d\bar{\theta}}{dF} \\ \frac{d\bar{H}}{dF} \\ \frac{d\bar{m}}{dF} \end{bmatrix} = \begin{bmatrix} b_3 \\ -(1 - x_8) \\ b_3 \end{bmatrix} \tag{25}$$

Applying Cramer's rule, we get

$$\frac{d\bar{\theta}}{dF} = \frac{b_3\alpha_3\alpha_8 - \gamma\left[(1 - x_8)\alpha_8 + \alpha_2 b_3\right] - ab_3\alpha_3}{|\Delta|} \tag{26}$$

with $\frac{d\bar{\theta}}{dF} < 0 \quad \text{if } b_3\alpha_3\alpha_8 < \gamma\left[(1 - x_8)\alpha_8 + \alpha_2 b_3\right] + ab_3\alpha_3$

$$\frac{d\bar{H}}{dF} = \frac{b\left[(1 - x_8)\alpha_8 + \alpha_2 b_3\right] - b_3(\alpha_1\alpha_8 - \alpha_2\alpha_5) +}{|\Delta|}$$
$$\frac{+ a\left[b_3\alpha_1 + \alpha_5(1 - x_8)\right]}{|\Delta|} \tag{27}$$

with $\frac{d\bar{H}}{dF} > 0 \text{ if } \alpha_1\alpha_8 < \alpha_2\alpha_5$

$$\frac{d\bar{m}}{dF}=\frac{-b\alpha_3 b_3+\gamma\left[\alpha_1 b_3+\alpha_5\left(1-x_8\right)\right]-b_3\alpha_5\alpha_3}{|\Delta|} \quad (28)$$

with $\frac{d\bar{m}}{dF}<0 \quad if\ \gamma\left[\alpha_1 b_3+\alpha_5\left(1-x_8\right)\right]<(b\alpha_3 b_3+b_3\alpha_5\alpha_3)$

Short-run Effects and Transitional Dynamics:
We consider equation (24).

$$\begin{bmatrix} \dot{\tilde{\theta}} \\ \dot{H} \\ \dot{m} \end{bmatrix}=\begin{bmatrix} b & \gamma & -a \\ -\alpha_1 & -\alpha_3 & -\alpha_2 \\ -\alpha_5 & 0 & -\alpha_8 \end{bmatrix}\begin{bmatrix} (\theta-\bar{\theta}) \\ (H-\bar{H}) \\ (m-\bar{m}) \end{bmatrix} \quad (24)$$

The positive roots are ignored to ensure the saddle path stability of the system. This amounts to setting the coefficients of positive roots equal to zero. Suppose that $-\beta_1, -\beta_2$ ($\beta_1>0, \beta_2>0$) are two negative characteristic roots. The solutions for expected future paths of θ, H and m in level form, as t goes from 0 to ∞, are

$$\left.\begin{array}{ll} \theta(t)-\bar{\theta}(t)=\exp(-\beta_1 t)[\theta(0)-\bar{\theta}(0)]+ & \\ \quad +\exp(-\beta_2 t)[\theta(0)-\bar{\theta}(0)] & (29.1) \\ H(t)-\bar{H}(t)=\exp(-\beta_1 t)[H(0)-\bar{H}(0)] & \\ \quad +\exp(-\beta_2 t)[H(0)-H(0)] & (29.2) \\ m(t)-\bar{m}(t)=\exp(-\beta_1 t)[m(0)-\bar{m}(0)]+ & \\ \quad +\exp(-\beta_2 t)[m(0)-\bar{m}(0)] & (29.3) \end{array}\right\} \quad (29)$$

Alternatively, we can write equations (29.1), (29.2), & (29.3) as

$$\left.\begin{array}{l} \dot{\tilde{\theta}}=-(\beta_1+\beta_2)(\theta-\bar{\theta}) \\ \dot{H}=-(\beta_1+\beta_2)(H-\bar{H}) \\ \dot{m}=-(\beta_1+\beta_2)(m-\bar{m}) \end{array}\right\} \quad (30)$$

Combining equations (25) and (30), we get

$$-a\left(m-\bar{m}\right)+b\left(\theta-\bar{\theta}\right)+\gamma\left(H-\bar{H}\right)=-\left(\beta_1+\beta_2\right)\left(\theta-\bar{\theta}\right)$$

$$\theta=\bar{\theta}+\frac{a}{\beta_1+\beta_2+b}(m-\bar{m})-\frac{\gamma}{\beta_1+\beta_2+b}(H-\bar{H}) \quad (31)$$

Differentiating equation (30) with respect to agricultural output and considering the short-run stickiness of H and m, we get

$$\frac{d\theta}{dF}=\frac{d\bar{\theta}}{dF}+\frac{a}{\beta_1+\beta_2+b}\frac{d\bar{m}}{dF}-\frac{\gamma}{\beta_1+\beta_2+b}\frac{d\bar{H}}{dF}$$

$$\frac{d\theta}{dF}-\frac{d\bar{\theta}}{dF}=\frac{a}{\beta_1+\beta_2+b}\frac{d\bar{m}}{dF}-\frac{\gamma}{\beta_1+\beta_2+b}\frac{d\bar{H}}{dF} \quad (32)$$

Overshooting or undershooting depends on the sign of $\frac{d\bar{m}}{dF}$ and $\frac{d\bar{H}}{dF}$. Suppose we consider that θ decreases as F increases. Thus, if $\frac{d\theta}{dF}-\frac{d\bar{\theta}}{dF}<0$, we can say that initially, θ decreases more than its long-run value; that is, there will be undershooting of θ. It is also observed that this undershooting occurs if $\frac{d\bar{m}}{dF}<0$ and $\frac{d\bar{H}}{dF}>0$; that is, the real money supply decreases and the stock of primary commodity increases as agricultural output increases.

3.2. *Devaluation:*

Extensive literature focuses on various channels by which devaluation might be contractionary in emerging economies (Edwards, 1989; Lizondo & Montiel 1989). In this paper, devaluation produces stagflationary effects along with a fall in the stock of primary commodities. The intuition is as follows. The rise in the nominal exchange rate causes improvement in trade balance and makes $\dot{m}>0$ provided that the export elasticity is greater than one. As a result, the real money balance increases. Consequently, we get $\dot{\theta}<0$ from the equilibrium condition in the financial market. Hence, the terms of trade increases, which in turn causes an increase in the real wage anda fall in industrial employment and output. On the other hand, a rise in the nominal exchange rate along with an increase in the terms of trade and the real money balance lead to an increase in demand for food, and hence, $\dot{H}<0$. Therefore, H has to decrease to maintain the steady state.

Long-run Effects:
Considering long-run equilibrium equations (14), (17) and (20), differentiating them with respect to the

nominal exchange rate(s) and arranging them in matrix form, we get

$$\begin{bmatrix} b & \gamma & -a \\ -\alpha_1 & -\alpha_3 & -\alpha_2 \\ -\alpha_5 & 0 & -\alpha_8 \end{bmatrix} \begin{bmatrix} \frac{d\bar{\theta}}{ds} \\ \frac{d\bar{H}}{ds} \\ \frac{d\bar{m}}{ds} \end{bmatrix} = \begin{bmatrix} 0 \\ \alpha_4 \\ -\alpha_9 \end{bmatrix} \quad (33)$$

Applying Cramer's rule, we get

$$\frac{d\bar{\theta}}{ds} = \frac{\gamma(\alpha_4\alpha_8 + \alpha_2\alpha_9) + a_9\alpha_3}{\Delta} > 0 \quad (34)$$

$$\frac{d\bar{H}}{ds} = -\frac{b(\alpha_4\alpha_8 + \alpha_9\alpha_2) + a(\alpha_1\alpha_9 + \alpha_5\alpha_4)}{\Delta} < 0 \quad (35)$$

$$\frac{d\bar{m}}{ds} = \frac{b(\alpha_3\alpha_9) - \gamma(\alpha_1\alpha_9 + \alpha_4\alpha_5)}{\Delta} > 0 \quad (36)$$

if $b(\alpha_3\alpha_9) > \gamma(\alpha_1\alpha_9 + \alpha_4\alpha_5)$

3.3 Fiscal Policy:

Contractionary fiscal policy will produce a favorable macroeconomic outcome in this model. Reduction in government expenditure on industrial goods reduces industrial price inflation (following from equation 11). Starting from the initial steady state, we get $\dot{\theta} > 0$, and hence, θ begins to fall. This in turn reduces real wage, measured in the unit of industrial goods, and hence, employment rises.

3.4: Capital Mobility and its Effects:

The model can explain how monetary liquidity through capital flow may generate adverse side effects in terms of inflation, output contraction and a rising unemployment rate. Greater capital flow (increase in J) leads to an increase in the stock of real balance (which follows from equation 18). It follows from the asset market (equation 10) that food price rises, and the terms of trade move in favor of the agricultural sector (from equation 13). The resulting increase in the real wage (measured in the unit of industrial goods) leads to a fall in employment, and contraction of the industrial sector ensues. Thus, capital flow produces adverse macroeconomic outcomes.

4. Conclusion:

The paper offers some insights on the relationship between money, commodity prices, terms of trade and unemployment. The existence of different dynamic adjustments in terms of trade and the rate of growth of the real balance may provide an explanation for the change in relative prices between agricultural goods and industrial goods and for unemployment. Now, we sum up the findings of our paper. The rise in agricultural production may reduce terms of trade and hence give rise to industrial employment and output. The effects on the stock of primary commodities and the real money balance are ambiguous. Overshooting or undershooting in terms of trade depends on the adjustment in the stock of primary commodities and real money supply. Devaluation produces a stagflationary effect along with a fall in the stock of primary commodities.

Contractionary fiscal policy will produce a favorable macroeconomic outcome in this model.

Again, monetary liquidity through capital flow may generate adverse side effects in terms of inflation, output contraction and a rising unemployment rate. In this section, we examine how different policies may reduce not only agricultural price volatility but also unemployment.

The broad policy message is that the long-term solution to commodity price volatility, inflation and unemployment is sustained agricultural growth. We also show that contractionary fiscal policy in the form of reduced expenditure on industrial output is also an effective policy. Moreover, both devaluation and greater capital flow might be counterproductive in controlling commodity price volatility and checking unemployment.

References

Bakucs, L. Z., & Ferto, I. (2005, August). Monetary impacts and overshooting of agricultural prices in an open economy. Paper presented at the XIth International Congress of European Association of Agricultural Economists (EAAE), Copenhagen.

Belke, A., Bordon, I. G., & Hendricks, T. W. (2009). Global liquidity and commodity prices – a cointegrated VAR approach for OECD countries. *Applied Financial Economics, 20*(3), 227–242.

Belke, A., Bordon, I. G., & Volz, U. (2013). Effects of global liquidity on commodity and food prices. *World Development, 44*, 31-43.

Buffie, E. F. (1986). Devaluation, investment and growth in LDCs. *Journal of Development Economics, 20*(2), 361-379.

Bureau for Development Policy. (2011, September). Poverty reduction. Towards human resilience: Sustaining MDG progress in an age of economic uncertainty. Retrieved from http://www.undp.org/content/dam/undp/library/Poverty%20Reduction/Towards_SustainingMDG_Web1005.pdf

Cashin, P., Liang, H., & McDermott, C. J. (2000). How persistent are shocks to world commodity prices? *IMF Staff Papers, 47*(2), 177-217.

Frankel, J. A. (1986). Expectations and Commodity Price Dynamics: The overshooting model. *American Journal of Agricultural Economics, 68*(2), 344-348.

Gordon, J. D. (1987). Expectations and commodity price dynamics: The overshooting model: Comment. *American Journal of Agricultural Economics, 69*(4), 852-55.

Goswami, B., & Nag, R. N. (2012). Macroeconomics of agricultural trade liberalization. *Global Economic Review, 41*(3), 233-242.

Jacks, D. D., O'Rourke, K. H., & Williamson, J. G. (2009). Commodity price volatility and world market integration since 1700 (Working Paper No. 14748). National Bureau of Economic Research. Retrieved from http://www.nber.org/papers/w14748.pdf

Lai, C. C., Hu, S. W., & Wang, V. (1996). Commodity price dynamics and anticipated shocks. *American Journal of Agricultural Economics, 78*(4), 982-990.

Lence, S. H., & Hayes, D. J. (2002). U.S. farm policy and the volatility of commodity prices and farm revenues. *American Journal of Agricultural Economics, 84*(2), 335-351.

Lizondo, S. J., & Montiel, P. J. (1989). Contractionary devaluation in developing countries: An analytical overview. *IMF Staff Papers, 36*(1), 182-227.

Morrison Paul, C. J., & MacDonald, J. M. (2003). Tracing the effects of agricultural commodity prices and food costs. *American Journal of Agricultural Economics, 85*(3), 633-646.

Moutos, T., & Vines, D. (1992). Output, inflation and commodity prices. *Oxford Economic Papers, 44*(3), 355-372.

Nag, R. N., & Goswami, B. (2005). Dual economy interlinkage in a monetary framework:
A post WTO perspective. *Journal of Economic Integration, 20*(3), 497-513.

Nag, R. N., & Goswami, B. (2008). Macroeconomics of commodity price fluctuations: A structuralist approach. *Trade and Development Review, 1*(2), 49-72.

Orden, D., & Fackler, P. (1989). Identifying monetary impacts on agricultural prices in
VAR models. *American Journal of Agricultural Economics, 71*(2), 495-502.

Rattsø, J., & Torvik, R. (2003). Interactions between agriculture and industry: Theoretical analysis of the consequences of discriminating agriculture in Sub-Saharan Africa. *Review of Development Economics, 7*(1), 138-151.

Saghaian, S. H., Hasan, M. F., & Reed, M. R. (2002). Overshooting of agricultural
prices in four Asian economies. *American Journal of Agricultural Economics, 34*(1), 95-109.

Taylor, L. (1991). *Income distribution, growth and inflation: Lectures of structuralist macroeconomic theory*. Cambridge, MA: MIT Press.

UNCTAD. (2012, April 30). Excessive commodity price volatility: Macroeconomic effects on growth and policy options. Contribution from the UNCTAD secretariat to the G20 Commodity Markets Working Group. Retrieved from http://unctad.org/en/Docs/gds_mdpb_G20_001_en.pdf

15

The External Sector Vulnerability Monitoring Index (Λ): The Case of Chinese and Asean-5 Economies

Mario Arturo Ruiz Estrada[1], Diwa Samad[1], Yew Joe Ho[2]

ABSTRACT This paper introduces an alternative indicator to evaluate the external sector behavior of a country or region. The objective of this indicator, titled "The External Sector Vulnerability Monitoring Index" (henceforth ESVM) (λ), is to offer policy-makers and researchers a new analytical tool to study the external sector trends and stages of any country from a global perspective. The ESVM-index (λ) is not intended to be a forecasting model. It is focused on showing the past and present economic situation in any country's external sector performance. It can provide a general idea of the situation and evolution of the foreign sector performance of any country. Therefore, the application of the ESVM-index (λ) is based on the characteristics, conditions and historical moments that any country presents in its external sector development. ESVM-index (λ) acts as a simulator that allows the application of a series of different scenarios and phases of external sector performance of any country. In our case, we apply the external sector vulnerability monitoring index (λ) on the Chinese and ASEAN-5 economies.

KEY WORDS: Trade liberalization, Openness, International Trade, ASEAN, China

[1] University of Malaya - Economics, Malaysia; [2] Universiti Malaysia Sabah - Labuan Faculty of International Finance, Malaysia

1. Introduction

In the last thirty years, many economists and policy makers have attempted to build alternative indicators to measure the external sector behavior and trends using terms of trade (ToT)[1] or openness index (Oi)[2]. It is important to mention that the abovementioned indicators have significantly contributed to the study of external sectors to date. In the literature, the application of these indicators has been focused on multi-cross-country comparative analysis and forecasting to explain the link between openness, growth, and income distribution. These indicators include (i) trade dependency ratios; (ii) the rate of growth exports (Balassa, 1985); (iii) the Heritage Foundation Index (Edwards, 1998); (iv) the Sachs and Warner Openness Index (Sachs et al., 1995); (v) Leamer's Openness Index (Barro, 1991); (vi) the Trade Liberalization Index (Lopez, 1990); (vii) Average Coverage of NTB -QR- (Edwards, 1993); (viii) black market premium (Harrison, 1996); (ix) the index of real exchange rate variability; (x) the index of real exchange rate distortion (Dollar, 1992); trade restrictiveness (TRI) under the uses of CGE modeling (Anderson & Neary, 1992; 1994; 1996; 2003; 2007); MTRI or Overall Trade Restrictiveness Index (OTRI) (Anderson & Neary, 2003).

Correspondence concerning this article should be addressed to: **Mario Arturo Ruiz Estrada**, University of Malaya - Economics, KL 53600, KL, Malaysia. E-mail: marioruiz@um.edu.my

Table 1. Comparison of Terms of Trade, Openness, and ESVM-Index (λ)

Concept	Measures	Function	Advantage	Disadvantage
Terms of Trade **-ToT-**	**X Price/M Price** **X = Export Index Price** **M = Import Index Price**	To study the relationship between exports price ratio and imports price ratio to find the deteriorating terms of trade among countries	Permits the visualization of the relationship between various international prices in the international market	Difficult to be applied to many countries and goods simultaneously
Openness **-Oi-**	**TV/GDP x 100%** **TV = X+M**	To measure the level of trade liberalization and the orientation of trade policy	Gives a general idea about how open an economy is in its international trade	It is focused to study how open is an economy from the specific trade point of view
The External Sector Vulnerability Monitoring Index (λ)	$\lambda = \varepsilon_i / \sigma'$	To measure the level of trade liberalization and investment mobility simultaneously	Observes the trends of the external sector from international trade and finance sector from both perspectives of international trade and finance simultaneously	Difficult to monitoring the FDI mobility in the short term

Source: Adapted from "External Sector Development Index," by M. A. Ruiz Estrada 2011a, *International Journal of China Studies*, 2(1), 55-70.

Edwards (1997), in a landmark paper titled "Trade Policy, Growth and Income Distribution", applied trade policy indices such as (i) Deviation from Actual Trade Shares; (ii) Trade Liberalization Index; (iii) Sachs and Warner Openness Index; (iv) QR; (v) deviation of the black market rate; (vi) black market exchange rate premium; (vii) the real exchange distortions and variation; (viii) the coefficient of Gini to prove the link between openness and income distribution. Edwards concluded that there was no evidence linking openness or income per capita increases in inequality.

However, we are interested in presenting a new indicator of analysis that is oriented to monitoring the behavior of the external sector of any country or region with a new perspective. The proposed index in this research is positioned to improve on the limitations of the indicators discussed in the literature review in this research paper. The ESVM-Index (λ) is a single indicator that uses multidimensional graphs. This new measurement of the external sector vulnerability can show the trend and stages of any country or region external sector. The main aim of ESVM-Index (λ) is to offer policy makers and researchers with a new alternative analytical tool to monitor the behavioral aspect of the external sector of any country from a holistic perspective. At the same time, this new indicator can generate alternative policies to improving the external sector performance of any country or region (Ruiz Estrada, 2011b).

The ESVM-Index (λ) has four objectives. The first objective is to measure the vulnerability of the external sector of any country. The second objective is to evaluate the external sector performance. The third goal is to analyze the relationship between the external sector leading (εi) and the GDP marginal rate (σ'). The fourth objective is to evaluate the external sector cycle based on the table of possible combinations between (εi) and (σ'). The ESVM-Surface is strongly affiliated with ESVM-Index (λ) results. The difference between these two indices is that in the measurement of ESVM-Index (λ) replaces absolute values by the first partial derivative. These first partial derivatives are the trade volume marginal rate (α'), the foreign direct investment marginal rate (β'), and the GDP marginal rate (σ'). The ESVM-Index (λ) analysis will also introduce a new variable called "the external sector main variable (ε_i)." The εi is equal to the trade volume marginal rate (α') plus the foreign direct investment marginal rate (β') (see Diagram 1).

The next objective discusses the relationship between ESVM-Index (λ) and (σ'), while the last one claims the evaluation of the ESVM-Index cycle based on the table of possible combinations between ESVM-Index (λ) and (σ'). Even though the three indicators (ToT, Oi, and ESVM-Index (λ)) have a different focus of analysis, they still share evaluation of the external sector as a mutual objective (see Table 1). The external sector vulnerability monitoring index (ESVM-Index) is an alternative tool for studying the trend of external sector in any country or region. The ESVM-Index (λ) is directly linked to the openness index. The difference between these two indices is that the ESVM-Index (λ) involves the foreign direct investment marginal rate (β') in its analysis, while the openness index does not. This research paper considers (β') as an import item in any country. In the measurement of ESVM-Index, the three primary annual growth rates are the trade volume marginal rate (α'), the foreign direct investment marginal rate (β'), and the GDP marginal rate (σ'). The simultaneous application of these three marginal rates help us visualize the trend of the external sector in any country or region.

2. The External Sector Vulnerability Monitoring Index (λ)

The objective of this indicator, titled as "The External Sector Vulnerability Monitoring Index" (henceforth ESVM) (λ), is to offer policy-makers and researchers a new analytical tool to study the external sector trends and stages of any country from a global perspective. These three fundamental variables are (i) the trade volume marginal rate (α'); (ii) the foreign direct investment marginal rate (β'); and (iii) the GDP marginal rate (σ').

Two specific growth rates represent the external sector of the ESVM-Index (λ) are the trade volume marginal rate (α') and the foreign direct investment marginal rate (β'). In this part of our research, the trade volume is equal to the sum of exports flows (Ψ) plus imports flow (θ) in billions of US$ per year. On the investment side, it is represented by the variation of the FDI annual growth rate between two years. The idea to include the foreign direct investment marginal rate (β') and the trade volume marginal rate (α') together into the study of the external sector is to create a more inclusive analysis of the sector. The computation of the ESVM-Index (λ) requires six steps detailed below (see Diagram 1).

Step-1: The Trade Volume Marginal Rate (α')
The trade volume marginal rate (α') is equal to the first derivative between the trade volume of a given year in billions of US$ $(\Psi + \theta)_{n+1}$ and the trade volume of the previous year in billions of US$ $(\Psi + \theta)_n$.

$$\alpha' = \frac{\partial (\Psi + \theta)_{n+1}}{\partial (\Psi + \theta)_n} \tag{1}$$

Step-2: The Foreign Direct Investment Marginal Rate (β')
The Foreign Direct Investment Marginal Rate (β') is equal to the first derivative between the foreign direct investment volume of a given year in billions of US$ $(\beta)_{n+1}$ and the foreign direct investment of previous year in billions of US$ $(\beta)_n$.

$$\beta' = \frac{\partial(\beta)_{n+1}}{\partial(\beta)_n} \tag{2}$$

Step-3: The GDP Marginal Rate (σ')
The GDP marginal rate (σ') is equal to the first derivative between the growth domestic product of a given year in billions of US$ $(\sigma)_{n+1}$ and the growth domestic product of the previous year in billions of US$ $(\sigma)_n$.

$$\sigma' = \frac{\partial(\sigma)_{n+1}}{\partial(\sigma)_n} \tag{3}$$

Table 2. Possible combinations between α' and β' to Final ε_i Results

ΔFDI/ΔT	$+\alpha'$	$-\alpha'$	$\alpha' = 0$
$+\beta'$	$\alpha' + \beta' = \varepsilon_{i+}$ Good	▲$(-\alpha')$ + ▼$\beta' = \varepsilon_i$- Poor ▼$(-\alpha')$ + ▲$\beta' = \varepsilon_{i+}$ Good	$0 + (\beta') = \varepsilon_{i+}$ Good
$-\beta'$	▲α' + ▼$(-\beta') = \varepsilon_{i+}$ Good ▼α' + ▲$(-\beta') = \varepsilon_{i-}$ Poor	▲$(-\alpha')$ + ▼$(-\beta') = \varepsilon_i$- Poor ▼$(-\alpha')$ + ▲$(-\beta') = \varepsilon_i$- Poor	$0 + (-\beta') = \varepsilon_{i-}$ Poor
$\beta' = 0$	$\alpha' + 0 = \varepsilon_{i+}$ Good	$-\alpha' + 0 = \varepsilon_{i-}$ Poor	$0 + 0 = \varepsilon_i = 0$ Null

▲ = Higher ▼ = Lower β' = The Foreign Direct Investment Marginal Rate (β')
σ' = The Trade Volume Marginal Rate (-) = Negative and (+) = Positive
ε_i = External Sector Main Variable 0 = Zero
Source: Adapted from "External Sector Development Index," by M. A. Ruiz Estrada 2011a, *International Journal of China Studies*, 2(1), 55-70.

Step-4: The External Sector Main Variable (ε_i)
The external sector main variable (ε_i) is equal to the sum of trade volume annual growth rate (α') and foreign direct investment annual growth rate (β') (see Table 2).

$$\varepsilon_i = \alpha' + \beta' \quad (4)$$

If any value is located in ε_{i+} then this value can get the category of good performance in the external sector. If any value is located into ε_{i-} then this value can get the category of poor external sector performance. Finally, if εi = 0 then this value can get the category of null.

Step-5: The External Sector Vulnerability Monitoring Index (λ)
The External Sector Vulnerability Monitoring Index (λ) is equal to the external sector main variable (ε_i) divided by the GDP annual growth rate (σ')

$$\lambda = \frac{\varepsilon_i}{\sigma'} \quad (5)$$

The results from the external sector vulnerability monitoring index (λ) is evaluated according to these parameters:

High Vulnerability

If ε_i and σ' are in the range ($+\varepsilon_i/\sigma'$) or ($-\varepsilon_i/-\sigma$), then the (λ) can be classified into the category of high vulnerability (see Table 3). Within the high vulnerability range, the ε_i and σ' are moving in the different directions. This category may display a strong link between (ε_i) and (σ').

Null Vulnerability

If (ε_i) and (σ') are located into these parameters such as (0/0), (0/+ σ'), (0/- σ'), ($-\varepsilon_i$/0), ($+\varepsilon_i$/0) then the (λ) can be classified into the category of null vulnerability (see Table 3). The category of null vulnerability can show how (ε_i) is equal to 0 and grow faster than the (σ'). This result will show how the external sector depends on the world trade trend, but it cannot be affected positively or negatively on the (σ').

Lower Vulnerability

If (ε_i) and (σ') are in the following range ($-\varepsilon_i/+\sigma'$) or ($+\varepsilon_i/-\sigma'$) then the (λ) can be classified into the category

Table 3. ESVM-Index (λ) Cycles Level Table

σ'/ε_i	$+\sigma'$	$-\sigma'$	$\sigma'=0$
$+\varepsilon_i$	**Level-1.1** Higher Vulnerability $+\varepsilon_i/+\sigma'$	**Level-1.2** Lower Vulnerability $+\varepsilon_i/-\sigma'$	**Level-1.3** Null $+\varepsilon_i/0$
$-\varepsilon_i$	**Level-2.1** Lower Vulnerability $-\varepsilon_i/+\sigma'$	**Level-2.2** Higher Vulnerability $-\varepsilon_i/-\sigma'$	**Level-2.3** Null $-\varepsilon_i/0$
$\varepsilon_i=0$	**Level-3.1** Null $0/+\sigma'$	**Level-3.2** Null $0/-\sigma'$	**Level-3.3** Null 0/0

Variables: ▲ = High ▼ = Low σ' = GDP annual growth rate
ε_i = External Sector Main Variable (-) = Negative and (+) = Positive 0 = Zero
Source: Adapted from "External Sector Development Index," by M. A. Ruiz Estrada 2011a, *International Journal of China Studies*, 2(1), 55-70.

of lower vulnerability (see Table 3). The category of lower vulnerability can show how (ε_i) growth is lower or higher than the (σ'). This result will clearly show that the external sector is not the main key factor to affect the (σ') of any country.

Step-6: The External Sector Vulnerability Monitoring Surface (λ -*Surface*)
The construction of the external sector vulnerability monitoring surface (λ -Surface) is using the (λ) results and the mega-surface coordinate space (see Expression 6 below). The (λ) is a three-by-three matrix that contains the individual results of all nine variables (taken from Table 3). However, the nine variables are plotted onto a three-by-three array with the vertical value on the (λ) (see Figure 1). The intent is to produce a surface for a quick pictorial representation of the overall propensities for any one country external sector behavior. The main idea here is to use the results of nine variables in the (λ) to build a symmetric surface. When the λ-surface-coordinate-system (η) has strictly the same number of rows as the number of columns, then the ESVM-Index rates can always be perfectly symmetric.

$$\eta = \begin{pmatrix} \lambda_1 & \lambda_2 & \lambda_3 \\ \lambda_4 & \lambda_5 & \lambda_6 \\ \lambda_7 & \lambda_8 & \lambda_9 \end{pmatrix} \qquad (6)$$

The final analysis of the λ-Surface depends on any changes that the surface can experience in a fixed period. The evaluation of the λ-Surface is classified in two distinct levels of vulnerability (see Table 3): (i) Level 1: High vulnerability: (+λ); Level 2: Low vulnerability: (- λ).

3. The External Sector Vulnerability Monitoring Index (λ)

The ESVM-Index (λ) analyzed the ASEAN-5's (Indonesia, Malaysia, Philippines, Singapore, Thailand) and China's external sector performance and vulnerability between 2005 and 2015. The reason for applying the ESVM-Index (λ) is to observe the performance and vulnerability of the external sector of any country or

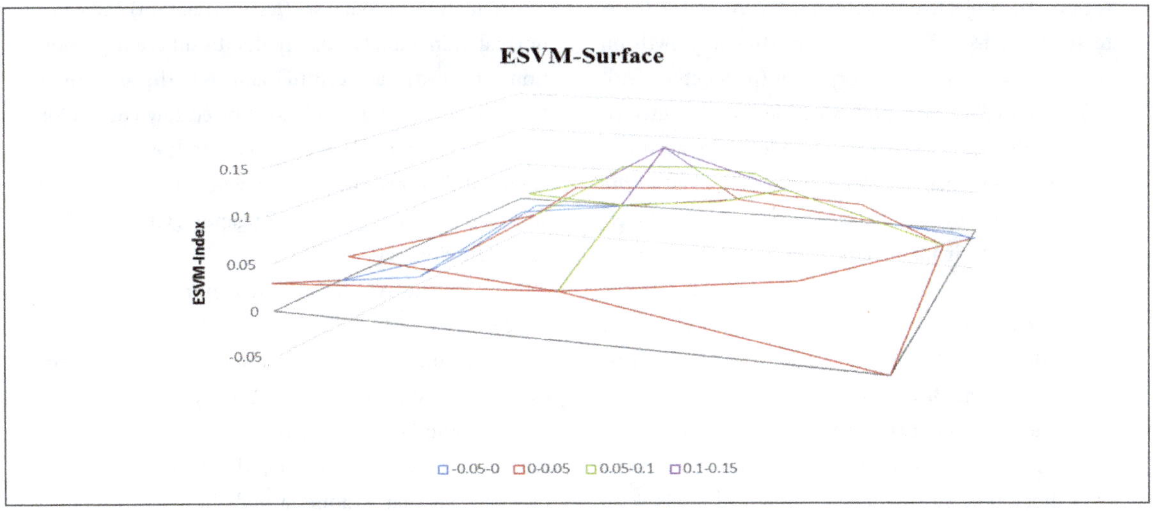

Figure 1. λ-Surface

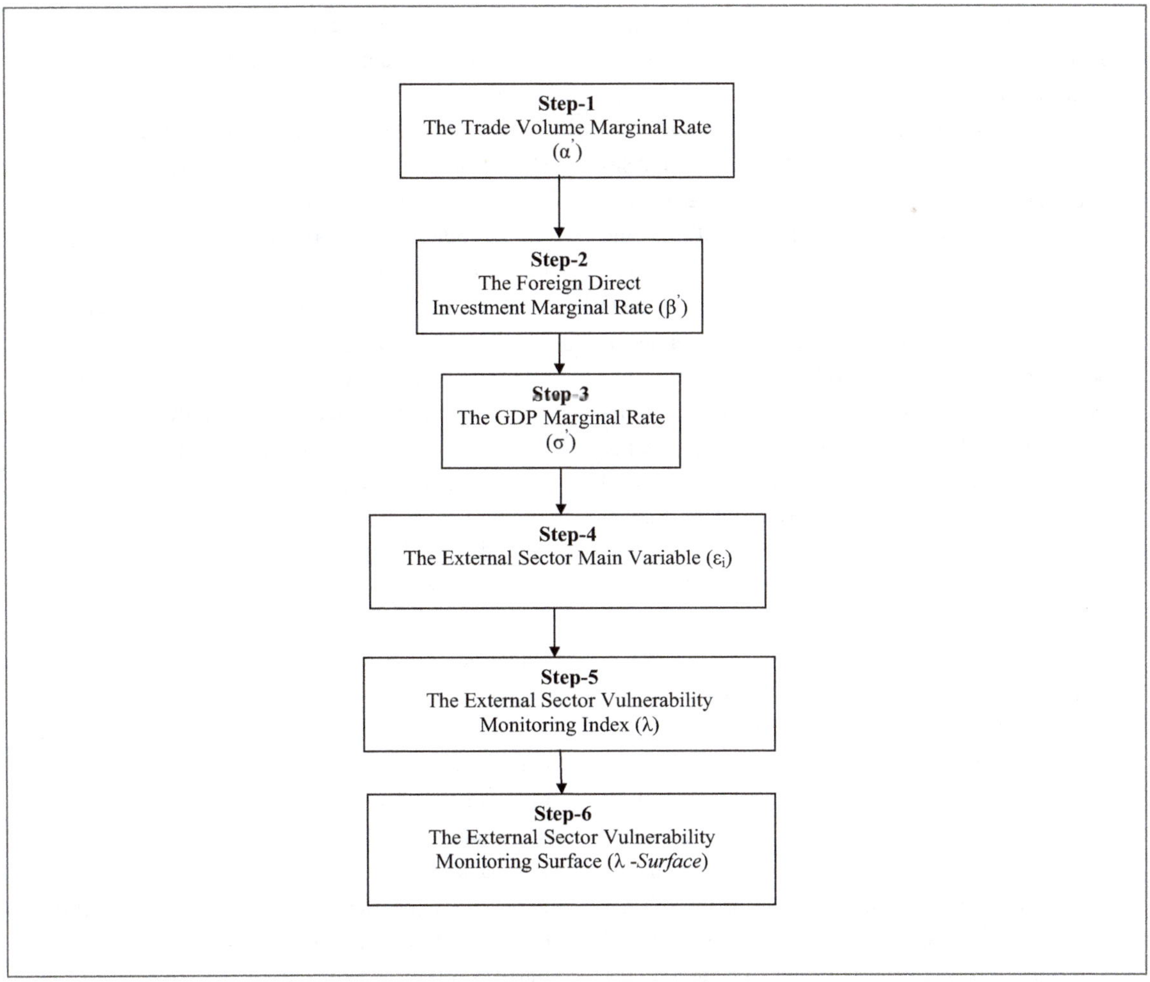

Diagram 1. Procedure to Measure the Si-Index

region. The objective in applying ESVM-Index (λ) is to see the effect of trade and investment growth on the (σ'). The reason to incorporate (β') together with (α') is to analyze how both variables can be affected by possible broad international trade or financial crisis. Specifically, the ESVM-Index (λ) is applied to the ASEAN-5 members as well as China to observe the effect of the 2008 financial crisis. The main reason for using ASEAN-5 (five members or five original members) and China is because of missing or inconsistent data from other ASEAN members such as Vietnam, Cambodia, Myanmar, Brunei, and Laos.

The application of the ESVM-Index (λ) to the selected countries in this study shows that the countries most affected by the 2008 financial crisis were the Philippines λ_{2008} = -0.08 (See Table 8), Singapore λ_{2008} = -0.18 (See Table 5), Thailand λ_{2008}= -0.16 (See Table 7), Malaysia λ_{2008}= 0.10 (See Table 6), Indonesia λ_{2008}= -0.18 (See Table 4) and China λ_{2008}= 0.00 (See Table 9).

In the case of China (2008), it was affected by the financial crisis but not at the same level as ASEAN-5 members. The results show high dependency of ASEAN-5 members to the external sector. The results also point to China's vulnerability to global fiscal crisis and business cycles. In the period of 2005-2015, we can show that the foreign sector of ASEAN-5 members and China illustrated an acceptable external sector performance, but two ASEAN-5 members displayed irregularities in their external sector behavior between 2008 and 2015. These countries are the Philippines (low participation of the external sector in world trade) and Singapore (high exposure of the foreign sector in world trade). From a comparative stance, China's external sector outperformed ASEAN-5 members between 2005-2015.

Next, we discuss how (ε_i) and (σ') are correlated. Our analysis in China (r^2 = 0.78), Malaysia (r^2 = 0.57) and Indonesia (r^2 = 0.52) indicated there exists a strong correlation between (εi) and (σ'), while Singapore (r^2 = 0.95), Thailand (r^2 = 0.83) and Philippines (r^2 = 0.89) displayed a higher correlation. Correlation results show that China and ASEAN-5 economies are highly dependent on external sector performance on (α') and (β') together. Singapore's external sector is classified as a high vulnerable category, mainly due to a higher trade volume and FDI from the U.S.

An analysis of Malaysia (less correlation) indicated normal vulnerability, mainly due to different proportions of growth between (α') and (β'). The analysis of the Philippines and Thailand showed low correlation between (εi) and (σ'), which points to the low vulnerability of their external sectors, where (α') and (β') are slow and small compared to Singapore, China, Malaysia, and Indonesia.

Considering ASEAN-5 and China, ESVM-Index (λ) cycles between 2005 and 2015 (10 years) indicate the following results: Thailand showed the poorest performance in Level-1.1 (4 years), Level-2.1 (5 years) and Level-2.2. (1 year) according to Table 7. Among ASEAN-5 members, the ESVM-Index cycles showed that Indonesia had the worst outcome in Level-1.1 (6 years) and Level-2.1 (4 years) (See Table 4). On the other hand, Singapore showed fair behavior in its ESVM-Index (λ) cycle; Singapore had Level-1.1 (3 years), Level-2.2 (1 year), and Level-2.1 (6 years) (See Table 5), and Malaysia featured Level-1.1 (3 years), Level-2.1 (6 years) and Level-2.2. (1 year) (See Table 6). In the case of China, it was located in Level-1.1 (6 years) and Level-2.2 (4 years). The reason why China shows different results in the ESVM-Index (λ) cycles is due to high dependency on international markets, especially with the U.S. (See Table 9). In the case of the Philippines, which was located in Level-1.1 (4 years) and Level-2.2 (6 years) (See Table 8), their unique position was due to low participation of its external sector in the world economy. It has few export products with high value to international markets.

4. Concluding Remarks

This research paper has presented the External Sector Vulnerability Monitoring Index (λ). It is focused on diagnosing the external sector vulnerabilities of any country. With the application of the ESVM-Index (λ) to the study of trade liberalization and openness, it is possible to observe that (α') and (β') need to be joined into a single variable to explore the external sector of any country or region. The single variable is called the external sector leading variable (εi). Thus, the ESVM-Index (λ) can be used as an alternative index to study trade liberalization cycles. In our opinion, the ESVM-Index (λ) may be considered as a complementary analytical tool together with terms of trade (ToT) and the

	2005	2006	2007	2008	2009	2010	2011	2012	2013	2014	2015
Exports	95	107	122	146	125	167	213	211	205	199	205
Export Growth	0.00	0.13	0.14	0.20	-0.14	0.34	0.28	-0.01	-0.03	-0.03	0.03
Imports	86	87	101	136	104	145	199	213	211	202	210
Import Growth	0.00	0.01	0.16	0.35	-0.24	0.39	0.37	0.07	-0.01	-0.04	0.04
Total Trade	181	194	223	282	229	312	412	424	416	401	415
ΔT	0.00	0.07	0.15	0.26	-0.19	0.36	0.32	0.03	-0.02	-0.04	0.03
FDI	-5,271,257,208	2,188,448,467	-2,253,330,000	-3,418,723,399	-2,628,247,483	-11,106,333,135	-11,528,394,762	-13,716,225,988	-12,170,055,179	-15,502,233,989	##########
ΔFDI	0.00	-1.42	-2.03	0.52	-0.23	3.23	0.04	0.19	-0.11	0.27	0.10
ΔGDP	0	5.5	6.3	6	4.6	6.2	6.2	6	5.6	5	5.10
Ei	0.00	-1.34	-1.88	0.78	-0.42	3.59	0.36	0.22	-0.13	0.24	0.13
	2005	2006	2007	2008	2009	2010	2011	2012	2013	2014	2015
ESVM-INDEX	0.00	-0.24	-0.30	0.13	-0.09	0.58	0.06	0.04	-0.02	0.05	0.03
Ei Performance	0	Poor	Poor	Good	Poor	Good	Good	Good	Poor	Good	Good
ESVM-Vulnerability	0	Lower	Lower	Higher	Lower	Higher	Higher	Higher	Lower	Higher	Higher
ESVM-LEVEL	0	L-2.1	L-2.1	L-1.1	L-2.1	L-1.1	L-1.1	L-1.1	L-2.1	L-1.1	L-1.1
T = ΔTRADE/ΔGDP	0.00	0.01	0.02	0.04	-0.04	0.06	0.05	0.00	0.00	-0.01	0.01
FDI = ΔFDI/ΔGDP	0.00	-0.26	-0.32	0.09	-0.05	0.52	0.01	0.03	-0.02	0.05	0.02
ESVM-Index TEST	0.00	-0.24	-0.30	0.13	-0.09	0.58	0.06	0.04	-0.02	0.05	0.03

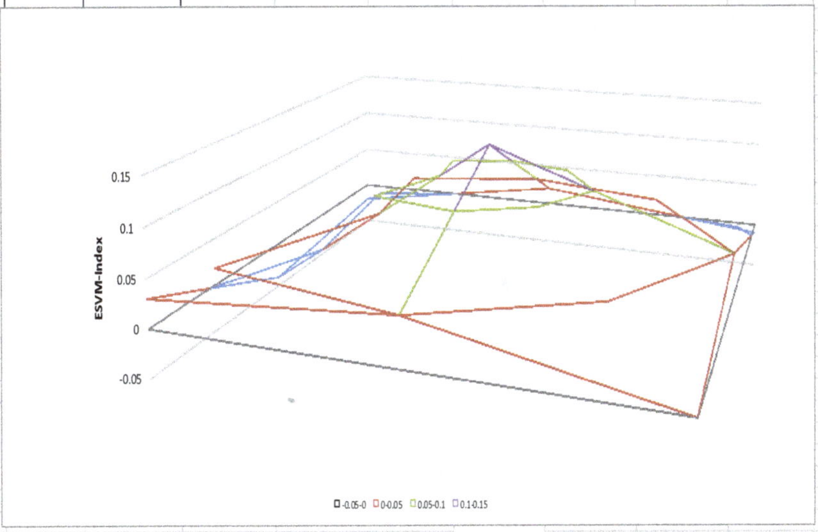

Source: World Development Indicators, World Bank
http://data.worldbank.org/indicator/BX.GSR.GNFS.CD?page=2
http://data.worldbank.org/indicator/BM.GSR.GNFS.CD
http://data.worldbank.org/indicator/BN.KLT.DINV.CD
http://data.worldbank.org/indicator/NY.GDP.MKTP.KD.ZG

Table 4. Application of the trade terms, openness index and ESVM-index in Indonesia
Figure 2. ESVM-Surface of Indonesia (2006-2014)
Source: Adapted from "Annual report GDP Growth (Annual %)" by The World Bank (2015a). Retrieved from http://data.worldbank.org/indicator/NY.GDP.MKTP.KD.ZG; "Annual report Exports of Goods and Services (BoP Current Prices)" by The World Bank (2015b). Retrieved from http://data.worldbank.org/indicator/BM.GSR.GNFS.CD; "Annual report Imports of Goods and Services (BoP Current Prices)" by The World Bank (2016a). Retrieved from https://data.worldbank.org/indicator/BM.GSR.GNFS.CD; "Foreign direct investment, net (BoP, current US$)" by The World Bank (2016b). Retrieved from http://data.worldbank.org/indicator/BN.KLT.DINV.CD

	2005	2006	2007	2008	2009	2010	2011	2012	2013	2014	2015
Exports	286	340	386	443	369	471	554	567	579	578	590
Export Growth	0.00	0.19	0.14	0.15	-0.17	0.28	0.18	0.02	0.02	0.00	0.02
Imports	86	296	331	402	324	409	482	501	509	502	510
Import Growth	0.00	2.44	0.12	0.21	-0.19	0.26	0.18	0.04	0.02	-0.01	0.02
Total Trade	372	636	717	845	693	880	1,036	1,068	1,088	1,080	1,100
Trade Growth	0.00	0.71	0.13	0.18	-0.18	0.27	0.18	0.03	0.02	-0.01	0.02
FDI	-6,502,052,545	-18,285,978,015	-10,836,097,100	-5,395,159,595	2,417,713,597	-21,698,437,242	-23,511,978,991	-41,512,193,196	-35,979,301,526	-26,863,107,218	##########
FDI Growth	0.00	1.81	-0.41	-0.50	-1.45	-9.97	0.08	0.77	-0.13	-0.25	-0.90
GDP Growth	0	8.9	9.1	1.8	-0.6	15.2	6.2	3.4	4.4	2.9	3.10
ESi	0.00	2.52	-0.28	-0.32	-1.63	-9.70	0.26	0.80	-0.11	-0.26	-0.88
	2005	**2006**	**2007**	**2008**	**2009**	**2010**	**2011**	**2012**	**2013**	**2014**	**2015**
ESVM-INDEX	0.00	0.28	-0.03	-0.18	2.71	-0.64	0.04	0.23	-0.03	-0.09	-0.28
Ei Performance	0	Good	Poor	Poor	Poor	Poor	Good	Good	Poor	Poor	Poor
ESVM-Vulnerability	0	Higher	Lower	Lower	Higher	Lower	Higher	Higher	Lower	Lower	Lower
ESVM-LEVEL	0	L-1.1	L-2.1	L-2.1	L-2.2	L-2.1	L-1.1	L-1.1	L-2.1	L-2.1	L-2.1
T = ΔTRADE/ΔGDP	0.00	0.08	0.01	0.10	0.30	0.02	0.03	0.01	0.00	0.00	0.01
FDI = ΔFDI/ΔGDP	0.00	0.20	-0.04	-0.28	2.41	-0.66	0.01	0.23	-0.03	-0.09	-0.29
ESVM-Index TEST	0.00	0.28	-0.03	-0.18	2.71	-0.64	0.04	0.23	-0.03	-0.09	-0.28

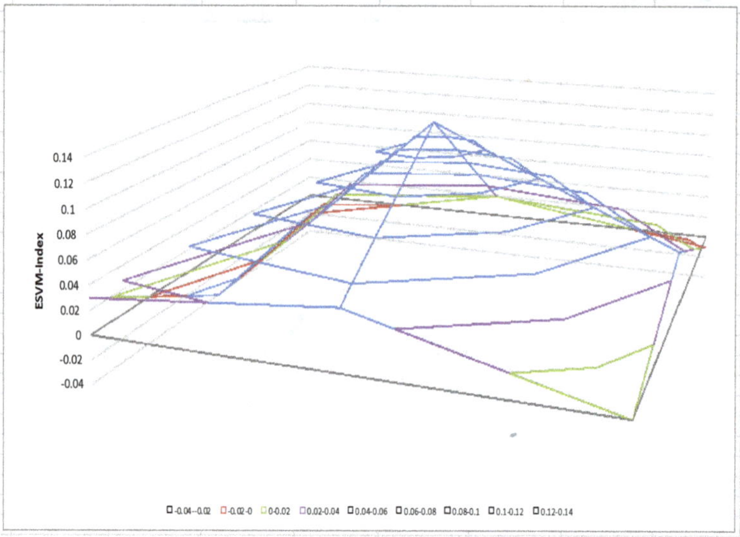

Source: World Development Indicators, World Bank
http://data.worldbank.org/indicator/BX.GSR.GNFS.CD?page=2
http://data.worldbank.org/indicator/BM.GSR.GNFS.CD
http://data.worldbank.org/indicator/BN.KLT.DINV.CD
http://data.worldbank.org/indicator/NY.GDP.MKTP.KD.ZG

Table 5. Application of the trade terms, openness index and ESVM-index in Singapore

Figure 3. ESVM-Surface of Singapore (2006-2014)

Source: Adapted from "Annual report GDP Growth (Annual %)" by The World Bank (2015a). Retrieved from http://data.worldbank.org/indicator/NY.GDP.MKTP.KD.ZG; "Annual report Exports of Goods and Services (BoP Current Prices)" by The World Bank (2015b). Retrieved from http://data.worldbank.org/indicator/BM.GSR.GNFS.CD; "Annual report Imports of Goods and Services (BoP Current Prices)" by The World Bank (2016a). Retrieved from https://data.worldbank.org/indicator/BM.GSR.GNFS.CD; "Foreign direct investment, net (BoP, current US$)" by The World Bank (2016b). Retrieved from http://data.worldbank.org/indicator/BN.KLT.DINV.CD

	2005	2006	2007	2008	2009	2010	2011	2012	2013	2014	2015
Exports	161	183	206	230	186	231	265	266	259	250	238
Export Growth	0.00	0.14	0.13	0.12	-0.19	0.24	0.15	0.00	-0.03	-0.03	-0.05
Imports	131	147	167	179	145	189	217	229	231	240	223
Import Growth	0.00	0.12	0.14	0.07	-0.19	0.30	0.15	0.06	0.01	0.04	-0.07
Total Trade	292	330	373	409	331	420	482	495	490	490	461
Trade Growth	0.00	0.13	0.13	0.10	-0.19	0.27	0.15	0.03	-0.01	0.00	-0.06
FDI	-993,682,960	-53,139,541	2,744,191,223	7,827,500,376	6,626,128,852	4,464,001,483	2,989,026,889	7,147,825,588	1,416,056,518	6,626,128,852	##########
FDI Growth	0.00	-0.95	-52.64	1.85	-0.15	-0.33	-0.33	1.39	-0.80	3.68	-0.33
GDP Growth	5.3	5.6	6.3	4.8	-1.5	7.4	5.3	5.5	4.7	6	5.00
ESi	0.00	-0.82	-52.51	1.95	-0.34	-0.06	-0.18	1.42	-0.81	3.68	-0.39
	2005	2006	2007	2008	2009	2010	2011	2012	2013	2014	2015
ESVM-INDEX	0.00	-0.15	-8.34	0.41	0.23	-0.01	-0.03	0.26	-0.17	0.61	-0.08
Ei Performance	0	Poor	Poor	Good	Poor	Poor	Poor	Good	Poor	Good	Poor
ESVM-Vulnerability	0	Lower	Lower	Higher	Higher	Lower	Lower	Higher	Lower	Hihger	Lower
ESVM-LEVEL	0	L-2.1	L-2.1	L-1.1	L-2.2	L-2.1	L-2.1	L-1.1	L-2.1	L-1.1	L-2.1
T = ΔTRADE/ΔGDP	0.00	0.02	0.02	0.02	0.13	0.04	0.03	0.00	0.00	0.00	-0.01
FDI = ΔFDI/ΔGDP	0.00	-0.17	-8.36	0.39	0.10	-0.04	-0.06	0.25	-0.17	0.61	-0.07
ESVM-Index TEST	0.00	-0.15	-8.34	0.41	0.23	-0.01	-0.03	0.26	-0.17	0.61	-0.08

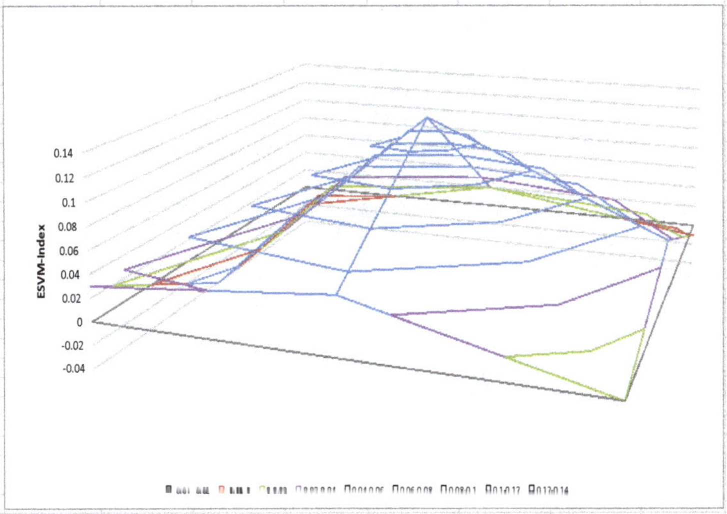

Source: World Development Indicators, World Bank
http://data.worldbank.org/indicator/BX.GSR.GNFS.CD?page=2
http://data.worldbank.org/indicator/BM.GSR.GNFS.CD
http://data.worldbank.org/indicator/BN.KLT.DINV.CD
http://data.worldbank.org/indicator/NY.GDP.MKTP.KD.ZG

Table 6. Application of the trade terms, openness index and ESVM-index in Malaysia

Figure 4. ESVM-Surface of Malaysia (2006-2014)

Source: Adapted from "Annual report GDP Growth (Annual %)" by The World Bank (2015a). Retrieved from http://data.worldbank.org/indicator/NY.GDP.MKTP.KD.ZG; "Annual report Exports of Goods and Services (BoP Current Prices)" by The World Bank (2015b). Retrieved from http://data.worldbank.org/indicator/BM.GSR.GNFS.CD; "Annual report Imports of Goods and Services (BoP Current Prices)" by The World Bank (2016a). Retrieved from https://data.worldbank.org/indicator/BM.GSR.GNFS.CD; "Foreign direct investment, net (BoP, current US$)" by The World Bank (2016b). Retrieved from http://data.worldbank.org/indicator/BN.KLT.DINV.CD

	2005	2006	2007	2008	2009	2010	2011	2012	2013	2014	2015
Exports	129	153	181	208	181	226	260	275	284	280	268
Export Growth	0.00	0.19	0.18	0.15	-0.13	0.25	0.15	0.06	0.03	-0.01	-0.04
Imports	133	147	163	204	155	207	254	272	274	253	248
Import Growth	0.00	0.11	0.11	0.25	-0.24	0.34	0.23	0.07	0.01	-0.08	-0.02
Total Trade	262	300	344	412	336	433	514	547	558	533	516
Trade Growth	0.00	0.15	0.15	0.20	-0.18	0.29	0.19	0.06	0.02	-0.04	-0.03
FDI	-7,554,132,823	-8,480,341,310	-8,312,493,362	-4,445,056,066	-683,125,957	-4,487,865,221	4,729,978,070	1,327,896,204	-1,901,956,499	-4,973,347,772	##########
FDI Growth	0.00	0.12	-0.02	-0.47	-0.85	5.57	-2.05	-0.72	-2.43	1.61	-0.40
GDP Growth	4.2	5	5.4	1.7	-0.7	7.5	0.8	7.3	2.8	0.9	1.10
ESi	0.00	0.27	0.13	-0.27	-1.03	5.86	-1.87	-0.66	-2.41	1.57	-0.43
	2005	2006	2007	2008	2009	2010	2011	2012	2013	2014	2015
ESVM-INDEX	0.00	0.05	0.02	-0.16	1.47	0.78	-2.33	-0.09	-0.86	1.74	-0.39
Ei Performance	0	Good	Good	Poor	Poor	Good	Poor	Poor	Poor	Good	Poor
ESVM-Vulnerability	0	Higher	Higher	Lower	Higher	Higher	Lower	Lower	Lower	Higher	Lower
ESVM-LEVEL	0	L1.1	L1.1	L.2.1	L2.2	L1.1	L2.1	L2.1	L2.1	L1.1	L2.1
T = ΔTRADE/ΔGDP	0.00	0.03	0.03	0.12	0.26	0.04	0.23	0.01	0.01	-0.05	-0.03
FDI = ΔFDI/ΔGDP	0.00	0.02	0.00	-0.27	1.21	0.74	-2.57	-0.10	-0.87	1.79	-0.36
ESVM-Index TEST	0.00	0.05	0.02	-0.16	1.47	0.78	-2.33	-0.09	-0.86	1.74	-0.39

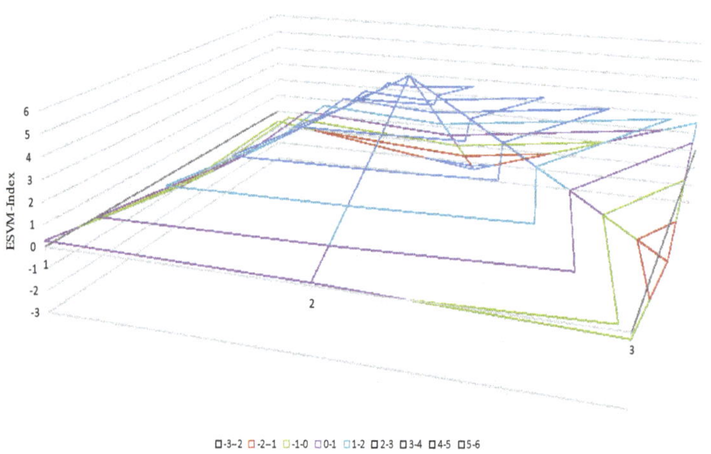

Source: World Development Indicators, World Bank
http://data.worldbank.org/indicator/BX.GSR.GNFS.CD?page=2
http://data.worldbank.org/indicator/BM.GSR.GNFS.CD
http://data.worldbank.org/indicator/BN.KLT.DINV.CD
http://data.worldbank.org/indicator/NY.GDP.MKTP.KD.ZG

Table 7. Application of the trade terms, openness index and ESVM-index in Thailand

Figure 5. ESVM-Surface of Thailand (2006-2014)

Source: Adapted from "Annual report GDP Growth (Annual %)" by The World Bank (2015a). Retrieved from http://data.worldbank.org/indicator/NY.GDP.MKTP.KD.ZG; "Annual report Exports of Goods and Services (BoP Current Prices)" by The World Bank (2015b). Retrieved from http://data.worldbank.org/indicator/BM.GSR.GNFS.CD; "Annual report Imports of Goods and Services (BoP Current Prices)" by The World Bank (2016a). Retrieved from https://data.worldbank.org/indicator/BM.GSR.GNFS.CD; "Foreign direct investment, net (BoP, current US$)" by The World Bank (2016b). Retrieved from http://data.worldbank.org/indicator/BN.KLT.DINV.CD

	2005	2006	2007	2008	2009	2010	2011	2012	2013	2014	2015
Exports	34	42	46	48	43	55	57	67	68	73	70
Export Growth	0.00	0.24	0.10	0.04	-0.10	0.28	0.04	0.18	0.01	0.07	-0.04
Imports	44	49	54	64	52	66	71	80	78	84	91
Import Growth	0.00	0.11	0.10	0.19	-0.19	0.27	0.08	0.13	-0.03	0.08	0.08
Total Trade	78	91	100	112	95	121	128	147	146	157	161
Trade Growth	0.00	0.17	0.10	0.12	-0.15	0.27	0.06	0.15	-0.01	0.08	0.03
FDI	-7,554,132,823	-8,480,341,310	-8,312,493,362	-4,445,056,066	-683,125,957	-4,487,865,221	4,729,978,070	1,327,896,204	-1,901,956,499	-4,973,347,772	##########
FDI Growth	0.00	0.12	-0.02	-0.47	-0.85	5.57	-2.05	-0.72	-2.43	1.61	-0.40
GDP Growth	4.8	5.2	6.6	4.2	1.1	7.6	3.7	6.7	7.1	6.1	6.50
ESi	0.00	0.29	0.08	-0.35	-1.00	5.84	-2.00	-0.57	-2.44	1.69	-0.37
	2005	2006	2007	2008	2009	2010	2011	2012	2013	2014	2015
ESVM-INDEX	0.00	0.06	0.01	-0.08	-0.91	0.77	-0.54	-0.09	-0.34	0.28	-0.06
Ei Performance	0	Good	Good	Poor	Poor	Good	Poor	Poor	Poor	Good	Poor
ESVM-Vulnerability	0	Higher	Higher	Lower	Lower	Higher	Lower	Lower	Lower	Higher	Lower
ESVM-LEVEL	0	L1.1	L1.1	L2.1	L2.1	L1.1	L2.1	L2.1	L2.2	L1.1	L2.1
T = ΔTRADE/ΔGDP	0.00	0.03	0.01	0.03	-0.14	0.04	0.02	0.02	0.00	0.01	0.00
FDI = ΔFDI/ΔGDP	0.00	0.02	0.00	-0.11	-0.77	0.73	-0.56	-0.11	-0.34	0.26	-0.06
ESVM-Index TEST	0.00	0.06	0.01	-0.08	-0.91	0.77	-0.54	-0.09	-0.34	0.28	-0.06

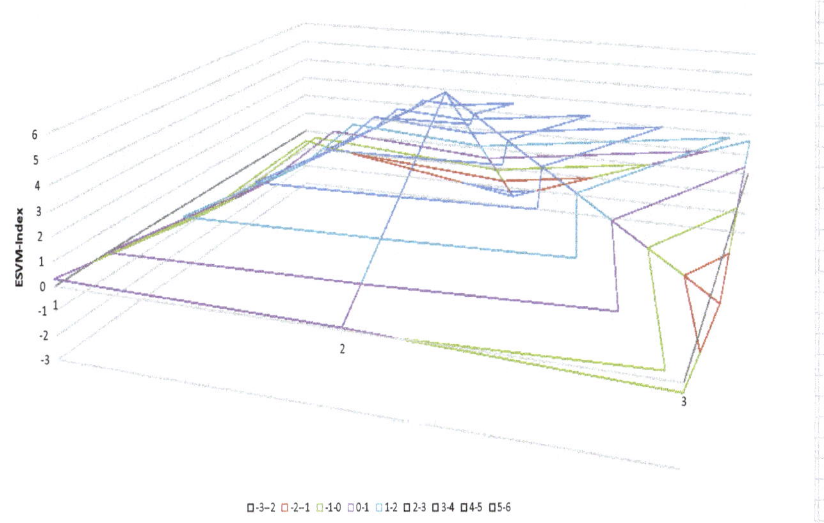

Source: World Development Indicators, World Bank
http://data.worldbank.org/indicator/BX.GSR.GNFS.CD?page=2
http://data.worldbank.org/indicator/BM.GSR.GNFS.CD
http://data.worldbank.org/indicator/BN.KLT.DINV.CD
http://data.worldbank.org/indicator/NY.GDP.MKTP.KD.ZG

Table 8. Application of the trade terms, openness index and ESVM-index in Philippines

Figure 6. ESVM-Surface of Philippines (2006-2014)

Source: Adapted from "Annual report GDP Growth (Annual %)" by The World Bank (2015a). Retrieved from http://data.worldbank.org/indicator/NY.GDP.MKTP.KD.ZG; "Annual report Exports of Goods and Services (BoP Current Prices)" by The World Bank (2015b). Retrieved from http://data.worldbank.org/indicator/BM.GSR.GNFS.CD; "Annual report Imports of Goods and Services (BoP Current Prices)" by The World Bank (2016a). Retrieved from https://data.worldbank.org/indicator/BM.GSR.GNFS.CD; "Foreign direct investment, net (BoP, current US$)" by The World Bank (2016b). Retrieved from http://data.worldbank.org/indicator/BN.KLT.DINV.CD

	2005	2006	2007	2008	2009	2010	2011	2012	2013	2014	2015
Exports	770	973	1,256	1,494	1,260	1648	1,991	2,188	2,363	2,450	2189
Export Growth	0.00	0.26	0.29	0.19	-0.16	0.31	0.21	0.10	0.08	0.04	-0.11
Imports	646	765	947	1,145	1,040	1,425	1,809	1,956	2,127	2,223	2135
Import Growth	0.00	0.18	0.24	0.21	-0.09	0.37	0.27	0.08	0.09	0.05	-0.04
Total Trade	1,416	1,738	2,203	2,639	2,300	3,073	3,800	4,144	4,490	4,673	4,324
Trade Growth	0.00	0.23	0.27	0.20	-0.13	0.34	0.24	0.09	0.08	0.04	-0.07
FDI	-90,379,127,564	-100,150,000,000	-139,095,000,000	-114,792,000,000	-87,167,067,370	-185,750,000,000	-231,652,000,000	-176,250,000,000	-184,972,000,000	-170,000,000,000	##########
FDI Growth	0.00	0.11	0.39	-0.17	-0.24	1.13	0.25	-0.24	0.05	-0.08	0.05
GDP Growth	11.4	12.7	14.2	9.6	9.2	10.6	9.5	7.8	7.7	7.3	6.90
ESi	0.00	0.34	0.66	0.02	-0.37	1.47	0.48	-0.15	0.13	-0.04	-0.03

	2005	2006	2007	2008	2009	2010	2011	2012	2013	2014	2015
ESVM-INDEX	0.00	0.03	0.05	0.00	-0.04	0.14	0.05	-0.02	0.02	-0.01	0.00
Ei Performance	Acceptable	Acceptable	Acceptable	Acceptable	Acceptable	Acceptable	Acceptable	Weak	Weak	Acceptable	Acceptable
ESVM-Vulnerability	0	Higher	Higher	Hihger	Lower	Higher	Higher	Lower	Higher	Lower	Lower
ESVM-LEVEL	0	L1.1	L1.1	L1.1	L.2.1	L1.1	L1.1	L2.1	L.1.1.	L.2.1	L.2.1
T = ΔTRADE/ΔGDP	0.00	0.02	0.02	0.02	-0.01	0.03	0.02	0.01	0.01	0.01	-0.01
FDI = ΔFDI/ΔGDP	0.00	0.01	0.03	-0.02	-0.03	0.11	0.03	-0.03	0.01	-0.01	0.01
ESVM-Index TEST	0.00	0.03	0.05	0.00	-0.04	0.14	0.05	-0.02	0.02	-0.01	0.00

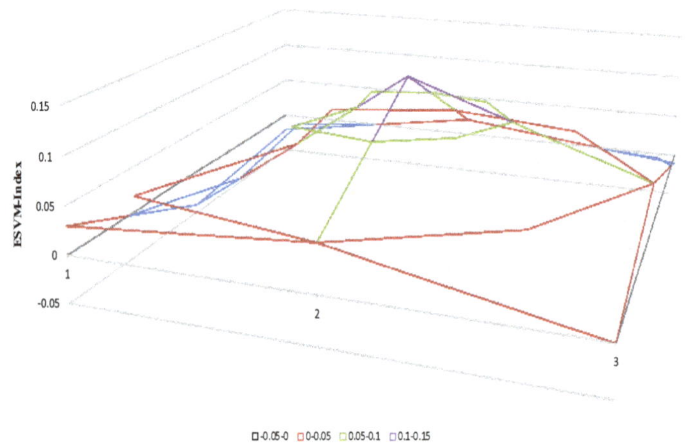

Source: World Development Indicators, World Bank
http://data.worldbank.org/indicator/BX.GSR.GNFS.CD?page=2
http://data.worldbank.org/indicator/BM.GSR.GNFS.CD
http://data.worldbank.org/indicator/BN.KLT.DINV.CD
http://data.worldbank.org/indicator/NY.GDP.MKTP.KD.ZG

Table 9. Application of the trade terms, openness index and ESVM-index in China

Figure 7. ESVM-Surface of China (2006-2014)

Source: Adapted from "Annual report GDP Growth (Annual %)" by The World Bank (2015a). Retrieved from http://data.worldbank.org/indicator/NY.GDP.MKTP.KD.ZG; "Annual report Exports of Goods and Services (BoP Current Prices)" by The World Bank (2015b). Retrieved from http://data.worldbank.org/indicator/BM.GSR.GNFS.CD; "Annual report Imports of Goods and Services (BoP Current Prices)" by The World Bank (2016a). Retrieved from https://data.worldbank.org/indicator/BM.GSR.GNFS.CD; "Foreign direct investment, net (BoP, current US$)" by The World Bank (2016b). Retrieved from http://data.worldbank.org/indicator/BN.KLT.DINV.CD

openness index (Oi). Additionally, the ESVM-Index (λ) offers a new type of graph to observe the index ESVM-Surface (λ-Surface). The ESVM-Index (λ) provides an opportunity for policy makers and researchers on international trade issues to observe and analyze the trends and stages of the external sector in any country from a new perspective.

References

Anderson, J. & Neary, J. P. (1992). Trade reform with quotas, partial rent retention, and tariffs. *Econometrica: Journal of the Econometric Society, 60*(1), 57-76. https://doi.org/ 10.2307/2951676

Anderson, J., & Neary, P. (1994). Measuring the restrictiveness of trade policy. *The World Bank Economic Review, 8*(2), 151-169. https://doi.org/10.1093/wber/8.2.151

Anderson, J., & Neary, P. (1996). A new approach to evaluating trade policy. *The Review of Economic Studies, 63*(1), 107-125. https://doi.org/10.2307/2298117

Anderson, J., & Neary, P. (2003). The Mercantilist index of trade policy. *International Economic Review, 44*(2), 627-649. https://doi.org/10.1111/1468-2354.t01-1-00083

Anderson, J., & Neary, P. (2007). Welfare versus market access: the implications of tariff structure for tariff reform. *Journal of International Economics, 71*(1), 187-205. https://doi.org/10.1016/j.jinteco.2006.02.004

Balassa, B. (1985). Exports, policy choices, and economic growth in developing countries after the 1973 oil shock. *Journal of development economics, 18*(1), 23-35. https://doi.org/10.1016/0304-3878(85)90004-5

Barro, R. (1991). Economic growth in a cross section of countries. *The Quarterly Journal of Economics, 106*(2), 407-443. https://doi.org/10.2307/2937943

Dollar, D. (1992). Outward-oriented developing economies really do grow more rapidly: evidence from 95 LDCs, 1976-1985. *Economic development and cultural change, 40*(3), 523-544. https://www.jstor.org/stable/1154574

Edwards, S. (1993). Openness, trade liberalization, and growth in developing countries. *Journal of Economic Literature, 31*(3), 1358-1393. https://www.jstor.org/stable/2728244

Edwards, S. (1997). Trade policy, growth, and income distribution. *The American Economic Review, 87*(2), 205-210. https://www.jstor.org/stable/2950881

Edwards, S. (1998). Openness, productivity and growth: what do we really know? *The economic Journal, 108*(447), 383-398. https://doi.org/10.1111/1468-0297.00293

Harrison, A. (1996). Openness and growth: A time-series, cross-country analysis for developing countries. *Journal of Development Economics, 48*(2), 419-447. https://doi.org/10.1016/0304-3878(95)00042-9

Lopez, R. (1991). Economic growth, capital accumulation and trade policy in LDCs. *Trade Policy Division, Country Economics Department, WPS 625. Retrieved from* http://documents.worldbank.org/curated/en/256911468766773672/pdf/multi-0page.pdf

Ruiz Estrada, M. A. (2011a). External Sector Development Index. *International Journal of China Studies, 2*(1), 55-70. Available at https://ssrn.com/abstract=2572041

Ruiz Estrada, M. A. (2011b). Policy Modeling: Definition, Classification, and Evaluation. *Journal of Policy Modelling 33*(4), 523-536. https://doi.org/10.1016/j.jpolmod.2011.02.003

Sachs, J. D., Warner, A., Åslund, A., & Fischer, S. (1995). Economic Reforms and the Process of Global Integration. *Brookings papers on economic activity, 1995*(1), 1-118. https://doi.org/ 10.2307/2534573

The World Bank. (2015a). Annual report GDP Growth (Annual %). *Retrieved from* http://data.worldbank.org/indicator/NY.GDP.MKTP.KD.ZG

The World Bank. (2015b). Annual report Exports of Goods and Services (BoP Current Prices). *Retrieved from* http://data.worldbank.org/indicator/BM.GSR.GNFS.CD

The World Bank. (2016a). Annual report Imports of Goods and Services (BoP Current Prices). *Retrieved from* https://data.worldbank.org/indicator/BM.GSR.GNFS.CD

The World Bank. (2016b). Foreign direct investment, net (BoP, current US$). *Retrieved from* http://data.worldbank.org/indicator/BN.KLT.DINV.CD

Endnotes

1. $ToT = IP_x/IP_m \times 100\%$
2. $O_i = X+M/GDP \times 100\%$

Permissions

All chapters in this book were first published in CE, by University of Finance and Management, Warsaw; Vistula University; hereby published with permission under the Creative Commons Attribution License or equivalent. Every chapter published in this book has been scrutinized by our experts. Their significance has been extensively debated. The topics covered herein carry significant findings which will fuel the growth of the discipline. They may even be implemented as practical applications or may be referred to as a beginning point for another development.

The contributors of this book come from diverse backgrounds, making this book a truly international effort. This book will bring forth new frontiers with its revolutionizing research information and detailed analysis of the nascent developments around the world.

We would like to thank all the contributing authors for lending their expertise to make the book truly unique. They have played a crucial role in the development of this book. Without their invaluable contributions this book wouldn't have been possible. They have made vital efforts to compile up to date information on the varied aspects of this subject to make this book a valuable addition to the collection of many professionals and students.

This book was conceptualized with the vision of imparting up-to-date information and advanced data in this field. To ensure the same, a matchless editorial board was set up. Every individual on the board went through rigorous rounds of assessment to prove their worth. After which they invested a large part of their time researching and compiling the most relevant data for our readers.

The editorial board has been involved in producing this book since its inception. They have spent rigorous hours researching and exploring the diverse topics which have resulted in the successful publishing of this book. They have passed on their knowledge of decades through this book. To expedite this challenging task, the publisher supported the team at every step. A small team of assistant editors was also appointed to further simplify the editing procedure and attain best results for the readers.

Apart from the editorial board, the designing team has also invested a significant amount of their time in understanding the subject and creating the most relevant covers. They scrutinized every image to scout for the most suitable representation of the subject and create an appropriate cover for the book.

The publishing team has been an ardent support to the editorial, designing and production team. Their endless efforts to recruit the best for this project, has resulted in the accomplishment of this book. They are a veteran in the field of academics and their pool of knowledge is as vast as their experience in printing. Their expertise and guidance has proved useful at every step. Their uncompromising quality standards have made this book an exceptional effort. Their encouragement from time to time has been an inspiration for everyone.

The publisher and the editorial board hope that this book will prove to be a valuable piece of knowledge for researchers, students, practitioners and scholars across the globe.

List of Contributors

Karol Szomolányi, Martin Lukáčik and Adriana Lukáčiková
University of Economics in Bratislava - Department of Operations Research and Econometrics, Slovakia

Valeska V. Geldres-Weiss
Universidad de La Frontera, Chile

Joaquín Monreal-Pérez
Murcia University, Spain

Dirceu Tornavoi-Carvalho
University of Sao Paulo, Brazil

Jorge Tello-Gamarra
University of Rio Grande, Brazil

Sin-Yu Ho and Bernard Njindan Iyke
University of South Africa - Economics, South Africa

Kizito Uyi Ehigiamusoe and Hooi Hooi Lean
Universiti Sains Malaysia - Economics Program, School of Social Sciences, Malaysia

Anselm Komla Abotsi
University of Education, Winneba - Department of Economics Education, Ghana Arts Centre, Accra, Ghana

Alexandru Capatina, Adrian Micu and Nicoleta Cristache
Universitatea Dunarea de Jos din Galati, Romania

Angela Eliza Micu
Universitatea Ovidius din Constanta, Romania

Raluca Vasilache and Madalin Darie
Dunarea de Jos" University of Galati, Romania

Enock Nyorekwa Twinoburyo and Nicholas M Odhiambo
University of South Africa, South Africa

João Estevão, Clara Raposo and José Dias Lopes
Advance/CSG-ISEG, Universidade de Lisboa, Portugal

Wiesław Dębski
University of Finance and Management in Warsaw, Poland

Ewa Feder-Sempach, Szymon Wójcik
University of Lodz, Poland

Xiaoxin Yang
Ocean University of China, China

Adriana Grigorescu
National University of Political Studies and Public Administration - Public Management, Romania

Elisabeth Bustos Contell and Gregorio Labatut-Serer
Department of Accounting, University of Valencia, Spain

Salvador Climent-Serrano
Department of Financial and Actuarial Economics, University of Valencia, Spain

Israa A. El Husseiny
Economics Department, Faculty of Economics and Political Science, Cairo University, Egypt

Jonaki Sengupta
Charuchandra College, Kolkata - Economics, India

Ranjanendra Narayan Nag
St. Xavier's College (Autonomous), Kolkata - Economics, India

Bhaskar Goswami
The University of Burdwan - Economics, India

Mario Arturo Ruiz Estrada and Diwa Samad
University of Malaya - Economics, Malaysia

Yew Joe Ho
Universiti Malaysia Sabah - Labuan Faculty of International Finance, Malaysia

Index

P

R

S

T